CAESAR

AND THE
FADING
OF THE
ROMAN
WORLD

Peter Baehr

CAESAR
AND THE
FADING
OF THE
ROMAN
WORLD

*A Study in Republicanism
and Caesarism*

Transaction Publishers
New Brunswick (U.S.A.) and London (U.K.)

Library of Congress Catalog Number: 97–16701
ISBN: 1–56000–304–9
Printed in the United States of America

Library of Congress Cataloging-in-Publication Data

Baehr, P. R. (Peter R.)
    Caesr and the fading of the Roman world : a study in
Republicanism and Caesarism / Peter Baehr.
        p.   cm.
    Includes bibliographical references and index.
    ISBN 1–56000–304–9 (cloth)
    1. Political science—History.   2. Casearism—History.
3. Republicanism—History.   I. Title.
JA81.B243   1997
321.9—dc21   97–16701
                                                        CIP

Contents

Acknowledgements

I first became interested in Caesarism some years ago when I was pursuing doctoral work at the University of Leicester on Max Weber. In the summer of 1994, I decided to return to some of the questions this work had originally provoked, but which, innocent as I then was of the republican tradition, I had been unable to answer. I would never have made this trip back to earlier concerns without the resolution of Irving Louis Horowitz. I am particularly grateful to him for encouraging me to revise earlier ideas and giving me the opportunity to present the results to a wider audience. Moreover, though this book bears little resemblance, in either argument or structure, to my doctoral thesis I must thank my supervisor Clive Ashworth for his initial guidance and great intellectual generosity.

Second, I am keen to acknowledge the individuals who read parts of the manuscript, proffered other kinds of advice on its content, or whose linguistic skills I often had need to call on: Charlene Agar, David Beetham, Jeff Bursey, James Butrica, Hilary Campbell, Kathleen Buckley, Anne Furlong, Rita Kindl, Helen Morgan, Barbara Neis, Marina Orsini, Thomas Pustow, John Selby, John Scott (University of Essex), Peter Sinclair, Duleepa Wijayawardhana, but especially Volker Meja, and Gordon C. Wells. Hedda Schuurman has been a particularly important interlocutor for me over the last couple of years, while to a continuing dialogue with Volker Meja I owe many insights and clarifications. I am also indebted to Geoffrey de Ste. Croix for the time and trouble he took to clarify a number of issues of Roman history, to Adrian Tronson for his astute comments on those parts of the text I asked him to read, and to Stuart Pierson who endured the onerous task of reading the manuscript in its entirety. His remarks helped improve the book in countless ways. Errors of judgment and of fact that remain are obviously my own responsibility.

Financial backing was provided by Memorial University under a program that allowed me to hire for a short but productive period two talented students, Yit Kay Moong and Martha Goosney, as research associates. I gratefully acknowledge their help as I do the support of Judi Smith and Annette Carter, the secretaries of the Department of Sociology, and that of the university more generally.

At the heart of a book on society and culture lies a paradox that will be familiar to all who have attempted to write one. While the subject matter of one's work is social relations, the activity actually demanded by the writing process itself normally requires long stretches of peace and quiet, asocial if not often plain antisocial behavior. It follows that my most keenly felt obligations are to the three people—*Caesare clementiores*—who have supported me in this enterprise: Hedda Schuurman, my mother Anne Baehr, and especially Hilary Campbell who lived with this work during its embryonic and most exasperating stages. The book is dedicated to her with love and gratitude.

St. John's, Newfoundland, June 10, 1996

Introduction

The Soothsayers' Vindication

There is a moment in the early political career of Julius Caesar that has become famous to historians of ancient Rome. Trudging the rounds of the assize circuit in Spain, Caesar came across a statue of Alexander the Great in the town of Gades. According to Suetonius, the thirty-two-year-old Caesar "was overheard to sigh impatiently, vexed, it seems, that at an age when Alexander had already conquered the whole world, he himself had done nothing in the least epoch-making. Moreover, when on the following night, much to his dismay, he had a dream of raping his own mother, the soothsayers greatly encouraged him by their interpretation of it: namely, that he was destined to conquer the earth, our Universal Mother" (Suetonius I.7 = 1980:15).[1]

Suetonius' story may, of course, be apocryphal; even if true, its chronology has often been disputed by historians. What is beyond doubt is that the soothsayers' prediction was insufficiently bold. For Julius Caesar not only went on to conquer "the earth"; his reputation then proceeded, for almost two millennia, to impose itself on the imagination of the Western world.

To document Caesar's notoriety is a secondary, if nonetheless prominent, objective of the present study. Its main purpose is to examine the trajectory and outcome of a particular European debate bound up with Caesar's name: the Caesarist debate of the second half of the nineteenth century. During this period, controversy in European educated circles turned around "Caesarism," a novel political formation exemplified in the regimes of Napoleon III and, to a lesser degree, Bis-

1

marck. The debate about Caesar*ism*—a term coined in the late 1840s, popularised in the 1850s, and a key word till the end of the century—is best distinguished, however, from a much longer argument about what one might call the "Caesar-question."

For many centuries before the nineteenth, Caesar was a name that evoked strong feelings among educated people. Some of these responses were laudatory, as in those interpretations that imagined Caesar's "monarchy" to be a preparation for the Kingdom of God. Of particular relevance to this book, however, is one discourse and tradition—political "republicanism"—that envisaged Caesar as an historical symbol for some of the most dangerous tendencies a polity could experience. The term "republicanism" is a slippery one, and is not to be confused with the American political party of the same name. But as a first approximation we can define it as a political idiom that received its most potent and influential (post-Roman) expression in the Florentine Renaissance—its *locus classicus* is Machiavelli's *Discourses*—was thereafter appropriated by the English republicans or "Commonwealthmen" of the seventeenth century (for instance by Henry Neville, John Milton, and James Harrington), was then adapted by Montesquieu and Rousseau in the eighteenth, and, in a plurality of mediations, became an integral element in the discourse of the American revolutionaries and constitution-builders, and of their counterparts in France.

Typically, "republicans" opposed hereditary monarchy and emphasized the collective political obligations citizens owed to their city or commonwealth. Those obligations entailed active involvement in, and responsibility for, the affairs of public life; for instance, citizens were expected to defend their own country, not hire mercenaries to defend it for them. The chief political mechanism for managing a healthy polity was considered to be a "mixed" constitution; that is, one that incorporated into the commonwealth all its various social and political forces, an achievement that was held to be one cause of the Roman Republic's greatness during its zenith. Another cause of its exalted position was the ethos the paradigmatic Roman citizen was claimed to carry in his heart, an ethos that later republicans enjoined their fellow citizens to cultivate: "virtue," or *virtù*, as the Florentine republicans called it, (from the Latin *virtus*) that is, manly patriotic commitment, courage and devotion, qualities necessary to subdue the tempestuous goddess Fortune without whose support honour, glory and greatness were unlikely ever to be acquired. Dedication to the *res publica*, to a polity that belongs to all its member citizens, was supposed to transcend or override every other earthly consideration, domestic and instrumental; it was to be the prime source of one's identity and the center of one's loyalties. And it was also commonly argued that devotion to the commonwealth, especially through the provision of public service, was itself a condition of both collective *and* individual freedom. For without a viable, healthy, and secure body politic, every citizen's liberty is potentially in danger from external enemies or civil conspiracy, calamities that imperil private as much as public life: it is hard to protect one's family or property if the walls of one's city are being knocked down, or if one's country is being invaded. At the same time, republicans were the first to acknowledge that such devotion to the commonwealth was by the nature of things precarious and unstable. The achievement and preservation of civic greatness is inevitably a strenuous activity, yet humans are not inherently virtuous or altruistic beings. Or even if, as Cicero remarked in the *Tusculan Disputations* (1945:227), the "seeds of virtue are inborn in our dispositions" they soon fall on the stony ground of social deception and prejudice. Citizens, because they are also human, have pronounced tendencies to forget their own wider and common interests, to confuse the commendable quest for renown and preeminence with vain ambition, to reduce the search for greatness to petty gain, and to become sated and complacent; in short, they are dangerously predisposed towards moral and physical "corruption." For this reason, it was necessary to fashion laws that coerced people to recognize and carry out their political duties, and to foster leaders of outstanding merit. Such leaders, exemplars of political virtue, were important not only in their capacity as active lawgivers, charged with the monumental task of building the foundations or framework of political life; but also as agents capable of reconstructing these foundations and returning the state to first principles wherever civic torpor had set in. In contrast, the worst kind of laws were those that, while purporting to express republican liberty, were simply a sham to cover the naked fact that a people had delivered itself into bondage and tyranny; while the most heinous kinds of individuals were those who fuelled human corruption, and who promoted not conflict per se, but rather the negative and factious dissension that drained the vigor of republican mores and manners.

Such a simplified portrait of "republicanism" is bound to be a cartoon; we shall see significant departures from it, and hybrids with other doctrines, by and by. Moreover, the pervasiveness of a classical symbolic universe and "the habit of deriving values from a classical past or associating them with it" (Pocock 1976:261) did not mean that everything from that past was idealized by republican-oriented thinkers; decadence, luxury, corruption, and hubris were prominent motifs. Nor did it mean that they were unaware of the need to appreciate distinctively modern problems or achievements. Montesquieu, for example, contrasting the Roman habit of exterminating the citizens of conquered cities with the more limited political and civic domination exerted by the French monarchy of the eighteenth century, was in no doubt that "here homage must be paid to our modern times, to contemporary reasoning, to the religion of the present day, to our philosophy, and to our mores" ([1748] 1989:139; cf. xliii, 140, 147, 162–64). At the same time, it was obvious to Montesquieu, as it was to Machiavelli, Harrington, and Rousseau, that "one can never leave the Romans" (172), that the history of the Roman and Greek world provided a frame of reference—cognitive and ethical—so fundamental that no person could be called civilized or learned who was ignorant of it. Even rejecting that world, in part or more generally, required that one understand what one was renouncing. With this in mind, republicans stressed the need for prudence and a commitment to the "public" world; propounded a theory of human inclinations and of social cycles; narrated stories of heroism and resilience, freedom and sacrifice, glory and greatness. That these models and values often related to the "real" Rome and Greece—slave-holding, belligerent and predatory, imperialistic—in the most tenuous and incomplete way is not the point here. What is the point is that a construction of the Graeco-Roman world was palpably *present*, alive, in the imagination and sensibilities of the educated; and that this construction furnished a storehouse of symbols, allegories, "lessons," arguments, and archetypes that were every bit as substantial as the earth they trod on.

Here lies the significance of Julius Caesar, probably the most notable symbolic foil of this tradition—and of other currents of thought that, though not necessarily "republican" in the sense that I have been using the term, also looked back with admiration to the Roman Republic and to personifications of republican "virtue." For it was Caesar, more than anyone, who was depicted as the man who presided over, and contributed decisively to, the ruin of the Roman Republic.

His defense of Catiline the conspirator, his demagogic manipulation of the common people, his opportunist alliances with thugs and warlords, his "usurpation" by force of arms of senatorial authority, his design to become a monarch—this is how Caesar is typically indicted by republican writers. Yet while Caesar was repeatedly summoned as the negation of republicanism, there was always a paradoxical sense in which he was being employed to uphold and reaffirm it. By symbolizing a cluster of behaviors and inclinations that decent people were urged to renounce, Caesar's example provided an antimodel against which genuine political "virtue" could be measured.

Within republican thinking, moreover, Caesar's name frequently operated in two striking ways. First, it possessed what might be called "polarity," that is, the ability of a term to generate its antithesis. To depict Caesar as a demonic figure, in other words, invited a contrast with those individuals who embodied all that he so singularly lacked, and who could be as lionized as Caesar was condemned: men like Junius Brutus, the legendary founder of the Roman Republic who put his country even above his own family; or Fabius Maximus Verrucosus, the "Shield of Rome," who wore down Hannibal's forces and helped to save Rome in one of its darkest hours; or Cato the Younger, the very paradigm of unflinching republican rigorism. Second, the use of Caesar's name in republican discourse is remarkable for its "recursive" properties, for its power to make itself virtually identical with concepts it then comes to enshrine. What this means is that Caesar is treated in republican discourse not just as an example of, for instance and notably, "usurpation," but as its very quintessence; and this to such a degree that when republican writers mention the word "usurpation," they typically do so to mean something like "the illegitimate seizure of power as epitomized by Julius Caesar"; while when they invoke Caesar, they want us to understand the horrors of "usurpation": each term functions as a virtual reflex of the other, so that even when Caesar is not specifically mentioned, a term like "usurpation" can summon him up to the republican mind.

Assuredly, the republican depiction of Caesar—to which I devote chapter 1—was more complex, more "sociological," as we would now say, than this: everyone was aware that structural fissures in the Roman Republic had provided Caesar, and precursors like Marius and the Gracchi brothers, with their opportunities. In any case, the republican reading itself was quite often contested, for instance, by champions of monarchy who hailed Caesar's dictatorship as a vindication of one-person rule: Caesar, they would say, wisely imposed on Rome the discipline and sound government it so sorely required. And by the eighteenth century we begin to see the ground being cleared for a more sympathetic assessment of Caesar's accomplishments, notably in Nathaniel Hooke's *Roman History* (4 vols., 1738–1771) which both deflated the achievements of the canonical republican figures, and insisted on Caesar's essential greatness. But this is still a minority position. We have to wait till the nineteenth century to see a major shift in Caesar's reputation, and in the use to which his name was put.

In this shift, two developments become apparent. On the one hand, Caesar enjoyed a major rehabilitation in the literary culture and historiography of the nineteenth century, interrogated ambivalently by Lord Byron, praised by Thomas De Quincey, honored by the younger Victor Hugo, proclaimed by Nietzsche, and exalted by Vincenzo Gioberti, Theodor Mommsen, and James Froude as the greatest statesman of his age. According to Friedrich Gundolf, more was written about Caesar in "the Bourgeois Century" than in all earlier centuries combined (Gundolf [1924] 1928:301). On the other hand, Caesar's name continued to function as a term of polemic in the emergence of a new debate on what came to be called "Caesar*ism*." Rehearsed in the salons, clubs, reading rooms, and newspaper columns of Europe in the second half of the century, this debate typically focused on the career of Louis Napoleon who, following *"l'opération Rubicon"*[2]—a coup d'état in 1851 against the Second Republic of which he was president—became, in December 1852, Napoleon III, emperor of France for the next eighteen-and-a-half years. Interest in this regime was intense in Europe, not only because of its unusual longevity, but because it appeared to constitute a novel political formation, one that was both economically "progressive" (bourgeois) and socially conservative, massively popular but harshly authoritarian, "democratic" but hierarchical. In particular, while "the Caesarism of Napoleon III" legitimated all its actions in the name of "popular sovereignty," it functioned de facto as a police state, prompting Robert Michels later to describe its ideology as "the theory of individual dominion originating in the collective will, but tending to emancipate itself of that will and to be become sovereign in its turn" ([1911] 1959:216–17). Was this regime a historical idiosyncrasy, a product of unique national conditions? Or was it the prototype of a new political order towards which all the European nations were heading? These questions were often asked and variously answered. Contention was also evident wherever the merits of this "Caesarism" were discussed. Critics feared the emergence of a new kind of tyranny, but one more invasive than anything known hitherto. Conversely, supporters praised Caesarism for being a type of regime capable of commanding popular support while ensuring order ("peace"), securing property, extending empire. Yet the rehabilitation of Julius Caesar in historiography and literature, did not translate in any straightforward way to admiration of the Caesarism of Napoleon III. Theodor Mommsen is only the most obvious case: a historian who saw in Julius Caesar a man of "perfect harmony" ([1854–7] 1911:428), but whose view of Napoleon III was extremely ambivalent.

Still, whatever the contending parties sought to explain, commend or indict, it soon became evident that the Caesarism debate had only the most tenuous links with earlier republican thought. It is true that the classical referent remained, though already becoming somewhat sloganized. But the key problems addressed were no longer a mixed constitution, political virtue and the like. They hinged much more on the "social question," on proletarian insurgency, or, in the vernacular of the day, on the "masses" and how to discipline, mobilize, or restrain them. Napoleon III's regime assumed significance because it appeared to have a firm, though unorthodox, response to this question: authoritarianism *and* "democracy" (populism). Julius Caesar could be invoked in this context not as a foil for the enunciation of republican values, but as a vague analogy of the current political situation: like Caesar, it would be said, Napoleon III was a democratic monarch, a proletarian king, a military demagogue. "A sphinx without a riddle," was Bismarck's more laconic judgement.

The debate on Caesarism, then, is of interest not only in its own right, but also as a window through which to view the enfeeblement of the republican tradition. The transformation of Caesar's image is a sure sign of changes within the wider political culture and evidence, too, of the emergence of new problems and challenges.

Phases of Caesarism

It is this nineteenth-century cultural conversation—its nature, its trajectory and its outcome in the twentieth century—that is the main subject of this book. Its nature I have already said something briefly about. Its trajectory and its twentieth-century fate call for some further comment.

The career of Caesarism as a concept has passed through roughly three phases. The initial phase—the subject of chapter 2—spans the period from around 1850 to 1871, the period of Napoleon III's hegemony in France, when the term Caesarism circulated effortlessly in the linguistic currency of educated people. My concern here is to pose and answer the following sorts of questions: When was the term Caesarism first coined and by whom? What did the word originally mean, both to the persons who first employed it, and to those who recognized in it something of pertinence to their contemporary situation? Why did the term become popular in the political vernacular of the day? If speech can be conceived of as "human relations turned into sound"; if concepts "grow and change with the group whose expression they are"; if they "live as long as this crystallization of past experiences and situations retains an existential value...that is, as long as succeeding generations can hear their own experiences in the meaning of the words" (Elias [1939] 1978:117, 6–7); then we will want to know what Caesarism meant to those who used the term, and what social and political forces sustained it during its heyday.

The second phase, which takes us up to the end of the First World War, is examined in chapters 3 and 4. This period marks the development of a more abstract and taxonomic approach to Caesarism; which is to say that the term finds its way into political or sociological treatises as a species of a genus, an item of some more encompassing classificatory grid; "tyranny" or "democracy" or "plebiscitary domination," for instance. Nonetheless, classical resonances remain, as evidenced in the neo-Aristotelian and neo-Polybian frameworks that inform the analyses of writers like Albert Schäffle and Wilhelm Roscher; so, too, do the connections to contemporary debates and everyday usage, in part because of the recent history of Napoleon III's "militarism" (Ferrero [1898] 1902), in part because of the ongoing and turbulent processes associated with the extension of democracy and citizenship to the working class and little-propertied, but also because Caesarism begins to be attached to the late emperor's nemesis, Otto von Bismarck. My approach to this phase will be similar to my treatment of its predecessor: I shall seek to retrieve a series of debates, map out a range of arguments, and explicate their significance and implications.

The third period in Caesarism's career, which comprises the remainder of the twentieth century, is significantly different from the phases it superseded. Specialist research on Caesar as a historical figure has never been more prodigious, a fact amply attested to in Helga Gesche's Caesar bibliography, embracing just over 1900 titles of scholarly works (Gesche 1976:207–325).[3] Twenty years later, hundreds more articles and books could be cited. Moreover, public interest in Caesar, though far less widespread and vigorously polemical than in the nineteenth century, has by no means lost its buoyancy. One might consider the recent reappearance of Caesar in the "popular" historical novel—notably Colleen McCullough's trilogy (1991, 1992, 1994),—examples of a genre that is in some respects redolent of Rex Warner's Caesar narratives (1958, 1960). But it was particularly during the thirties, forties, and fifties, that Caesar proved to be a valuable resource for those with a taste for historical allusion: José Ortega y Gasset in *The Revolt of the Masses* ([1929] 1957); John Dos Passos in the *USA* trilogy ([1930–36] 1960); and more pointedly for an era that witnessed the momentary triumph of fascism, Kurt Weill's "Caesar's Death" from *Der Silbersee* (premiered simultaneously in Leipzig, Magdeburg, and Erfurt on February 18, 1933 just days before the Reichstag fire); Alfred Neumann's *Der neue Cäsar* (1934); Bertolt Brecht's unfinished Caesar novel, begun in 1937, but only published twenty years later[4]); Thornton Wilder's *The Ides of March* (1948). The thirties, too, saw the longest ever run of Shakespeare's *Julius Caesar*: Orson Welles' antifascist production in New York in 1937 which clocked up 157 performances (Ripley 1980:9). In fact no single work has done more to keep Julius Caesar alive in the public mind of the English-speaking world of the twentieth century than Shakespeare's tragedy.[5] This is not only because of Shakespeare's "canonical" status in the school and college curriculum. During the twentieth century, as in the three previous centuries of its performance, the play itself has shown an outstanding theatrical versatility:

> At one moment it has served as a star-vehicle; at another, a clothes-horse for pageantry; at still another, a political medium. The script has been endlessly chopped and changed; individual roles have been adjusted up or down to suit the whims of stars; and spectacle has been added or subtracted as fashion dictated. Yet audiences remained consistently loyal, whatever its form. Early seventeenth-century theatre-goers were ravished by the play and left the theatre in wonder, Leonard Digges [the seventeenth-century poet] tells us. Three centuries on, their successors made it the most frequently-requested item in the Old Vic repertoire. (Ripley 1980:9)

And the play's possibilities as a "political medium" were dramatically advanced by a radical twentieth-century development in communication: the feature film. In 1953, the same year that Joseph McCarthy (that "pathological character assassin" as Truman once called him) became Senate chairman of the Permanent Subcommittee on Investigations, John Houseman produced, and Joseph Mankiewicz directed, the MGM screen version of *Julius Caesar*. The cast was impressive: Marlon Brando as Mark Antony, James Mason as Brutus, John Gielgud as Cassius, and Louis Calhern as the eponymous Roman. Deborah Kerr and Greer Garson were also drafted in to play the roles of Portia and Calpurnia. Though MGM, flush with the box-office success of *Quo Vadis* (1951), may have expected some simple patriotic theme, or even sheer escapism, Houseman and Mankiewicz offered something more subtle: a movie that parried the attack on communists and liberal "fellow travellers" by depicting Brutus as the man of principle refusing to bow either to the imperious Caesar or the rabble-rousing, cynical Antony, and, in consequence, provoking the anathema of the mob— and ultimately inviting his own death. In this way the film delivered a powerful message aimed at a cold war audience: that those who are called "traitors" may actually be the victims of ruthless manipulators; and that true patriotism may well involve risking infamy and ruin at the hands of the unscrupulous (Lenihan 1992:48–50).[6]

I have been commenting on the reception of Caesar in historical scholarship, the popular novel and the arts to help me now underscore the point that Caesar*ism* has received palpably less attention in the period I have been sketching. Though still employed as a term with political connotations, Caesarism tends to become increasingly marginal to political debate. Few theorists seek to integrate it into their analytical schemata; and even fewer commentators find it helpful as a conceptual device to make sense of the modern period. There are exceptions to this generalisation: Antonio Gramsci's coded analysis of "Caesarist" parliamentary coalitions in *The Prison Notebooks* ([1929–35] 1971), a usage that was resurrected by British Marxists in the 1980s; Franz Neumann's contrast between "Caesarist" and "totalitarian" dictatorships (Neumann 1964); the rather disparate group of writers on American politics who, up to the present, have continued to detect the specter of Caesarism in presidential power. So Caesarism does not die as the twentieth century unfolds. Nonetheless, it undergoes a striking metamorphosis: it becomes more esoteric, more remote from everyday political conversation, in short, more academic—and more chaotic, a sure sign that it has lost its anchor in any major tradition or group of traditions.

Since twentieth-century usages aim to furnish a working concept of Caesarism for political analysis and sociology, my earlier emphasis on descriptive reconstruction becomes combined in chapter 5 with a stance that is more directly critical in import. As we shall see, the historical and logical cogency of most modern treatments of Caesarism leaves much to be desired. This in turn raises the question of the concept's contemporary status. Is it advisable to embark on yet one more theoretical quest to define what Caesarism "really" is or was? Or should we relinquish all efforts to "operationalize" the term, and treat it instead as a political and cultural item affording us insight into a nineteenth and early twentieth-century debate? I think the latter course is more credible, a position I shall defend in the concluding chapter of this book.

The Significance of Max Weber

Bestriding the Caesarism debate like a colossus stands the imposing figure of Max Weber (1864–1920). No other social and political thinker is more symptomatic of Caesarism's tortuous metamorphosis than Weber, and for this reason he receives more attention in this book than any other author.

Ralph Waldo Emerson once remarked that "the greatest genius is the most indebted man," that "great men are more distinguished by range and extent, than by originality" ([1850] 1990:328). How applicable are these dicta to Weber? It is well known that the German thinker possessed a formidable "range and extent" and with it a prodigious ability to assimilate, weed out, re-argue, and refashion the dominant ideas and shifting frameworks of the age. We will not be surprised, then, that in invoking Caesarism in his correspondence and *political* writings—notably, in the critique of Bismarck—he made use of standard nineteenth-century motifs and echoed the negative connotations that mostly attached to them. In this way, Weber was deeply "indebted" to his time, and the previous generation that helped shape it: in my terms, the Caesarism debate in its initial phase.

Largely coeval with this older usage, however, Weber gradually reshaped the concept of Caesarism in a significantly new and fateful way. This took place between 1913 and 1919 (thus during the second phase of Caesarism's career); and not in the political writings, but in the lexicon and "ideal-types" Weber fashioned for the science of sociology. First, Caesarism is demoted as a concept and becomes gradually *absorbed* into the much more expansive notion of "charisma." Second, Caesarism is not only ingested into charisma, thereby losing its previous distinctiveness; it is also *renamed* as "plebiscitary" or "leader democracy." And third, and most importantly, the traditional problem of Caesarism, and the much older republican argument attending the "Caesar-question," is radically *redescribed*, such that what was once seen as a highly contentious and dangerous phenomenon now becomes normalized as the inevitable accompaniment of modern democracy.

It is true that in intellectual terms Weber died intestate, leaving no testament to proclaim or school to carry forward his diverse explorations. During his own lifetime, and in the twenties and thirties, his influence was muted both in Germany and elsewhere. However, though Weber's particular theses on charisma and "plebiscitary democracy" had little influence on his contemporaries, his project of constructing a new language for sociology was of great moment in the longer term, playing its part in the destruction of an older way of viewing and describing the world. Refracted through multiple prisms, and carried through numerous mediations, Weber's vision has become part of the common sense of modern "social science." And because of that influence and appropriation, there is also a sense in which Weber intrudes into what I have been calling the third phase of Caesarism. He does so indirectly by a process of theoretical constitution and deflection, for inasmuch as academics think in Weberian terms, they think on the conceptual terrain he constructed. To that extent, the conventional depiction of Weber as a "founder" of sociology is entirely accurate. What is typically missing from that expression, however, is an understanding of what it was that Weber left behind.

It is also worth adding, in view of the continuing scholarly effort to locate Weber's work in Western traditions, that no project was less "republican" than Weber's sociology; and even to envisage Weber's broader political analysis as republican—as Wilhelm Hennis appears to do by linking it to "the ancient sense of *politics*," and the tradition of "Machiavelli, Rousseau and Tocqueville" ([1987] 1988:196–67)— must involve one in a mode of interpretation so selective, and so general, as to be highly misleading. It must, to take only the most obvious case, omit Machiavelli's crucial argument for involving the entire male citizen body in political life as actors animated by *virtù*, as distinct from treating them as a passive "mass" to be mobilized by what Weber identified as the plebiscitary leader. It must disregard Rousseau's protracted attempt to reconstruct "modern" politics on the antique model of small, homogeneous states, a model Weber believed impossible to replicate under contemporary conditions. And it must leave unsolved the mystery for any sound textual claim of Weber's relationship to Tocqueville, that none of Weber's major works—in politics or sociology—so much as mention him. No one doubts that Weber was a champion of the constitutional state. But the participatory strains evident, though everywhere qualified, in the republican view of political citizenship, are absent from Weber's leader-centered analysis. This point will bear some elaboration.

Despite some very inconsequential qualifications to the contrary, the weight of Weber's definition of politics falls on "the leadership, or the influencing of the leadership, of a political association, hence today, of a state" ([1918] 1970a:77, emphasis omitted). Moreover, Weber takes it for granted that, under modern conditions, only "a relatively small number of men are primarily interested in political life and hence interested in sharing political power" (1970a:99). So exclusive, indeed, is the sphere of the political thus conceived, that political action "is always determined by the 'principle of small numbers,'" or "the superior political maneuverability of small leading groups. In mass states, this Caesarist element is ineradicable" (Weber [1918] 1978a: 1414). The obverse of this position is Weber's contention, nicely summarized by Harvey S. Goldman (1993:176), that "collectivities cannot be empowered, but only used as the tool of charismatic domination. It is impossible within Weber's schema to envision, for example, the public creation of purposes and goals or innovative social and political action originating in social movements, mass efforts, or associations." Weber's "schema," it is true, is not always consistent with his practice: for instance, his discussion of the achievements of the *zemstvo* movement in Russia ([1906]:1995a). But this is unusual. Typically, Weber's understanding of the modern political arena is rigidly tripartite in delineation: there are individual leaders who rule, their immediate disciples who constitute the leader's apparatus or "machine," and the "irrational masses" who form the subpolitical material of the leader's designs.

Weber's point could of course be rephrased to say that modern liberal democracies are characterized by great political apathy; that politics requires effort, energy, and leadership; and that some individuals are more willing and more gifted to lead than others. Thus phrased, the point is unexceptional, indeed, banal; it simply states some of the empirical properties and tendencies of modernity, leaving open the possibility of greater public participation in political life. But this is not *Weber's* point. On his account, politics by definition, centers on individual leadership; everything outside such leadership may be *relevant* to politics as a condition of its existence (for example, a following to recruit and discipline), but does not *constitute* politics itself. In its turn, political leadership is understood to be about ruling and domination, a conceptualization that follows a long tradition in Western and Near Eastern thought. The implications of this emphasis are important to grasp: in stressing politics as rulership and domination, other human beings must be envisaged as essentially the material of a creator-leader. The talented and willful ruler is akin to a sculptor imposing form on brute matter, a fashioner of the resources or "mass" at his disposal that he uses as the means to realize his own "higher" ideals and projects (cf. Arendt, 1958:220–30).

To this it might be objected that Weber sought to offer a descriptive rather than a normative account of political life; that, in other words, whether we like it or not, he was simply specifying modern political realities. But Weber did more than this. He offered not merely a theoretically informed description, but a definition that appears to be both tautologous and exclusive: tautologous because, as Carl Schmitt once pointed out, "The state thus appears as something political, the political as something pertaining to the state—obviously an unsatisfactory circle" (Schmitt [1932] 1976:20); exclusive because statecraft or governance on the one hand, and politics on the other, are in effect conflated—a narrative procedure that would have struck most republicans since Machiavelli as bizarre and dangerous. For while none of them would have denied the obvious fact that a major part of statecraft is, and always has been, about ruling and violence, or that people can behave like a "mass" under certain conditions, or that leadership is vital to a thriving body politic and involves onerous responsibilities, none would want to have taken the further step and reduce politics more generally to such considerations.

This I take to be the key explanation for Hannah Arendt's studied reticence towards Weber, the reason why she could never share the enthusiasm for the German scholar of her mentor, Karl Jaspers. Arendt, a modern republican theorist, did not seek to "refute" Weber's fabricator model of politics, any more than she attempted to refute Carl Schmitt's friend-enemy distinction as the criterion of the political; one cannot falsify a model or definition, only offer a substitute and consider the degree to which it is cogent, which is to say coherent, illuminating, fertile. In Arendt's counter-conception, politics is best seen as a discursive activity, and a public space, in which people articulate and clarify common concerns, though from different points of view. The state is (or can be) one of these spaces, but it is not the only one; indeed, any activity can become political—a neighborhood protest against the dumping of toxic waste, a trade union meeting, a conference. The specific means of politics is not "violence," but "power," rendered by Arendt as an energy and dynamism that derives from collective action; violence, in contrast, is an antipolitical force, substituting coercion and isolation for action in concert. What is more, the vital condition of politics is not a mass to dominate, or a following to recruit, but the equality that citizenship confers on human beings, and the "plurality" of human beings themselves: "the fact that men, not Man, live on the earth and inhabit the world" (Arendt 1958:7). Political and legal institutions are the frameworks that lend form, accommodation, and durability to human plurality, both giving room to human initiative while also providing a crucial degree of stability in an unpredictable world.

Arendt's account of politics—of which only the baldest summary has been offered here—is not without its own problems. Weber's account of politics is not without its superb contributions; I would simply refer to his discussion of political ethics, his surgical exposure of the constitutional deficiencies of the *Kaiserreich*, his magisterial investigations into the fragmentation of Western "life-orders," his deep seriousness about the demands of political life for the person who wants to live it honestly, with inner control and discipline. Arendt's peculiar importance lies, however, in seeking to make distinctions that Weber elided, and in reappropriating a republican sense that politics is not something that belongs to rulers or leaders, or any group, but is a space in which all citizens can potentially find a home and make an active contribution (Canovan 1992:208).

"Foreign Nations"

My subject, then, is Caesar's significance for republican thought, the specific debate around Caesarism in the nineteenth century and the transmutation of this debate during the twentieth. But why should this be of interest now? Certainly, the Caesar question, and the Caesarism debate, tells us much about the hopes and fears of our predecessors. But it also tells us more, since the controversy around Caesar's name is significant for what it reveals, by default, about modern times. The gradual loss of Caesar as a potent symbol of argument in Western civilization during the twentieth century is actually indicative of a much deeper transformation in our condition: the development not of a postmodern, but of a postclassical, postrepublican political culture. It follows that any serious attempt to rethink or revive republicanism today will need to recognise not only the limitations of its precursors but also the very different conditions under which it would now have to be realized.

The fading of the Roman world in the social memory of the West, has in some quite evident respects emancipated us from a dream of liberty that could only become a dangerous caricature when applied to conditions for which it was never intended or fit. Notably, it has put paid to those political experiments that, with antiquity as their model, attempted to transpose onto modern conditions the ethos and exemplars of the early republics. Graeco-Roman republicanism was a martial, expansionist, patriarchal, activist tradition to a large extent predicated on homogeneous communities. Benjamin Constant's ([1814] 1988:105–9) devastating portrait of those "modern imitators of the republics of antiquity," like Robespierre and the Abbé de Mably, who "believed themselves charged with the regeneration of the human race," stands as an eloquent witness by a contemporary observer to the perils of political anachronism. Infatuation with regulations, and the need to subject all actions to their sway, total supremacy of the legislative arm of government, crime dressed up in the raiment of patriotic duty, hatred of idiosyncracy and privacy, the equation of private property with social evil, justification of dictatorship: these, Constant reminds us, are the malevolent offspring of attempts to turn the many into One. Of course this was not what post-Roman republicanism—the republicanism of Machiavelli, Harrington, Montesquieu, the federalists, and anti-federalists—in the main stood for; quite the reverse. And it is also true that republicanism, combined with other doctrines such as liberalism and Christianity, could be a force for greater individual freedom: the American Revolution and its aftermath can be summoned as obvious corroboration. Even so, Constant's depiction of the Jacobin terror does offer us an object lesson of the potential for an ideal to become ludicrous and lethal when extrapolated from one historical setting to another. Today we no longer have to be reminded what the attempt to create a monolithic community would look like: we have already seen it in totalitarian movements, tribal carnage, and in the new barbarism of "ethnic cleansing."

And classicism itself—republican or otherwise—had a darker side to it than is at first apparent. Over many centuries, educated people in Europe and North America grew up with, and drew on, a common stock of knowledge about the ancient world. Schooling and the demands of cultivation entailed familiarity with the basic texts of Greek and Roman philosophy, literature, and history. Such an education enabled republican and other thinkers to excavate the human experiences that lie encrusted in antique vocabularies. It furnished them with insights into the rise and disintegration of cultures that helped them appreciate human vulnerability and transience, the cosmic counterpoint to greatness and glory. To the degree that we have lost capacities like these, we have also lost contact with our own historicity and with a mythological grid whose power to bridge past and present has no analogue in modern times. An example may serve to highlight the point.

The enormous gulf that separates modern experience from the classical and republican vivacity of our forbears is epitomized by a single canto, of a single poem, written by someone who is typically thought of as a romantic rather than a neo-classicist: the finale of Byron's *Childe Harold's Pilgrimage*. Purporting to be the pilgrim's reflections on the grandeur and fate of Italy, the fourth and last canto appeared at a time—1818—when Byron had already become a pariah of refined society, a bitter contrast to the tumultuous praise he had received in 1812 when, at the age of twenty-four, the first two cantos had appeared in print and within a year had passed through four editions. (The third canto was published in 1816). What is remarkable about the fourth canto, and indeed the poem as a whole, is not only the scope of its references to the ancient world by a man who was still so young.[7] What is just as striking is the realization that its composition would be virtually unthinkable today by a writer wishing to reach a literate public. Without a substantial apparatus of notes to guide the modern reader, the poem's unremitting stream of allusions to ancient Greece and Rome is likely to be nearly incomprehensible. Who today would even imagine comparing George Washington to "Pallas, arm'd and undefiled"—Pallas the virgin goddess (Washington was born in Virginia) of Greek mythology who "sprang armed from the head of Zeus" (Tozer 1885:313)? More than this, Byron's classical pathos, and the resonance he could hope to expect from sympathetic readers—rightly, since in continental Europe, much more than in Britain, Byron's radicalism was admired and appreciated—is something clearly of a bygone age. When Byron thought of the classical world he contemplated liberty, its destruction and yet its redemptive tenacity; he saw Cromwell—"the sagest of usurpers"—in the figure of Sulla; and he summoned republican heroes like the Scipios, Tully (Cicero), and Brutus to remind his audience of those who, in an earlier age, had sought to protect Rome against its enemies. The enemy Europe had recently faced, of course, was Napoleon, that "fool of false dominion—and a kind of bastard Caesar, following him of old with steps unequal." Though Byron never repudiated the French Revolution, he despised the arrogance and bloodletting that had followed it, and that had proclaimed liberty at the same time as it had snuffed it out. But Napoleon, and the reaction that had followed his eclipse, could not extinguish liberty for ever:

> Yet, freedom! yet thy banner, torn, but flying,
> Streams like the thunder-storm *against* the wind;
> Thy trumpet voice, though broken now and dying,
>   The loudest still the tempest leaves behind;
> Thy tree hath lost its blossoms, and the rind,
> Chopp'd by the axe, looks rough and little worth,
> But the sap lasts,—and still the seed we find
> Sown deep, even in the bosom of the North;
> So shall a better spring less bitter fruit bring forth.
> (*Childe Harold* IV.98.874–82.)

Byron wrote these lines in Venice, inspired by the Italian trip he had recently completed, and using this inspiration as a source of, and occasion for, contemporary comment. A repetition of any thing like this mood and inspiration is as improbable today as a repetition of the singular genius who produced *Childe Harold*.

Yet the very structure of thought that enabled Byron to call up the classical world with such evocative force, coexisted with another tendency—call it classical fetishism—whose passing modern people will be less likely to mourn. Over two centuries earlier it had compelled Francis Bacon—yearning to free his contemporaries from the straitjacket of fossilized Aristotelianism—to present his own doctrines as if they were a rediscovery of antique fables; naturally, *De Sapientia Veterum* ("On the Wisdom of the Ancients," 1609), like the *Novum Organum* (1620), was written not in English but in Latin, the lingua franca of European cultivated circles. And even after Byron's death, the penchant for seeing the contours of antiquity in the topography of modern times remained remarkably tenacious. We have the chagrin of Fustel de Coulanges, Emile Durkheim's teacher at the Ecole Normale Supérieure, to vouch for the fact:

> In our system of education, we live from infancy in the midst of the Greeks and Romans, and become accustomed continually to compare them with ourselves, to judge of their history by our own, and to explain our revolutions by theirs. What we have received from them leads us to believe that we resemble them. We have some difficulty in considering them as foreign nations; it is almost always ourselves that we see in them. Hence spring many errors. We rarely fail to deceive ourselves regarding these ancient nations when we see them through the opinions and facts of our own time. ([1864] 1916:9–10)

For Fustel de Coulanges, the best way to approach ancient Greece and Rome was to recognize that they were "absolutely inimitable; nothing in modern times resembles them; nothing in the future can resemble them." Only from that standpoint could the delusions of the "last eighty years"—*The Ancient City* was first published in 1864—be avoided, a period that encompassed the French Revolution and its imperial aftermath, the Bourbon Restoration, the Orleanist monarchy of Louis Philippe, the Second Republic, and just over half of the life of the "Caesarist" Second Empire that the author himself was writing under.

It is important to add, however, that while Fustel de Coulanges wanted to understand modern times with new concepts and formulations, it would never have occurred to him to relinquish classical learning to do so.[8] On the contrary, such learning was crucial since man was an historical being: "take him at any epoch, and he is the product, the epitome, of all the earlier epochs. Let him look into his own soul, and he can find and distinguish these different epochs by what each of them has left within him" ([1864] 1916:13). So the protest against intellectual sclerosis of someone like Fustel de Coulanges, one could say, was an educated one because he still had one foot in the classical culture only the *abuses* of which he was repudiating. Today there is no real protest or repudiation because the basis on which it could sensibly be made—the ability to compare cogently the antique and modern with the tools afforded by classical linguistic competence—has gradually contracted not only in the wider educated culture but also within the academy itself. Today classicism is a fringe interest, the preserve of a coterie of specialist scholars in the universities. Our civilization is the poorer for this.

I have been arguing that attempts to rethink republicanism for modern times will need to be aware of the limitations of its precursors, the dangers of political anachronism, and the very ambivalent legacy of classical modes of thinking. However, any contemporary republican project has to face not only problems of the past but of modernity itself.[9] I will focus on one such problem: the erosion of moral and political obligation.

Christianity, Republicanism, and the Obligated Self

When one turns to consider the nature of modern life, especially as it is lived by highly educated people in the west—academics, many groups of professionals, people involved in the knowledge and culture industry, in short, the potential readers of this book—one comes across a particular contrast with the ages that preceded it. For many centuries, post-Roman republicanism existed in the deepest and most aggravated tension with Christianity. Part of this tension was political, and concerned the role of the Church as a worldly power with highly secular ambitions; another part of it was ethical and doctrinal. In a famous passage, contrasting favorably the "pagan" religion of the Romans with the type of Christianity encouraged by the Church of his day, Machiavelli complained:

> the old religion did not beatify men unless they were replete with worldly glory: army commanders, for instance, and rulers of republics. Our religion has glorified humble and contemplative men, rather than men of action. It has assigned as man's highest good humility, abnegation, and contempt for mundane things, whereas the other [Roman religion] identified it with magnanimity, bodily strength, and everything else than conduces to make men very bold....This pattern of life, therefore, appears to have made the world weak, and to have handed it over as a prey to the wicked, who run it successfully and securely since they are well aware that the

generality of men, with paradise for their goal, consider how best to bear, rather than how best to avenge, their injuries. ([1550] 1970:278)

Machiavelli made his point with a complete lack of humbug. Nonetheless, what is surely striking in retrospect—that is, from the vantage point of our own time—is just how much the "classical republicanism" of Machiavelli and the general tradition of Christianity had morphologically in common, how they worked together to shape a certain kind of social self, and how both of them have declined together in the social memory and sensibilities of the highly educated. Each of them, for instance, generated doctrines of duty, virtue, sacrifice, in a word *service*; each offered descriptions of human perversity, warnings against hubris or spiritual pride, corruption and laziness, amnesia and entropy; each emphasized the significance of remembrance; each offered consolation, either in the records of historians, or in the glory that the believer partakes in by entering God's Kingdom. In both cases, the individual was important as an agent, understood to be egoistic, restless, and internally at war; but also understood to be a vehicle of ideals whose higher purpose he or she was enjoined to serve. And the notions of service and charity had nothing to do with a belief in natural human altruism. Machiavelli, to the contrary, viewed individuals as basically self-interested; the point was to make them understand the connection between, on the one hand, their own particular interests and, on the other, a vibrant city-state that must sometimes override what they spontaneously wish for, but whose welfare and greatness is the ultimate precondition of their security and liberty. The Christian concept of charity acknowledges that there is little spontaneous about giving to others; charity is a discipline, the exercise of a certain kind of practical love; it takes effort to relinquish or transfer scarce resources, energy, and time.[10] Together, or by themselves, such ideas contributed to a notion of self as an entity attached to, obligated to, something beyond its own limited purview: the welfare of the city or commonwealth; the demands of God, the "Servant King."

In our own time, it has become fashionable in intellectual and cultural circles to ridicule such notions, to see contingency not simply as a property of the world, but as an end-in-itself, and to construe a belief in God as a vestige of intolerant and myopic premodern superstitions. In most cases, this kind of dismissal is trivial and unreflective. But there is another side to it that any candid reckoning must acknowledge. After what we have witnessed this century, the very mention of an "obligated" self or a self as a "vehicle" is going to make any reasonable person nervous. It will remind them of the countless millions of people who have been murdered, and are still being murdered, because of the elevated beliefs of others in the "laws" of history or race, or in the imperatives of the nation.[11] The notion of an "obligated self" will also evoke the bigotry, religious and secular, that so often lurks beneath the idea. And it may well even garner the suspicion that moral injunctions, such as the call to service or to deeper responsibility, are little more than what Nietzsche once designated, in a malicious but telling phrase, as "the moral hypocrisy of the commanders." Nietzsche was referring to those individuals who, unable to carry honestly the burden of their own independence and dominion, feel compelled to practice the deceit that they are only obeying some higher power. Such people

> know no way of defending themselves against their bad conscience other than to pose as executors of more ancient or higher commands (commands of ancestors, of the constitution, of justice, or the law or even of God), or even to borrow herd maxims from the herd's way of thinking and appear as "the first servant of the people" for example, or as "instruments of the common good." ([1886] 1973:102)

All this is well taken, but it is not the last word. If the moral hypocrisy of the commanders is a danger—a real danger—so too is nihilism, vacuity, triviality, irresponsibility, narcissism—issues Nietzsche could himself only resolve conceptually in the most grotesque and unconvincing way. Neither republicanism nor Christianity, of course, could offer any solace to him. For while republicanism was precisely that absurd philosophy that still held out some hope for the "herd," Christianity was the religion of moral hypocrisy par excellence. Pulsating with *ressentiment*, Christianity was a doctrine, Nietzsche claimed, that attracted those who hated life and dreaded suffering, a "slave morality" that employed its own weakness to exert power over the strong through the evocation of guilt and through the secretion of values of humility and submissiveness that had imprisoned civilization for almost two millennia. At this point, the resonances with Machiavelli's critique might seem palpable, but actually they are quite superficial. Machiavelli was aware of the tension between Christian and political virtue, and of the diabolic paradoxes of "goodness"; as he once pointed out, "an evil should never be allowed to continue out of respect for a good when that good may easily be overwhelmed by that evil" ([1550]

1970:393). But Machiavelli's characteristic target was not the "slave morality" of the Gospels so much as the orthodox way of teaching the Christian religion, and the Church of Rome's divisive interventions into the Italian politics of his epoch (ibid: 144–45).[12] As for Nietzsche's answer to nihilism and to the "herd" and its philosophy—the eternal recurrence and the *Übermenschen*—Machiavelli would have seen this, had he even been able to comprehend it, as a dangerous abdication of political responsibility, a vertiginous descent into monomania and madness.

More generally, it is important to stress in the context of historical "republicanism" that our commonsense division between "sacred" and "secular," or between a consistent Christianity and a "serious" politics, or between world-renunciation and world-affirmation, or between religious and civic virtue, is something of a modern caricature. Such a stark dualism would have surprised the American anti-federalists (those who opposed the Constitution of 1787) who, as we shall see in the next chapter, were able to combine republican, liberal, and Christian motifs, in a highly combative repertoire. It would have also flabbergasted an English republican like John Milton, the poet and defender of tyrannicide, whose Arminianist conviction led him to believe in the "dependence of men's salvation upon the free exercise of their reason and choice," and whose fire was intended for the established clerisy, not for the religion he claimed they had purloined. As Blair Worden records, Milton:

> described the service of the gospel as "rational, manly and utterly free;" he could equally well have applied the phrase to his conception of political service. He may have wanted to divorce church from state, but he did not think religion divisible from politics. He knew that the causes of civil and religious liberty were "inseparably knit together"...No government, he declared in 1660, came "nearer" to the "precept of Christ, than a free commonwealth." The gospel speaks "much of liberty, a word which monarchy and her bishops both fear and hate, but a free commonwealth both favours and promotes." (Worden 1990:230–31)

Before Milton and Machiavelli, their humanist precursors took it for granted that Christianity and civility existed together; the point was how to articulate them. One might consider, for instance, Maurizio Viroli's discussion of Italian political writers of the thirteenth and fourteenth centuries. The context of his remarks is the humanist appropriation of Cicero, particulary his *De Officiis* ("On Duties") and his *Somnium Scipionis* ("Scipio's Dream"), an appropriation in which

Macrobius sought to integrate Roman republican values into the idiom of Christianity:

> In a well-known passage of the *Somnium*, Cicero argues that for all the great men who devoted themselves to the good of their *patria* there is a place in the heavens where they enjoy perennial *beatitudo*. Macrobius' explanation for this passage is that God loves the *civitas* above all else and thus Cicero is perfectly right in saying that the good *rector civitatis* will immediately return to the heavens whence all men came. By ordering the laws and ensuring justice, political men lead their fellows to live a life of virtue which is in turn the pathway to true happiness. The true *politici*, concludes Macrobius, fully deserve the perennial enjoyment of *beatitudo*. (Viroli 1990: 163)

I have quoted these scholarly sources at some length to show not only the crudeness of much modern dualistic thinking about Christianity and politics, but also to emphasize what seems embarrassingly obvious once stated: that the New Testament has provided succour to, and doctrinal authority for, some of the most intense struggles for political liberty ever waged in our past. To look to God for ultimate redemption, to treat the Gospels "seriously," is not the same thing as, nor does it logically entail, turning one's back on the political world; one might ask Václav Havel, or Adam Michnik or Desmond Tutu what they think about that equation. One can be devoted to each, though in different ways. Indeed, it is *through* the world of social relations and "culture," through for instance our duties to our "neighbours" (our fellow citizens, as republicans would say) that Christians carry out God's will for humans. Further, it is precisely the world of social relations that sustains a Christian existence, by furnishing those intermediaries or *metaxu*—"home, country, traditions, culture" that "warm and nourish the soul and without which, short of sainthood, a *human* life is not possible" (Simone Weil [1947] 1963:133). Nor, Simone Weil went on to say elsewhere, was even a religious life possible in most cases: deprive people of the "nourishment" of the social world, insert them into bondage, break them in drudgery, narrow their vision to the satisfaction of immediate needs, and you leave them spiritually desolate. It would seem to follow, then, that our responsibilities to others are enhanced, not diminished, by such a perspective.

What the Gospels remind us of most forcefully, then, is not the antithesis between the world and God, but rather the *distinction* between them; that attempts to be a god, or to create a society like a god, are insane projects; that people "must soberly and modestly distinguish between things divine and human, between the oracles of sense and of faith; unless they mean to have a heretical religion and a fabulous philosophy" (Bacon [1609] 1860:155). Moreover, despite all the evils to which Christianity has been prone over the centuries, there is a sense in which Christian belief remains one of the great impediments to ideological thinking. This lies in its ability to distinguish between the necessary dissonance of this world and the harmony of the other world. We cannot expect, here, the end of suffering, malignity, and social evil, though we can build fortifications against them to limit their power and scope. For the believer perfection lies elsewhere; but precisely because it does exist, there is hope for humanity. Conversely, wherever the political and sacred are simply collapsed into one another, we can be certain that zealotry and tyranny are never very far behind.

It will be said that such a collapse is not a danger that most modern intellectuals face, since their skepticism towards religion inoculates them against conflating the religious and political spheres. On the contrary, it appears to be a common trait of the intellectual mind, apparently so scornful of the transcendental, to sublimate sacred longings into politics: thus the utopian impulse, with its characteristic oscillations between cynicism and high moralism. And even if it were possible to expunge the sacred in human affairs, to create a culture of contingency, play, fantasy, vicissitude, desire, as some of the more fashion-conscious culture critics like to imagine, it is hard to see what ethical obligations towards others could come from this. Indeed, such a culture would be likely to encourage the flight from obligation, and plunge its proponents even deeper into the vacuity of an extractive self.

It is true that the obligated self is not dead, any more than God is dead. In some ways the extent of obligation has grown, and in ways that would never have occurred to early republicans and Christians: the obvious case is environmentalism which has "expanded the circle" (Singer 1981) of commitment to embrace the nonhuman animal world and nonhuman nature. Conversely, the extractive self is not new: few cultures were more predatory and parasitic than the Roman, while the Judaic-Christian tradition has a sorry record in its attitude and practice towards the nonhuman world, which it has invariably seen as a resource to plunder. However, it is arguable that modern capitalist relations of production, the bureaucratic managements that serve them, and modern "rights"-centered philosophies of life that appear to be their defensive reflex, are changing the meaning of obligation in important ways, and weakening it accordingly. With the decline of continuous employment in one job or profession, the ethos of vocation to which it was necessarily tied is dying; it is being replaced by the proliferation of "mission statements" whose commitments to the public world are about as convincing as the pompous language in which they are clothed. With the growing subordination of the "labor market" to anonymous, centrifugal, and prodigal economic forces, and the growing marginalization of the poor and the unemployed, the very idea of "service" will sound hollow and ridiculous for most people, a euphemism for servitude. Even where a sense of obligation exists for some collective good or purpose, its connotation is very different from that of classical republicanism or Christianity. Today we do not seek "political virtue" or "political goodness," ideas that seem quaint and foreign to us; we follow "causes" or pursue particular interests. But causes are often ephemeral and dislocated; they are advanced and dropped, subject not only to the natural limitations of human energy, but also to fashion. Even where they persist, they normally fail to generate an inclusive citizen ethic for to do so today would fall foul of "the politics of difference." It is not obvious that republicanism can flourish on such ground.

* * *

In this concluding section I have been attempting to spell out some of the broader, contemporary implications of this study. I must now return to the hero and antihero with whom these reflections began.

Notes

1. For a different version of the events, see Plutarch I (1992:206, 221).
2. This is how Louis Napoleon himself described the coup preparations: see Philip Thody (1989:51).
3. Of the 1,907 multilingual entries listed by Helga Gesche, a few are devoted to figures other than Caesar (e.g., there are entries on contemporaries like Cato and Pompey) and some refer to nineteenth century sources.
4. See Brecht ([1957] 1969); also the references to Caesar in the two versions of the Solomon Song: *The Threepenny Opera* III/7 (premiered in Berlin in 1928, Brecht [1979:64–65]), *Mother Courage*, scene 9 (premiered in Zurich in 1941, Brecht [1980:75–76]). Brecht's essay "Caesar and His Legionary" ([1949] 1961:61–77) is also worth consulting.

For a thorough documentation of Brecht's interest in Caesar, see Hans Dahlke (1968), and the more critical analysis by Keith Dickson ([1978] 1994:127–38).
5. For a recent collection of articles mostly (though not exclusively) on Shakespeare's Roman tragedy, see Harold Bloom (ed.,) 1994.

Bernard Shaw's *Caesar and Cleopatra*, first performed in Chicago in 1901, also continues to help keep Caesar's name alive among students of literature and those who attend the theater. On Caesar's "greatness," see Shaw's "Notes to Caesar and Cleopatra" in Shaw (1963:477–79); also the analysis by Charles Berst (1994).
6. Another film production of *Julius Caesar*—Stuart Burges' 1970 version—sought to modify the audience's sympathy by portraying Mark Antony, played by Charlton Heston, as a sincere and sympathetic figure; for details, again see Lenihan (1992:50–51).
7. Byron's contemporary, Thomas De Quincey ([1832] 1877:i) claimed to have written his work on "The Caesars" almost entirely from memory, "with the exception of a few penciled extracts in a pocket-book from the Augustan history." Covering unevenly the period from Julius Caesar to Diocletian, De Quincey's essay constitutes 245 pages of the 1877 Riverside Edition that I am using here.
8. The same is true of Marx, Durkheim, and Weber: the exponents of "classical sociology," as we now think of it, were all intimately familiar with the ancient world. While they, like Fustel, rebelled against classical atavism, and while they, too, sought to understand what was distinctive about modern times, they remained steeped in, and continued to rely on, classical learning and competences. Marx's doctoral thesis contrasted Democritus's and Epicurus's philosophy of nature; later he read Aeschylus and Thucydides in Greek for recreation. Though Durkheim's main dissertation was "The Division of Labour in Society" (1893), he was also required to compose his second, shorter thesis on Montesquieu in Latin, a stipulation of French universities in the nineteenth century; carrying the title *Quid Secundatus Politicae Scientiae Instituendae Contulerit* (1892)—"What Secundatus [i.e., Charles Louis de Secondat, Baron de La Brède et de Montesquieu] Contributed to the Founding of Political Science"—it had to wait till 1937 to be translated into his own native tongue. Weber's *Habilitationsschrift*—the second thesis German scholars were obliged to complete to be eligible as teaching faculty—was on Roman agrarian history.

On Marx as a classical scholar, and on his particularly high regard for Aristotle, see Geoffrey de Ste. Croix (1981:23–25), and George E. McCarthy (1990:57–119); also McCarthy (ed.) (1992). It should be added, however, that while Marx adapted some aspects of ancient Greek epistemology, ethics and what we would now call "class" theory, he was not a "republican" in either the antique Graeco-Roman or Machiavellian senses. I return to this point in chapter 2.
9. Objections to modern republicanism—both in regard to its desirability and its feasibility—are honestly rehearsed in Sandel (1996:57–74), especially at 69–70.
10. For probably the most powerful evocation of charity or "love" (both terms are used to translate the Greek *agapē*)in the Christian tradition, see 1 Corinthians 13. The stringent demands made on life by a commitment to charity explain why St. Paul elevates it above hope, and even, faith as the cardinal Christian practice.
11. The language of sacrifice was a prominent motif of National Socialism, as J.P. Stern (1975:28–34) has eloquently reminded us.

Oswald Mosley (1968:322) would also claim, in a speech delivered in March 1933, that "the fascist principle is private freedom and public service."
12. Hannah Arendt ([1963] 1990:286) nicely puts into thematic context Machiavelli's

oft-quoted remark in the *Histories of Florence*, III, 7, commending Florentine patriots who, in their defiance of the Pope, showed "how much higher they placed their city than their soul." "The question, as Machiavelli saw it, was not whether one loved God more than the world, but whether one was capable of loving the world more than one's own self. And this decision indeed has always been the crucial decision for all those who devoted their lives to politics. Most of Machiavelli's arguments against religion are directed against those who love themselves, namely their own salvation, more than the world; they are not directed against those who really love God more than they love either the world or themselves."

1

Caesar Within the Republican Imagination

Caesar: Founder, Destroyer

In an essay on Shakespeare's Greek and Roman plays, Tony Tanner remarks on a feature of *Julius Caesar* that has puzzled commentators for quite some time: "the appropriateness of naming a play after a character who has such a small part (some 130 lines out of 2,500) and who dies in the middle of the action."

> Visibly, audibly, Caesar appears on stage for a shorter period than any other major Shakespearian protagonist. Yet his *name* occurs, re-echoes, throughout the play on *more* occasions than that of any other major protagonist: 211 times to Brutus' 130. This is a non-trivial point. The body goes: the name lives on. . . . Monument, reputation, image, name—spirit—these are phenomena which can outlast corporeal terminations. (Tanner 1993: xli, xliii)[1]

Caesar's "corporeal termination"—his murder in 44 B.C.—put an end to the life of Rome's greatest general and *popularis*. Almost simultaneously it began a remarkable transfiguration of his name and those of his rivals. It is likely that not only Caesar's deeds, but their timing, enabled him to play this role.

Caesar has come to symbolize two momentous and conjoined transitions in world history. His life was on the threshold of both, and for both he could be made to claim, however anachronistically, some responsibility. The first transition was from the "pagan" to the Christian world; the second was from the Roman Republic to Augustus' Principate and thence to Empire. In each case Caesar could be perceived to be either a destroyer or a founder, or both simultaneously.

Associated with a new stage in the history of occidental civilization, and of Rome which was at its epicenter, Caesar's reputation assumed monumental proportions. Here was a man, it was alleged, whose life coincided with, and contributed decisively to, the demolition not just of a particular polity but a *system*, perhaps even a model, of politics—antique republicanism—and who established not just a quasi-monarchy, as Sulla had temporarily achieved de facto before him, but a monarchical *template* that Caesar's adopted son, Octavian (Augustus) consolidated, extended, and finessed. Thereafter, "Caesar" became a synonym for civil authority itself. Supporters of this momentous shift discerned in it nothing less than the work of God. Critics saw a tragedy on a massive scale. To use a formal distinction that John Locke articulated in the late seventeenth century but that, as intuition, long preceded him, Caesar was more than a "usurper"—a person who engaged in the "Domestick Conquest" of a polity over which he had no right to rule. He was also a "tyrant." For while usurpation involves "a change only of Persons," tyranny entails a revolution in "the Forms and Rules of the Government." In addition, just as "Usurpation is the exercise of Power, which another has a Right to; so Tyranny is the exercise of Power beyond Right, which no Body can have a Right to" (Locke [1689–90] 1960:415–6).[2]

This interstitial position of Caesar—a world-transforming figure who closes one era and opens another—explains in part why, over the centuries, such different characterizations could be made of him; and perhaps why, too, he could play alternately, and sometimes in the career of the same writer—Petrarch, Salutati, and Vergerio are examples (Baron [1954] 1966)—the parts of scourge or savior. As the pivot of transformations that deeply shaped civilization, he was bound to become deeply implicated in how these transformations were perceived in any one age. And since, for centuries, the merits of Christianity, Monarchy, Empire, and Republic were passionately argued over as subjects of urgent contemporary political importance, Caesar's name was never far from the firestorm of disputation.

I said above that Caesar symbolized two transformations, one religious, the other political; in practice, though, the distinction was often compounded. Wherever Caesar was seen positively as the pacifier of republican turmoil, and the harbinger of the monarchy consolidated by Augustus, there was also the tendency to associate him with, or link him to, Christianity. This was exactly Hegel's point when he noted that Caesar "calmed the internal strife" of a moribund Republic, and when he went on to accuse Brutus of indulging the "remarkable hallucination" that led him and his compatriots to believe that "if this one individual were out the way, the Republic would be *ipso facto* restored." On the contrary, Caesar's assassination proved "that only a *single* will could guide the Roman state." It also proved more:

> Rome was the Fate that crushed down the gods and all genial life in its hard service, while it was the power that purified the human heart from all speciality. Its entire condition is therefore analogous to a place of birth, and its pain is like the travail-throes of another and higher Spirit, which manifested itself in connection with the *Christian Religion*. (Hegel [1830–31] 1956:312, 313, 318–19)

Hegel's philosophy developed this thought in distinctive ways that need not detain us here. But the core idea of Caesar as a "single" will, and the peculiar isomorphism of that will with the one "higher Spirit" that was to follow, had a long and distinguished pedigree. In medieval tradition, it was a commonplace of theological argument to proclaim that Caesar was "the founder of the divinely instituted universal state," and that monarchy was "that form of human government . . . which most closely corresponds to the rule of the world by the one Divine Lord" (Baron [1954] 1966:119, 148–49). Even where that tradition found itself under mounting attack—as in the early Italian Renaissance—its resilience is startling. Of many examples, one can consider the career of Coluccio Salutati. A champion of Florentine liberty in one of its darkest periods—the struggle against the Visconti of Lombardy between 1390 and 1402—Salutati was also known for his earlier tracts supporting Cicero, and for his attempt to demolish, through painstaking scholarly deconstruction, the legend that Florence itself had been founded by Julius Caesar. Against this interpretation, Salutati sought to establish Florence's impeccable republican origins by proving that the city had originally been founded by veterans of Sulla's armies (Baron [1954] 1966:63). Yet in 1400 Salutati, then chancellor of a free republic under attack from a tyrant, could also write a defense of Caesar in which many of the medieval religious motifs are recapitulated. The dénouement of Salutati's tract comes at the point where he is defending Dante's decision to place in the deepest and most wretched extremities of Hell the spirits of Brutus, Cassius, and Judas Iscariot, mangled in the three-headed mouths of Lucifer (*Inferno*, canto 34).[3] For Salutati:

> It was a reasonable idea to plunge Judas, Cassius and Brutus into the same place to which the prince of the world of demons, who through pride had rebelled against God his maker, was relegated in the plan of the poem. For Judas betrayed the God-man, and Cassius and Brutus treacherously slew Caesar, the image, as it were, of divinity in the rightfulness of his rule . . . Further, since that most learned and Christian author [Dante] saw from the logic of events—the most certain witness of the divine will—that God had decreed that all the affairs of men should be brought under the one single government of the Romans, was he not bound to place among the damned, as men working against the divine plan, those who tried in every possible way to oppose this order? (Salutati 1925:113–14)

Dante's fictive guide to the depths of Hell is Virgil; and it is evident why both Dante and Salutati would find in that "Poet of the Gate" to the Christian centuries (Knight 1958:11) exemplary anticipation for the coming of God. For had not Aeneas, in his own journey to the underworld, been instructed to look at his "own true Romans"? And what had he found? "Caesar, and all the line of Iulus, who are destined to reach the brilliant height of Heaven. And there in very truth is he whom you have often heard prophesied, Augustus Caesar, son of the Deified, and founder of golden centuries once more in Latium" (*The Aeneid* VI.790–94 = Virgil 1958:171).

It is no exaggeration to say, then, that from one standpoint Caesar became the pagan saint of Christendom. And since the cognomen "Caesar" was adopted as the official title of the Roman emperors after Augustus, the name also became associated with the political structures of the Empire, particularly those that extended citizenship—and thus juridical protection—to those outside Rome itself. It is true that for the early Christians, the name Caesar, like the name Herod, could often be a term of abuse, a symbol of the persecution they endured periodically until Constantine's conversion in 312 A.D. At the same time, "Caesar" evoked another connotation: the possession of Roman citizenship and the recourse to Roman, as distinct from provincial, "justice" such access allowed. This, as readers of the Acts of Apostles will recall, was the import of St. Paul's famous appeal to Caesar (Acts 25:11).[4] For on this occasion Paul could escape his persecutors, and find legal sanctuary, only because he could claim to be a subject of Rome.[5] James Froude, reflecting on Paul's experience many centuries later, drew what he took to be the obvious conclusion that "Had Europe and Asia been covered with independent nations, each with a local religion represented in its ruling powers, Christianity must have been stifled in its cradle" (1879: 435; cf. Fowler [1891] 1904: 382–

84). And although Froude may have shocked his Victorian contemporaries with what he concluded three paragraphs later, he was in one sense only returning to an earlier orthodoxy:

> Strange and startling resemblance between the fate of the founder of the kingdom of this world and of the Founder of the kingdom not of this world, for which the first was a preparation. Each was denounced for making himself a king. Each was maligned as the friend of publicans and sinners; each was betrayed by those whom he had loved and cared for; each was put to death; and Caesar also was believed to have risen again and ascended into heaven and become a divine being. (1879:436)

Strange resemblances indeed, though Froude had at least the discretion not to remind his readers of another one: the fact that the initials of the founders' names, as conventionally cited, are identical.[6]

Shades of "Republicanism"

I have been commenting on Caesar's apotheosis in some currents of the Western tradition, and on the manner in which his name was associated both with the rise of the Empire and Christianity. But if Caesar could be revered as the demiurge of Empire and of the one God, he could also be castigated as the man who ruthlessly and with cold calculation broke the Roman Republic's back. It is to this counterinterpretation of Caesar that the rest of this chapter is devoted.

From the early fifteenth century to the end of the eighteenth, Caesar's name was repeatedly invoked by European and American "republican" thinkers, or by those who at least subscribed to a republican reading of Roman history, as an object of vilification. The term "republican" is a notoriously complex one, actually covering many distinct currents of thought and national traditions, and allowing various admixtures with other doctrines (contractual, liberal, Enlightenment, Christian, even pacifist). Before I can deal with the republican critique of Caesar explicitly, I must clarify what the term "republicanism" actually means.

Most often, republicanism is described as a doctrine, or set of doctrines, which, minimally, was opposed to hereditary monarchy; which, almost invariably, was anticlerical and tended towards religious skepticism; which, more positively, insisted that the fundamental source of political authority lay in the consent of the citizen body or "the people";[7] and which sought to remodel society and government in ways that would revive public spiritedness and patriotism, uphold the rights of citizens, encourage civic greatness, and promote constitutional balance. Such is what a rough definition will provide. Nonetheless, historians will immediately caution us that the antique republicanism of, say, the late Roman Republic or of its vestiges in the early Principate, is identical neither with the "classical republicanism" generally associated with the Florentine Renaissance, the discourse of English "Commonwealthmen" of the seventeenth century, nor French and American republicanisms of the eighteenth. The caveat is well taken and prompts the qualifications that follow.

1. Post-Roman Republicanism—the subject of this chapter—is best understood as a language, or an idiom, or a set of discursive conventions rather than as a clearly enunciated program or philosophical system (Pocock 1977:15).[8] As such one can expect to find it wedded to, and affected by, a variety of other discourses that circulate within a society and political culture at any given time. Thus during the heated deliberations in 1787–88 that produced the constitution of the American Republic, both federalists and anti-federalists repeatedly drew on at least four idioms, "the languages of republicanism, of Lockean liberalism, of work-ethic Protestantism, and of state-centered theories of power and sovereignty." "None dominated the field, and the use of one was compatible with the use of another by the very same writer or speaker" (Kramnick 1988:4; cf. Appleby, 1986:22ff; Lutz 1984:190 ff). Equally, a particular strand of thought or doctrine might be given prominence in one republican tradition, and minimized in another. An example of this is the saliently monotheistic Christianity one finds in American anti-federalist arguments—the Book of Deuteronomy was the most frequently cited text of the founding era (Lutz 1984:192)— but which is attenuated almost to the point of insignificance in a "classical republican" writer like Machiavelli. In Machiavelli, the god— or rather goddess—who pervades the workings of humanity, and who men are wise to beguile or subdue, is the deity of the Roman moralists: Fortune (Skinner 1981:24–31). Further, conventional Christian education is for Machiavelli thoroughly nonpolitical inasmuch as it has "assigned as man's highest good humility, abnegation, and contempt for mundane things" and dissipated the moral and physical strength "to do bold things" and pursue "worldly glory" (Machiavelli [1550] 1970: 278). Rousseau went even further, transforming Machiavelli's historical distinction into a categorical opposition: the

idea of a Christian republic, Rousseau avers, is actually a contradiction in terms (Rousseau [1762] 1993a:304–6).[9]

2. "Republican" traditions are heterogeneous across time and space, shaped by the historical moment and the broader political culture in which they find expression. The highly imperialistic and expansionist character of Grecian or Roman antique republicanism may have had some resonance for the colonial policy of English Commonwealthmen in the late seventeenth century (Robbins 1969:43; Worden 1982:196–200), but it would have been quite repugnant to many of those who, a century later, wished to establish a pacific yeoman republic in America. Even the question of monarchy could inspire radically different responses. What Englishmen like John Milton and Algernon Sidney objected to principally was that perversion of monarchy that had accompanied its transition from the elective office of "Gothic" times, to the hereditary and tyrannical office of their own (Worden 1991:447–48). In contrast, fierce opposition to kingship—elective or otherwise—was one of the central motifs of American thought after the Revolution, and, as we shall see later, was one of the key reproaches levelled against those who drafted the Constitution of 1787.

3. Even within a single region and a single century, republicanism could take on distinctive hues. Montesquieu's "republican" idea of the separation of powers—an adaptation of theories of mixed governance traceable to Aristotle, Polybius, and Cicero, among others[10]—is a far cry indeed from the unitary view of republicanism that one finds in Rousseau's later theory of the Social Contract. Similarly, while Montesquieu argued forcefully that large states require that "the people must have their representatives do all that they themselves cannot do" (Montesquieu [1748] 1989:159), Rousseau adamantly claimed the opposite: that while the executive power could and should be delegated, "law being purely the declaration of the general will" could not. For Montesquieu, the practice of representation was one of the great advances of political liberty. For Rousseau, the very idea of representation was compromised by its genesis in feudal government, "that iniquitous and absurd system which degrades humanity and dishonours the name of man" (Rousseau [1762] 1993a:266).

4. A republican *reading* of ancient Rome—an expressed preference, nominal or substantial, for the republic's "virtue" and senatorial institutions over the Imperial order that followed—was by no means confined to active self-professed republican *partisans*. The notion that

Caesar was a tyrant, that Roman virtue was at its zenith during the war with Hannibal and declined thereafter, that, with the possible exception of Augustus, the Julio-Claudian emperors were depraved: none of these fairly commonplace attitudes need commit a person to that celebration of republican "liberty" and active citizenship that we find in men like Machiavelli or Harrington. In late seventeenth- and eighteenth-century England, for instance, it was possible for both "country-party" critics of Hanoverian rule, men like John Trenchard and Thomas Gordon who drew on the Machiavellian Commonwealthmen tradition, *and* "court-whig" supporters of the first two Georges—Conyers Middleton and Thomas Blackwell may serve as examples—to invoke republican history sympathetically as they saw fit. Each, in his differing way, sounded the Republic's praises, invoking Tacitus or Cicero to do so; each deduced different lessons from its destruction. The former drew parallels between the disintegration of Roman liberty and contemporary England under the Whig ascendancy; they fulminated against "excessive commercialism, a large national debt, a standing army, placemen in parliament, and an overly strong central executive authority sustained by patronage and novel financial structures." In contrast, Whig apologists preferred a different analogy between "the ancient Roman and modern British nobility," suggesting that "wise modern Whig ministers . . . embodied Ciceronian public virtue" (Turner 1986:579–80).

Another way of putting this is to say that the "Republican myth" (Ward 1964:420) was a phenomenon much more inclusive than the politics we associate with "classical republicans" and their ideological offspring. The myth showed itself capable of the most remarkable suppleness, so that in eighteenth-century England both the Oxford-Bolingbroke ministry *and* that of Walpole's, could be depicted as Caesarean—by Jonathan Steele and Alexander Pope respectively (Ward 1964:422–25). Nor should it surprise us that such elasticity could function in ways completely unexpected by an author whose work helped to promote the myth. A nice illustration of this point is provided by Joseph Addison, and his tragedy *Cato*. Though work on the play began around 1687, it was not first performed until 1713, a year before the end of the War of the Spanish Succession (1701–14). Tories tended to oppose the war, Whigs to support it, and they interpreted Addison's hero in the light of their own political sympathies. "Whigs identified Cato in Addison's drama with Marlborough, while the Tories identified Marlborough with Caesar" (Litto 1966:434–35). As for Addison himself, he had sought assiduously to avoid giving political offence:

> The Prologue and Epilogue were divided, respectively, between Pope, a Tory sympathizer, and Samuel Garth, a Whig. Addison also requested and got the leading Tories, Oxford and Bolingbroke, to read the script and give their approval some days before the first production. More than this, when the Queen hinted that she would not be averse to the author's dedicating the published version of the play to her, Addison "tactfully ignored" the hint, fearing that such an act would imply his support of the Tory interpretation of the play, i.e., that it was hostile to Marlborough with whom the Queen had recently quarrelled. By publishing the play without dedication, Addison left it neither Whig nor Tory. (Litto 1966:434; drawing on Loftis 1963)

Yet once the drama migrated to a different milieu, the thirteen colonies of America, Addison's caution was for naught. There, in the 1760s and 1770s *Cato* was gradually appropriated as a revolutionary play, its great republican protagonist transformed into "a symbol of colonial resistance to British tyranny" (Litto 1966:440).

5. An additional complicating factor is that a republican reading of Rome, one that minimally accepted that Rome was at the height of its greatness during the republican epoch, that "the Romans, after the fall of the Republic, combated only for the choice of masters," (Gibbon [1776–88] 1910:116) need not even embrace a negative view of Julius Caesar! Illustrative in this regard, and to remain with the eighteenth century, is the treatment of "the first and greatest of the Caesars," in *The Decline and Fall of the Roman Empire*. The context of Gibbon's discussion is Herodian's suggestion that "the uncommon abilities and fortune of Severus" (emperor between 193–211 A.D.) were reminiscent of those of Caesar, a suggestion from which Gibbon vigorously dissents. Blessed with "commanding superiority of soul," and "generous clemency," Caesar was able to "unite the love of pleasure, the thirst of knowledge, and the fire of ambition." In fact, Gibbon adds mockingly, Caesar's magnificence is best exhibited by one his most virulent detractors: Lucan. Lucan's description of Caesar in the tenth book of the *Civil Wars* is normally read as an attempt to demonize the Roman dictator. But by showing the villain "at the same time, making love to Cleopatra, sustaining a siege against the power of Egypt, and conversing with the sages of the country," the poet wrote unwittingly "the noblest panegyric" that could be penned (Gibbon [1776–88] 1910:113 and n.2). There could be no judgments less typically "repub-

lican" than these, even while they anticipate the sort of eroticized and mercurial Caesar that attracted Byron and Nietzsche.

In contrast, Gibbon's portrait of Augustus is crushing, and re-roots the Enlightenment historian in the hallowed ground of republican traditions. A man with no firm principles—"His virtues, and even his vices, were artificial"—Augustus had a superb grasp of what was required to maintain power: "When he framed the artful system of the Imperial authority . . . [h]e wished to deceive the people by an image of civil liberty, and the armies by an image of civil government." And in this stratagem "that subtle tyrant" was supremely successful. Ever "sensible that mankind is governed by names,"[11] Augustus understood that "the senate and people would submit to slavery, provided they were respectfully assured that they still enjoyed ancient freedom" (Gibbon 1910:70–71). In this way, if only by implication, Gibbon distanced himself from one of his key sources, Cassius Dio, who had concluded his own frank, but much more sympathetic account of Augustus's fabrications, with the remark that thereby the constitution had been reformed "for the better, and greater security . . . achieved" (*Roman History* 53.19 = Cassius Dio 1987:142).[12]

6. Finally, one should note that thinkers whom we normally think of as subscribing to some version of republicanism could diverge quite radically on a fundamental issue: the question of whether antique models were still relevant for contemporary politics. Machiavelli, the seventeenth-century English republicans who, in the words of John Milton, had sought to build "another Rome in the west" (cited in Worden 1982:200), and Rousseau believed that such models were applicable (again, for different reasons); Montesquieu and the framers of the American Constitution typically concluded otherwise. For Montesquieu, it was England, not Rome, that offered Europe a model of political and civic freedom. While the distinctive "purpose" of the Roman state was expansion, and that of the Lacedaemonian (i.e., Spartan), war, England was the only "nation in the world whose constitution has political liberty for its direct purpose" (Montesquieu [1748] 1989:156; cf. 325–33). A chief mechanism in the exercise of this liberty was the practice of representation, and this too was not an antique invention. On the contrary, the English had not the classical world to thank for it, but rather the "Germanic nations" that had overrun and subordinated the Roman Empire to "Gothic government" (Montesquieu [1748] 1989:167).

Similarly, for the American framers, the ancient city-states of antiquity were no exemplars waiting for modern emulation. Generally, Rome was treated more favorably than the Greek *polis* that had preceded it, but even in the case of Rome there was no serious attempt to duplicate her institutions—neo-classical architecture, and the nomenclature of the "Senate," notwithstanding (Burns 1954:144–46; Shklar 1990:274–76). The point was not to copy the ancient world, but to learn how to avoid its unremitting militarism and bloodletting, the fragility induced by the relatively small size of its republics, the wild oscillations that typified its governance. What would save the American Republic from the fate of its predecessors was its *novelty*, said James Madison in *Federalist* 15, though at the same time as he proclaimed America's freedom from the "blind veneration for antiquity, for custom or for names," he evoked, almost despite himself, an older idiom. It was the "glory" of Americans, Madison continued, that they were a people who learned from their own situation and experience, and did not require permission or precedent before they embarked on some new path. In consequence of this "manly spirit," Americans had bequeathed to the world countless benefits "in favour of private rights and public happiness." The challenge ahead was to continue in this spirit, to draw inspiration from the leaders of the Revolution whose "noble course" had led them to effect a transformation with "no parallel in the annals of human society."

* * *

For the historian of ideas, the above differences and distinctions will be of signal importance. They arise from the different aims and contexts of republican-inspired thinkers (a pure "republican thinker" is an epistemological phantom) and the differing obstacles they felt compelled to overcome. However, my objective in this chapter is not to write a history of republican thought but rather document how republican ideas in many varieties were formed, delineated, or dramatized in a confrontation with Caesar's reputation; to show, in other words, what republican thought—in any of its numerous guises—*did* with Caesar's name and to what purpose. This differentiated and pragmatic approach has two justifications. First, by examining a *range* of writers expounding republican arguments, it resists the impulse to create a caricature of republicanism that, with the professed aim of identifying "core elements" of the phenomenon, would only impose a spurious unity upon multiple, protean traditions. Second, a focus on *usage* is actually consistent with the way that Caesar was himself treated in the greater part of this tradition. Writers inspired by republican arguments were not generally interested in the "real," flesh-and-blood Caesar; they were not especially concerned, that is, to retrieve and reconstruct the person as "he actually was" in all his complexity. Instead, Caesar was employed for symbolic and allegorical purposes: to instruct, to admonish, to tell a story, to exhort the virtues of republican heroes through denigration of their antipode. Moreover, what Addison Ward has said of the "Republican myth" in Britain during the eighteenth century has a much broader applicability:

> One rarely finds, in the early eighteenth century, a writer who recognizes that [the republican reading] of Roman history is an *interpretation*—who sees that this is not the only meaning the facts could be made to yield. The quasi-religious venera-tion of the heroes of the Republic stands squarely in the way of any attempt to assess in non-partisan terms the events which transformed Rome from Republic to Empire; only when the "Republican myth" has been discredited does it become possible to write anything like a modern history of Rome. (Ward 1964:415)

The point, then, was to appropriate Caesar for a particular project, to which, in effect, he became subordinated. My strategy in what follows is to show how this worked. Inevitably, I will have to be selective. To expedite it, I will concentrate on the "classical republicanism" associ-ated with Machiavelli, on its amendments in Montesquieu, and on a particular case study of republican thought in action: the debate on the American constitution of 1787. The choice is not arbitrary. If Machiavelli's indebtedness to precursor traditions is no longer in doubt (Kristeller 1961; Skinner 1978, vol.I:23–112; Viroli: 1990), neither— following the major studies of Caroline Robbins (1959), Felix Raab (1964) and J.G.A. Pocock (1975) among others—is his status as the principal theorist of "classical republicanism," and as the decisive in-tellectual influence on many later versions of republicanism. Montesquieu, too, played a salient, if posthumous, role in practical republican politics. In America between 1760 and 1805, no European author was cited more often than he; further, such citation was more or less evenly distributed between those who supported, and those who opposed, the constitution of 1787 (see the tables in Lutz 1984:194, 195). In revolutionary France, the picture was similar: according to Harold Parker's tabulation of the records of debates in the National (or the "Constituent") Assembly (1789–1791), the Legislative Assembly

(1791–1792), the National Convention (1792–1795), and of a sample of revolutionary news papers, Montesquieu's works were more frequently invoked than any other eighteenth-century figure, and indeed almost twice as often as Rousseau's (Parker [1937] 1965: 18–19).

Choosing the American example as a case study also requires explanation. Though the analysis of particular treatments of Caesar across republican traditions may be illuminating in showing how widespread such a practice was, it can obscure as much as it reveals. The reason is obvious. Comparative analysis tends to highlight pertinent usages without adequate sensitivity to the contexts in which they are more complexly embedded, and to the precise intentions that formed them. Moreover, the comparative method encourages the worst excesses of sociological reasoning. Human experience becomes "data" for pseudo-scientific classification, while unique events and configurations lose their vitality to become merely one subset of a more inclusive phenomenon. Historians will rightly recoil from this kind of reductive theorizing. They will want to say, among other things, that any one republican tradition is internally dynamic—consider the four "stages" of English republicanism delineated by Blair Worden (1991:444)—and characterized by various tensions: for instance between a conception of politics as an activity animated by the self-interested quest for power, *and* "an idealization of civic virtue" (Wootton 1986:70). By looking at the American case I hope to be able to give some historical depth to what would otherwise be a somewhat abstract investigation. In addition, America is important for this book more generally because nowhere in the world has the Caesar problem remained, to the same extent, a topic of discussion, a point to which I return in chapter 5.

Finally, I shall also draw on those writers of the ancient world to whom later republicans so often appealed: men with a deep aversion to the loss of senatorial power—Cicero is the key source—or who, like Sallust, Livy, Tacitus—"a good writer, and firm opponent of tyrants," Milton called him ([1658] 1991: 167)—and Plutarch, documented both the ethos and decline of republican virtue; or who, like Polybius, were read as cardinal authorities in explaining "by what means and by virtue of what political institutions almost the whole world fell under the rule of one power, that of Rome, an event that is absolutely without parallel in earlier history" (*Histories* VI.2 = Polybius 1979:302).

Caesar and Republican Demonology

I have already remarked on the obloquy that attaches to Caesar's name in republican thought. But what did such detestation *do*? What was its purpose as a narrative token within republican discourse? Caesarian demonology served, first, to shore up key republican *values*, second to furnish important *distinctions* regarding highly prized human attributes, and, third, to offer cautionary tales or markers about *social and political tendencies* that Caesar's career could be honed to exemplify. That Caesar could be a vehicle for all these matters should not, in principle, surprise us. Most doctrines and stories require actors to embody or represent them in some way, so as to lend flesh and blood to what would otherwise be abstract, anemic categories. And though today it is commonplace among academics to deride historical narratives that seek to dispense the appropriate moral "lesson" we have to remember that this is a recent reflex. Before the twentieth century, moral and political instruction was a vital objective of historical study, indeed, probably its main objective. Let us now see how this worked in the case of Caesar.

Values

To begin with, Caesar's name was recurrently employed to dramatize the contrast between his actions and those motivated by republican *values*.

Among the most cherished of these values was a commitment to political liberty, typically envisaged both as freedom from "external aggression and tyranny" and as freedom to "take an active part in the running of the commonwealth," to contribute, in other words to its internal, self-regulating vitality (Skinner 1978:157, 77). It is true that republican thinkers differed among themselves when they came to consider how this liberty was best to be translated into actual governance. While some writers recommended vesting authority in a well-educated and wealthy elite, others embraced a more inclusive vision in which citizens of all ranks were to be encouraged to participate in the life of the commonwealth in some defined capacity. In either case, Caesar could be depicted as the destroyer of republican liberty and political institutions, and pilloried accordingly. Thus for all the differences between Francesco Guicciardini and Machiavelli, both could basically concur that "those who set up a tyranny are no less blame-worthy than are the founders of a republic or a kingdom praisewor-thy," (Machiavelli [1550] 1970:134) and both could invoke the "de-testable and monstrous" Caesar (Guicciardini 1965:77) as a prime example of the former.

For republican liberty and government to thrive, however, it was not enough that cities establish workable institutions. The citizens them-selves must also share and celebrate a specific kind of sensibility that could animate these institutions, breathing vigor and energy into them. The sensibility and ethos to which classical republican thinkers most often returned was *virtù*, a term that enjoyed multiple connotations in republican thought: virility, courage, prudence, intelligence, frugality, and the dedication of all these capacities to the public good, which is to say the good of commonwealth and country. *Virtù* in these senses had nothing to do with humility or self-effacement. Rather it valorized the kind of heroic sacrifice in which the self, far from being obliter-ated, is elevated to glory through the achievement of great deeds, of which war,[13] speech and the acts of founding and restoring, immortal-ized through remembrance, are the principal expressions. The greatest glory of all was to serve and protect the homeland. And though few thinkers put it as bluntly as Machiavelli—"when the safety of one's country wholly depends on the decision to be taken, no attention should be paid either to justice or injustice, to kindness or cruelty, or to its being praiseworthy or ignominious" (Machiavelli [1550] 1970:515)—it remained pivotal to republican discourse that, of all earthly consid-erations, patriotism was of fundamental importance.

To say, however, that the most glorious of actions were those de-voted to the supreme good of one's homeland, was not to suggest that only brilliant deeds counted as evidence of political virtue. On the contrary, a republic was at its most healthy when virtue was an inte-gral part of the maxims and reflexes of everyday life and governance. Nor was political virtue a property of rank or a function of learning; in principle, it was something open and amenable to everyone of what-ever station, however elevated or lowly, because at root, said Montesquieu, it is something very simple, "love of the republic," and as such "a feeling and not a result of knowledge" (Montesquieu [1748] 1989:42). In its turn, Montesquieu continued, love of the republic is love of equality, an emotion predicated on the conviction that while people cannot render their homeland equal services, they can and should "equally render it services" (43). This principle of equality, however, is inherently unstable, subject to a dual malaise. On the one hand, it can simply fade away, leading to aristocracy or monarchy. On the other, it is prone to degenerate into a parody of itself: "extreme equality." But, Montesquieu continued, as "far as the sky is from the earth, so far is the true spirit of equality from the spirit of extreme equality. The former consists neither in making everyone command nor in making no one command, but in obeying and commanding one's equals" (114). Where the latter conditions prevail, a republic opens itself up to all kinds of demagogue—the allusion to Caesar and his precursors is unmistakable—who "speak only of the people's greatness," (113) thereby concealing the tawdry fact of their corruption and avarice.

There is most certainly a danger in lumping together different notions of political virtue into one republican stew, as I have just been doing. At the same time, there are obvious and important continuities in republican thinking that help give it some inner coherence as a discourse. Looking ahead, Montesquieu's emphasis on virtue as a feeling of love, is echoed by Rousseau in his essay *Political Economy* ([1755] 1993b:139–43) albeit with a more coercive emphasis: "Make men, therefore, if you would command men: if you would have them obedient to the laws, make them love the laws, and then they will need only to know what is their duty to do it." Looking backwards, Montesquieu himself is drawing on a long tradition of thought. A striking example of this comes in one of his more obviously indignant ripostes to those who had misunderstood what he had meant by "virtue." In the foreword to the 1757 edition of *The Spirit of the Laws*—published two years after his death, and six years after his treatise had been put on the Index—Montesquieu insists that the value and capacity of which he speaks is not religious ("Christian") but *political* virtue. And this prompts him to make the corresponding distinction between the "Christian good man," which is not his concern in *Spirit* to discuss, and "the political good man" who, in part, is his subject: the man who possesses "political virtue," that is, who loves his homeland, true equality and who acts accordingly (xli-ii).

Now the expression "political good man" itself had a venerable lineage, going back to the thirteenth century, but particularly to adaptations in fourteenth and fifteenth century Italy of Cicero's doctrine of moderation (Viroli 1990:163–66). In this tradition, the *bonus vir* or the *uomo buono* is the man who is judicious, wise, and disciplined; the man who knows how to act appropriately for the good of his city, to which he is utterly committed, and who seeks to mobilize all forces, and find a place for all ranks, in its preservation. The talents of this good man are especially evident in his powers "to speak, persuade and deliberate with prudence"; and they are called for most urgently in those cases where a city requires to be reconstructed and revitalized. It was this tradition that influenced humanists like Leonardo Bruni; it also influenced Machiavelli, even as he sought to make the further, unorthodox, argument that there are times of extremity in which the good man must know how to be bad without, however, losing his essential goodness, that is, his commitment to the noble goal of a thriving and free commonwealth.[14]

This brings us back to Montesquieu—and to Caesar, the very antithesis of the political good man "who loves the laws of his country and who acts from love of the laws of his country" (Montesquieu 1989:xli-xlii). J.G.A. Pocock has described Catiline as a "figure one shade darker than Caesar's in the spectrum of republican demonology" (1975:529), but this is doubtful. Catiline's conspiracy failed: Caesar's succeeded.[15] And in that success, it was the Roman "usurper," more than anyone, who helped undergird the concept of *uomo buono* by incarnating its opposite. Republican advocates had to go no further for confirmation of Caesar's "conspiracy" against his own homeland (Machiavelli 1970:420–21) than the third book of *De Officiis* ("On Duties"), in the course of which Cicero appears to add the charge of insanity to that of cynicism and hubris in his indictment of Caesar and his apologists:

> Here you have a man who longed to be king of the Roman people and master of every nation; and he achieved it! If anyone says that such a greed is honourable, he is out of his mind: for he is approving the death of laws and liberty, and counting their oppression—a foul and hateful thing—as something glorious. But if anyone admits that it is not honourable to reign in a city that has been free and ought to be so, but says that it is beneficial to the man who can do it—what reproach, or rather what abuse, can I use to try to tear him for so great an error? Immortal gods! Can the most disgusting, the foulest of parricides, that of one's fatherland, be beneficial to anyone? Can it be so, even if the man who took it upon himself is named "father" by the citizens he has oppressed? (III.83 = Cicero 1991:131–32)

It followed that the action of Caesar's assassins, in resisting someone "not merely aiming at monarchy, but actually reigning as monarch," "was superhumanly noble in itself" one destined for "immortality"

(*Philippic* II.44 = Cicero 1971:151)—a conclusion that Milton took up enthusiastically in his defence of regicide: "From this it is clear that all the most outstanding men among the Romans not only killed tyrants in whatever way and whenever they could, but that, like the Greeks formerly, they held that deed as worthy of the greatest praise" (Milton [1651] 1991:170–71).

Moreover, while few republicans could doubt Caesar's courage, fortitude, and military genius—well-documented in even the most hostile sources—it was not so very difficult to paint other ostensibly admirable qualities as dissimulations. For instance, Caesar's famous liberality and munificence—the sumptuous banquets and spectacular games he hosted—could be interpreted not as evidence of generosity but as a device to solidify alliances, create or further indebten clients, buy votes (Plutarch II 1992: *Caesar*:214, 218–19; cf. Plutarch I 1992: *Coriolanus*:300). Worse, by stimulating men's insatiable appetites for wealth and luxury, Caesar's practices gravely offended the value of republican frugality, typically seen as a vital bulwark against corruption. Even Caesar's habit of forgiving his enemies, it was claimed, was tactical or feigned, irrelevant or humiliating. It was not necessary to stoop to the lurid character assassination that takes place in Lucan's *Civil War*, in which we witness Caesar gloating over the carnage of the battlefield at Pharsalia, and weeping crocodile tears at the spectacle of Pompey's severed, mummified head (*Civil War* IX = Lucan 1956:222–23). Montesquieu's view, though more restrained, was ultimately just as damning: "Caesar," Montesquieu remarked in *Considerations on the Causes of the Greatness of the Romans and their Decline* ([1734] 1965:108–9) "pardoned everyone, but it seems to me that moderation shown after usurping everything does not deserve great praise." Basically, Caesar's "clemency . . . was insulting," indicating the "almost ridiculous" loss of senatorial power. Under these undignified conditions "Caesar did not pardon" so much as he "disdained to punish." A later historian amplified the point: "'Clementia' is the virtue of a despot, not of a citizen and an aristocrat. What right had Caesar to exercise pardon? His enemies resented the assertion of power and magnanimity, or denied it utterly: the son of Domitius Ahenobarbus refused to be pardoned" (Syme 1964:119).[16]

The reputation of Caesar as a dissembler, as a man with a "designing temper . . . and ambition for absolute power" that he cloaked under the "disguise of good humour and affability" (Plutarch II 1992: *Caesar*:24), would become a familiar theme in republican literature. It was also extended, in a somewhat different way, as we saw above, to Caesar's adopted son Octavian (Augustus). Julius Caesar's duplicity is most evident, the republican reading seems to say, in the strategy he contrived to acquire absolute dominion. Once installed in power, on the other hand, he became irascible and careless, finding it hard to hide his contempt for senatorial authority. Octavian, too, was adept at machinations in his quest to become lord of Rome. But it was in his actual governance that the great trick of concealment was performed, as Augustus allowed the form and trappings of senatorial authority to persist while ruling *de facto* as a tyrant.[17]

Distinctions

So far I have been examining the way in which the alleged characteristics of Julius Caesar could be adapted as a foil to the republican values of liberty, virtue, and equality. In order for republican values to become vivid and lifelike, however, it was never enough simply to recite or preach them and their antitheses abstractly. They required bearers to exemplify their significance and here again Caesar could play an important role either through being elided with figures that republicans deemed contemptible—Cromwell is the ubiquitous case for later republican thought—or contrasted with republican heroes. Let me concentrate on the latter.

In republican mythology, the paragons of republican virtue are simple but extraordinary men and, more rarely, women:[18]simple, in their austerity, sometimes in their poverty, in the unsullied strength of their conviction; extraordinary in their courage, their skill, and their outstanding contribution to republican life. As such, they represent the very antithesis of Caesarean extravagance and corruption. While they are not beyond practicing the stratagems of deceit where necessary, such dissimulation is not self-serving or based on simple mendacity, but is always for a higher purpose: the life of the republic itself. More specifically, they are *founders* not destroyers of republics, men like Lucius Junius Brutus "the father of Rome's liberties" (Machiavelli 1970:390; 155, 530–31) who having expelled the Tarquin kings from Rome and established the Republic, found himself as consul in 509 B.C. faced by a conspiracy of his own sons that he met by ordering, and superintending, their execution (Livy II.1–5 = Livy 1971:105–10).

The republican icons are thus the supreme embodiments of patriotism, willing to subordinate every private and domestic consideration to the good of the commonwealth. And founding is not the only area in which republican heroism can be made manifest. It also reveals itself in those *saviors* of republics at moments of extreme peril, men like Lucius Quinctius Cincinnatus who, legend has it, answered his country's call to defend it against the Aequi, assumed the dictatorship in 458 B.C., and after prevailing over Rome's enemies resigned his office, and returned to his four-and-a-half-acre farm (Machiavelli: 1970:475; cf. Livy III.26–29 = Livy 1971:213–16[19]). Third, republican heroism is evident among those *restorers* and revivers of virtue, who return the republic to first principles, men like "Horatius Cocles, Scaevola, Fabricius, the two Decii, Regulus Attilius, and several others, whose rare and virtuous examples wrought the same effects in Rome as laws and institutions would have done" (Machiavelli 1970:388). And finally, if fortune has decided that they can be neither founders, saviors nor restorers of republics, they can at least be their heroic champions, *defenders* of republican rigourism and conservatism, like Cato the Younger, even as they fall magnificently to defeat (Machiavelli 1970: 389).

It is true that discussion of republican titans often takes place at a remove from any direct reference to Caesar. Nonetheless, writers sympathetic to the republic at its pre-Gracchan zenith—few were sympathetic to the Republic in its final phase—all knew how the story was to end: that is, in its destruction, so that Caesar, and precursors like Marius and the Gracchi, are an imaginative presence in republican writing and hero-construction even where they are not explicitly mentioned. In any event, examples of direct character juxtaposition are not so very hard to find. Here we have the "polarity" that I mentioned in the introduction to this book: the ability of Caesar's name to evoke persons who stand for his complete negation. The latter need not always be republican. Caesar could be forcefully contrasted with Alexander the Great (356–323 B.C.) precisely because he had so much wanted to be like him. This, presumably, is what Plutarch's missing "comparison" of Caesar and Alexander would have provided. Montesquieu made up for the loss in a passage that, explicitly, and through allusion, highlights the divergence between the Macedonian king and the Roman usurper. While Caesar sought monarchy as an ornament of ostentation, wishing to "imitate the kings of Asia," and while the Romans "conquered all in order to destroy all," Alexander wanted to conquer all in order to preserve all, and in every country he entered, his first ideas, his first designs, were always to do something to increase its prosperity and power. He found the first ways for doing this in the greatness of his genius; the second, in his own frugality and his own economy; the third, in his immense prodigality for great things. His hand was closed for private expenditures; it opened for public expenditures. Was it a question of regulating his household? He was a Macedonian. Was it a question of paying soldiers' debts, of letting the Greeks share in his conquest, of making the fortune of each man in his army? He was Alexander. (Montesquieu 1989:150–51)

All the same, it is more usual to find Caesar contrasted not with kings—it was, after all, his aspiration to kingship or his *de facto* achievement of it that most often offended republican sensibilities— but with their most fervent enemies: for instance, Scipio and Cincinnatus (Machiavelli 1970:135, 474–75); Cato the Elder ("compared with Caesar and Pompey, Cato seems a god among mortals," Cato who "defended his country, its liberty, and its laws, against the conquerors of the world, and at length departed from the earth, when he had no longer a country to serve": Rousseau 1993b:143); and especially Cato the Younger. Of him, Cicero would eulogize: "what strength there is in character, in integrity, in greatness of soul, and in that virtue that remains unshaken by violent storms; which shines in darkness; which . . . is radiant always by its own light and is never sullied by the baseness of others" (*Pro Sestio* XXVIII.60 = Cicero 1958:115). The opposition between Marcus Cato and Caesar—personal and paradigmatic—is also touched on in Tacitus (*Annals*: IV.34, XVI.22 = Tacitus 1977:174, 391) snakes its way throughout Plutarch's lives of Caesar and Cato the Younger, and is the pivot of Book IX of Lucan's *Civil War* in which "Cato and Caesar are presented as contrasting personifications of the Stoic idea of virtue and vice, or liberty and tyranny" (Lily Ross Taylor 1949:181). Later this polarity would become a commonplace of the "republican myth," even if it meant contradicting a key documentary source: Sallust's admiring comparison of both figures—"They had the same nobility of soul, and equal, though quite different, reputations"- in the *Conspiracy of Catiline* (LIV.1 = Sallust 1963:226).[20] The response to Sallust, who had added insult to injury by seeming to deprecate Cicero's contribution to Catiline's rout, was to brush aside his account as idiosyncratic and perverse; Cicero and Cato hagiography simply left little room for an evenhanded approach to their great rival. As Addison Ward, citing William Rose, remarks of the British scene:

Eighteenth-century editions and translations of Sallust show the pains which were taken to correct the deviation: introductions remind the reader of Sallust's vicious personal life, his supposed quarrel with Cicero, his abject subservience to Caesar. Often Cicero's four Catilinarian Orations are appended in order to do "full justice to the superior abilities, the undaunted courage, the unwearied diligence, and uncommon sagacity, whereby Cicero baffled so desperate a conspiracy, and saved Rome from one of the greatest dangers that had ever threatened her." (Ward 1964:416)

Similarly, in a school edition of Sallust, students were instructed that "Cato was a brave and worthy patriot. And to compare two such men together, whose characters were as opposite to one another, as black and white, in the manner Sallust has done, was vile dawbing, setting a gloss upon the most extreme wickedness to give it the air and lustre of virtue" (417, and n. 11).

Such character juxtaposition—Caesar pitted against Cicero, Cato, Brutus, or Cincinnatus—had an immense historical resonance, not only in England, but also in France, and in America at the time of its revolution and constitution-building. I shall return to this theme in the next section of this chapter. For the moment, however, let us examine a particular problem republican-oriented writers had to face as they sought to come to terms with Caesar's reputation.

Republican critiques of Caesar were confronted with a peculiar, and very revealing, quandary that arose from the very values republicans themselves espoused. The more ferocious attacks on Caesar became, and the more he was conspicuously singled out as a destroyer of the Republic, the more extraordinary, remarkable, and fantastic he might appear to history. In other words, there was a danger that such assaults on Caesar—by their very prominence and tenacity—would increase his fame, a highly prized human attribute in classical culture. The danger was compounded by an ambiguity in the concept of fame itself.

In the ancient world, and in many later appropriations of its language, "fame" did not mean, as it does today, anything that is massively appreciated, however ephemeral or manufactured that appreciation happens to be. Instead it could assume at least three meanings. From one angle, "fame" (*fama*) was one of a cluster of terms—cognates included glory, reputation, renown, distinction, conspicuousness—that could be employed to refer to achievements so monumental, praiseworthy, and deserving of human emulation, that they were destined to outlast, not only their progenitors, but their epoch. Here, then, "fame" belongs to a long tradition of terms and ideas that denote accomplishments of the highest order. A precedent for the Roman preoccupation with fame is readily noticeable in Pericles' funeral oration, in which the assembled Athenians are reminded that those who had formed the character of the city "won praises that never grow old, the most splendid of sepulchres—not the sepulchre in which their bodies are laid, but where their glory remains eternal in men's minds, always there on the right occasion to stir others to speech or to action. For famous [*epiphanes*[21]] men have the whole earth as their memorial" (*Peloponnesian War* II.43 = Thucydides 1972:149). Or, as Sallust put it in a Roman context, "The truth is that no man really lives or gets any satisfaction out of life, unless he devotes all his energies to some task and seeks fame by some notable achievement or by the cultivation of some admirable gift" (*Catiline* II.9 = Sallust 1963:176). Moreover, because fame or renown was itself dependent upon historical record for its immortalization—dependent, that is, on the arduous task of finding "words worthy of your subject" (*Catiline* III.2 = Sallust 1963:176)—it followed for both Greeks and Romans alike that he who documented such renown also thereby participated in it.[22]

From another angle, however, "fame" was something dangerous or diabolical, which accounts for such English-language derivations as "infamy" or "defamation." In the *Aeneid*, *fama* is personified as the force of rumour, which "is of all pests the swiftest"—"Fama, malum qua non aliud velocius ullum." It is she who "strikes dread throughout great cities, for she is as retentive of news which is false and wicked as she is ready to tell what is true" (see IV.173–97 = Virgil 1958:102–3).[23] This background explains why Francis Bacon, in his unfinished fragment "Of Fame" ([1625] 1909b:140–42), could say that while "The poets make Fame a monster," he would speak of "What are false fames; and what are true fames"; and why Goethe, in the early erotic poem-cycle, the *Roman Elegies*, could observe that "between Love who commands me/And the goddess *fama* there is, I know, bitter strife" (Goethe [1795] 1988:89).[24]

Finally, "fame" might be defined as neither honorable nor pestilential, but as simply equivalent to great renown, to a person's success in being remembered, irrespective of the grounds of that success (Adair [1967] 1974a:11). Here, then, fame is not equated with particular outcomes, but rather with any outcome that transforms a man into a colossus and thereby allows him to rise above the "silent obscurity" (Sallust) induced by our own animal appetites, to transcend the oblivion that otherwise follows man's fleeting presence on the earth. The reason that both good and bad deeds might find asylum under a single concept lies deep within classical ontology where ambition and the quest for preeminence were seen as entirely natural human attributes (cf. Syme 1964:117). Ambition, Sallust explains, may be a fault under some circumstances, but it is a fault that comes close to being a virtue. For "distinction, preferment, and power are the desire of good and bad alike—only, the one strives to reach his goal by honourable means, while the other being destitute of good qualities, falls back on craft and deceit" (*Catiline* XI.1–2 = Sallust 1963:182).[25]

How, then, was Caesar to be treated in republican-minded literature? His military achievements could not be gainsaid, nor could his popularity with his soldiers and the common people. Similarly, Caesar's command of language—as orator-advocate and as the author of the *Commentaries*—often found commendation even among those who in other respects were his enemies or critics. In short, Caesar was simply too cultivated and talented to be depicted as a simple thug. However, if Caesar's renown could not be denied, it could certainly be circumscribed in such a way as to preserve its bearer's reputation for wickedness and folly; and this stratagem could be secured in a number of ways. First, and most evidently, it was always feasible to distinguish between aspects internal to Caesar's character and career that were meritorious, and those that deserved censure. This is the treatment that Caesar receives in Plutarch, who offers a much more rounded and complex picture of his subject than most of the secondary literature on the Greek writer would lead one to suppose. Indeed, it is the extent of the praise for Caesar that is remarkable. We get a sense of it in a passage in which Plutarch is describing Caesar's feats in the Gallic Wars: "For if we compare him with the Fabii, the Metelli, the Scipios, and with those who were his contemporaries, or not long before him, Sylla, Marius, the Luculli, or even Pompey himself, whose glory, it may be said, went up at that time to heaven for every excellence in war, we shall find Caesar's actions to have surpassed them all" (Plutarch II 1992:209; cf. 210, 215). Alongside this portrait, however, Plutarch can flatly describe Caesar as the man whose "ambition for absolute power" resulted in "the altering of the whole constitution" of Rome and thereby the destruction of the Republic (201). Another example of this kind of narrative stratagem is provided in the course of Cicero's contrast of Antony with Caesar:

In him [Caesar] there was genius, calculation, memory, letters, industry, thought, diligence; he had done in war things, however calamitous to the State, yet at least great; having for many years aimed at a throne, he had by great labour, great dangers, achieved his object; by shows, buildings, largesses, banquets he had conciliated the ignorant crowd; his own followers he had bound to him by rewards, his adversaries by a show of clemency: in brief, he had already brought to a free community—partly by fear, partly by endurance—a habit of servitude. (*Philippic* II.45 = Cicero 1926:179–80)[26]

Second, it was always possible for republican partisans to distinguish between types of renown, reserving the most important for republican heroes, and assigning the most dubious to the miscreants of Rome. This was what Cicero sought to convey in his distinction between "true glory" and the mere "shadowy phantom of glory" of the kind Caesar managed to achieve (*Tusculan Disputations* III.1.3–4 = Cicero 1945:227–29).[27] It was also the strategy that Machiavelli adopted in *The Art of War* ([1521] 1965:17) when he put into the mouth of Fabrizio Colonna the observation that while Caesar and Pompey "acquistarono fama come valenti uomini"—that is, acquired fame as skilful men—they were not good men, that is, good citizens. In contrast, those who had flourished before and during the Second Punic War when *virtù* was at its zenith, "won glory [*gloria*] by being both civic-minded and skillful" (cf. Viroli 1990:168–69). However, it is in the *Discourses* that Machiavelli's views about Caesar's reputation become particularly translucent.

Unlike Guicciardini[28] who is willing at least to distinguish between Caesar's "good qualities," even "great" ones (1965:77, 123) and his ruinous ambition, Machiavelli is unrelenting and total in his hostility.[29] Even Caesar's fame, he makes clear, was badly compromised by what he did. People "deceived by the false semblance of good and the false semblance of renown," should understand "what fame, what glory" attaches to those who "might have founded a republic or a kingdom to their immortal honour" and what "infamy, scorn, abhorrence, danger and disquiet" comes to those who destroy a polity. More specifically:

Nor should anyone be deceived by Caesar's renown when he finds writers extolling him before others, for those who praise him have either been corrupted by his fortune or overawed by the long continuance of the empire which, since it was ruled under that name, did not permit writers to speak freely of him. (Machiavelli 1970:135–36)

What is required in the case of Caesar, then, is a perspective that cuts through all idealisation and sycophancy and appreciates what Caesar's legacy represents. From that vantage point a person

> will see Rome burnt, its Capitol demolished by its own citizens, ancient temples lying desolate, religious rites grown corrupt, adultery rampant throughout the city. He will find the sea covered with exiles and the rocks stained with blood. In Rome he will see countless atrocities perpetrated; rank, riches, the honours men have won, and, above all, virtue, looked upon as a capital crime. He will find calumnia-tors rewarded, servants suborned to turn against their masters, freed men to turn against their patrons, and those who lack enemies attacked by their friends. He will thus happily learn how much Rome, Italy, and the world owed to Caesar. (Machiavelli 1970:137–38)[30]

Machiavelli's many allusions to incidents that postdated Julius Caesar's death indicate that Caesar is here being employed as an historical symbol to evoke the horrors of postrepublican turmoil; or, more pre-cisely, those periods lacking the wisdom and skill of a Nerva. But Caesar is also used by Machiavelli as a *symptom* of the republic's malaise; we are told that Caesar "complete[d] its spoliation" (138) rather than being himself responsible for its destruction. The effect of such a remark, and similar ones, [31] albeit somewhat in tension with Machiavelli's previous demonization, is to deflate Caesar's fame by absorbing it into its (dire) conditions; and this is the third way that Caesar's fame can be handled. According to Machiavelli, there were two major, underlying causes of the republic's eclipse; both of them established the essential conditions under which Caesar's ambition could have had the devastating impact it did. The first arose from disputes arising between plebs and patricians over the Agrarian Law (486 B.C.), an attempt at land redistribution that specified the maxi-mum amount of land a person could own, and that provided for grants of conquered land to the Roman people. The plebs, egged on by their tribunes, supported such a law; the nobles cursed and resisted it, find-ing it an unwelcome impediment to the accumulation of wealth and power. The result was class conflict, initially checked by the fact, among other things, that the land expropriated through conquest tended to be far from Rome, often resistant to successful cultivation, and thus less attractive to the plebs than closer, more fertile land would be. However, after lying "dormant until the time of the Gracchi," the conflict flared up again with increased bitterness and eventually "spelt the complete destruction of Rome's liberty" (Machiavelli 1970:202).

Second, republican Rome became increasingly subject to the unintended consequences of its own success. In particular, imperial expansion had the effect of protracting military command; armies fighting at distances more and more remote from Rome were difficult to control from the center and required ever greater periods in the field. In consequence, the pool of men actually able to attain military experience and reputation diminished; and with extended tenure of military command, and its growing exclusivity, soldiers became clients of their generals, as distinct from being the arm of the Senate.[32] Marius and Sulla saw the possibilities for grandeur and acted on them; in earlier times "they would have been crushed at the very outset of their careers." But it was Caesar, "Rome's first tyrant" who showed himself able "to reduce his country to subjection."[33]

Machiavelli's analysis of Caesar is, when considered carefully, more subtle than its vituperative prose would suggest. On the one hand, Caesar *is* depicted to be a unique figure for it is he, as we have just seen, who is considered to be "Rome's first tyrant." (This is a departure from Tacitus for whom "despotism" had already been established by the time of Marius and Sulla; it was they who "destroyed the republican constitution by force of arms," [*Histories* I.37 = Tacitus 1964:103]). On the other hand, by embedding Caesar's career in what sociologists would call "structural" conditions, Machiavelli can ensure that Caesar does not appear too heroic. Caesar's alleged greatness can be punctured by showing him to be the culmination of causes and consequences—corruption, prodigality, class hatred—whose product in the final analysis he is.

Social and Political Tendencies

We have just seen that one way of managing Caesar's fame was to portray it as the outgrowth of conditions for which he was not responsible but that he typified and accentuated nonetheless. This conveniently brings me to the final way in which Caesar could function within republican-oriented discourse. For Machiavelli was by no means the only thinker who would treat Caesar symptomatically, as an abbreviation for social and political tendencies or transformations. On the contrary, the practice was widespread among writers sympathetic to the republican tradition. One thinks of James Harrington's extension of Donato Giannotti's division of Italian government into a universal schema. The "whole series of government" is divisible, Harrington claims, "into two times or periods":

> The one ending with the liberty of Rome, which was the course of empire, as I may call it, of ancient prudence, first discovered unto mankind by God himself in the fabric of the commonwealth of Israel, and afterward picked out of his footsteps in nature and unanimously followed by the Greeks and Romans. The other beginning with the arms of Caesar which, extinguishing liberty, were the transition of ancient into modern prudence, introduced by those inundations of Huns, Goths, Vandals, Lombards, Saxons which, breaking the Roman Empire, deformed the whole face of the world with those ill features of government which at this time are become far worse in these western parts, except Venice.([1656] 1992:8; cf. 43)

However, in republican traditions Caesar did far more than simply mark a transformation of types of "government"; he also represented a variety of syndromes to which all republican political formations might be subject. In order to understand this point more clearly, it is worth looking briefly at its context in classical thought—particularly, the trinitarian formula and the cyclical theory of social and political change that attended it.

The trinitarian formula, a child of Greek political theory, refers to a division of political "constitutions" into three elemental types, each of which has a strong internal tendency to degenerate into perversions (*parecbaseis*) of its true nature. Herodotus, Plato, and Aristotle all espoused versions of this formula; but it is Polybius's popularization and amendment of it that proved especially influential, and for that reason I shall concentrate on it here.

Polybius followed his forebears in distinguishing between kingship (preceded by "monarchy," the original, most primitive form of rule that develops into kingship), aristocracy, and democracy (Aristotle, had said "polity"—*politeia*), for which the corresponding deviations were tyranny, oligarchy, and ochlocracy (mob rule). In addition, he argued not only that each of these three principal forms of constitution degenerated "through an inevitable law of nature" (*Histories* VI.10 = Polybius 1979:310), but that all six of them followed each other in historical succession. This political cycle or *anacyclosis* could not be permanently avoided; but it could be forestalled through human ingenuity, meritorious deeds, and the playful, and ultimately unfathomanable, workings of Fortune (*Tyche*) that tie all human threads into one organic pattern, and that it is the job of the "universal" historian to decipher. The glory of the Roman constitution lay in the fact that it had proved able to suspend history's anacyclotic course, an achievement that Polybius reckoned to have reached its zenith by the time of the Second Punic War (218–201 B.C.). The crux of this accomplishment was Rome's ability to "mix" monarchy, aristocracy, and democracy, normally divergent forms, into one integrated constitution by assigning the three principles of rule to a different element of the "state": respectively, the consuls, Senate, and the plebs. This was a wonder, but given "the cycle of political revolution, the law of nature according to which constitutions change, are transformed, and finally revert to their original form" (VI.9 = 309), it was one that not even Rome could perform forever.

An additional and salient motif of Polybius's cyclical theory, is the predisposition of humans to forget why their current constitution was established, to forget the trials that had originally accompanied it, to forget its value. This social amnesia occurs, Polybius makes plain, as the beneficiaries of a legitimate polity become increasingly removed from the original act of liberation: the arrogance that follows inheritance proves to be their doom. So long as the contemporaries of a shift from say, tyranny to aristocracy, are alive, the constitution remains stable and vibrant: both the aristocracy which assumes authority, and the people at large who support it, play their role in the smooth functioning of the new legitimate order. In contrast, the rulers of later generations, pampered and privileged, gradually forsake their duties and begin to govern arbitrarily and licentiously, in short, oligarchically. The upshot is a rebellion that deposes them, and sets up a democracy—which itself then degenerates because of complacency, forgetfulness, and corruption, and is overthrown—and so the cycle continues.

All republican writers of any stature knew virtually by heart the trinitarian theory; we find it propounded at length in Books I and II of Cicero's *De Re Publica* that Romanizes the Greek distinctions, in Machiavelli and Montesquieu, indeed, in all the major currents of republican thought up to the end of the eighteenth century. Its emphasis on the perishability of political constitutions[34] was not its only contribution. What Polybius and his Greek predecessors offered was a way of locating individual action in a fairly rigid set of political categories, a device that was simultaneously organizational and temporal. That is, figures like Caesar could be envisaged as examples of syndromes to which all political societies were prone. Many instances of this phenomenon could be cited, but we can restrict ourselves to a detailed discussion of one case study: America during the founding era and the great constitutional debate between "federalist" and "anti-federalist" protagonists that accompanied it. To prepare the way for that discussion, however, it is necessary first to say something about the prominence of antique models in the cultural life of the thirteen colonies, and to offer some remarks on the terms "federal" and "republic" in the early American context. With those tasks completed, I can then proceed directly to the Caesar question in America.

Antiquity in the New World

Historians and other interpreters of early America have for some decades recognized the importance of ancient Greece and Rome to the men and women of the revolutionary and founding period. This importance lay not in any simple imitation of antiquity whose models were in fact often criticized and deemed alien. Nor, *a fortiori*, did it lie in a wholesale adoption of a classical discourse; on the contrary, classical and republican idioms coexisted with, and were mediated by, many other cultural traditions: liberal, Christian, radical Whig, Enlightenment for instance. Rather the significance of ancient Greece and Rome consisted in the cultural materials it offered for thought and practice. As Gordon Wood has remarked: "it was not as scholarly embellishment or as a source of values that antiquity was most important to Americans in these revolutionary years. The Americans' compulsive interest in the ancient republics was in fact crucial to their attempt to understand the moral and social basis of politics" ([1969] 1972:50).[35] What this entailed was the attempt to understand how and why the ancient republics had thrived and collapsed, and what role virtue on the one hand, and luxury and corruption on the other, had played in this historical tragedy.

The school and college curriculum was by no means the only, or the most important, medium through which this "compulsive interest" was disseminated. Nor was the appeal to—and of—antiquity simply a matter of elite sensibility. On the contrary, classicism proved capable of arousing more general enthusiasm largely because its province of inspiration was not restricted to the book. "All but a few knew their ancient history, much as medieval believers knew their biblical history, through ritual and icons and theater." Indeed, even among the educated of the eighteenth century "classicism was less a matter of accurate scholarship than of political mythmaking" (Wills 1984:133). Ritual, icons, and theater were effective means, both somatic and semantic, of reliving and reenacting significant episodes of the ancient world, compressing the space and time between contemporary events and classical templates. College students, for instance, might adopt classical names in the secret literary societies to which they belonged— Princeton's Cliosophic Society has been ably researched—and then role-play the characteristics associated with their heroes (by no means always classical).[36] A speaker at a public meeting might don a Roman toga, as Joseph Warren did in a speech delivered to commemorate the fifth anniversary of the Boston Massacre in 1770, thereby directing "a complex, multileveled sign to his audience." The sartorial appearance of the Ciceronian speaker, as much as his ringing declamations against "luxury" and "corruption," activated in the minds of the audience, one author conjectures, "the 'cultural code' that constituted the living classical tradition of the America of the 1770s" (McLachlan 1976:83).

Dramatic and theatrical enactment of Roman republican virtue could also take more standardized forms. In the thirteen colonies, few plays were more celebrated than Joseph Addison's *Cato* ([1713], 1928)—it went through nine editions in America before 1800—and reached an apotheosis of sorts in its performance in front of George Washington and his troops at Valley Forge on May 11, 1778.[37] Constructed to present the quintessence of republican integrity, patriotism, courage, and fortitude—"My life is grafted on the fate of Rome" (II.1 = 1928:21)—Addison's Cato is the uncompromising, iron foe of Caesar. While Cato is stalwart in virtue and the personification of the steadiness of law and principle, Caesar is voracious, restless, unstoppable.[38] And while Addison himself would doubtless have been astonished by the American reception of the play, its popularity suggests it furnished a source of inspiration and contemporary parable to the audience who watched and reflected on its performance. When, in the tragedy, Caesar sends his ambassador Decius to Cato offering clemency, but in effect demanding capitulation, the parallel is unlikely to have been lost on the embattled colonists. In response to Caesar's proposal of "friendship," Cato states his impossibly honorable terms: "Bid him disband his legions,/ Restore the commonwealth to liberty,/ Submit his actions to the public censure,/ And stand the judgment of a Roman senate./ Bid him do this, and Cato is his friend" (II.1 = 21).

Classical pseudonyms among essayists and publicists, so often derived from Plutarch's *Parallel Lives*,[39] were another device to paint an individual in Greek or Roman colors. To adopt a pseudonym, in these conditions, was to do more than simply decorate a pertinent theme, protect oneself from the possibility of state prosecution, or strike a gentlemanly pose; it was to show the synchronicity between a contemporary discourse and a reconstructed ideal that the nom de plume itself served to abbreviate. The practice was widespread in eighteenth-century America, notably among both supporters and opponents of the Constitution thrashed out in Philadelphia in 1787. The opponents, so called anti-federalists, were often quick to wear the badge of Agrippa, Brutus, or Cato; but even those advocates of the new Constitution who were convinced that antiquity had little positive to offer an expansive American republic, evinced a similar proclivity. For while the political structures of the ancient republics were not to be emulated, this did not mean that persons of that epoch had nothing to offer as symbols of heroic qualities and as capsules of historical instruction. Alexander Hamilton, James Madison, and John Jay published the *Federalist Papers* under the nom de plume "Publius" (the reference is to Publius Valerius, or Publicola, one of Rome's first consuls; he is compared with Solon in Plutarch). Hamilton also at various times before 1800 adopted the pseudonyms of Phocion, Tully (i.e., Cicero), Camillus, (all from Plutarch) and Titus Manlius (from Livy) (Adair 1974b:275).[40] All of the Roman figures could, in different ways, be seen as exemplars of *virtus* or as enemies of demagogy—as such, all were of an anti-Caesarean ilk. And although it was claimed by Paul Leicester Ford ([1892] 1970:281), and later often repeated, that Hamilton was the author of the two "Letters of Caesar" published in the New York *The Daily Advertiser* of October 1787, the textual grounds for this contention have been largely discredited by subsequent research (Cooke 1960; Storing *CAF* [= *Complete Anti-Federalist*[41]] vol. 2:103, 126–27). The view that Hamilton's imperial ambition, and his desire to attain presidential office, led to his growing identification with the Roman dictator[42] is equally implausible. Hamilton, to be sure, is proverbial for his love of glory and fame. But true fame and glory, he declared, were to be distinguished from "ambition without principle," a view reminiscent of Plutarch's judgment of Caesar. Hamilton also hated political demagogy; and, contrasting Cato with Caesar maintained that "the former frequently resisted—the latter always flattered the follies of the people."[43] Moreover, it is also highly improbable psychologically that Hamilton could, at one and the same time, identify with Caesar and yet couple him to Catiline[44], or associate Caesar's name with individuals or situations he deplored: for instance Daniel Shays, leader of the so-called Shays' Rebellion in Massachusetts (1786)—Shays is linked to Caesar and Cromwell in *Federalist 21*—and Hamilton's nemesis Aaron Burr, the man to whom, on July 11, 1804, he would fall in a duel.[45]

Finally, if the names of classical figures could be adopted, they could also be assigned, a fate to which George Washington's career so singularly attests. He was compared with Moses, and also with both Cato and Fabius, but it was "Cincinnatus" that seemed the most appropriate designation for many of his contemporaries. What enabled Washington's deeds to be linked to the early republican savior of Rome was his patriotic commitment to lead the American Army against the British between 1775 and 1782 while refusing pay; and his decision, executed in December 1783 to "retire from the great theatre of Action"—to resign his commission now that the war had ended so that he might, at the pinnacle of his achievements and prestige, return to civil life (Wills 1984:12–13). By so doing, he created a sensation at home and in Europe, and through what Garry Wills has called "the creative power of surrender" showed his radical distance from the likes of Julius Caesar with whom, incidentally, he "was always contrasted" (Wills 1984:3, 138).

Caesar in America

The expression "anti-federalist" normally denotes a position opposed to the "federal" constitution drafted in Philadelphia during the summer of 1787 by the Constitutional Convention, presented to the Continental Congress (the central authority of the day) in September of that year, and then submitted to the thirteen American states for ratification. Anti-federalists tended to view the new constitution as having been put together by men who had exceeded their legal warrant as state delegates;[46] and they preferred, though they also understood many of the limitations of, the more decentralized Articles of Confederation, the constitution that had emerged from the War of Independence, and that had become operative in 1777.[47] It was the Articles of Confederation that the new constitution replaced; and it did so through a more integrated, hierarchical, and centrist political structure.

During the ratification debate that followed the Convention's deliberations, terms like "federalist" and "republic" were hotly contested
and appropriated to be consistent with the interests and ideologies of
the polemicists. Thus, anti-federalists could claim that it was they who
were the real federalists—believers in a decentralized or confederated
body politic that reserved equal and final powers to the sovereign
individual states that composed it—and their opponents averse to federalism in their desire to replace the federal principle by a unitary,
"consolidating" or "general" one. In response, the framers of the constitution could counter, as Madison did in *Federalist* 39,[48] that federal
and "national" principles were balanced in the new constitution to the
benefit and harmony of both. Failure to achieve this balance, Madison
also argued, would not produce genuine federalism, but civil anarchy
and the subjection of the states to the pressure of "majority" factions,[49]
domestic alliances and foreign intervention. Further, as the idea of a
"federal *authority*" began to supersede the earlier notion of a "federal
principle" (Storing, *CAF,* vol.1:10) it was the constitution-makers at
Philadelphia who assumed the mantle of true "federalism," while their
critics found themselves steadily compelled to fight back employing
an essentially negative self-description.

And there was a related battle over the meaning of "republic," a
term that until around the time of the constitutional debate, had only
rarely been invoked positively.[50] It is important not to caricature—or
sentimentalize—anti-federalist thinking on this subject. Anti-federalist
arguments, like those of their adversaries, were neither straightforward
nor monolithic but rather combined various propositions, idioms and
sensibilities. For instance, behind much of the talk about "virtue" and
the common good was the powerful liberal notion that both were
valuable in as much as they served individual freedom (Storing, *CAF*:83
n. 7). At the same time, these critics of the Convention often invoked
ideas and values of a recognisably antique or classical republican lineage. Notably, they championed the values of simplicity and moderation; and they were particularly concerned, echoing one interpretation
of Montesquieu, that states should not become too large and thereby
heterogeneous. Size was a critical factor, anti-federalists claimed, because to the degree that states grew larger they became less able, by
their very impersonality, to secure the devotion and loyalty of their
citizens; less qualified because of their remoteness to express the political will of the latter; and, in consequence of both factors, more

inclined to rule by force than through persuasion. Small republics mitigated these ills through inspiring in people the justifiable conviction that they controlled their own destiny. Where representation was necessary (as anti-federalists often conceded it was) the imperative mandate for delegates, short tenure of office, rotation, etc. should attend it.[51] And small republics were also more likely to preserve the people's homogeneity: a homogeneity of blood, education, middling wealth, and civic virtue underpinned by religious instruction, elements that an expanded republic, on the model of the new constitution, would be bound to destroy (Storing, *CAF,* vol.1:15–23).

In addition, anti-federalists raised the familiar republican critique of pseudo-constitutionalism. For "A Columbian Patriot," the whole constitution was a sham, "a heterogeneous phantom," "a Republican *form* of government, founded on the principles of monarchy" (Storing, *CAF,* vol.4:275). "Centinel" concurred: "but of what avail will be the *form* without the *reality* of freedom?" Evidently, the Convention had learned their lesson from "that profound, but corrupt politician Machiavel, who advises any one who would change the constitution of a state, to keep as much as possible to the old forms":

> for then the people seeing the same officers, the same formalities, courts of justice, and other outward appearances, are insensible of the alteration, and believe themselves in possession of their old government. Thus Caesar, when he seized the Roman liberties, caused himself to be chosen dictator (which was an ancient office) continued the senate, the consuls, the tribunes, the censors, and all other offices and forms of the commonwealth; and yet changed Rome from the most free to the most tyrannical government in the world (Storing, *CAF,* vol.2:157).

Hitting back against this kind of argument, the authors of the *Federalist* could also claim to be recommending institutions consonant with republican history and principles, though as we shall see, it was the break with classical republicanism, rather than its continuation, that was the most signal feature of the federalist achievement. Even so, in *Federalist* 39 Publius insisted that the government to be established by the new constitution was republican in that it was to be "a government which derives all its powers directly or indirectly from the great body of the people, and is administered by persons holding their offices during pleasure for a limited period, or during good behavior. It is *essential* to such a government that it be derived from the great body of the society, not from an inconsiderable proportion of a favored class of it." Equally, the government was republican "in its absolute prohibition of titles of nobility" (255–56)—not, as it happens, an actual prerequisite of republican forms. But the really daring part of the argument, as breathtaking as it was disingenuous, had come earlier in the series. There, in *Federalist* 10, Publius sought in a remarkable *coup d'essai* to recast the traditional meaning of republic through making representation, extensiveness and diversity its definitive features. On this account, a republic was to be contrasted with a "pure democracy . . . a society consisting of a small number of citizens, who assemble and administer the government in person" (126; cf. 141f). Though "theoretic politicians" might laud such a government, its practice was execrable. A pure democracy, far from being the precondition of individual liberty was actually its negation: intense in the emotions it generated, authoritarian and intolerant of dissent, no respecter of property or life. Nor could one even rely on its longevity since its failure to accommodate plural interests fostered indignation, tumult, and ultimately revolt. A genuine "republic" was superior in every way. The commission of government to a relatively small number of elected representatives, free to deliberate with detachment on matters of weight, would "refine and enlarge the public views by passing them through the medium of a chosen body of citizens, whose wisdom may best discern the true interest of their country and whose patriotism and love of justice will be least likely to sacrifice it to temporary or partial considerations." The intrusion of local prejudices, petty interests, and intrigues into great matters of national governance—common federalist complaints about state behavior under the Articles of Confederation—would be commensurately diminished and corrected by such a system.

Similarly, geographical and political extensiveness would draw in to the political arena the most diverse "parties and interests" thereby making it that much more difficult for any one group, however large, to impose its views on the whole: "Extend the sphere [of republican government] and . . . you make it less probable that a majority of the whole will have a common motive to invade the rights of other citizens; or if such a common motive exists, it will be more difficult for all who feel it to discover their own strength and to act in unison with each other" (127; cf. *Federalist* 51 = 321).

Madison's compatriot, Hamilton, took the argument a bracing step further in his defence of the executive power, the arm of government anti-federalists feared most. Tackling head-on the idea "that a vigorous executive is inconsistent with the genius of republican government," Hamilton sought to prove such an executive was essential to it. Had not even the Roman Republic required the office of "dictator" to protect it from domestic intrigue, public sedition and foreign menace? However, dictatorship—"the absolute power of a single man"—was not what the new constitution intended to establish; its multiple checks and balances were expressly designed to avoid this exigency. What it would establish was an executive capable of providing the "energy" necessary for "good government." Such energy in the executive required the concentration of executive authority in the hands of a single magistrate (the chief magistrate, i.e., the president); a reasonable period of time (four years) in which his proposals could be formulated and administered; the inducement of presidential reeligibility which, among other advantages, would reward excellence and experience; fixed remuneration adequate to the discharge of his responsibilities; and powers sufficient to rule justly and effectively, for example, powers to strike-down "improper laws" through the use of a qualified veto, to conduct war, make treaties, appoint officials.[52]

Something else should be noted about Hamilton's defence of an energetic executive. In the numbers of the *Federalist* that I have just summarized, Hamilton's main point is not that executive *energy* is a phenomenon unique to republican government, but rather that energy or vigor is necessary for all "good government."[53] To the degree, then, that a republic is to have good government, it must have an energetic one. The specifically "republican" element he emphasises is not energy, but "safety": the safety of the body politic from an imperious magistrate (435–36). This feat was to be secured by means of legislative restraint (e.g., the ability of Congress to override the presidential veto by a two-thirds majority), judicial compulsion (e.g., the provision of impeachment) and by the fact that the president was, of course, dependent on public support to be reelected. All the same, there is a very real and integral sense in which energy *was* conjoined, if not to republics *per se*, then certainly to republican traditions. First, Hamilton was clear that "the vigor of government is essential to the security of liberty" (*Federalist* 1 = 89), and it was liberty, as we have seen, that was the perennial concern of republican arguments.[54] Second, energy is a precondition of that greatness and fame that were as important to Hamilton—the "love of fame," he says in his own now famous defence of presidential reeligibility, is "the ruling passion of the noblest minds" (*Federalist* 72 = 414)—as they were to antique and classical republicanism. As Douglass Adair noted, the quest for fame suggests dynamism, "it rejects the static complacent urge in the human heart to merely *be* and invites a strenuous effort to *become*—to become a person and force in history larger than the ordinary." Unlike "honor," which can be inherited, or "glory," which can be seen as a gift of God, "fame has to be earned" ([1967] 1974:11).[55]

Yet, because of the elasticity of the republican idiom, it was always possible for one motif to collide, or come into uncomfortable tension, with others—for instance, those that insisted on political equality and social homogeneity. Hence anti-federalists were not averse to fame or greatness in themselves, particularly where they were being claimed for some collective agent: a country, a generation—or the dissenting minority in the Philadelphia Convention.[56] Juxtaposed to such a view, however, was a strong belief in what Isaac Kramnick (1987:44) has called "the mirror theory of representation," a theory that achieved an almost pristine expression in the arguments of Melancton Smith. In an oft-quoted speech delivered to the ratifying convention of New York in June 1788, Smith maintained that "when we speak of representatives," a particular idea suggests itself: "that they resemble those they represent; they should be a true picture of the people; possess the knowledge of their circumstances and their wants; sympathize in all their distresses, and be disposed to seek their true interests." The problem with the proposed constitution, and especially the small number of representatives to be elected to the House of Representatives (one member for every thirty thousand people), was that the elite of society ("the natural aristocracy") would in practice come to govern the country. This would occur because "the influence of the great"—on account of their wealth, status, and capacity to organize—would be most strongly felt during election time, and because it would meet little serious or concerted resistance. On the one hand, the "poor" or the "common people," bereft of time and resources, would fragment or, even worse, fall under the sway of "some popular demagogue, who will probably be destitute of principle." On the other, the "middling class," typified by the "substantial yeoman of sense and discernment," would be disinclined to put themselves forward: their frugal manners and general style of life would deter them from joining the ranks of the "elevated and distinguished." But it was precisely the "middling class" that a country like America needed to represent it. A House of

Representatives that had little room for this class would become "a government of oppression":

> I do not mean to declaim against the great, and charge them indiscriminately with want of principle and honesty.- The same passions and prejudices govern all men. The circumstances in which men are placed in a great measure give a cast to the human character. Those in middling circumstances, have less temptation—they are inclined by habit and the company with whom they associate, to set bounds to their passions and appetites—if this is not sufficient, the want of means to gratify them will be a restraint—they are obliged to employ their time in their respective callings—hence the substantial yeomanry of the country are more temperate, of better morals and less ambition than the great. (Storing, *CAF*, vol.6:157–58)

It is true that Smith was making an argument against the creation of what today we would call a ruling class, not against the quest for "fame" or "glory." But an important connection remains. The middling classes, consisting of men "who have been used to walk in the plain and frugal paths of life" (158), are not an entity disposed to seek glory or fame; as we have seen from the above quotation, their passions are bounded, as is their ambition. Smith, in praising this class, emphasizes the republican ideas of equality, moderation, prudence, and temperance (compare Montesquieu 1989:43–48)—not "distinction," another republican idea picked up by Hamilton. The hero seeking fame and using power to acquire it, or the president infused with the energy of office, sounded too haughty and grandiose for anti-federalists. It made them think not of the selfless patriot representing the common good, but of the person seeking renown, preeminence and dominion at the expense of his fellow citizens.

At this point, and against this background, we can return to the Caesar question. Both federalists and anti-federalists raised it in highly negative contexts, but they did so in their own peculiar and revealing ways. For anti-federalists, the main problem summed up in the name "Caesar" was the abuse of the executive arm of government. On their account, the constitution drafted at Philadelphia aggravated this problem in several ways. In particular, constitutional critics damned the office of president as a massive, unjustifiable, and menacing accretion of power (cf. Wood 1972:521–22).

One of their most common complaints was that the sheer number and extent of powers to be enjoyed by a president made him comparable to a monarch: "tell me what important prerogative the King of Great-Britain is entitled to, which does not also belong to the president during his continuance in office," asked "An Old Whig" rhetorically.[57] The accusation was bound to be incendiary. America had only recently emerged victorious in a war against the British crown. To suggest that the framers had created a monarchical system in the aftermath of that triumph, was not only to impugn their patriotism— "Agrippa" suggested nothing less than perfidy when he claimed to notice the "pretty strong attachments to foreign nations" evident among some of the Philadelphia Convention's leaders (Storing, *CAF*, vol.4:92)—but to imply further that, should their draft be ratified, the War of Independence would had been for fought for nothing.[58] Aside from the formidable array of powers at his disposal, the president was likened to a monarch in two chief respects.[59]

In the first place, his tenure of rule appeared to be potentially unlimited so long as he was alive. Though the president was initially elected for a four-year term, this could be extended indefinitely since the constitution allowed for presidential reeligibility. This provision alarmed anti-federalists like "Denatus" who sought to restrict reeligibility to two terms[60] and so ensure that "after governing he [the president] ought to be governed, to prevent his despotic principles from making head." More generally: "The conduct of Dejoces, Julius Caesar, Oliver Cromwell . . . ought ever to be held in view when the powers of this president are in contemplation" (Storing, *CAF*, vol.5:266).

Second, the office of president looked distinctly regal to anti-federalists because of the way its incumbent was to be selected. Chosen by an electoral college, rather than elected directly by the people, the president embodied a remoteness inimical to that "maxim in republics" which stated that "the representative of the people should be of their immediate choice." Adopt this system, "Cato" warned, and "you will incline to an arbitrary and odious aristocracy or monarchy" (Storing, *CAF*, vol.2:115, 117). Furthermore, the fact that the presidency was an elected office, rather than an hereditary one, did not make it any less monarchical or abhorrent for anti-federalists. When "An Old Whig" observed that the president was "a KING as much *a King as the King of Great-Britain*," this did not mean he was the same kind of king. On the contrary, he was a sovereign "of the worst kind;—an elective King." A hereditary monarchy may be repulsive to republican feeling, but it had at least the advantage in principle of enabling dynastic power to pass smoothly and peacefully from one family member to another. In contrast, the president of the putative American

Republic, as "an elective King," suggested "a scene of horror and confusion." Such a ruler would be typically ill-disposed to return to the travails and trivialities of everyday life. Especially perilous to liberty would be a situation in which he was "a favorite with his army" while lacking "the virtue, the moderation and love of liberty which possessed the mind of our late general [Washington])." And if such a man's moral failures were to be compounded, as were Caesar's, by a combination of indebtedness and ambition, he "would die a thousand deaths rather than sink from the heights of splendor and power into obscurity and wretchedness." It was this ominous prospect that the constitutional draft had created: "under pretence of a republic" it had laid "the foundation for a military government, which is the worst of all tyrannies" (Storing, *CAF*, vol.3:37–8).

The reference to "military government," for which Caesar so often stood as a codeword, and vice-versa, is worth pursuing further because it was so often raised by anti-federalist writers. The potential for militarism in the new constitution was believed to derive from a number of sources. The first was the presidential office itself which conferred on its incumbent the power of commander-in-chief and by so doing gave him direct constitutional control over the forces of coercion, be they at the national or state level (*Federalist* 74). Second, in failing to prohibit the existence of a "standing army" in peacetime,[61] the new constitution was asking for trouble: it would allow the president a military instrument not only formally separate from and independent of the state militias, but one in a position, it was alleged, to dominate them. The idea of a commander-in-chief ruling over a "standing army" during peacetime was horrific to anti-federalists. "It always hath been and always will be the grand machine made use of to subvert the liberties of free states. *Pisistratus and Caesar* are not forgotten" warned "A Federal Republican."[62] Whereas militias "composed of the yeomanry of the country have ever been considered as the bulwark of a free people," said "John DeWitt," it "is universally agreed, that a militia and a standing body of troops never yet flourished in the same soil. Tyrants have uniformly depended upon the latter, at the expense of the former." Standing armies were an "engine of oppression" as the examples of Pisistratus, Dionysius, and Caesar, among others, showed persistently enough (Storing, *CAF*, vol.4:37–38).

The danger came from two directions: on the one hand, rulers of a state might use the army for their own malevolent purposes; or, on the other, the *army itself* might "subvert the forms of the government, under whose authority, they are raised, and establish one, according to the pleasure of their leader."[63] According to "Brutus," the army was an especial problem for a free state because military discipline, being stringent and compelling, was invariably able to override a soldier's patriotism. Indeed, "every lover of freedom" need look no further for confirmation of this menace than the experiences of Rome and Britain, "the two most powerful nations that have ever existed in the world; and who are the most renowned, for the freedom they enjoyed, and the excellence of their constitutions":

> In the first, the liberties of the commonwealth was [sic] destroyed, and the constitution overturned, by an army, lead by Julius Cesar [sic] who was appointed to the command, by the constitutional authority of that commonwealth. He changed it from a free republic, whose fame had sounded, and is still celebrated by all the world, into that of the most absolute despotism. A standing army effected this change, and a standing army supported it through a succession of ages, which are marked in the annals of history, with the most horrid cruelties, bloodshed, and carnage . . .
>
> The same army, that in Britain, vindicated the liberties of that people from the encroachments and despotism of a tyrant king, assisted Cromwell, their General, in wresting from the people, that liberty they had so dearly earned. (Storing, *CAF*, vol.2:413)[64]

Elective kings and military despots: these, then, were the main tendencies that Caesar's name abbreviated. Each issued from, or amounted to, an abuse of executive power. But why should such an abuse appear likely? Behind the criticism of the draft's particular articles was another deeper, more encompassing, ontological objection in which Biblical tradition (see Lutz 1984:192) and Polybian determinism joined forces. The enormous powers vested in the new order by the Convention took insufficient account of human nature and the lessons of human history: "sir, we know the passions of men, we know how dangerous it is to trust the best of men with too much power. Where was a braver army than that than under Jul. Caesar?" ("Brutus," in Storing, *CAF*, vol.2:407). "We are not sure that men have more virtue at this time and place than they had in England in the time of George the 2d" affirmed "A Newport Man."

> If to take up the cross and renounce the pomps and vanities of this sinful world, is a hard lesson for divines, 'tis much harder for politicians,—a Cincinnatus, a Cato, a Fabricious [sic], and a Washington, are rarely to be found . . . [;] whether human nature be less corrupt than formerly I will not determine; but this I know that

Julius Caesar, Oliver Cromwell, and the nobles of Venice, were natives and inhabitants of the countries whose power they usurped and drenched in blood. (Storing, *CAF*, vol.4:252)

"Cato" agreed. The "general presumption that rulers will govern well is not a sufficient security," he advised, asking his readers to cast naivety and innocence aside. An American is fully capable of being a tyrant, for "Americans are like other men in similar situations, when the manners and opinions of the community are changed by the causes I mentioned before, and your political compact inexplicit, your posterity will find that great power connected with ambition, luxury, and flattery, will as readily produce a Caesar, Caligula, Nero, and Domitian in America, as the same causes did in the Roman empire" (Storing, *CAF*, vol.2:117–8).[65]

Indeed for many anti-federalists there was something distinctly anti-Christian and idolatrous about the Convention's handiwork. Attempts to find in the constitution "the finger of God" were, according to "Helvidius Priscus" opportunistic rationalizations by men whose belief in the Creator was doubtful in the extreme. Men of "the fashionable sceptical race," like Dr. Benjamin Rush, should avoid "impious affectation." Even here, a Caesarean parallel could be invoked to damn the ungodly. "While the Roman usurper was ravaging Gaul, whenever it was convenient for their purposes, his commissioners consulted the Pagan oracles, and when the people were prepared by their love of pleasure, and prostration of principle, to bow to the yoke of servitude, he was pronounced from the lip of the Cybles, the destined master of the world" (Storing, *CAF*, vol.4:155–6). The charge was clear: Caesar's manipulation of religion for political purposes—his assumption in 63 B.C. of the head of the Roman state religion (the Pontifex Maximus) is specifically mentioned—was being imitated by the Convention's supporters for reasons of pure expediency. But just as Caesar was a man without "much religion" and was happy to dispense with religious precedent when it suited "the purposes of the tyrant," the same could be expected from those who had drafted the constitution.

Publius against Polybius

Of course, to federalist writers such accusations—especially those regarding the fiduciary character of the Convention's proposals—were a travesty of their position. Far from being sanguine about human nature, their aim was to design institutions best able to cope robustly with its imperfections and perversity, "supplying, by opposite and rival interests, the defect of better motives (*Federalist* 51 = 320).[66] "Why has government been instituted at all?" Publius enquired in *Federalist* 15. "Because the passions of men will not conform to the dictates of reason and justice without constraint" (149). The point was not to rely on a people's altruism, but to do precisely the reverse: to mobilize their natural, restless inclination to pursue their own individual interests in such a way as to maximise the common good. To do this required a finely balanced constitution which fully recognized the predilections of the "constitution of man." "Ambition must be made to counteract ambition" (*Federalist* 51 = 319). Translated into institutional terms this meant "contriving the interior structure of the government as that its several constituent parts may, by their mutual relations, be the means of keeping each other in their proper places." Though "each department should have a will of its own" it was important that the constitution "be so constituted that the members of each should have as little agency as possible in the appointment of the members of the others" (318–19).

And what of the danger of a Caesar figure? Though in the *Federalist Papers* Caesar is alluded to on several occasions, his name is mentioned explicitly only once (*Federalist* 21 = 174). Why might this be? One possibility is that the framers, being more theoretically creative and innovative than their conservative rivals, being freer of an imaginative cosmos dominated by the Polybean wheel, felt far less afraid of a Caesarean terminus. As such, they had less reason to invoke it. I return to this below. But another answer is also plausible. Earlier in this chapter, I wrote of the "polarity" of Caesar's name: its ability to generate antitheses. We now come to a second power it possessed which, for want of a better word, can be called recursiveness. By this expression, I mean more than the simple connotational force enjoyed by the term "Caesar" and by means of which it summoned-up such concepts as "usurpation," "demagogy," and "military despotism"; I mean its ability to make these concepts virtually its own. To be sure, this kind of elision and adhesion—the ability of a name to stick to a concept so as to make both virtually indistinguishable—will appear dubious to the logician who will want to tell us that Julius Caesar's mode of rule is best thought of a species of the genus "usurpation," or "demagogy," or "military despotism"—all expressions that the framers employ when they are looking for a Caesar analogue. But in linguistic practice this kind of analytical distinction is of little import. The reason is that, from the standpoint of republican conventions, Caesar is thought of not primarily as one modality of, say, "usurpation"; rather he is considered *sub specie aeternitatis*, that is, as the very exemplification of it. Accordingly, species and genus to all intents and purposes collapse into one another in a process of linguistic implosion. Cromwell also played this role for republican thought, but significantly he is almost always mentioned alongside his great Roman progenitor. One explanation, then, for the paucity of direct reference to Caesar in the *Federalist Papers* is simply that such direct reference was unnecessary. Mention of "usurpation" and its cognates would do the work that was required, for within the linguistic conventions of the time this would conjure up the figure of Caesar in the reader's mind. Still, what is clearer than these conjectures, is the actual shape of the framers' argument, and it is to this I must now turn.

For Publius, the main threat to liberty and the American polity came not from a fortified executive branch designed along the lines proposed by the Philadelphia Convention, but from its *absence or insufficiency*, a salient feature of the constitutional status quo under the Articles of Confederation. Under the Articles, as Publius saw it, three conditions of tyranny or dissolution (the latter would lead ineluctably to the former) were being fostered: the cancerous growth of legislative authority; a power vacuum at the center; and demagogy. Caesar is by implication linked to the last two of these conditions. But in a move analogous to Publius's radical redefinition of "democracy" and "republic" the Caesar problem is turned on its head. Now it is extensive popular participation and decentralized state-legislative supremacy that is claimed to be the locus of Caesar-like situations, and a vigorous, though balanced, executive its most vital impediment. Let us see how this argument works.

Federalist writers were far more anxious about "legislative usurpations" (*Federalist* 48 = 309),[67] than executive ones. "It is one thing to be subordinate to the laws, and another to be dependent on the legislative body" (*Federalist* 71 = 410).[68] Specifically, the problem of "legislative authority" lay in its tendency "to absorb every other" branch of government:

> The representatives of the people, in a popular assembly, seem sometimes to fancy that they are the people themselves, and betray strong symptoms of impatience and disgust at the least sign of opposition from any other quarter; as if the exercise of its rights, by either the executive or judiciary, were a breach of their privilege and an outrage to their dignity. They often appear disposed to exert an imperious control over the other departments; and as they commonly have the people on their side, they always act with such momentum as to make it very difficult for the other members of the government to maintain the balance of the Constitution. (*Federalist* 71 = 410–11)

Moreover, the fact that the legislature consisted of many members was no guarantee of civic and political freedom. Quoting part of a paragraph from Thomas Jefferson's *Notes on the State of Virginia* (1787),[69] Publius concurred that "One hundred and seventy three despots would surely be as oppressive as one. . . . An *elective despotism* was not the government we fought for; but one that should not only be founded on free principles, but in which the powers of government should be so divided and balanced among several bodies of magistracy, as that no one could transcend their legal limits, without being effectually checked and restrained by the others."[70] But, surely, a confederated "democracy," maximizing popular participation at every level of government, would be able to avoid despotism, "elective" or otherwise? Publius did not think so. Direct, decentralized democracies were far more prone to despotism than "representative republics" for at least two reasons. First,

> In a democracy, where a multitude of people exercise in person the legislative functions and are continually exposed, by their incapacity for regular deliberation and concerted measures, to the ambitious intrigues of their executive magistrates, tyranny may well be apprehended, on some favorable emergency, to start up in the same quarter. (*Federalist* 48 = 309)

In other words, if there were anything to be feared from executive abuse, it should be levelled at direct democracies which were especially prone to it; the reason for this was that the "multitude" was incompetent to rule and would sooner or later find itself compelled, on some pretext or in some emergency, to relinquish its functions.

Second, the Articles of Confederation actually encouraged the rise of Caesar-figures, Publius implied, because they made no provision for truly national (pan-state) institutions and their corollary, a truly national executive. Under the Articles, there was simply no way for the existing central government, the Continental Congress, to "exact obedience" from intransigent states unwilling to obey the law it enacted; and there was no power, either, to intervene in cases where a particular state was riding roughshod over the liberties of its own members and menacing its neighbours. Reversing the received wisdom that a decentralized political system was an obstacle to tyranny, Publius insisted that such a system was a stimulus to it:

> Usurpation may rear its crest in each State and trample upon the liberties of the people, while the national government could legally do nothing more than behold its encroachments with indignation and regret. A successful faction may erect a tyranny on the ruins of order and law, while no succor could constitutionally be afforded by the Union to the friends and supporters of the government. The tempestuous situation from which Massachusetts has scarcely emerged [the reference is to the so-called Shays' Rebellion] evinces that dangers of this kind are not merely speculative. Who can determine what might have been the issue of her late convulsions if the malcontents had been headed by a Caesar or by a Cromwell? Who can predict what effect a despotism established in Massachusetts would have upon the liberties of New Hampshire or Rhode Island, of Connecticut or New York? (*Federalist* 21 = 173–4)[71]

The conditions that led to a Caesar-like situation, then, were those of political impotence. As a matter of historical contingency, a Caesar or a Cromwell had not as yet emerged, but a vacuum of power, rather than its energetic and expeditious exertion, had created the possibilities for such an appearance. A strong, national executive authority, vested in the office of the presidency, and as provided for under the new Constitution, was the proper remedy for these political ills. It was also a remedy for those associated with a "standing army."

Both federalists and anti-federalists equated Caesar with what we would now call militarism (the word itself did not yet exist[72]) but, again, their view of this equation differed. Anti-federalists, as we have seen, traced it to the existence of a commander-in-chief in control of a standing army. For Publius, on the other hand, a "military despotism of a victorious demagogue" was much more likely to originate in "anarchy, civil war, [and] a perpetual alienation of the States from one another" (*Federalist* 85 = 486) than from the constitution favoured by the Philadelphia Convention. Again and again, the framers hammered home the message that it was national division that was the real threat to liberty, not consolidation, and that the values defended by the anti-federalists would actually be undone by their own proposals. Hence a *proliferation* of "standing armies" *and* an irresponsible executive would be the inevitable outcome of America's fragmentation:

Frequent war and constant apprehension, which require a state of as [sic] constant preparation, will infallibly produce them. The weaker State, or confederacies, would first have recourse to them to put themselves upon an equality with their more potent neighbours. They would endeavor to supply the inferiority of population and resources by a more regular and effective system of defence, by disciplined troops, and by fortifications. They would, at the same time, be necessitated to strengthen the executive arm of government, in doing which their constitutions would acquire a progressive direction towards monarchy. It is of the nature of war to increase the executive at the expense of the legislative authority. (*Federalist* 8 = 115)

Finally, a strong, consolidated nation-state would act as a prophylactic against demagogy, another major tendency of democratic and "pure republican" types of government. For:

a dangerous ambition more often lurks behind the specious mask of zeal for the rights of the people than under the forbidding appearance of zeal for the firmness and efficiency of government. History will teach us that the former has been found a much more certain road to the introduction of despotism than the latter, and that of those men who have overturned the liberties of republics, the greatest number have begun their career by paying an obsequious court to the people, commencing demagogues and ending tyrants. (*Federalist* 1 = 89)

The reference to Caesar is unmistakable and it was no coincidence that Publius should in this incarnation be Hamilton, a man whose aversion to demagogy was often ventilated.[73] However, when it came to the issue of demagogy there was much more than personal predilection at stake.

A prominent theme of the framers' arguments was the danger to a state of "popular fluctuations," that "sudden breeze of passion" and "transient impulse which the people may receive from the arts of men, who flatter their prejudices to betray their interests."[74] Regular elections to the House of Representatives and the Senate were one thing; direct appeals on high matters of state quite another. The latter were to be particularly eschewed where the relations between the various branches of state were concerned because complex and delicate problems required the careful exercise of political judgment, not the hysteria and bamboozling most likely to eventuate from the engagement of society as a whole. Further, the direct involvement of the people in such matters, far from inspiring confidence in a government's receptivity to the popular will, actually worked to the detriment of its legitimacy: "as every appeal to the people would carry an implication of some defect in the government, frequent appeals would, in great measure, deprive the government of that veneration which time bestows on everything, and without which perhaps the wisest and freest governments would not possess the requisite stability" (*Federalist* 49 = 313–14).

The same kind of logic—avoid or attenuate the unmediated intrusion of "the multitude" into the political arena wherever possible[75]— applied with equal force to the office of the chief magistrate. Far better to appoint the president through an electoral college than to submit his candidacy without the mediation of "men chosen by the people" for this "special purpose." "A small number of persons, selected by their fellow citizens from the general mass, will be most likely to possess the information and discernment requisite to so complicated an investigation" (*Federalist* 68 = 393). In fact the impact of the citizen body as a whole was to be quadruply diluted, and thus quadruply cushioned from the clutches of the Caesarean demagogue. First, it was the *legislature* of each state, rather than the people *en masse*, that would decide how the presidential "electors" were to be chosen. Second, the "electors" (whose number was to be equal to the sum of a particular state's representatives and senators) would, by definition, make up a *plurality* of members, as distinct from a single person on whom passions could focus: "The choice of *several* to form an intermediate body of electors will be much less apt to convulse the community with any extraordinary or violent movements than the choice of *one* who was himself to be the final object of the public wishes." Third, on a day to be decided by Congress, these "electors" would cast *their* ballot for the presidential candidate of *their* choice. (The totality of states' votes would then be recorded by the president of the Unites States' Senate.) Fourth, the process of voting was to take place, not in some central location, but *in the electors' own state*: "this detached and divided situation will expose them much less to heats and ferments, which might be communicated from them to the people, than if they were all to be convened at one time, in one place" (*Federalist* 68 = 393).

Moreover, once the president was chosen he was to be given powers, a duration of office, and a fixed remuneration sufficient to resist demagogy forcefully and with confidence. The president is not, according to Publius, the incarnation of the vox populi, but a leader positioned "to dare to act his own opinion with vigor and decision." For:

When occasions present themselves in which the interests of the people are at variance with their inclinations, it is the duty of the persons whom they have

appointed to be the guardians of those interests to withstand the temporary delu-
sion in order to give them time and opportunity for more cool and sedate reflection. Instances might be cited in which a conduct of this kind has saved the people
from very fatal consequences of their own mistakes, and has procured lasting
monuments of their gratitude to the men who had courage and magnanimity enough
to serve them at the peril of their displeasure. (*Federalist* 71 = 410)

It should be clear, then, that the president was never intended to be
what later centuries would call a "Caesarist" or a "plebiscitarian" leader.
The language used to describe the president's relation to the people, is,
if anything, quasi-Platonic: the chief magistrates of the future are to be
like the ruler-"guardians," clear-sighted, wise, discerning, disciplined,
"devoted to what they judge to be the interests of the community, and
never prepared to act against them" (*Republic* IV.1 = Plato 1955:157).
His office does not rest on the direct choice or instantaneous legitimation of the collectivity. Unmediated appeals to the citizen body on
constitutional questions appear to be barred to him. Nor is he the
mouthpiece or expression, real or nominal, of the sovereign people.
For the framers, a Caesar-like figure, and the situation that produces
him, are pathologies of democracy, fragmentation, public credulity.[76]
To design a constitution that avoided these problems was a salient
objective of their proposals.

It was remarked previously that anti-federalists opposed the Philadelphia Convention's work not just on the basis of particular objections, but on that of a grand objection: they contended that it took no
account of the frailties and the darker propensities of human nature. It
was also observed that federalists would have been aghast at such an
allegation since their view of humanity was as vigorously unsentimental as it is possible to be. The constitution they drafted or supported
was intended to acknowledge human weakness and depravity, mobilize human energies, and produce a system of government as stable as
it was powerful. Yet how, with such a view of human nature, could
the framers have believed that such a constitution was actually possible? How might one be able to halt the Polybean wheel in America?
Whence came this confidence?

If is of course entirely possible that while the framers' confidence
was quite limited, their sense of urgency was intense; and that it was
this impulse more than any other that lent fire to their arguments. Men
like Madison, Hamilton, Washington, John Jay, Robert Morris, James
Wilson, Henry Knox, James Duane, and Gouverneur Morris were all

people who had been deeply shaped by the war, derived from it continental, not simply state-bound, experience, and served the nation in a continental capacity: as officers in the Continental Army, members of and diplomats for the Continental Congress, leading lights of committees devoted to the military effort (Elkins and McKitrick 1961:202). Eleven years younger on average than their most illustrious anti-federalist rivals, they had less invested in the structure of politics before 1776 (the year of the Declaration of Independence) and even less sympathy for the provincialism of state-centered politics that, during the war, caused them so many frustrations. It was the Revolution itself that brought them national prominence and that expanded their vision of what a modern nation-state needed in order to function in the world. Minimally, it required a central authority, with a stable financial base, and powers to implement and enforce its laws: elements that the Articles of Confederation and state particularism so lamentably impeded (Elkins and McKitrick 1961:203–6).

In short, the sense of emergency and frustration that was produced from the cauldron of war, together with the new vision it created, would have been enough to convince many people that a constitution on the lines of the Philadelphia Convention was required. Yet there was more. In a penetrating account of the constitutional achievement,[77] Gordon Wood (1972:593–615) points out that federalist protagonists had initiated not simply a profound change in the political structure of America, but also in its imaginative and theoretical underpinnings. What was more, they were aware of the scale and novelty of their own accomplishment. The document that emerged from the Philadelphia Convention contained with it a series of features that broke profoundly with the older, "classical" and republican ideology. The notion that a constitution was most stable when it was based on the integration of various rankings or "orders" of society was replaced by the idea—and constitutional provisions to secure it—that all branches of government were the "grants of the people" at large (Wood 1972:597, quoting James Wilson). The executive and judiciary, as much as the legislature, were the people's agents and representatives; stability and freedom from tyranny were to be promoted through the separation of these agencies, energy by their competition and rivalry. The constitution itself embodied the people's sovereignty, vesting powers in government that were partial, tentative, and provisional. As such, the constitution was a compact among and between the people, as distinct from a vertical agreement between rulers and ruled. However, the "people" that were referred to in these contexts were understood not as a homogenous entity—save in the senses that all were to enjoy equal rights, and that their legal standing was not compromised by rank, order or title—nor an entity primarily animated by, or in modern conditions capable of being primarily animated by, virtue. On the contrary, the "people" comprised a plurality of interests and "factions" seeking advantage and power. The point of government was not to repress such interests for the common good, but instead to recognise that the common good itself was in at least some respects a mean of diverse interests. Security was best attained by a federal republic in which "the society itself will be broken into so many parts, interests and classes of citizens, that the rights of individuals, or of the minority, will be in little danger from interested combinations of the majority." Just as religious rights were protected by the "multiplicity of sects," so civil rights were safeguarded by the "multiplicity of interests" (*Federalist* 51 = 321). Moreover, liberty became increasingly to denote, not, as it had for the classical republicans, participation in government and security from external enemies, but the liberty of individuals to pursue projects in civil society, and to go about their daily private lives, free from government infringement and intervention. It was naive to think that political virtue could substitute for interest and faction. "America would remain free not because of any quality in its citizens of spartan self-sacrifice to some nebulous public good, but in the last analysis because of the concern each individual would have in his own self-interest and personal freedom. The really great danger to liberty in the extended republic of America, warned Madison in 1791, was that each individual may become insignificant in his own eyes—hitherto the very foundation of republican government" (Wood 1972:612).

Underlying these formulations, another conviction fortified federalist writers, to wit, their belief in the novel possibilities afforded by science for political agency. Concretely, this meant that an intellectual aristocracy versed in the "science of politics," would be able to perform great deeds hitherto believed to be impossible. The rationalist faith in logical reasoning, and the empiricist faith in the lessons of experience, are both evident in Publius' statements regarding the "wholly new [political] discoveries" of modern times; the "primary truths, or first principles" as basic to ethics and politics as to geometry; the benefits to be gained by "quitting the dim light of historical research, and attaching ourselves purely to the dictates of reason and good sense," while not forgetting how important are time, experience and experiment in correcting the errors to which human beings inevitably fall prey.[78] It is not hard to see why the harnessing of science to politics could be an extraordinarily liberating belief. Once properly understood, the primary truths "that every power ought to be commensurate with its object; that there ought to be no limitation of a power destined to effect a purpose which is itself incapable of limitation" could plausibly lessen that "excess of jealousy and timidity" that issues in "absolute skepticism and irresolution" (*Federalist* 31 = 216, 219). For the framers it was not the sheer sum of power that led to its abuse, but rather its faulty organization, unbalanced distribution, or thoughtless application. There was nothing to dread about power as such; "the danger of usurpation ought to be referred to the composition and structure of the government, not to the nature and extent of its powers" (*Federalist* 31 = 219).[79] It was ignorance of science that condemned humanity to the endless repetition of the Polybean wheel. Armed with the kind of experimental attitude that science proffered, republics were no longer doomed to terminal decay. The merit of the new American republic was not that it solved every problem once and for all, but rather that it contained the reformatory mechanisms necessary to confront problems as they arose, lending to politics the suppleness and dynamism that the republics of antiquity had so parlously lacked. Anti-federalists might invoke the dark shadows of the ancient past. For those, conversely, who saw the dynamic relation between "an interest in the progress of political science and the cause of true liberty," (Madison)[80] even the Caesar question might at last be resolved.

Conclusion

In this chapter I have sought to show how writers influenced by republican arguments employed Julius Caesar as a potent symbol of danger and decay. Discussion of the Caesar question offers an index of republican thinking, demonstrating how various writers grappled with such issues as political liberty, the nature of human character, the symptoms of virtue and corruption. Yet, as we have seen in the American case, the old ideas of republicanism were already being radically recast by the end of the eighteenth century. In the nineteenth, new problems would tower over the political landscape. With them would come a fundamental reappraisal of Caesar's qualities, and an urgent debate that would once more bear his name.

Notes

1. For an acute reading of Shakespeare's *Julius Caesar* that brings out its "republican" motifs, see Jan H. Blits (1981).
2. Locke does not mention Caesar explicitly in this passage, though he does apply the concept of "usurpation" to Cromwell (Locke [1689–90] 1960:219, 247). As we shall see below, the names were often linked.
3. I am using the version of *The Divine Comedy* in Paolo Milano ed.([1947] 1977), translated by Laurence Binyon, with notes by C.H. Grandgent. The *Inferno* can be found on pages 3–187, the thirty-fourth Canto on 181–87.
4. See also *Acts* 22:25–26, where Paul seeks to escape the scourging that provincial law allowed, but that Roman law forbade: "And as they bound him with thongs, Paul said unto the centurion that stood by, Is it lawful for you to scourge a man that is a Roman, and uncondemned? When the centurion heard that, he went and told the chief captain, saying, Take heed what thou doest: for this man is a Roman."
5. His native Tarsus had been elevated to a free city by Augustus (McKenzie 1965:747).
6. The historical relationship between Jesus and Caesar (Julius, Augustus, or the Roman emperors more generally) has proved an enduring source of speculation. In Germany, Bruno Bauer (1877) devoted a whole book to the question, and then, in a pamphlet, returned to rebut critics of his basic thesis that the nature of the Roman emperors as masters over life and death, over mercy and damnation, closely corresponds to the Christian savior (who is victorious over nature and who vanquishes his enemies). On Jesus and the "masses" see Bauer (1880:67–78).

   For representations of Caesar as a *Satanic* figure, and representations of Satan as a Caesarean figure, see Blissett (1957); cf. Gundolf ([1924] 1928:41).
7. Cicero has Scipio say that "a commonwealth is the property of a people [*res publica res populi*]. But a people is not any collection of human beings brought together in any sort of way, but an assemblage of people in large numbers associated in an agreement with respect to justice and a partnership for the common good." As Cicero makes plain, it is the act of "mutual agreement" that transforms "a scattered and wandering multitude" into "a body of citizens" (*De Re Publica* I.25 = Cicero 1928:65).
8. Pocock is referring specifically to English republicanism, but the point is valid more generally.
9. "But I am mistaken in speaking of a Christian republic; the terms are mutually exclusive. Christianity preaches only servitude and dependence. Its spirit is so favourable to tyranny that it always profits by such a regime. True Christians are made to be slaves, and they know it and do not much mind: this short life counts for too little in their eyes" (Rousseau [1762] 1993a: 306).
10. See Montesquieu ([1748] 1989:156–66). Also Fink (1945:1–27); Bailyn (1992 [1967]:71–72, n.16).
11. Gibbon's remark is itself probably an adaptation of Montesquieu's comment that "les hommes ne sont guère touchés que des noms" ([1734] 1967:61). More gener-

ally, the notion of the "Augustan charade" (Shklar 1990:265–67) was a prominent theme of both republican thought and of those who subscribed to a republican reading of Roman history.

12. Francis Bacon was another admirer of Julius Caesar. Of Bacon it has been said that he was "as important for defining the character of the American Revolution and the regime to which it eventually gave birth as were Locke and Montesquieu" (Rahe 1992: 347). Evidently, the impact of Bacon's advocacy of scientific method, and his withering criticisms of scholasticism, more than compensated for his praise of Caesar's combination of "military virtue and learning," and the "sovereign honour" he achieved in being a founder of a state (Bacon [1605] 1974:51–54, at 53; Bacon [1625] 1909a:129–30).

13. The close relationship in Machiavelli's writings between political and military *virtù*, is helpfully clarified by Price (1973:326–35).

14. Machiavelli also broke with Ciceronian doctrine in not accepting the *concordia ordinum*—the ideal of social harmony and concord—as the basis of a secure and great republic. Machiavelli, to the contrary, envisioned internal strife, discord, conflict as "a prime *cause* of freedom and greatness" (Skinner 1990:130, 136; also Crick in Machiavelli 1970:33–41).

15. Machiavelli (1970:136) would say: "Caesar is the more blameworthy of the two, in that he who has done wrong is more blameworthy than he who has but desired to do wrong."

16. Syme adds that the word "clemency" (*clementia*) acquired "an invidious connotation. Caesar is himself careful not to use it in the books on the Civil War" (Syme 1964:119).

17. This interpretation of Augustus, particularly influenced by Tacitus, was a topos of the "republican myth" and found many expressions. One of them was the concept of "legal tyranny" finessed by the Country Tory Charles Davenant. Writing during the reign of William III, Davenant was among a host of writers concerned that government corruption, and its cancerous effects on the commonwealth more generally, was repeating the pattern of the late Roman republic. The Glorious Revolution of 1688—the uprising that ejected the Stuart, catholic James II, replaced him by the protestant William of Orange, and effectively set up the basis of a constitutional monarchy—had avoided, everyone agreed, the peril of continental absolutism. But Davenant and other critics maintained that the new order, while offering a show of liberty and virtue, was becoming increasingly fraudulent. Cupidity at the upper reaches of society, and passivity and opportunism at the lower, were encouraging a sham constitutionalism in which people were gradually relinquishing their freedom, and enslaving themselves. As he put it:

> A tyranny that governs by the sword, has few friends but men of the sword; but a legal tyranny (where the people are only called upon to confirm iniquity with their own voices) has on its side the rich, the fearful, the lazy, those that know the law and get by it, ambitious churchman, and all those whose livelihood depends upon the quiet posture of affairs. (cited in Gunn 1983:16–17)

Montesquieu ([1734] 1965:108–9, 122–23, 126n.7; cf. [1748] 1989:309) continued this tradition, but when he attacked what Judith Shklar (1990:265) has called the "Augustan charade," he was addressing the very different politics of his own country: Montesquieu's targets were the eulogists of Louis XIV and the legacy of absolute monarchy. "In the seventeenth-century version of the Augustan pretence":

> a good prince not only possessed all the great stoical and republican virtues of selfless patriotism, abnegation of all personal inclinations in favour of the

public good, stern repression of all ambitions other than public ones, impartial justice for all, and so on, but the courtiers also displayed republican virtues by just serving him as selflessly as he serves the state. For he is the republic now. (Shklar 1990:266)

It was this pretence that Montesquieu strove to expose, and he could do so through historical allusion to ancient Rome—"while tyranny fortified itself under Augustus, people spoke of nothing but liberty" (Montesquieu [1734] 1965:123)—and through political analysis of the "spirit of the laws" which demonstrated that "republican virtue was possible only in genuinely popular non-monarchical republican regimes and that political virtue had never been the effective ideology of any monarchy, whose 'principle,' that is, active political ethos, was that of personal honour, and not virtue" (Shklar 1990:266).

18. Women play a strong role as defenders of republican virtue in Plutarch's *Coriolanus*, where particularly the protagonist's mother, Volumnia, is willing to give her country priority over her treacherous son. In the main, however, women are players within the sphere most distant from republican life: the household. Their primary role is to take care of everyday needs, to provide domestic order, not to enter the light of the polis as equal citizens with men and acquire fame. One recalls Pericles' admonition to the mothers of the dead Athenians: "'Your glory will be great if you show no more than the infirmities of your nature, a glory that consists in being least the subjects of report among men, for good or evil'"(*History of the Peloponnesian War* [II.46]; I am using, for this extract, the Benjamin Jowett translation, revised by P.A. Brunt, in Knox [1993a:343]). See also Knox (1993b:49ff).

19. Livy says a three-acre farm (Livy III.26 = Livy 1971:213).

20. Ronald Syme points out that even in the *Conspiracy of Catiline*, Cato is depicted as the more honourable and practical figure of the two (Syme 1964:115).

21. *Epiphanes* might also be rendered as "conspicuous."

22. See also *Peloponnesian War* (I.22 = Thucydides 1972:48).

23. Compare with *Metamorphoses* (XII.39–63 = Ovid 1955:269).

24. See also the distinction between *"fama"* and *"existimatio,"* in Yavetz ([1979] 1983:214–27).

25. Not all republicans shared this enthusiasm for glory, preeminence, ambition. James Harrington's ambivalence towards them is nicely described in Rahe (1992:417).

26. This is a different translation of Cicero (1971).

27. "For true glory is a thing of real substance and clearly wrought, no shadowy phantom: it is the agreed approval of good men, the unbiased verdict of judges deciding honestly the question of pre-eminent merit; it gives back to virtue the echo of her voice. . . . The other kind of glory, however, which claims to be a copy of the true, is headstrong and thoughtless, and generally lends its support to faults and errors; it is public reputation, and by a counterfeit mars the fair beauty of true honour. By this illusion human beings, in spite of some noble ambitions, are blinded and, as they do not know where to look or what to find, some of them bring about the utter ruin of their country and others their own downfall."

Such a view could be applied, in various ways, by both republican partisans and those who, though not "republican" in their political sympathies, still subscribed to a republican reading of ancient Rome. Thus one might compare a modern republican thinker, Hannah Arendt, who also "denies that *bad* acts can be glorious" (Canovan 1992:193; Arendt 1958:77) with someone like Alexander Pope who, in the Prologue to Joseph Addison's *Cato* ([1713] 1928:5) remarks that Caesar is "ignobly vain, and impotently great."

28. Or, later, Montesquieu (1965:106).
29. I must reemphasise that this is the Machiavelli of the *Discourses*—the "philosopher of liberty," as Quentin Skinner dubs him (1981:48)—that we are discussing. In *The Prince* ([1532] 1972:99), on the other hand, Machiavelli is more than willing to describe Caesar as one of those "excellent men" who was willing prudently to imitate those most "praised and honoured" before him (notably, Alexander the Great). Similarly, in *The Art of War* (1965:55–56, 111, 120, 178–79, 211) Caesar's military skill is highly praised.
30. The passage is taken almost verbatim from Tacitus' *Histories* (I.2 = Tacitus 1964:22).

    Machiavelli and Tacitus are describing not the Caesarean interlude, but the period 69 A.D. to the end of the Flavian dynasty in 96 A.D., that is, the period that spans Galba's assumption of imperial authority (and murder) to Domitian's death.
31. For instance, Machiavelli (1970:158).
32. Guicciardini (1965:123–24) argued, against Machiavelli, that it was not the prolongation of command that was a principal cause of the republic's collapse, so much as its context: the widespread corruption of Rome. "Hence I conclude that while Rome was not corrupted, the prolongation of commands and the continuation of the consulship which they resorted to frequently in times of great difficulty, were useful and virtuous measures. But once the city was corrupted, civil discord began and the seeds of tyranny, even without the prolongation of the command. And so one can conclude that even if there had not been the extensions as well, neither Caesar nor the others who usurped the republic would have lacked the idea or the opportunity of seizing power by some other means."
33. The quotes come, respectively, from Machiavelli (1970:428, 203 [cf. 193], 474).
34. On this phenomenon, see Rousseau (1993a:257–60); and Montesquieu (1989:166).
35. This is a weaker claim than that made by Charles F. Mullett (1939–40) or Richard M. Gummere (e.g., Gummere 1962) but a stronger claim than that made by Bernard Bailyn ([1967] 1992:26) who remarks that while the "classics of the ancient world are everywhere in the literature of the Revolution," they "are everywhere illustrative, not determinative, of thought. They contributed a vivid vocabulary but not the logic or grammar of thought, a universally respected personification but not the source of political and social beliefs. They heightened the colonists' sensitivity to ideas and attitudes otherwise derived." This way of phrasing matters seems to me questionable because we are invited to make a choice—between "illustration" and "grammar"—without knowing the criteria under which to make it in this particular case. If an "illustration" is used again and again—as the Caesar figure is, for instance—has it not become *part* of the "logic or grammar of thought"? Moreover, if we see the classical world as something mediated by and refracted through other traditions, then even on Bailyn's account it appears to be formative and integral rather than simply "illustrative." For instance, see Bailyn (42–45, 102, 113–14, 131, 133, 135–37, 141–42, etc). A sensible attempt to address these issues is found in Rahe (1992:570–72).
36. See McLachlan (1976).
37. Details in Litto (1966: 435, 447).
38. "Alas," says the senator Sempronius, "thou know'st not Caesar's active soul,/ With what a dreadful course he rushes on/ From war to war. In vain has nature formed/Mountains and oceans to oppose his passage" (I.3 = 1928:11).
39. According to Douglass Adair (1974b:274 n.6), the John Dryden translation (1683–86), which I have been using thus far, was the standard one for early American

readers; this is contradicted by Meyer Reinhold (1975:41) who maintains that Sir Thomas North's translation (1579)—based not on the Greek, but on Jacques Amyot's (1559) French rendering—was more often consulted than Dryden's.

40. Hamilton in 1803 also began signing himself as Pericles, an indication, says Adair, of his imperial designs.

41. Herbert J. Storing's *The Complete Anti-Federalist* is a misnomer; it contains, according to Bernard Bailyn (1992:327) "only about 15 per cent of the total available antifederalist material." However, Storing's six volume compilation (the seventh volume is an index) will suffice for my purposes here.

42. See Adair (1974a:15–22, 1974b:279–85); cf. Stourzh (1970: 98–99, 119, 239 n.85); Pocock (1975:529–32).

43. This and the previous statement are cited in Stourzh (1970:99).

44. See the remarks cited in Govan (1975:477).

45. Thomas Govan's bibliographic study of Caesar references in the writings of Alexander Hamilton, shows that with only one exception, and even this is neutral rather than positive in meaning, Hamilton's remarks on Caesar "uniformly carry an opprobrious connotation" (Govan 1975:476).

Further doubt is cast upon Hamilton's supposed Caesarian aspirations by Mackubin T. Owens, Jr. (1984).

46. See "Cato" in Storing (*CAF*, vol.2:108); "Centinel" in Storing (*CAF*, vol.2:156–57).

47. For instance, see Smith, in Storing (*CAF*, vol. 6:150).

48. Because of the multiple editions of the *Federalist* (1788), I have resorted to citing, in the first instance, the relevant essay number. All page references are to the Penguin Classics edition, edited by Isaac Kramnick (1987). References to Kramnick (1987), are to his excellent Editor's Introduction. In the bibliography, the *Federalist* is cited under James Madison, Alexander Hamilton and John Jay.

49. We are accustomed to think of a faction as a minority grouping, but to Publius "By a faction I understand a number of citizens, whether amounting to a majority or minority of the whole, who are united and actuated by some common impulse of passion, or of interest, adverse to the rights of other citizens, or to the permanent and aggregate interests of the community" (*Federalist* 10:123).

50. Isaac Kramnick (1987:41) points out that "None of the eighteen constitutions adopted by the thirteen American states between 1776 and 1787 . . . used the word 'republic.'"

51. See, for example, the arguments of "The Federal Farmer" in Storing (*CAF*, vol.2:304).

52. The relevant *Federalist Papers* are 70–77 = 402–36.

53. Madison agreed in *Federalist* 37 = 243–44.

54. Cf. Machiavelli's *Discourses*, book 11, and part 2 of Montesquieu's *The Spirit of the Laws*.

55. Compare with the preface to *The Jugurthine War* (I.1–3 = Sallust 1963:35).

Paul Rahe (1992:565–66) argues that while Hamilton may have used the classical lexicon of "nobility" and "fame," "Nowhere did [he] insist that the love of fame is a spur to the pursuit of virtue or an echo of the universal longing for true excellence." For a contrasting view in which patriotism and "true excellence," appear to be part of what Hamilton intended in his evocation of "fame," see Stourzh (1970:99–106), and the revealing quotations from Washington and Pickering (103).

56. See "Cato," "Centinel," and "Helvidius Priscus" in Storing (respectively, *CAF*, vol.2:117; vol.2:155; vol.4:156).

57. Storing (*CAF*, vol.3:38; cf. "Cato" in *CAF*, vol.2:115, 117).
58. The monarchical allegation was contemptuously dismissed by Publius in an outburst of bitterness unmatched in the *Federalist Papers*. See *Federalist* 67 = 389–392.
59. The vice president's powers were also considered dangerous; see, for instance, Storing (*CAF*, vol.2:12, 115; vol.5:44, 117).
60. In time, "Denatus" would have his way: see, section 1 of the twenty-second amendment (1951) of the Constitution:"No person shall be elected to the office of the president more than twice" etc.
61. The constitution did not specify the creation of a standing army, but nor did it specifically prohibit one: see *Federalist* 8 = 115. It was the absence of such a prohibition that anti-federalists attacked.
62. Storing (*CAF*, vol.3:76). The author does not mention the president in this context, but rather the powers of Congress.
63. Remarked "Brutus" in Storing (*CAF*, vol.2:413).
64. See also the comparison between Caesar and Cromwell in Storing (*CAF*, vol.2:407–8).
65. See also "An Old Whig": Storing (*CAF*, vol.3:48).
66. Reliance on human goodness is rare in the *Federalist Papers*. Where it appears, as in *Federalist* 55 and 76 (= 339, 431), it manifests itself as a *deus ex machina* to supply, as federalists might have put it, the defect of better arguments.
67. Compare with Montesquieu (1989:166): "Since all human things have an end, the state of which we are speaking [England] will lose its liberty; it will perish. Rome, Lacedaemonia, and Carthage have surely perished. This state will perish when legislative power is more corrupt than executive power."
68. Or as Benjamin Rush remarked ([1777] 1947:71) "It has been said often, and I wish the saying was engraven over the doors of every statehouse on the Continent, that 'all power is *derived* from the people,' but it has never yet been said that all power is *seated* in the people. Government supposes and requires a delegation of power: It cannot exist without it." Attempts to involve the people on a mass scale in, specifically, the judicial arm of government, were monstrous and counterproductive, Rush contended. "All history shows us that the people soon grow weary of the folly and tyranny of one another. They prefer one to many masters, and stability to instability of [sic] slavery. They prefer a Julius Caesar to a Senate, and a Cromwell to a perpetual Parliament."
    See also Rush ([1779] 1951, vol.1:235) where Caesar and Cromwell are also invoked in a highly negative context.
69. Which in the paragraph's entirety contains a negative reference to Caesar.
70. Jefferson (1787), in Peterson (1975:164 = *Federalist* 48 = 310–11).
    See also Jefferson's very interesting letter, dated January 26, 1811, to Destutt de Tracy, in which he defends the Philadelphia Convention's decision to create a "singular" rather than a plural *executive*. The failure of the French to do so, he argues, was the key cause for the collapse of the Directory, and the rise of Napoleon. And Jefferson continues: "You apprehend that a single executive, with eminence of talent, and destitution of principle, equal to the object, might, by usurpation, render his powers hereditary. Yet I think history furnishes as many examples of a single usurper arising out of a government by a plurality, as of temporary trusts of power in a single hand rendered permanent by usurpation." The real guarantee of liberty was not a plural executive, but strong state governments. In contrast, the "republican government of France was lost without a struggle, because the party of "*un et indivisible*" had prevailed; no provincial

organizations existed to which the people might rally under authority of the laws, the seats of the directory were virtually vacant, and a small force sufficed to turn the legislature out of their chamber, and to salute its leader chief of the nation" (Jefferson, in Peterson [1975:520–25]).

71. See also "Cassius" in Ford ([1892] 1970:34–35).

72. The word was coined around 1816–18, but was then left in abeyance until Pierre-Joseph Proudhon employed it in 1861. By the late 1860s it was firmly on its way to becoming a keyword of European political discussion. On the term's origins and trajectory, see Volker Berghahn ([1981] 1984).

73. It was thus appropriate and in character that one participant at the Convention should portray him as "a convincing Speaker" but no "blazing Orator." This is part of a sketch of Hamilton by Major William Pierce, a fellow member of the Philadelphia Convention. See Hunt and Scott ([1920] 1970:lxxxviii-lxxxix).

74. The quotes come, respectively, from *Federalist* 63 and 71 = 371, 409–10.

75. On the dangers for the polity of over-large representative assemblies, see *Federalist* 55, 58, 63 = 336, 351, 370ff.

76. They were also a pathology of proletarianization: see Burns (1954:162–63) on Hamilton's and Madison's fears about this, and the Caesar parallel on which both writers allegedly drew.

77. On which I rely heavily in the following two paragraphs.

78. *Federalist* 9, 31, 70, 85 = 119, 216, 404, 486.

79. See also *Federalist* 23 = 187.

80. The statement comes from Madison's will, printed in part in Hunt and Scott ([1920] 1970:v).

2

The Advent of Caesarism

Exoneration

The Victorian Age, it has justly been said, was an era of redefinitions. "Sins became crimes; crimes, diseases; diseases, social problems" (Gay 1993:213). What, then, did the Caesar-question become? The question admits of no easy answer since it depends on who examined it, when, and through what lenses.

Aesthetically, Caesar emerges against the backdrop of the romantic, pantheistic affirmation of earthly life, and the revolt against bourgeois and Christian morality. Depicted as the man free of onesidedness, the man of word and deed, the man willing to suffer and risk everything for personal transcendence over the banal, this is the Caesar who caught Byron's attention even before the Victorian Age proper began. Byron's troubled ambivalence towards the dictator ensured that his enthusiasm could never match that of Thomas De Quincey, for whom Caesar's "reforms, even before his Pompeian struggle, were the greatest ever made by an individual…and during that brief term which his murderers allowed him, transcended by much all that in any one century had been accomplished by the collective patriotism of Rome" ([1832] 1877:312; cf. 50–64). Byron, conversely, knew that Caesar's "substance left graves enough, and woes enough, and fame more than enough to track his memory": this is how the Mephistopheles-like Stranger describes Caesar to Arnold the hunchback in *The Deformed Transformed* (1824) just before himself assuming the name of the eponymous Roman. Yet elsewhere, contrasting Napoleon with Caesar, Byron depicts the Roman's mind as "modell'd in a less terrestrial mould/With passions fiercer, yet a judgement cold/And an immortal instinct which redeem'd/The frailties of a heart so soft, yet bold/ Alcides with the distaff now he seem'd/At Cleopatra's feet—and how himself he beam'd/ And came—and saw—and conquer'd!" (*Childe Harold* IV.90.805–11). It was almost as if what Giuseppe Mazzini ([1839] 1908a:68) celebrated in Byron's distinct type of egoism—the "pride of power, freedom and desire...inhaling existence at every pore, eager to seize 'the life of life'"—was what Byron found himself compelled to see in Caesar.

He was not alone, as Friedrich Gundolf ([1926] 1968) pointed out long ago in a work that to this day stands as the most acute, if most idiosyncratic and maddening, analysis we have of nineteenth-century literary, artistic and historicist appropriations of Caesar. Taking us on a tour of personalities so otherwise diverse as Gioberti, the younger Victor Hugo, Stendhal, Heine, Quinet, Balzac, Delacroix, Gautier, Sue, Flaubert, Sainte-Beuve, Baudelaire, Anatole France, Mommsen, Merivale among many others, Gundolf showed how each found in Caesar what he sought to idealize of past achievements or lacerate in modern times and mores. The apogee of this revaluation came from Friedrich Nietzsche. This was not, of course, out of romantic attachment which he often repudiated, but rather derived from his own peculiar purposes, Dionysian and prophetic. The Caesar Nietzsche loved was not simply the master of Latin style and composition, though this would have been an understandable affection from one of the most brilliant philologists of the century. Nor was he simply the man of action; the impulse for action alone Nietzsche distrusted as a "flight from oneself," a longing to be absorbed into some project in order to escape the tensions of personal existence ([1881] 1982:221). Instead Caesar was mostly praised by Nietzsche as the man of titanic inner strength, discipline, and plenitude: Caesar who, shunning the sedative of happiness, embodied "irreconcilable drives"; Caesar the genius of "self-control, self-outwitting" ([1886] 1973:103; [1889] 1968:84, 93), exemplar of Roman aristocratic warrior values, antithesis of the priestly, plebeian, life-abnegating values of Jewishness which, after the life of Christ, had vanquished and tamed the Roman world. Periodically, Nietzsche remarked in *The Genealogy of Morals*, the glory of the Roman world and its brightest light had reasserted itself. When the French Revolution "collapsed under the weight of vindictive popular instincts," when, that is, plebeianism seemed once more triumphant, something wholly unexpected happened: the ancient classical ideal appeared incarnate and in unprecedented splendor before the eyes and conscience of mankind. Once again, stronger, simpler, more insistent than ever, over against the lying shibboleth of the rights of the majority, against the furious tendency toward levelling out and debasement, sounded the terrible yet exhilarating shibboleth of the "prerogative of the few." Like a last signpost to an alternative route Napoleon appeared, most isolated and anachronistic of men, the embodiment of the noble ideal...Napoleon, that synthesis of the brutish with the more than human [*diese Synthesis von Unmensch und Übermensch*]. (Nietzsche [1887] 1956:186–87 = Nietzsche 1966 2:796–7)[1]

By the time Nietzsche wrote these lines, the identification of Napoleon with Caesar had been a platitude for at least fifty years. Conversely, so powerful was that association that the "aesthetic and literary image of Caesar" himself "was dominated by the impression of Napoleon" (Gundolf 1968:292). The Napoleonic interpretation of Caesar also penetrated historical writing. "Napoleon's halt to the bickerings of the corrupt French Directory, his imposition of efficient laws and administration on France, his expansion of the French Empire, and his overturning of the old regime across much of the Continent" not only invited "the drawing of parallels between himself and Caesar" but also encouraged a mostly positive revaluation of Caesar's own historical significance (Turner 1986:589–90).

The Roman's rehabilitation, however, was never simple or definitive; on the contrary, it found itself complicated and compromised by a major political debate. If many could celebrate Napoleon as a Caesar-like figure, then it was always possible for others to abhor the Corsican for roughly the same reason. And this controversy became accentuated when, in a remarkable political extrapolation, the Caesarean mantle of Napoleon fell on the shoulders of his nephew, Louis Bonaparte. Between 1850 and 1871, Louis Bonaparte's career became enmeshed in a major dispute about "Caesarism," a term that, until Bismarck, it made virtually its own. To examine this debate is the principal task of this chapter. But first we must briefly return to the man who paved the way for it. For while the "Caesarism" controversy had to wait until Napoleon Bonaparte's death to be born, the Napoleon-Caesar mythology on which it partly depended, was of an older provenance. Many thinkers and propagandists contributed to that mythology; not least among them was Napoleon himself.

Classicism Without Republicanism:
Caesar, Napoleon and the "Great Parallel"

Few analogies can have proved more historically seductive than the one linking the political achievements of Julius Caesar and Napoleon Bonaparte, a resemblance that has exercised the imagination of scholars, journalists, artists, and propagandists for almost two centuries. True, Napoleon I was not the only person in revolutionary France to find himself compared with ancient Rome's most famous dictator—Mirabeau had earlier claimed this mantle for Lafayette (Soboul [1965] 1977:55); nor was Julius Caesar the only model that commended itself to those with a penchant for heroic parallels: Alexander, Charlemagne, and Cromwell,[2] to name but three, were all identified, at one time or another, as figures whose monumental deeds bore affinity with those of the Corsican. But if one name was to stick to Napoleon more than any other it was that of Caesar. There is evidence that the emperor of the French would not have been too downcast by the association.

The parallel often crossed his own fantastically inventive mind, albeit sometimes defensively. Consider Napoleon's own description of the events surrounding his coup of the Eighteenth Brumaire (November 9, 1799).[3] France, he tells us, was a country in a shameful state when he arrived back from Egypt, dogged by the weakness and oscillation of the Directory's policies whose bankruptcy was evident both in the domestic turmoil that gripped the nation, and in the humiliating military reverses suffered in Italy, Switzerland, and Germany. The agitation of the people was palpable; a crackle of expectation charged the air: the French nation looked for a savior, its own "tutelary genius" to deliver it from its misery. It would not have to look for long. Everywhere he travelled, the reception was rapturous—"It was not like the return of a citizen to his country, or a general at the head of a victorious army, but like the triumph of a sovereign restored to his people"—hurrahed by crowds of people ecstatic that at last a leader had been sent to them to restore the glory that was their birthright. Lyons, apparently, was in "an universal delirium," while the unfortunate Baudin, a deputy from the Ardennes "died of joy when he heard of my return"![4] Emboldened by this display of support, Napoleon continued, he resolved to save France from both the weaklings in the Directory and the Jacobin "men of blood," a decision that after a few weeks of scheming culminated in the coup d'état of the Eighteenth ("prepared with a cunning as skilled as Nazi management of the Reichstag fire"[5]). The next day, a few hours before his stormy confrontation with a hostile Council of the Five Hundred, who would greet his entry into the chamber with "angry shouts of 'Down with the tyrant!' 'Down with Cromwell!' 'Outlaw the dictator!'" (Barnett 1978:69) Napoleon attempted to justify his action to the Council of Ancients. "You stand," he thundered,

> upon a volcano; the Republic no longer possesses a government; the Directory is dissolved; factions are at work; the hour of decision is come...I know that Caesar, and Cromwell, are talked of—as if this day could be conquered with past times. No, I desire nothing but the safety of the Republic, and to maintain the resolutions to which you are about to come. (Napoleon Bonaparte [1823] 1986:375–76)

In less guarded moments Napoleon's antique model—or at least one of them, since he had several[6]—could reveal itself more blatantly. Five years after the coup, smarting from George III's rebuff of Bonaparte's "peace" overtures, he promised Josephine: "I will take you to London, madam...I intend the wife of the 'modern Caesar' shall be crowned at Westminster,"[7] while he would later advise Goethe (1966:72) "to write a tragedy about the death of Caesar—one really worthy of the subject, a greater one than Voltaire's. That could be the finest task you undertook."[8]

Yet there was always a residue of ambivalence. In the same year (1809) as he remarked to the sculptor Canova "What a great people were these Romans, especially down to the Second Punic War. But Caesar! Ah, Caesar! That was the great man!"[9] Napoleon turned down a request from the Institute to award him the titles of Augustus and Germanicus with the following disquisition on ancient Roman history:

> The Institute proposes to give the Emperor the titles of "Augustus" and "Germanicus." Augustus only fought one battle—Actium. Germanicus may have appealed to the Romans through his misfortunes: but the only famous thing he did was to write some very mediocre memoirs.
> I can see nothing to envy in what we know about the Roman emperors. It ought to be one of the principle endeavours of the Institute, and of men of letters generally, to show what a difference there is between their history and ours. What a terrible memory for future generations was that of Tiberius, of Caligula, of Nero, of Domitian, and of all those princes who ruled by no laws of legitimacy, or rules of succession, and who, for what reasons it is needless to specify, committed so many crimes, and burdened Rome with such a weight of misfortunes!
> The only man who distinguished himself by his character, and by many illustrious deeds—and he was not an emperor—was Caesar. If the Emperor desired any

title, it would be that of "Caesar." But the name has been dishonored (if that is possible) by so many pretty princes, that it is no longer associated with the memory of the great Caesar, but with that of a mob of German princelings, as feeble as they were ignorant, not one of whom is familiar to the present generation.

The Emperor's title is "Emperor of the French." He does not want any name carrying alien associations—neither "Augustus," nor "Germanicus," nor "Caesar."

The inscriptions ought to be written in French. The Romans sometimes used Greek for their inscriptions, but that was only a relic of the Greek influence upon Roman arts and sciences. French is the most cultivated of all modern tongues: it is more widely spread, and more exactly known, than the dead languages. Nobody, then, wants any other language to be used for these inscriptions.[10] (in Thompson 1954:224)

Napoleon's self-perceptions can never be known with any certainty, nor is it particularly important to know them for our purposes. What is more pertinent to understand in an essay of cultural interpretation is how others perceived him, and why they perceived him as they did. That the Caesar analogy was alive and well during his own lifetime is copiously attested to in various contemporary sources. Some were straightforwardly propagandist in intent, as evidenced for instance in Louis Fontanes's pamphlet of November 1800, penned only a year after Napoleon's pious renunciation in front of the Council of Ancients. Entitled "Parallel between Caesar, Cromwell, Monk and Bonaparte" the pamphlet drew attention to a contemporary topos (and accusation), only to insist that "Caesar was the chief of demagogues… Bonaparte on the contrary rallied the class of property owners and educated men against a raging multitude….The First Consul, far from overthrowing all the conservative ideas of society, restores them to their ancient splendour."[11] Later, David and Ingres developed the Roman theme, though a composition like "Napoleon I on the Imperial Throne" is more a tribute to Napoleon as Charlemagne than as Julius Caesar. Others were less impressed by the fruits of Napoleon's beneficence. For William Blake, Napoleon's tyranny meant the end of his hopes for the French Revolution, a despair he registered in the haunting "Auguries of Innocence": "The Strongest Poison ever known/Came from Caesar's Laurel Crown/Nought can deform the Human Race/Like to the Armour's iron brace." But even before Napoleon ascended to power and fame the ground had been laid for a version of classicism that in a very real sense both anticipated and helped frame his significance.

The tendency to depict political relations in the language and forms of antiquity was, as we saw in the previous chapter, a compelling motif of European and American culture from the Renaissance to the eighteenth century. It did not stop there. But during the Enlightenment and the nineteenth century an important shift of emphasis becomes apparent. Increasingly, the point behind this "great parallel," as Dieter Groh aptly calls it in a discussion to which this chapter is considerably indebted, was not a celebration of the values of "virtue" and self-governing political activity that had been the mark of republican thought since Machiavelli's time; nor was it, to put the matter in a different way, an attempt to summon up the memory of Rome during its prime. On the contrary, the Roman Republic was now more often invoked as a warning, as something to be feared, not emulated; accordingly, its demise and aftermath, not its zenith, comes to be accentuated. Traces of the great parallel figure conspicuously in the political predictions of Diderot, Friedrich II, and von Moser; their reading of the Roman Republic's collapse, together with their understanding of Cromwell as "the first modern usurper of hereditary monarchy," did not persuade them to be sanguine about the future (Groh 1972:732). For decades afterwards major currents of political theory and polemic across the ideological spectrum would attempt to make sense of contemporary events with the example of Rome as paradigmatic.[12] Recurring elements would include: the masses as the new barbarians, civil war, the Caesar figure as *bête noire* or savior, a popular, usurpatory militarism as the dominant type of state.

Yet if the French Revolution and Napoleon encouraged and animated such doomsday scenarios, they by no means necessitated them. Similarly, the "great parallel" was often raised not simply to affirm, but also to deny, its cogency: it is thus best to envisage it as a focus of political discourse, an issue to be debated, rather than a simple prediction or cliché. As evidence of this complexity, one might consider the way in which both legitimists and "liberals" questioned the French Revolution's "republican" complexion.

A common theme was the argument that the very concept of republicanism was illogical or anachronistic under modern conditions (or at least that it required considerable redefinition), though this did not stop such critics enlisting the figure of Julius Caesar to sound a more general alarm. Joseph de Maistre, answered his own question—"Can the French Republic Last?" with the reply that "It would be better to ask whether the Republic can exist." In a manner reminiscent of American anti-federalist writing, Maistre concluded that while a city-state might facilitate a republican government, a large and extensive state like France could not, even if it were to possess a representative system: "the phrase *large republic*, like *square circle*, is self-contradictory." The utter confusion in the country—three constitutions in five years—together with the "fear and apathy" that attended the turmoil, indicated that if France were a republic it was "a republic without republicans" ([1797] 1974:65–6, 72, 102). In any case, it was absurd for a people or assembly to believe, as the republican ideal of self-governing freedom encouraged them to believe, that they could actually control their own political destiny. Ultimately, it was God that controlled it, by, among other means employing "the masses...as a passive instrument" of His divine will.

> One may even notice...that the efforts of a people to obtain a goal are precisely the means that Providence employs to keep them from it. Thus the Roman people gave themselves masters while believing they were opposing the aristocracy by following Caesar. This is the image of all popular insurrections. In the French Revolution the people have continually been enslaved, outraged, ruined and mutilated by all parties, and the parties in their turn, working one against the other, have continually drifted, despite all their efforts, toward breakup at length on the rocks awaiting them. (1974:134–35)

The demands of popular "sovereignty" were not only heretical; they were futile because they ignored the fact that history unfolded according to God's purposes, not Man's—either as mass or as leader—and that divine Providence "makes sport of human plans." In the case of the Revolution, this meant that the attempts to subvert the Church and the monarchy were bound to climax in their "glorification."

Liberal thinkers challenged the French Revolution's "republican" model from a different angle. Madame de Staël and Benjamin Constant, for example, had no need of Maistre's brand of legitimism, nor were they ready to subscribe to an eschatology that saw the Revolution's bloodletting as a prelude to the expiation of the godless and the ultimate redemption of France. The great mistake of the Revolution and its ideologues, they agreed, was to try to recapitulate Graeco-Roman antiquity, to impose on modern "public opinion" what was no longer suitable for it. The contemporary Frenchman wanted peace, not military conquest; stability, not the constant, frenetic participation in government to which all his vital energies would be committed. The extent of France—geographic and demographic—meant that modern citizens could no longer find satisfaction in the attainment of fame that smaller societies had afforded. A nation the size of France could not do without the mechanism of political representation, and "where seven hundred men out of twenty-five million are called upon to deal with public affairs, the odds against ambition are too great to make it worth the bother." Moreover, in ancient Rome the well-being of the city had been coterminous with the well-being of its citizens because "the contribution of each individual was outweighed by the benefit he derived from the common weal." Under those circumstances, the patriotic sacrifice of individual interests to the common good made sense because each was imbricated in the other.[13] The concept of "liberty" in ancient times meant "everything that ensured citizens the largest share in the exercise of power." But since such extensive involvement was no longer feasible, the concept of liberty itself had to change—and it had changed. It had been replaced by the conviction that freedom was more threatened by the demands of government than protected by them; that liberty now meant rather the capacity and space to enjoy civil liberty, privacy, serenity, and the fruits of one's wealth free of government control: "In the present era liberty means everything that protects citizens' independence of the government." It was this that Rousseau and his followers had failed to understand with such disastrous consequences. They had lost sight of the fact that henceforth "public opinion will be based upon the love of tranquillity, the desire to acquire wealth, and the need to preserve it; that people will always be more concerned with administrative concepts than political questions because they bear more directly upon private life" (Madame de Staël [1906] 1964:99–100).[14]

It was left to Benjamin Constant, Madame de Staël's intimate collaborator, to elaborate on the consequences of ignoring the signal differences between the ancient and modern world. Constant refused to join those who blanketly condemned republican polities; if he criticized attempts to repeat antiquity, then he still found much to admire in the "energy and dignity" of the original model. Similarly, modern "republics" like Switzerland, Holland, and Geneva were excellent in a number of respects. However, the irony that Constant wished to expose was the fact that while a constitutional *monarchy* like England had developed into a bastion of relative freedom, a "republic" like France had degenerated into terror and arbitrariness. This led him to make a distinction between "monarchy" (a "regular" form of government typified by the Bourbon dynasty) and "usurpation" (an illegitimate regime-type embodied in Napoleon Bonaparte, with precedents in Cromwell and Julius Caesar). In the process, he anticipated many of the themes of the later "Caesarism" debate to which we shall be attending presently.

On the surface, Constant observed, monarchy and usurpation appear to be fundamentally similar entities, in that both appear to rest on "one man." Closer scrutiny reveals salient and fateful differences. The monarch of a venerable lineage is envisaged by his subjects not so much as a concrete person but as "an abstract being" coagulating "a whole race of kings, a tradition of several centuries."[15] Moreover, the hereditary monarch has no need to make an august reputation—he already has one. As the preeminent figure in the society he rules over he has no competitors, nor is he "compared with anyone else." His background and education may be no guarantee that he will rule wisely, but they at least prepare him for the functions he must discharge, and accustom him gradually to the supreme position he will, in time, fill. The "usurper," in contrast, is both a radically different political being from the traditional monarch, and finds himself in a correspondingly dissimilar moral and psychological situation. Usurpation is intrinsically bound up with a particular person, "and such individuality, because it is opposed to all preexisting interests, must be in a state of permanent defiance and hostility." Part of this springs from a defensiveness that does not plague hereditary monarchy: the usurper must "justify his elevation," avoid disappointing those whose expectations he has raised, guard himself against those who would drag him down. In consequence, he is impelled to engage in furious activity as he seeks to accomplish "great deeds" and thereby vindicate his claim to supremacy. Moreover, the character of the individual usurper is likely to accentuate the worst features of his governance. Usurpation requires "treachery, violence and perjury" and such acts become imported into the regime as normal, daily manifestations once it has become established. Taken together, such structural and characterological aspects help explain why the usurper must be in the centre of things, the focus of attention, whether he wants to be or not. A king can delegate military power to others on his behalf. The usurper, on the contrary, "must always be at the head of his Praetorian Guard. If he were not their idol, he would be the object of their contempt." In addition, the force that is necessary to consummate the initial act of usurpation must continue, transmogrified, into "incessant warfare" that allows the usurper to mobilize and discipline the army in his support, and "dazzle people's minds"; conquest must be substituted for legitimacy (Constant [1814] 1988:85–94). Distilled into its essential properties, then, usurpation is illegitimate—the "usurper sits with fear on an illegitimate throne, as on a solitary pyramid" (147)—derives from a seizure of power (158), and demands constant warfare, not only for the reasons previously given, but also because peace would reestablish commerce and communication between nations and hence the reintroduction of regular governance. To frustrate that eventuality was Napoleon's purpose in the Continental blockade and the assault on Russia (163).

However, not only is usurpation, as an irregular form of government, to be sharply distinguished from the monarchy it replaces; it is also markedly worse than conventional forms of "despotism." Despotism is at least transparent in its destruction of liberty. Usurpation, on the other hand, is deeply corrupting because it cleaves to the forms of freedom all the while destroying their substance; thus while despotism "stifles freedom of the press," usurpation "parodies" it. In some of the richest, and most memorable passages of the essay that I have been summarizing, Constant describes this "counterfeiting of liberty" as an all-encompassing crusade to penetrate every corner of privacy and "exact the signs of consent. The quiet are persecuted as indifferent, the energetic as dangerous; servitude has no rest, agitation no pleasure." "Despotism, in a word, rules by means of silence, and leaves man the right to be silent; usurpation condemns him to speak, it pursues him into the most intimate sanctuary of his thoughts, and, by forcing him to lie to his own conscience, deprives the oppressed of his last remaining consolation" (96–97).

> In thinking of the famous usurpers who are celebrated over the centuries, only one thing seems wonderful to me, and that is the admiration that people have for them. Caesar and Octavius, called Augustus, are models of this type: they began by proscribing all that was eminent in Rome; they continued by degrading everything that remained noble; they ended by bequeathing to the world Vitellius, Domitian, Heliogabalus and finally the Goths and the Vandals. (97)

And Napoleon? He too was a usurper, though one who combined in a hideous configuration all that was worst in despotism as well: namely, "arbitrary power" and with it the reduction of all political bodies to instruments of his sovereign will (95–96, 114, 129–31). With Napoleon, "despotism" became part of the apparatus by means of which he secured and perpetuated his regime. Yet in Constant's account, the merger of usurpation with despotism will be shown to be a fugitive and transient phenomenon: ultimately, despotism is destined to collapse and with it the usurpation it defended. In that sense usurpation was both new and outdated; new in the visage of Napoleon and the peculiar character he had given it; outdated in its incapacity to survive changing times. In particular, Constant believed that moral and economic conditions were bleeding usurpation of its parasitic power. Again, Constant returned to the differences between ancient and modern polities to illustrate his argument. Unlike ancient states, which had little sense of individual liberty, modern conditions tended to inculcate it, thereby giving people a new focal point of resistance to despotic and usurpatory governments. In addition, modern commerce makes the seizure and monopoly of property virtually impossible. This is because commerce "confers on property a new quality: the circulation of money" the fluidity of which makes it particularly difficult to control from any one power center. Even more, the expansion of credit, and the dependence of governments on it, make the latter especially vulnerable to public opinion. Credit cannot in the long term be coerced:

> against it, force is useless; money hides or takes flight. All the operations of the state are suspended. Credit had no such influence among the ancients; their governments were stronger than private citizens, while in our own time private citizens are stronger than political powers....Commerce has brought nations closer together and has given them virtually identical customs and habits; monarchs may still be enemies, but peoples are compatriots. (141)

To invoke the "great parallel" with antiquity, then, did not always mean that one subscribed to it; more that it was a problem that one had to confront, and take a stand on. A number of thinkers were concerned to stress the unique character of their time. But as the references to Caesar make plain, novelty and antique forms resided in the closest intellectual proximity. They had done so in the mind—or at least the rhetoric—of Napoleon himself. During the coup of Brumaire he had lectured the Council of Ancients: "let us not look into the past for examples of what is now going on. Nothing in history resembles the end of the eighteenth century; nothing in the eighteenth century resembles the present moment" ([1823] 1986:372). Yet, as we have seen, Napoleon often did later draw on and adapt classical frames of reference.[16]

His nephew would join him in a similar historical pot-pourri. Seeking to distill Napoleon's achievements as a combination of "ancient forms and new principles," Louis Bonaparte did not restrict himself to classical Roman precedents, even as he insisted that "Napoleon and Caesar...found themselves in analogous circumstances." In *L'Idée Napoléonienne* ([1840] 1856a),[17] a key text of the Napoleonic revival,[18] Louis sought to enshrine his uncle's achievement in a pantheon of other "great men"—namely, Moses, Mohammed, Caesar, and Charlemagne—who had "united" in themselves "the double character of founder and warrior." Each laid the tracks that civilization followed; thus, in spite of Caesar's murder, "his policy and [its] impetus maintained the unity of the Roman empire for six centuries, repulsed the barbarians, and extended the limits of the empire" (Louis Bonaparte ([1840] 1856a I:7).[19] The reference to religious figures in Louis's pantheon was hardly fortuitous, but does not quite prepare the reader for what comes next: the contention that the "Napoleonic idea has burst from the tomb of Saint Helena just as the moral of the Gospel has risen triumphantly, in spite of the torments of Calvary." That idea "sprang out of the French revolution as Minerva from the head of Jupiter: with a helmet on its head, and clad in mail." Its destiny was "to reconstitute French society, overthrown by fifty years of revolution, to conciliate order and liberty, the rights of the people, and the principles of authority." And Louis Bonaparte was its contemporary agent. For his own self-professed task was now to redeem in full the Napoleonic promise, and with it a system hierarchical but not hereditary in character, equalitarian but rewarding of merit, democratic but disciplined, free but strong, rational but active, and in such wise emancipated from the "two equally oppressive evils—tyranny and anarchy" that the first Napoleon had so majestically vanquished (Louis Bonaparte [1840] 1856a I:6–11).

Soon, this version of the Napoleonic idea and its multiple syntheses became associated with a new word in the political vocabulary: "Caesarism." Louis Bonaparte did not invent it, but between 1851 and 1870 no one was believed to exemplify it more than he. And even those who deliberately refused to use this classical-sounding appellation, and who cautioned against the imposition of old terms on a new reality, still found themselves caught up in an imaginative cosmos bound up with the great parallel. In *Democracy in America* ([1835, 1840] 1969) Alexis de Tocqueville pointed out repeatedly that the conditions his French contemporaries faced were novel, and that previous categories of thought were outdated (1969:12, 691, 703). Authority could no longer be based on privilege or tradition. The French must embrace democracy in their own way before the inexorable tide of equality and levelling eventuated in the rule of one man and a new kind of servitude. Yet even Tocqueville, searching for coordinates to make sense of the new, was occasionally compelled to fall back on the great parallel to do so:

> To find anything analogous to what might happen now with us, it is not in our own history that we must seek. Perhaps it is better to delve into the memorials of antiquity and carry our minds back to the terrible centuries of Roman tyranny, when mores had been corrupted, memories obliterated, customs destroyed; when opinions become changeable and freedom, driven out from the laws, was uncertain where it could find asylum; when nothing protected the citizens and when the citizens no longer protected themselves; when men made sport of human nature and princes exhausted heaven's mercy before their subjects' patience...I find those very blind who think to rediscover the monarchy of Henry IV or Louis XIV. For my part, when I consider the state already reached by several European nations and that toward which all are tending, I am led to believe that there will soon be no room except for either democratic freedom or the tyranny of the Caesars. ([1835]] 1969:314)[20]

Tocqueville was thinking here of the emperors who followed in the footsteps of Caesar and Augustus. It was not an isolated observation: he returned to it after Louis Bonaparte's coup of December 1851, an event he considered an unmitigated national humiliation and disaster.[21] In conversation with Nassau William Senior, Tocqueville insisted that the coup of December was unique to French history since this was "the first time that the army has seized France, bound and gagged her, and laid her at the feet of her ruler." The Eighteenth Brumaire of Napoleon Bonaparte had been quite different: it terminated, but did not begin, in "military tyranny," since there had been widespread support in the Councils and among the educated classes for the removal of the Directory. The Eighteenth Brumaire was, thus, "almost as much a civil as a military revolution." Louis Napoleon, to the contrary, was a much more isolated figure whose real support lay in the army. "For a real parallel you must go back 1,800 years" (Senior 1871, vol. II:227–8).[22]

Caesarism

Although the group of words to which "Caesarism" belongs has a long and complex history,[23] and though semantic elements of what came to be known explicitly as "Caesarism" had been anticipated in the eighteenth century, it was not until the nineteenth that the term became publicly available, first somewhat idiosyncratically, then in the vernacular of a political discussion that was particularly animated in France and Germany. Exactly when "Caesarism" was coined is a subject of some disagreement among historians and lexicographers, but it appears that it was not, as is often stated or assumed, originally a French creation.[24] Its first documented appearance in 1846[25] actually comes from a German pen, that of Johann Friedrich Böhmer (1868:278–79), a Lutheran, conservative thinker, who employed the word to criticize the tendency of the state to subordinate Church authority to its domination.[26] However Böhmer's usage was casual rather than theoretical, an aside in a private letter to a "military friend" rather than a manifesto or a political declaration. A more ambitious and systematic usage was not long in coming. It arrived in 1850 in a book by Auguste Romieu entitled *L'ère des Césars*, which though never translated into English, appeared in German a year after its French publication.[27] Henceforth "Caesarism" quickly gained vogue status throughout Europe, even if the domestication of the term was subject to no single Continental chronology.

Britain and Italy, for instance, were notably tardy in their adoption of the word. The *Oxford English Dictionary* records the first English use in a comment of Brownson (in 1857) equating Caesarism with "monarchical absolutism." A year later, the *O.E.D.* also informs us, the term attracted the ire of a contributor to the *Westminster Review* who complained of the "clumsy eulogies of Caesarism as incarnate in the dynasty of Bonaparte."[28] And in Italy "Caesarism" had to wait even longer to be taken up by political commentators (De Giorgi 1984:325).[29] It emerged as an explicit topic of discussion in a pamphlet, printed in 1862, written by the Italian member of parliament Giuseppe Lazzaro. Concerned with Napoleon III's meddling in Italian affairs (Nice and Savoy had recently been ceded to France) and with the insidious influence of the "Napoleonic idea," Lazzaro admonished *Cesarismo* for its fraudulence and debilitating properties. Posing as the executor of the people's wishes, the modern Caesar was in fact no more than their elected master (*padrone*). If under absolutism the people as body were, so to speak, politically murdered, under French Caesarism they had collectively committed suicide. For the real exemplars of Italian liberty, whatever the quarrels between them, it was to Cavour

and Garibaldi that one must look: Cavour, the consummate and influential diplomat; Garibaldi, whose "energy of heart," "divine intuition,"
and grandeur made him the very epitome of Italian patriotism (Lazzaro
1862:6–7, 23–24).

Lazzaro's analysis of Caesarism is of particular interest not only for
the varied definitions it provides (among other things, Caesarism is
"monarchical hypocrisy," a "hybrid" of absolutism and universal suffrage) but also because it contains an early mention of Bismarck as a
Caesarist figure; like Napoleon III, Lazzaro contends, the Prussian is
an autocrat masquerading as the people's benefactor and paying sham
homage to "progressive ideas" (Lazzaro 1862:17). However it was
only after the publication in France of Napoleon III's "biography" of
Caesar in 1865 that Italian writers turned to the concept of Caesarism
with any real focus or attention. The reception of both the biography
and the concept was overwhelmingly negative.[30] For Mazzini the problem was not only that Napoleon III's "mediocre" book on Julius Caesar misrepresented German historical criticism, and ignored English
scholarship altogether. It was also that it lent authority to a view of
progress and leadership that was basically untenable. Mazzini, like
Napoleon III himself, believed in progress. But the Italian patriot warned
that while progress can be slowed down or accelerated by men, its
tidal movement is essentially under the rule of God. The cult of the
individual leader—Alexander, Caesar, or Napoleon I—was objection-
able because it failed to understand what true leadership requires:
humility in the face of the Creator. Real leaders serve God and
people; they serve ideals like truth and morality, which themselves
are media of God's purpose for man. In contrast, men like Alexander,
Caesar, and Napoleon misspent their genius by becoming egoists;
each of them closed an epoch, rather than initiating one, and for this
reason all attempts to idolize them were profoundly mistaken (Mazzini
[1865] 1939:791–92, 798, 803–4). Napoleon III's biography also
stirred Giosue Carducci (1939:24–25) in September 1868, to pen two
sonnets on Caesarism. And while his idiom was more oblique than
Mazzini's, the contrast between Caesar the "*dittatore universo*" and
"*Santo Cato*" leaves the reader in little doubt where the poet's commitments lay.

Many other writers shared such views, but it is the volatile nature of
Caesarism, much more than its continuities, that makes it such a fascinating term to observe. Capable of assuming numerous mutations, no

constituency or ideology proved able definitively to colonize it. For example, it could be used as a term of praise or, and more usually, censure; seen as an accelerator or retarder of revolution;[31] envisaged as a peculiarly French (the view of Treitschke and Bagehot) or a European-wide phenomenon (as Droysen insisted).[32] There was an accompanying debate about the term's utility: though some found "Caesarism" an empirically fruitful coinage—Burckhardt ([1852] 1929:32, n.2) would say that he was "at a loss to know why the world of learning should prove so recalcitrant to this expression employed by Romieu since it describes a particular thing very well"[33]—others, like Marx and Mommsen, thought it execrable, piling fad upon historical obfuscation. Initially, to a lesser extent as time wore on, it was bound up with a group of other words, notably "Napoleonism," "Bonapartism"—and "imperialism," which originally meant not the international domination of one country by another, but the kind of internal rule, populist and authoritarian, typified by Napoleon III. In France during the Second Empire, the word "imperialism" had to be used with caution lest one be "suspect of...treasonable comment" (Koebner and Schmidt 1964:7–8). In Britain, during the 1870s, as "imperialism" was well on the way of assuming some of its modern connotations, it became an "anti-Disraeli slogan" employed by Gladstonian and other Liberals to depict the Conservative leader's administration in the detested colors of Napoleon III: an "alien form of a government that made use of direct appeals to the multitude, false military splendour, adventures abroad, Empire expansion, and [which] practiced arbitrary despotic rule." This was no way to help build, as Gladstone put it in the Midlothian campaign of 1879–80,[34] "a sisterhood of nations, equal, independent" (Koebner and Schmidt 1964:7–8, 147–48, 326).[35]

However the term "Caesarism" had a peculiar linguistic advantage for some writers that its cognates lacked. "Bonapartism" and "Napoleonism" smacked of a specific national location: France. Accordingly, such words seemed to suggest that the kind of regime Napoleon III represented was merely regional in character. But this is exactly what many people disputed as they sought to delineate the global tendencies of "Caesarism."[36] Such opinion was given added weight after Napoleon III's eclipse in 1870, the replacement of the Second Empire by the Third Republic, and hence the evaporation of a Napoleonic dynasty. Then "Caesarism" began to be extended to new targets, Disraeli's imperial program and the regime of Bismarck chief among them.

The currency of this term, then, cannot be gainsaid. Nor can the complexity of its usages and trajectory: if by 1866 "Everybody is now talking of Caesarism," as Ludwig Bamberger remarked,[37] they were clearly not all talking about it in the same way. This will become increasingly evident as this chapter unfolds. But first it will be useful to return to the work that introduced the concept in a sustained and deliberately polemical way: Romieu's *Age of Caesars* (Romieu 1850). An examination of this book is helpful not because its definition of Caesarism was particularly influential; even the book's author claimed it to have been much misunderstood.[38] Rather Romieu is important because his early formulation provides us with an expeditious benchmark by which to compare and contrast later appropriations of the concept. To understand the career of a word we require some sort of baseline from which to view it, and it is this that Romieu so vividly supplies.

Age of Caesarism, Age of Force

Romieu's *Age of Caesars* (written, he tells us, in July 1850)[39] is a book in which clarity is the occasional sacrifice to declamation, a lapse aggravated no doubt by the nature of a man whose interest in the imperial purple coexisted with a tendency to dye his prose a similar color. But difficulties of exegesis are eased somewhat if we begin by appreciating the prime objective of Romieu's polemic which is essentially an assault on what he calls the "liberal principle" (132) and its twin manifestations in philosophy—and culture more generally—and politics. In many respects, Romieu's intervention is reminiscent of the critiques of liberalism levelled by Maistre and Donoso Cortés but, as we shall see, it was no simple imitation of them.

Philosophically, Romieu argues, the liberal principle amounts to the denigration of faith and the celebration of Reason as the alleged guiding force of man. The problem is, however, that reason cannot guide but is capable only of fostering chronic doubt, dissension, uncertainty, and emotional and social chaos. This should not surprise us. For man, far from being a rational animal is fundamentally a creature of passion (82–85, 205), a being that requires, if his life is to be anchored, the certainties that only religious dogma provides.[40] But this is precisely what rationalism, and its materialistic and atheistic corollaries, has been busily attacking. The role of liberalism, as an intellectual attitude that promotes the love of abstraction and discussion, and that encourages contempt for all that is holy and sublime, is thus destructive of the human fabric. More than this, liberalism's philosophical doctrines are utterly false: man is not free but acts only within a predestined orbit decided for him by God, is not an angel but still a beast; the belief in moral progress trumpeted by liberal philanthropists is totally illusory. In undermining respect for the old truths in king and God, in transmitting, through secular education, its arrogance to the young and placing in their hearts a void that "the dry algebra of reason" (79) can never fill, liberalism has poisoned the mind of France and all those other European nations that have drunk from the same cup.

Predictably enough, Romieu blames the temporary intellectual ascendancy of "the cripple reason" (8) on the Enlightenment *philosophes*. However, the rot had begun at least two centuries earlier in the Reformation when Luther provoked the revolt of the mind against belief. It was he who proclaimed the right of free examination in religious affairs and this right, by a direct process of intellectual contagion, spread naturally to political questions also: "The deduction is simple: he who can discuss God can discuss man" (81).[41]

In the political arena, meanwhile, the liberal principle is incarnated in the "fashion" (*phase*) for constitutional, parliamentary government. Now Romieu's assessment of this kind of rule is somewhat ambivalent. On the one hand he accepts that some countries are more attuned to it than others: England and Spain, for instance, in their historically evolved political mix of democracy and aristocracy facilitate constitutional government, whereas in other countries where these conditions are absent—such as France—"constitutional government" (Romieu here means constitutional monarchy) is the "obligatory prelude to the Republic" (24).[42] On the other hand, Romieu finds the constitutional, parliamentary system deplorable in principle, since it deprives a nation of resolute leadership and puts in its place a cacophony of bickering voices whose only produce is verbiage, indecision, and cowardice. Besides, conceived of as a social practice, parliamentarism is completely alien to the normal way people conduct their affairs:

I will always ask myself, until we manage to apply the parliamentary form to the serious and ordinary actions of life, what is the peculiar cause of madness which makes us apply it to the things of government. I have never seen the navigation of a ship entrusted to an assembly; and I know why: it is because the ship and assembly would sink two leagues from the harbour. In that case the danger would be immediate and one would at all costs avoid putting the ship at such risk. But in a matter of politics, stupidities only have their effect after months and years. Their cause is soon forgotten. In the same way it has never occurred to anybody to place a regiment under the command of a commission. The regiment would be beaten by the national guard. In the family, which is the molecule of society, where is the vote, where is the ballot?...Everywhere, in every thing that touches him directly, man only proceeds with one will, so sure is he that he cannot act in a better or quicker way. And in this serious thing which is the conduct of the state, he decides in a bizarre way to reject this natural rule as imperishable as humanity! (19–20)

Romieu has no difficulty at all finding the main culprits for this modern malaise: it is the bourgeoisie who are primarily responsible. It is they who insinuated the liberal principle, as intellectual creed and set of political institutions, into the French body politic and European civilization more generally. It is from their ranks that the secular intelligentsia have come propagating, even more so after 1814, "the cult of the university" (14), that obsession with the sentence and the word, preposterously imagining they are the inheritors of the old Roman assembly tradition while forgetting that people like Cicero were simultaneously men of action. It is the bourgeoisie whose cupidity and ambition led them to oppose the restoration of legitimist governance because they visualized it leading once more to the "supremacy of the gentleman" (113). Worst of all, the bourgeois class it is which has prepared the ground for the organized insurrection of the masses, the "inner barbarians" (6, 77) by openly abandoning and mocking tradition, by teaching them dissatisfaction through the book, the pamphlet, the newspaper, the speech (92), and by fuelling their rapaciousness. This mass now stands poised to devour the creature that gave it birth for a "population to whom one has only taught revolution will never become peaceful. A population in front of whom one has laughed at God, from whom one has taken away belief will never be resigned to its laborious poverty in the presence of idle luxury; a population to whom one has preached equality as a dogma...will never admit the lords of yesterday, born of the bank and the gaming houses. This population will be a perpetual rebel, one hundred times more logical than those who formed it" (92). In short the custodians of the liberal principle have brought society to a state of civil war which can only temporarily be calmed.[43] The masses have been unleashed and their orgy of violence and hatred is imminent and inescapable (206).[44]

What will emerge from this turmoil? Even if Romieu's tirade, in the targets it chooses to attack and the ferocity of its invective, reads at times like a codicil to the last will and testament of legitimism, Romieu is no Ultra. Nowhere in his book does he entertain the hope that the past can be restored. Though hardly reconciled with the present, he, unlike Maistre or Cortés, is at least resigned to it. This is because Romieu subscribes to a cyclical philosophy of history, a commitment that he not only states explicitly on a couple of occasions (7, 162) but one that forms the basis of the many analogies between present and ancient conditions that Romieu is fond of citing: for example, the Roman world threatened by the "barbarian" and Christian invasions— "one killing the material wealth of the state, the other its moral wealth" (6)—and those invasions represented by the proletariat and bourgeoisie (6, 77); between ancient and modern military dictatorships spawned by democracy (3, 35–36); between the figures of a Caesar and a Napoleon (13, 34, 44, 130–32). Contemporary Europe, says Romieu, "finds itself placed in conditions nearly like those which characterized the epoch when the Caesars appeared" (5)[45] a statement necessarily incompatible with restorationist sentiment. Furthermore, Romieu accepts, even argues, that the faith in the old monarchical legitimacy (*"ce beau dogme"*: 111) is dead and cannot be resuscitated. Attempts to combine it with constitutionalism, as the Orleanist example shows, are doomed to futility and failure. For one cannot combine faith, which legitimacy rests upon and requires, with the purely ephemeral products of discursive reasoning and the ballot box (109–11). People have lost their sense of the divine, their spiritual convictions, and so "it is real childishness to look for social salvation in the combinations of the past" even if that past was "noble and beautiful" (195).

Legitimism, then, cannot be restored, nor liberalism be made to work; indeed liberalism itself marks an interregnum between the collapse of legitimism and a new order of things: "Caesarism." And what is "Caesarism?" One of Romieu's strategies in answering this question is to insist on what Caesarism is not, and it is not (hereditary) monarchy, for monarchy supposes legitimacy, legitimacy ultimately supposes faith in the divine, and faith, as we have seen, is moribund, a victim of the slavish rationalism of the liberal principle and its carriers (194–95). Caesarism, to be sure, does have a tendency to move towards a monarchical system but its dynastic aspirations are always confounded (193–94), as Napoleon's case reveals. For Bonaparte, while achieving the status of First Consul, could not establish a viable monarchy. "He had made himself Caesar on the 18th Brumaire and was never anything more...The anointment [as emperor] added nothing to his greatness; it only earned him some hatred and some sarcasm" (130), so that even this "demigod" was powerless to rejuvenate the attributes of royalty in an age when transcendental belief had been annulled. The "cult of which he was the idol, this fabulous admiration of which he was the object was for the hero and not for the sovereign" and this was because "there was no throne; there was only an all-powerful sword which could only, like that of Alexander, be given to the worthiest man, that is to say the strongest" (130–31). Monarchy, Romieu observes, lasts as long as it is believed in while Caesarism exists in and by itself alone (193–94).

Yet if Caesarism is not monarchy, neither is it "empire," "despotism," nor "tyranny" (30), though Romieu does not specify the exact meaning of these words.[46] Instead it is best conceived of as the modern rule of force (194), which replaces both the principle of discussion and that of heredity.[47] Force, indeed, is actually at the bottom of all institutions, their necessary guarantee, though liberalism hypocritically disguises this fact, while monarchy softens it with the sublime conviction and consolation that belief in it inspires. But with Caesarism force emerges in all its brutality: Caesarism is naked power: untrammelled might: coercion without apologetics. And it is in the nature of things that Caesarism should come in this form and at this time, for "Men have respect for two things, what is saintly and what is strong. The saintly element does not exist any more in this century. The strong element is of all times and it alone can reestablish the other one" (200)—though only after an indeterminate period of violence. The experience of the Napoleonic empire presaged this new era of undiluted force (132), and though periods of calm were subsequently regained, Caesarism remained immanent within the historical process. It will reemerge soon (193), in the midst of the protracted civil war that is destined to follow the liberal experiment's collapse into anarchy (150). And who is best fitted to rule in such an historical conjuncture? The army, naturally, whose turn it is to have its day.

Romieu makes a number of related points about the military that are worth brief consideration since the "man on horseback" theme is common to so many nineteenth-century conceptualizations of Caesarism. Like many later thinkers, most notably Wilhelm Roscher,

Romieu envisages the domination of the army springing directly from democratic foundations. He is convinced that "always and without exception," where public authority has its basis in discussion and the vote, a day will come when army commanders decide the result of the election on the battlefield (3). One of Romieu's points, if a minor one, is that military dictatorships are the natural consequences of the geographical expansion of states per se (3–4, 35); but the weight of his argument falls on the now familiar proposition that democracy brings in its train such bickering and disorder that the army, feeling keenly the humiliation experienced within civil society to a lesser extent, turns its eyes "toward the order and unity incarnated in its chief" (36; cf. 39–40). Two features in particular facilitate the army's ability to seize power: for one thing, its martial training, its discipline ("the army will obey...he who knows how to command it"), its relative distance from the dissensions of civil society, lend it an institutional coherence supremely adapted to survive the general social disintegration (158); for another, the soldiery had learned, since the June Days, a new and invigorating political axiom: "an army determined to fight always dominates an insurrection" (91).[48] Nonetheless, Romieu does not believe that, for the foreseeable future, one commander will be able to establish a stable and durable dynasty. On the contrary, the modern age of Caesars is an age of vicissitude, of habitual violence, where a "succession of masters" (196) will do battle for hegemony.

Before I leave this description of Romieu's thesis two aspects of his treatment should be recorded. To begin with, it is notable that when Romieu talks about the original "age" of Caesars, he omits the one military leader that from the title of his book, we all expect him to include: namely, Julius Caesar himself. But, for Romieu, the exploits of Julius Caesar are the culmination of a decadence and demagogy, stretching back at least as far as Marius (34), which *preceded* the age of Caesars and made it historically inevitable. Instead it is with Augustus that the era of the Caesars commences.[49] Augustus's reign was a golden age, a time when the evils that had plagued the late Republic were extirpated and when an unprecedented tranquillity (never again matched) settled on the Roman world (40)—a claim that stands in some tension, the reader may think, with Romieu's standard equation of the Caesars with force. Critically, it was Augustus's momentous achievement to have combined "the command of the army and the tribuniciary power. Rome was made one in the person of Caesar" (33).

In other words, the Caesars (and unless I have missed something Romieu never uses the word "Caesar*ism*" of antiquity, but speaks only of the "era," "epoch," "period," or "time" of the Caesars) refer to what we think of today as the Roman emperors.

My second observation concerns Romieu's attitude to the Bonapartes, uncle and nephew. There is no doubt at all in Romieu's mind that Napoleon I performed deeds that were similar to those of the Caesars and that the Corsican was a harbinger of Caesar*ism* to boot; this is a judgment Romieu constantly repeats (13, 34, 44, 130–32). Louis Bonaparte on the other hand (and remember that *L'ère des Césars* was written before the coup of December 2, 1851) is assigned a much more humble place in Romieu's schema. Louis's personal courage and integrity are acknowledged; the power of his name understood. But Romieu is convinced that Louis can only be a "temporary leader" and that the coups d'état "of which so much [has been] spoken would have no serious result....In one way or another one would arrive at a short interregnum, followed soon by unavoidable uprisings" (133). What is interesting here of course is not Romieu's limited powers of prediction—how could he have known that the "interregnum" would extend to almost two decades?—but the fact that in this early treatise Caesar*ism* does not apply to the man later writers would take to be its archetype—a clear sign already of the mutations that the concept of Caesarism would undergo in its curious evolution. Even so, there are a couple of themes in Romieu's work that did remain fairly constant in later discussions of Caesarism: the first is the issue of Caesarism's illegitimacy; the second is its relationship to the "masses."[50] I shall now discuss each in turn.

Caesarism and "Illegitimacy"

We have seen that, for Romieu, the modern age and the Caesarism that will overtake it, is essentially antithetical to any traditional idea of legitimacy. Legitimacy is capable of flourishing only in a climate of faith; it cannot thrive in the soulless ice age heralded by liberalism. In any case, Caesarism requires no prettying or comforting justification; force is its only rationale, and with it will come a violent new order, the regime of military commanders, and a quasi-permanent state of civil war as the normal form of future society.

Such a discussion of legitimacy and illegitimacy was itself part of a much broader debate in Europe that had taken place ever since the French Revolution,[51] the decapitation of Louis XVI and his wife, and the rise of Napoleon; I have already touched on aspects of it in my description of Constant's theory of "usurpation." It was not only that the Bourbon family, a noble house of Europe, had been the subject of revolutionary attack. Once Napoleon had become First Consul, his own monarchical proclivities had quickly manifested themselves; his habit of wearing a red coat—a badge of court society dress—,the Regent diamond that sparkled from his sword, and his preference for the "Tuileries of the kings to the Luxembourg of the Directors" (Bergeron [1972] 1981:13) all presaged the promulgation of the hereditary empire in May 1804, the promotion of his brothers Joseph and Louis to the status of princes shortly thereafter, and the coronation that followed in December 1804. The coronation itself—magnificently, if sycophantically captured by David[52]—was a remarkable affair, combining both traditional and innovative features. Napoleon's earlier Concordat with the Church—his attempt to uncouple Catholicism from Royalism—had enabled him to enlist that icon of ancestral legitimacy, the Holy See, in his investiture. However, by taking the crowns from tha altar in the Cathedral of Notre-Dame, and by placing one on his own head (and one on Josephine's) Napoleon showed that he could use tradition without submitting to it. Equally, while the ceremony at Notre-Dame invested Napoleon "with the ritual emblems of the early-medieval French monarchy: orb and sceptre, and sword" (Barnett 1978: 91), there was nothing medieval about Napoleon's resort to mass legitimation to endorse and solemnize his decisions: the plebiscite of 1804 that confirmed the hereditary empire—3,572,329 for, 2,569 against—repeated the earlier sanctions he had received for the Constitution of 1800 in which 3,011,007 had voted in support, and only 1,562 against (Cobban [1961] 1965:13; Gay 1993:566,n. 34).[53] Later, in exile, Napoleon would ridicule Brutus for assimilating Caesar to the ranks of "those obscure tyrants of the Peloponnesus who, with the help of a few schemers, usurped the authority over their cities. He refused to realize that Caesar's authority was legitimate because it was a necessary safeguard, because it assured the preservation of all the interests of Rome, because it was in fact the result of the popular opinion and will" (Herold 1955:59). It was an appropriate comment from a man who became not a medieval monarch but, as Chateaubriand put it, a "proletarian king" who "mounting the throne...seated the throne...seated the common people beside him" ([1848] 1961:329)[54] and one who, with an eye to his classical ancestor, chose the Roman Legion's eagle as the motif for the French army's Imperial colours (Barnett 1978:92).

All the same, it was exactly Napoleon's legitimacy and, even more, the legitimacy of the kind of regime he personified, that was the key point for his critics, both liberal and legitimist, and that formed an important bridge to the later discussions about the Caesarism of Louis Bonaparte. No one has tried to demonstrate this linkage more persuasively than the American political theorist Melvin Richter, in a series of articles (Richter 1981, 1982, 1988) that have been unjustly neglected by students of nineteenth-century political culture. Since his argument provides an important insight into the wider context and continuities of the Caesarism debate, and since this is also my subject here, it is worth examining what Richter has to say in some detail.

Richter is convinced that scholars can learn much about such heavily loaded notions as "legitimacy" and "liberty"—about the significance attributed to them by historical actors, about their role in constructing conceptual frames of reference—by an investigation into their antinomies. Indeed,

> My contention is that concepts of illegitimacy and total domination are as important, theoretically and in the actual practice of politics, as those concepts of legitimacy and liberty, to which they are related, but from which they cannot be derived. (Richter 1981:71)

The test case through which he seeks to demonstrate the relatedness of normative terms is the pair "legitimate regime" and "illegitimate regime" as it evolved in France during the years of "revolution, counterrevolution, restoration and imperial foundation" (1982:187) that span the period 1789–1853, a time characterized by a fierce ideological assault prosecuted by the enemies of the Bonapartist state. The battle that ensued between, on the one hand, restorationist and liberal critics of the Bonapartist regime and, on the other, Napoleonic partisans, was simultaneously cultural and political as each side struggled to contest that most coveted of political prizes: the claim to de jure governance. An assertion by one party to be legitimate, necessarily involved rubbishing the professions of its rivals as spurious; conversely a critique of a rival's illegitimacy, involved a justification of the superiority of one's own political values and constituency.[55] "In this unstable context, claims that a regime was legitimate or illegitimate could not be a matter of indifference to political actors, whether incumbents or contenders for power" (Richter 1982:187).[56]

It is against this backdrop that Richter invites us to consider "Caesarism" as part of a "negative model" or, alternatively, as one of a "family of concepts" (1981:63, 71)—encompassing "tyranny," "despotism," "absolute monarchy," "usurpation," and "totalitarianism"— which political thinkers have employed since antiquity to "designate a relationship between rulers and ruled strictly analogous to that of master over slave, or to some other form of servitude at least as severe" (1981:72). These concepts, viewed historically, were originally attempts to convey an extant mode of illegitimacy—for instance, the tyrannies of ancient Greece, the absolutist rule of eighteenth-century European monarchs—and, in the process condemn it as heinous. "Bonapartism" or "Caesarism" or "plebiscitary dictatorship" (1982:186, 191, 202)— there is a tendency for Richter to view these notions as broadly equivalent—were the nineteenth-century counterparts to earlier (and later) categories of illegitimate rule, typifying regimes thought to exemplify "the most dangerous potentialities of politics in the modern age" (1981:63). "Bonapartism," a term Richter dates as first used in 1816,[57] for a while "could mean either supporters of Napoleon or the regime he created"; "Caesarism," on the other hand "came into general use to refer to a regime type only after 1851, when Louis Napoleon repeated the sequence of taking over, by military coup d'état, a republic established by revolution. Like his uncle he sought legitimacy through plebiscites, established an empire, and lost it by military defeat" (1982:186).[58] After Louis's coup, Bonapartism and Caesarism tended progressively to merge with one another, such that nineteenth-century thinkers came to treat them as virtually synonymous.

Given that a vocabulary of negative terms already existed (tyranny, despotism, absolutism, usurpation) through which the odious character of a regime might be communicated, what was it exactly about nineteenth-century France that prompted the creation, or dissemination, of Bonapartism and Caesarism? What Richter suggests is that the old discourse carried associations that political theorists increasingly sensed to be inadequate to convey the new social reality that had burst forth around them. Recognising that a chasm had opened up between the language they had inherited and the situation they currently faced, a group of thinkers in the first half of the nineteenth century sought new

terminological coordinates: the result, eventually, was the birth of
Bonapartism and, later, Caesarism.

> Often it was argued that under such dictatorships [as Louis Bonaparte's], subjects
> were put under greater constraints than under tyranny, despotism, or absolute
> monarchy. The modern age was the first to use such effective psychological ma-
> nipulation, mass mobilization, the organization of enthusiasm by nationalistic ap-
> peals, and effective all-encompassing bureaucratic controls. And a single man was
> the focus of such loyalties. (Richter 1981:73)

Unfortunately, Richter does not say much more than this about
Caesarism, though his brevity is explicable for a couple of reasons. To
begin with, Caesarism as a concept in its own right is not his primary
concern; Richter is interested in it only insofar as it comprises one of
the "family" of notions that express illegitimate domination and whose
role in political thought and action he wants to understand. Second,
because Richter tends to concentrate on the sixty years before 1853
there is a sense in which his analysis deals mostly with Caesarism's
gestation rather than its actual appearance as a term. The two anti-
Bonapartist strains of thought he examines—the camps of Royalism
(Burke, Maistre, Chateaubriand, Bonald) and liberalism (Constant, Madame de Staël, Guizot)—were ones that certainly anticipated a number
of central motifs that Caesarism would later attract to itself, including
the theme "that there is an inevitable slide from revolutionary governments based on popular sovereignty into military domination by a
single commander" (1982:192)—the view of Royalists—and the contention that, where the people have politically abdicated, have re-
nounced their rights as individual citizens and instead entrusted supreme legislative and executive power to a supposed representative of
the general will, a lamentable condition of "democratic despotism"
(Guizot) ensues.[59] However, as Richter shows, none of the theorists
from either camp, used the term Caesarism; nor did Tocqueville, who
was also searching for a new word to express the new thing. It fell to a
later generation of thinkers—Bagehot, Lorenz von Stein, Jacob
Burckhardt, and Max Weber—to break new ground; it was they who,
pondering on the significance of Louis Bonaparte's reign for France
and modern politics more generally, would use and adapt (or, like
Marx, consciously discount) such terms as Caesarism, Bonapartism,
and plebiscitary dictatorship.

How is one to assess Richter's analysis? Of particular value is the historical depth it gives the treatment of Caesarism, which now appears to possess three dimensions: it exists as word, as concept (or idea), and as a member of a family of concepts. The *word*, we have already established, has its origins in the mid-to-late 1840s. With Louis Bonaparte's coup, the illegitimate connotations around the term hardened even further. Proudhon added juridical to political language in his condemnation of Caesarism: Caesarism, he wrote, was a "crime" that was "unpardonable" (*irrémissible*) because it imposed "despotism."

> And what is despotism? It is the substituting of an individual's arbitrary, violent, corrupt and murderous rule for the instinctive, spontaneous and free movement of society itself. (1883:40)[60]

Shortly after the coup, Victor Hugo employed similar terminology in his literary assault on *Napoléon le Petit* (1852).[61] And while Karl Marx accused the *Times* of rampant inconsistency in its response to Louis Bonaparte's "imperialism," he too could not resist quoting an editorial from that "Leviathan of the English press" of November 18, 1861 that poured scorn on the Emperor's legal credentials: "We will leave to others the task of congratulating Caesar on his admission that he is a finite and fallible being, and that, indisputably reigning by the power of the sword, he does not pretend to rule by virtue of Divine right. We had rather inquire what have been the financial results of ten years of Imperial sway" (Marx [1861] 1984:82). Moreover, the association of Caesarism or Napoleonism with "the embalmed air of rancid legitimacy," as Marx had earlier put it ([1856] 1980a:617) is one that proved to have considerable longevity. Consider the German case. In the thirteenth edition of F.A. Brockhaus' *Conversations Lexikon* we read:

> Caesarism has come into use mainly to characterize the Napoleonic system. In this sense it means a particular kind of monarchy, which is different from the absolute as well as the constitutional ones because of its democratic basis and lack of legitimacy. Its essence, however, is a personal autocratic regime which is based on the predominance of administration and the ruthless enforcement of state power. The constitutional authority of the legislative bodies is used for its disguise and it tries to surround itself with the dubious glamour of a self-created aristocracy. (Brockhaus 1883:38)

True, not everyone agreed with the details of such a formulation. Heinrich von Treitschke ([1897–1898] 1916 II:222–23), for instance, argued that precisely because "Caesarship was never a matter of legitimate inheritance" it was a tyranny not a monarchy. This fact was demonstrated he said by a simple point: Caesarism bore and emphasized the name of a man, not a dynasty. Nonetheless, though Treitschke's interpretation differed from Brockhaus in this respect, it agreed with it on the crucial issue that the Caesarist ruler holds his position "by no established right" and that "Roman Caesarism has found its modern counterpart in the Bonapartism of France." Similarly, as late as 1917, Ferdinand Tönnies, in the notes-cum-glossary appended to his book on the English and German political systems, wrote that "Caesarism (after Julius Caesar) is a form of state in which a leader of the people (usually a leader of the army) sets himself up as a sole ruler (*Alleinherrscher*)," adding immediately afterwards in parenthesis: "Illegitimate or irregular monarchy" (1917:210).[62]

The *concept* of Caesarism, however—or at least elements of it—has a longer lineage. Constant's theory of usurpation anticipated it. Burke, in 1790, was predicting in phrases that uncannily resemble some later theorizations of "Caesarism," that popular revolution in France (and, by extension, elsewhere) would result in a military takeover, the hegemony of a military leader: "In the weakness of one kind of authority, and in the fluctuation of all, the officers of an army will remain for some time mutinous and full of faction, until some popular general…shall draw the eyes of all men upon himself" (Burke [1790] 1968:342). Maistre and Bonald had said something similar.[63] Finally, the *family of concepts* expressing illegitimate governance, of which Caesarism (in some renditions) is but one, is as old as Western political theory itself—the lineage of the word "tyranny," for example, stretching back, in its Greek usage, to at least the mid-seventh century B.C. (Ste. Croix 1981:279).

All this is useful, but there is a problem in Richter's analysis the identification of which will give us a clearer understanding of the Caesarism debate. Richter's highly abbreviated treatment of Caesarism not only inevitably underplays the variety of meanings the idea could assume, a tendency that is compounded by the restriction of the analysis to France and the broad identification of "Caesarism" with "Bonapartism." More seriously, there is an asymmetry in the group or family of terms he considers. Tyranny, usurpation, and despotism have pejorative undertones that are nearly universal in political theory. Political writers might define these terms in various ways, but virtually all modulations have sought to convey forms of rule deemed highly dangerous and undesirable.[64] With Caesarism, on the other hand, the matter is more complex. Without doubt the term was employed as a label of disparagement in the vast majority of cases, in England, Italy, and of course France itself. The same is true of Germany, as Heinz Gollwitzer's pioneering study illustrates soundly enough. But Gollwitzer also points to a range of people of diverse intellectual backgrounds and political persuasions who envisaged the "Caesarism of Napoleon III" in ways quite different from what one might have expected from Richter's analysis. Consider German conservative thought of the period: overwhelmingly anti-Napoleonic it certainly was, but there remained plenty of space for recusancy. Hence conservative thinkers like Radowitz, Riehl, Manteuffel, Quehl, and Segesser—a heterogeneous group in themselves—congratulated Napoleon III's "Caesarism" for confronting the red menace, checking revolution and revolutionary fervor, reaffirming the sanctity of private property and for generally restoring "order."[65]

And liberal and socialist thinkers too were in particular instances not immune from some admiration, however equivocal, for Napoleon III, as the stances of Heine, Fröbel, Hillebrand, and Mundt (all liberals after a fashion) and the socialist Schweitzer reveal plainly enough.[66] Moreover, even in the French case, on which Richter concentrates, the matter is not clear cut. Romieu's usage of Caesarism is certainly "negative" in conjuring up a politically horrendous state of affairs, but it is also ambivalent; while Romieu prefers legitimism to Caesarism he, ostensibly at least, favors Caesarism over contemporary liberalism. Ambivalence is also evident in various French lexicons of a later date. Littré's *Dictionnaire* (1873:534), for instance, renders Caesarism as "domination of the Caesars, that is, princes brought to government by democracy but invested (*revêtus*) with absolute power," yet it goes on to add that Caesarism is the "[t]heory of those who think that this form of government is best." Furthermore, while the author of the entry on "Caesarism" for Larousse's *Grand dictionnaire universel du XIXe siècle* (1867:812) does not hide his own personal disdain for the phenomenon it is his task to define, he still records the view that "Caesarism implies *necessarily* the idea of a government *either good or bad* according to the person who will exercise it....It is one of the *progressive* forms of despotism, fitting to those peoples who cannot or do not know how to govern themselves" (my emphasis).[67]

Democracy without Liberty:
Caesarism and the Rise of the "Masses"

I observed earlier that Romieu's *Age of Caesars* sounded one theme that a variety of writers also rehearsed when they thought of Caesar and Caesarism: domination and illegitimacy. Later we will see how Max Weber helped transform the categories of this kind of analysis by arguing that Caesarism is not a pathology of modern states (the majority view throughout the nineteenth century), but a typical and normal feature of their development. For the moment, however, it is a second idea in Romieu's book that will engage my interest: the key linkage between Caesarism and the "masses."

In the whole history of the Caesarism discussion, from Romieu to Weber, from Weber to Oswald Spengler, from Spengler to Amaury de Riencourt no other linguistic association is more prominent or more enduring, no gravitational pull between concepts so strong, as this one. Between 1850 and 1920 in particular, their symbiosis was described by political commentators in various ways. As George Mosse has remarked, "Caesarism became involved with the new importance given to the masses as a political force in the post revolutionary age." More particularly,

> Caesarism as a concept is important in modern times because it became shorthand for a new political constellation arising during the nineteenth century. As a result of the French revolution, political theorists began to distinguish between two kinds of democracy: the rule of representatives, and the rule of the masses....A discussion of Caesarism leads necessarily to an analysis of the rise of mass democracy: if not yet within the reality of historical development, then, certainly, as either a fear or hope in the minds of men concerned with the trend of the politics of their time. (Mosse 1971:167–68)

And it was fear more than hope than tended to predominate whenever the question of the masses was raised in liberal and conservative circles. To liberals and conservatives alike, the emergence of a modern industrial proletariat, that is, of a class bereft of independent means of production, suggested not only a body lacking independent means of judgment, an "amorphous and indistinguishable" (Williams 1976:159) multitude unconstrained by the collective obligations that full membership of a body politic imposed on its propertied citizens. It also suggested something potentially explosive and unpredictable, in a word, "irrational." For this reason it is understandable that the term "mass"—

which carried the dual associations of formlessness and instability—
came to be employed to designate the new thing. While contemporary
labour historians and social scientists have accustomed us to speak of
the crowd's "moral economy," or of "collective action" rather than
mass behavior or mob rule, we have to remember that such academic
notions were utterly foreign to most strands of nineteenth-century opinion. The social psychology of the times, often jumbling mass, crowd,
and mob into one category, beheld a different spectacle—an atavistic,
homogeneous, and irrational multitude—and it is significant that even
those, like Scipio Sighele and Gabriel Tarde, who sought to go beyond
such simplifications, came to their subject matter from the angle of
criminology (McClelland 1989:155ff).

Within such a conceptual framework, political and scientific, the
cultivation of "virtue" beloved by classical and other republicans simply could not make sense. Nor could a polity permeated by the ethos
of self-governing liberty; a mass, by definition, is not an entity either
disposed or able to rule. It is something to be shaped and controlled.
For liberals and conservatives alike, the term "mass" tended to emphasize the problem of "order" and "stability" rather than the values of
"freedom" and "obligation." It evoked what Romieu himself referred
to as "*le spectre rouge*," the red menace, the threatening and intimidating rule of the street. And this took on particular urgency when the
franchise was not simply extended as part of a developmental and
piecemeal process but when it was granted instantaneously and wholesale. The reason why in Britain the Caesarism debate was not as
incendiary as it proved to be in France and in Germany was that it was
not as pertinent. For many British liberals and conservatives, Caesarism
was a Continental phenomenon arising out of Continental conditions.
Though the *Times* of December 8, 1851 stigmatized Louis's coup as a
heinous and disgraceful act, others among the British establishment
took the view that if the French will be French this had little to do with
the English. As Lord Malmesbury put it:

we should not measure his [Louis Bonaparte's] acts by an English standard, or ask
ourselves how we should like to see our Parliament shut up, the press abolished,
and everybody imprisoned at pleasure; for we must remember that the French are
more or less accustomed to such proceedings, and that Louis Napoleon put an end
to a system that everybody knew was a fraud and could not last. (Quoted in
Thompson [1955] 1983:126)

It is true that the rehabilitation of Caesar in British Victorian historical writing reflected, as it did elsewhere in Europe, major national issues and pressing political questions.[68] Hence the "mid-century authoritarian and pro-Caesar interpretations" in the historical work of Charles Merivale, John Williams, Henry G. Liddell, and Richard Congreve exposed the perception that a time that had witnessed the Anti-Corn Law League protest and Chartist demonstrations of the forties, and the Crimean War of the mid-fifties, required strong, able, and decisive leadership (Turner 1986:592). In such a context, Louis Bonaparte was not without his admirers.[69] During the 1870s, Caesar again became "a vehicle for attacking contemporary British politics" (Turner 1986:593) when James Froude commended the Roman general for rising above partisan and corrupt politics in a way that was lamentably absent among the politicians of his day. And if, as we saw previously, the 1870s was the decade when Disraeli's second administration (1874–1880) was accused of "imperialism," a term which in that particular context was often equated pejoratively with the Caesarism of Napoleon III, the newfangled "social imperialism" of the 1890s once more sought to redeem Caesar's reputation.[70]

However, while British historians and commentators had recourse to Caesar when turbulent, partisan, and indecisive times seemed to call for the celebratory revival of his memory, the situation faced by their counterparts in France and Germany[71] was significantly different; in consequence, it prompted the Caesarism question in a more agonizing manner. There was no equivalent in Britain of the February 1848 Revolution and the slaughter of the June days; no equivalent either of Louis Bonaparte's *putsch* and the repression that followed it: the mass arrests, censorship, prohibitions on assembly, purges of 3000–4000 teachers, and deportations: as late as 1859, 1,200 of the original 9,600 deportees were still languishing in Algeria (Goldstein 1983:204). Indeed, the 1850s—the decade that spawned the Caesarism debate—was a relatively tranquil time in British domestic politics: Chartism was to all effects over by 1848, and the Young Ireland movement had collapsed. There was also nothing comparable in Britain to the longevity of Louis Bonaparte's uninterrupted rule as president and then emperor: twenty-one years in all. And most evidently there was no parallel to the way that the franchise was granted, and then employed, in elections and plebiscites during the period from 1848 to 1871. In Britain, electoral reform was a gradual process whose development is marked by the milestone Acts of Parliament of 1832, 1867, 1884, and 1885. Inclusion of the male members of the "masses" came incrementally and the first strides towards franchise extension were, in quantitative terms, the shortest: the Reform Act of 1832 increased the electorate by only 2 percent (from 5 to 7 percent of the adult population). The Reform Act of 1867, following three decades of political education, roughly doubled the number of those entitled to vote, while the Act of 1884 further increased the British electorate but only to five million. To be sure, these dates and figures notoriously conceal the arguments, hopes, fears, and torments that animated debates among the propertied classes. To say the electoral process in Britain was "gradual" does not mean that it was smooth and unproblematic; nor should it suggest that there was a consensus on how, and at what pace, the workingman should be integrated into the parliamentary system.[72] Even so, there was nothing to compare in Britain with the wild leaps and oscillations that characterized franchise reform in France. Before the February revolution of 1848, there were less than 250,000 electors; by March this figure had swollen to over 8,000,000; by 1849 the electorate had increased by almost two million more; but then in 1850, alarmed by workers' support for republican and socialist candidates, the government rendered a sizeable bloc of mobile workers electorally impotent by imposing a three-year residence qualification on the right to vote: at a stroke, roughly three million of the ten million electors were effectively disenfranchised (Cole and Campbell 1989:18,45). The plebiscite, too, was a device untried in Britain, and, as such, the parliamentary "representative" system, in which electors are "subjects" of the Crown, could be contrasted with the direct "democracy" of French Caesarist ventriloquism that chose to speak in the name of the French "people."

It was largely taken for granted that the "people" were unable to speak wisely and prudently for themselves, an assumption shown with particular clarity whenever the relationship between "Caesarism" and the ignorant or irrational "masses" was discussed. Cutting across liberal as well as conservative thought, the formulation was available in both a weak and a strong version. In the first variant, Caesarism is envisaged as resting upon, or actively promoting, the ignorance of the "untaught masses,"[73] and it is in the work of Walter Bagehot that this position finds its most sardonic expression. In an essay entitled "Caesareanism as it now exists" first published in *The Economist* in

March 1865, Bagehot pondered on a regime that "stops the effectual inculcation of important thought upon the mass of mankind." Under the government of Napoleon III, Bagehot argued, intellectual culture may thrive and respect still be accorded to the achievements of scholarship. But outside of cultivated circles, a populace had been created that was totally unschooled politically—a consequence of the Second Empire's draconian censorship policy. As he put it, for "the crude mass of men...there are but two instruments penetrative enough to reach their opaque minds—the newspaper article and the popular speech, and both of these are forbidden" (Bagehot [1865] 1968a IV:113).[74] Almost five and a half years later, as Napoleon III's government tottered on the brink of the ignominy of Sedan, Bagehot returned to this theme in a formulation notable not only for its elaboration of his earlier view, but also for a definition of Caesarism that lassoes many of the meanings that, by 1870, that term had come to assume. After declaring that it is not "personal government" per se that has failed in France—for the "personal government" of the Prussian crown is steaming to victory—Bagehot proceeds to identify the miscreant: it is

Caesarism that has utterly failed in France,—meaning by Caesarism, [1][75] that peculiar system of which Louis Napoleon—still, we suppose, nominally the Emperor of the French—is the great exponent, which tries to win directly from a *plebiscite* i.e. the vote of the people, a power for the throne to override the popular will as expressed in regular representative assemblies, and to place in the monarch an indefinite "responsibility" to the nation, by virtue of which he may hold in severe check the intellectual criticism of the more educated classes and even the votes of the people's own delegates. That is what we really mean by Caesarism, [2]—the abuse of the confidence reposed by the most ignorant in a great name to hold at bay the reasoned arguments of men who both know the popular wish and also are sufficiently educated to discuss the best means of gratifying those wishes. [3] A virtually irresponsible power obtained by one man from the vague preference of the masses for a particular name—that is Caesarism...[4]...Caesarism,—i.e....the absence of all intermediate links of moral responsibility and cooperation, which such a system necessarily leaves between the throne and the people. It is the very object of the plebiscite to give the Emperor an authority which reduces all intermediate powers to comparative insignificance if they come into collision with his own. Consequently everything must depend on him, and if he be not practically omniscient there is no substantial check at all on the creatures whom he sets up to execute his will. (Bagehot [1870] 1968b, IV:155–56)[76]

Because all power and patronage is ultimately concentrated in the hands of one man, Bagehot continues, the errors, miscalculations, and inefficiencies of that person, (and under Napoleon III these were legion) have all-encompassing repercussions for his system. A more devolved order of governance on the other hand, such as that which existed within the Prussian military caste, where the king rules through his nobility, provides "a thousand checks against the dishonesty and corruption which seem to have undermined the French military system"—provides, that is to say, a mechanism of damage limitation.[77]

To many modern ears, Bagehot's remarks about the masses will sound patronizing and exaggerated, so it is important to add not only that they reflected commonly held views, but also that they at least sought a political explanation for the alleged vacuity. Even where the lexicon of the "masses" tended to give way to that of "electors" and "citizens," the linkage between "Caesarism" and ignorance—political or otherwise—remained remarkably durable. We see it reappearing, for example, as late as 1904 in Joseph Ferrand's *Caesarism and Democracy*. Ferrand's central argument was that "Caesarist" state centralization had produced a situation of political and administrative debility in France. Since Napoleon Bonaparte the central government had assumed responsibility for a plethora of local concerns—right down to the level of sanitation and cemeteries—without being able to discharge this responsibility efficiently and equitably. In consequence, municipal government was often weak, financially insecure, and a creature of patronage—in short, administratively emasculated. Moreover, since the days of the First Consul, two pernicious ideas had dominated French political life. First, that to deliberate is the responsibility of the many, but that action is the responsibility of a single individual. Second, that since government represents the "sovereign" people, it is impossible that the people could oppose it, for to do so would be to contradict themselves. It was little wonder, according to Ferrand, that such a model had led France disastrously to more or less institutionalize the coup d'état. For while the first idea was predicated on, and legitimized, a feeble and demoralized parliamentary system, the second issued in an electorate that was not encouraged to think— or indeed provided with the educational "instruments" to do so. The consequence was not a "sovereign" people but an alienated and apathetic one wielding the mass suffrage in a show of participation only. Napoleon III had made matters decidedly worse. Though he established a close relationship with the "masses," the latter were both "inconsistent in their new role, and inattentive in exercising it." Besides, universal suffrage offered precious little restraint to the "*erreurs*

de l'ignorance et de la passion" that the plural vote and the representation of minorities might have afforded (Ferrand 1904:1–15, 62–64).[78]

We have seen that, from one point of view, Caesarism has a particularly close affinity with a mass whose lack of education makes it
dangerously amenable to demagogy, irresponsibility and token participation in the political order. Caesarism both promotes and feeds off
such a state of affairs. The implication of such a depiction is that
without Caesarism, political education could begin or move forward;
or at least that the "masses" have the capacity, given time, leadership,
and more propitious conditions, to take their place on the political
stage. Such a conviction is to be distinguished from the second version
of the mass irrationality theme which contends that there is something
about the mass *as such* that renders it virtually imbecilic. We get a
sense of this perspective in Bismarck's reflections on the relationship
between Caesarism and the masses,[79] but it is in the political writings
of Heinrich von Treitschke, one of the Iron Chancellor's most fervent
admirers, that it emerges in a particularly crude and unsullied form.
Warmly endorsing Schiller's assertion that "Majorities are folly and
reason has always lodged among the few," Treitschke warned that
democratic government (that is, the masses in power), "must totally
lack certain finer attributes of political intelligence, and more especially the gift of foresight"; it is always subject to "that terrible demo-
niacal and base passion—envy." In addition, people in democracies
are "peculiarly responsive to direct and simple sensations, good or bad
alike and easily roused by a skillful demagogue" (Treitschke [1897–8]
1916 II:282–83, 289).[80] What is more, there is even a sense in which,
under Caesarism, leader and led deserve each other: while majorities
are "folly," the Caesarist ruler is prone to a kind of madness that
explains his tendency to pursue policies, especially in regard to foreign
affairs, that are plainly "contrary to reason" (Treitschke 1916 II:208,
221, 223). For Bagehot and Ferrand, Caesarism was at root a political
condition inviting a political solution. For Treitschke it was essentially
a problem of democratic social psychology; the implication was that
democracy, and not just Caesarism, was to be avoided at all costs.

Republicanism Overwhelmed

The discussion in European educated circles about Caesarism and
the masses is important not only as an index of incredulity and con-

cern among many witnesses of the nascent democracies. It sheds light also on the intellectual paucity of the republican tradition itself once confronted with a situation for which its concepts were singularly ill-adapted to deal. The essential problem of all European nineteenth-century states—the question of how to respond to the growing demands of the unpropertied for political inclusion and citizenship—had never been adequately worked out by European (or American) republican theorists, nor had there generally been any pressing need for them to do so. In consequence, critics of Napoleon III had few specifically republican conceptual resources to fall back on as they sought to address alternatives to the "Caesarist" model. Republican political theory had been conceived in different times; and these were not times of "democracy" as we think of it today, "representative," "plebiscitarian" or otherwise. On the contrary, "representation" was often contrasted with "democracy," and the latter was typically envisaged as both unworkable and demagogic.[81] Commonwealthmen like Neville, Algernon Sidney, and Harrington, for instance, certainly championed the expansion and entrenchment of civil and religious freedoms, but they had never dreamt of proposing universal manhood suffrage; political representation was not a matter of numbers—the alternative notion of Napoleonic "representation"[82] would have been barely comprehensible to them—but of ensuring that all members of the propertied, literate, and independent classes, had a vote. "That servants, fishermen, labouring men and 'rabble' should exercise such a privilege was never conceived by them" (Robbins 1969:49). Rousseau ([1762] 1993a:239–40) made the point differently but just as bluntly: "If we take the term in the strict sense," he remarked, "there never has been a real democracy, and there never will be. It is against the natural order for the many to govern and the few to be governed. It is unimaginable that the people should remain continually assembled to devote their time to public affairs," just as it was unthinkable that democratic-like conditions—simplicity of manners, equality in rank, the absence of luxury—could be recreated in a modern polity. Democracy supposes "a people of gods," not of men. So-called "pure democracies" had also been criticized, just as they had been redefined, in the *Federalist*, as we saw in the last chapter. The argument for a republic, rather than a "democracy" was an argument for delegated powers. "Nothing can be more fallacious than to found our political calculations on arithmetical principles," Madison had said in *Federalist* 55. Political assemblies needed to be of an optimum size to work effectively. If they were too small there was danger of oligarchy; but if they were too large they would simply encourage "the confusion and intemperance of a multitude. In all very numerous assemblies, of whatever characters composed, passion never fails to wrest the sceptre from reason. Had every Athenian citizen been a Socrates, every Athenian assembly would still have been a mob."[83]

Madison was here affirming the principle of representation that Rousseau himself so stridently attacked. But in both cases "democracy" was not a part of their rhetorical armory. And by the middle of the nineteenth century, the term "republican" itself had become exceedingly broad and vague. Hence while Proudhon, in 1840, could say that of course he was a republican, he also felt bound to add that "this word has no precise meaning. *Res publica*, that is, the public good. Now whoever desires the public good, under whatever form of government, can call himself a republican. Kings too are republicans" (Proudhon 1969:88). Exactly a decade later, in recollections that would only be published towards the end of the century, Tocqueville was identifying "the republican form of government" with an "ill-balanced form of government" dominated by "an elected executive branch"; he would also contrast it invidiously with the greater liberty allowed under constitutional monarchy ([1893] 1970:200–1). Marx and Engels's views on republicanism were even more complex.[84] Writing on the *Class Struggles in France:1848–50* ([1850] 1973a), Marx noted that while republicanism could be associated with the revolutionary politics of the workers' leadership—the "democratic republicanism" of an Auguste Blanqui and an Armand Barbès—it was just as capable of receiving a petty bourgeois and bourgeois appropriation;[85] indeed, even Legitimists and Orleanists would on occasion realize that the battle against the revolutionary proletariat "could only be joined in the name of the republic" ([1850] 1973a:56; cf. 41, 44, 62). The term "republican" Marx suggests again and again is largely a bourgeois label for bourgeois rule. Engels agreed with him. Moreover, while both Marx and Engels were willing to acknowledge that, in developmental terms, the "bourgeois republic" would typically need to precede, and prepare the conditions for, a postcapitalist society, this was simply another way of saying that republicanism was a *transitional form* of political association leading eventually to "revolutionary socialism."[86]

Even where, as in France, "republicanism" continued to attract supporters as a self-professed designation and creed, its doctrine had only superficial resemblances to its classical predecessors. Thus the "republicanism" of the Third Republic was predominantly a social, Kantian liberalism with the commitments to pursue educational reform along secular lines, promote social solidarity and mutual aid, reduce the excesses of competitive individualism, woo the workers from revolutionary Marxism and syndicalism, establish a peaceful and just society. (Bellamy 1992:58–74.)[87] It is true that such a project shared the anticlericalism of its republican namesake, as well as the Rousseauian desire to create a "civic religion." There the similarity ends, however. Indeed such attitudes, and the policies that flowed from them, led the Third Republican reformers to be accused by Catholic critics, like Eugéne Villedieu, of Caesarism. From such a perspective, "Caesarism" denoted not the negation of republicanism, but—in the metamorphosis of "Jacobin Caesarism"—its apotheosis.[88] According to Villedieu, "Caesarism is the self-expression and the inevitable result of the Revolution's doctrines," and the execution of such doctrines encouraged war, internal tumult and the violation of the rights of citizens. In particular, "Jacobin Caesarism" sought to rob citizens of the most important thing in their life: the Church. Whereas Napoleon's Concordat had at least moved towards some rapprochement with the Church, the new Jacobins of the Third Republic were busy undoing even that compromise. The rights of the Church to exist, to develop to its full potential, and its right to teach and establish new schools were all being attacked by "*le Césarisme Jacobin*." As such, the regime was attacking not just the Church as an institution, but God Himself (Villedieu 1880:1–17).[89]

This association of "Caesarism" with Jacobinism, and Jacobinism with the Third Republic is more evidence of the growing confusion surrounding the republican idea. For one thing, French social liberals of the Third Republic, like their forebears, were self-consciously *anti*-Jacobin (Bellamy 1992:60), yet here they were being tarred with the same brush on account of their policies towards the Church. For another, the more conventional view that Caesarism was exemplified in Napoleon I and III—figures who had moved to *crush* Jacobinism and republicanism alike—is here replaced by the contention that Caesarism and Jacobinism are, if perhaps not one and the same phenomenon, then nonetheless integrally linked. Moreover, the idea that Jacobinism was alive and well in the structures of the Third Republic was not restricted to domestic critics of the regime or to Catholic apologists. Towards the end of the century, the position would be recapitulated and refined by the Italian historian and political commentator Guglielmo Ferrero.

Ferrero opens his remarks on "Militarism and Caesarism in France" with the now predictable comment that "republic" is "a word signifying many and diverse things." Nominally, France is a "parliamentary and democratic republic," but the modern "republican constitution" that drapes its political system "still covers its original trunk and pith" which is Caesarism. For Ferrero, Caesarism is more than Napoleonism; it is the militarism of the "Jacobin lay State created by the Revolution in opposition to the Church." While the two Bonapartes certainly acted within, and intensified, this structure of relations, the Jacobin phenomenon also embraces the "republic" that ostensibly has replaced their empires. Originally, the Jacobin state had come about as a result of the deep contradiction the French Revolution had exposed between the new "enlightened" secular-minded rulers and those who still clung to Church authority. The former, "a small and bold minority" propagating ideals of popular sovereignty, rationalism, and discussion, found themselves in power not "through the force of their ideas" but because the decrepitude of the *ancien régime* had permitted their ascent by default. Once in charge, however, a nasty shock awaited them. Far from being welcomed as the liberators of society, the new reformers came face to face with an antagonistic or indifferent majority committed to traditional, deeply ingrained ideals and customs, and to a Church offering extensive social and welfare protection. So it was that:

> The Jacobin State, whose object was to give liberty to France, grew rapidly entangled in a grave contradiction, for it was compelled to establish a new protective system analogous to that of the Church, in order to raise itself from the condition of a feeble governmental minority engulfed in the midst of a vast hostile community. French society, accustomed for centuries to universal Church protection, would have found itself, when the Church was stripped of wealth and power…in a terrible position…Napoleon's reign saved France and the work of the Revolution, by definitely organizing, on the lines traced out by the Convention, the new universal secular protection of the Jacobin State in place of that formerly exercised by the Church. ([1898] 1972:206–7)

Bureaucratic gargantuanism, state paternalism and clientism, centralization, a mighty executive seeking to legitimize its authority through the incitement of patriotic fervor and thus inclining towards war—all these were the characteristic features of the French Jacobin State. So was Caesarism, the militarist impulse and attitude that had permeated each of nineteenth-century France's many governmental forms. The Third Republic was essentially no different. However, as the borders of Europe had changed, and France's ability to conduct war effectively in Europe frustrated, French militarism had been compelled to change with it. The result was the colonial policy of Ferrero's day that he decried as economically wasteful and politically antiquated.

I have been commenting on the growing opacity of the republican idea in the nineteenth century, and the conceptual limitations of the older republican tradition to deal creatively with the challenges associated with modern democracy. It remains for me to add that even where "democracy" and "the masses" enjoyed more favorable connotations, as the terms tended temperamentally to do in socialist or anarchist[90] thought, this had little to do with a republican conception of politics in spite of flourishes in that direction. Republicans had typically valued politics as something valuable in its own right: a space for the articulation of public goals; a nexus of rights and obligations; a stage for greatness and glory. Man's greatest dignity lay in his capacity for political action, in his ability to love, defend, and participate in his commonwealth. In contrast, the dominant strands of nineteenth- and twentieth-century socialist thought were, and have continued to be, highly reductive and laborist in character. For twentieth-century social democrats, politics has tended to be thought of in distributive and instrumentalist terms, as a mechanism embedded in the state to deliver social resources and to engage in projects of social engineering. In the nineteenth century, "social democracy" meant Marxism, but for classical Marxism, the point of engaging in politics was to end it, so as to introduce a society without exploitation and inequality. It has been said that when Marx and Engels "spoke of the 'dictatorship of the proletariat', they were using the term 'dictatorship' in its ancient Roman sense" (Medvedev 1981:41), but such a view will not stand close scrutiny. Certainly, the founders of Marxism conceived of a dictatorship as a crisis form of rule, employing extraordinary powers for a limited duration, the purpose of which was to superintend the transition from a late capitalist mode of production to at least the first stages of a socialist and classless society. However, the analogy with Rome is, more closely considered, quite superficial. In Roman constitutional theory, and in early republican practice,[91] the dictatorship was an office of an already established government (the Senate) empowered to take drastic action in order to reestablish normal political conditions. The dictatorship entailed the juridical *transfer* of power from the Senate to one of its magistracies. For classical Marxists, in contrast, the dictatorship of the proletariat was supposed to emerge from a *seizure* of power spearheaded by a revolutionary organization; it was, in a very real sense, the *first* legitimate government. Moreover, the dictatorship of the proletariat does not mark an interregnum designed eventually to reestablish the political *status quo ante* but the first stage in a process the end result of which is the termination of the state itself.[92]

In addition, the idea of law, as crucial for republicans as for liberals, was openly attacked in the classical Marxist tradition, as were legitimacy and love of country. Law was an ideological charade masking the repression of bourgeois rule; debates about legitimacy and patriotism were irrelevant cant so long as one class or one national bourgeoisie dominated another. "Brotherhood," rather than "citizenship,"[93] "internationalism" rather than "virtue," were the keynotes of Marxist praxis, and just for this reason the term "masses"—now suggesting solidarity and classless homogeneity—could take on positive associations. Classical republicanism, to the contrary, was a doctrine of political equality *and distinction*. That man's essential being lay in his activity as *homo faber*; that liberty must entail a fundamental rupture with traditional notions of legal obligation and the rule of law;[94] that one's primary loyalty was owed to a class rather to a commonwealth; such ideas would have made as little sense to classical republicans as the anarchist preference for society without a state.[95]

However, if opinion across the ideological spectrum read into the "masses" its own peculiar agenda, we have seen that it was mainly, though by no means exclusively, liberal and conservative thought that tied the term to Caesarism. While he who says Caesarism says the masses, the inverse relationship does not necessarily hold. This is because liberals and conservatives tended to see Caesarism as a reflex of mass behavior and intrusion; each appeared to entail the other. For this they had the impeccable source of Louis Bonaparte himself. In the *Extinction of Pauperism* ([1844] 1856cII:122), he had announced: "Today, the rule of castes is over: one can only govern with the masses. They should therefore be organized so that they can express their will, and disciplined so that they can be guided and enlightened as to [what constitutes] their own interests." The statement reformulated Louis's remark that "the Napoleonic idea"—the idea that Caesarism came in one prominent version to enshrine—"would use the influence it exercises over the masses, not in upsetting, but in calming and reorganising society. The Napoleonic idea is in itself peaceful rather than warlike, and it is an idea more in favour of reconstruction than of upheaval" (Louis Bonaparte [1840] 1856a I:12–13). Liberals and conservatives may, or may not, have seen such a program as bogus; but when they thought of the "masses," that is, when they thought of people *as masses*, the Caesar figure—Napoleon III, Bismarck—was never very far from their thoughts. For Marxism, in contrast, the relationship between Caesarism and "the masses" was much more open ended, not least because of the positive valence that the latter notion enjoyed in Marxist doctrine. Moreover, while Caesarism may have been a problem for some socialists and Marxists,[96] there was always the hope—virtually impossible in the thought-worlds of liberals and conservatives—that through education and leadership the masses would eventually be a problem *for Caesarism*.[97]

The Marxian Interpretation of Louis Bonaparte and the Second Empire

During the middle years of the nineteenth century, "socialism" was a term still very much in the flux of definition.[98] What made an idea or doctrine "socialist," was not necessarily its tendency to attack the institution of private property, let alone call for its abolition. Rather, the "central notion was concern with the 'social question' as distinct from concern merely with political liberalism, freedom, philosophic and religious radicalism, and such. The 'social question' was the plight of the masses of people in the new society of growing industry and bourgeoisification, and the need to do something about it" (Draper 1977 I:97).

It was in this context that Louis Bonaparte could himself, on occasion, be thought of as entertaining "socialist" ideas. Had he not, in the *Extinction of Pauperism*, sought to devise for the state a scheme of mass employment, entailing the cultivation of unused land, the creation of agricultural colonies, and tax and investment policies favorable to the working class? And was not this, in the parlance of the day, equivalent to at least one interpretation of "socialism"?[99] The editor of a British Napoleonic anthology certainly thought so:

It will be apparent that this project is only a modification of the principles of Socialism or of Communism (we are hardly clear which is which), and as such repugnant to all sound principles of political economy....[W]e will only add that, considering the views here advocated by the writer, it is certainly a remarkable inconsistency to find him, within half-a-dozen years afterwards, putting himself forward as one engaged upon a "mission" against Socialism. (Louis Bonaparte [1852] 1972 II:94)

Yet it was precisely the nature of this "mission," and more importantly the underlying conditions that sustained it, which were at that very moment being interrogated by a man whose socialist credentials have less often been in doubt. Karl Marx's analysis of Louis Bonaparte and the Second Empire[100] is distinctive on a number of counts, but it too was by no means totally immune to the "great parallel" with antiquity—a famous protestation of Marx's notwithstanding. In the 1869 preface to the second edition of *The Eighteenth Brumaire of Louis Bonaparte* ([1852] 1973b), he concluded his remarks with the "hope that my work will contribute towards eliminating the current German school master's phrase which refers to a so-called *Caesarism*." This "superficial historical analogy ignores the main point"

namely, that the ancient Roman class struggle was only fought out within a privileged minority, between the free rich and the free poor, while the great productive mass of the population, the slaves, formed a purely passive pedestal for the combatants.[101] People forget Sismondi's significant expression: the Roman proletariat lived at the expense of society, while modern society lives at the expense of the proletariat. The material and economic conditions of the ancient and the modern class struggles are so utterly distinct from each other that their political products also can have no more in common with each other than the Archbishop of Canterbury has with the High Priest Samuel.[102] (Marx [1869] 1973b: 144–45)

It followed that if one were to really understand the "political products" (*politische Ausgeburten*) that constituted Louis Bonaparte's regime, it would be necessary to reveal the peculiarly modern "material and economic conditions" that had created and thereafter sustained them. In addition, Marx insisted that the Bonapartist regime had to be framed within the class struggles of the time; it was such struggles that had "allowed a mediocre and grotesque individual to play the hero's role."

These comments are in one way misleading, but in another way faithful to Marx's aspiration to offer a truly conjunctural and modern analysis of Bonapartist rule. They are misleading in that both Marx and Engels frequently did resort to historical analogies that might have attracted the stigma of "superficiality." For while Marx, in 1869, looking back on almost the entire span of Louis Bonaparte's rule, could repudiate current analogies with ancient Rome as facile, a decade earlier he had shown little reluctance to exploit them. As Hal Draper (1977 I:466) observes: "Marx himself had made his own analogies with Caesarism more than once": in *New York Daily Tribune* articles of the 1850s "he had referred to the Bonapartist regime as 'the Caesarism of Paris,' and to 'military despotism, the rule of the Caesars' in contemporaneous Europe."[103] Similarly, Marx likened the growing domination of the army under Bonapartism to "the rule of the pretorians" (Marx 1986d). Considered from another perspective, however, Marx's self-description constitutes an accurate account of his own distinctive theoretical inclination. If he on occasion employed the expressions Caesarism or Bonapartism in ways that adopted some of the current associations the terms enjoyed—especially in regard to military rule—he at the same time distanced himself from the mainstream Caesarism debate in fundamental ways. For Marx, the secret of Louis Bonaparte's ascent to power and of the Second Empire that followed, lay in a particular crisis of property relations. Marx identified the problem of Bonapartism not primarily as a problem of "legitimacy," or Jacobinism or plebiscitary politics; certainly not as a problem of the corrosive impact of liberal ideas; and even less as a problem of the rise of some undifferentiated ignorant *proletarian* "mass"[104]—all formulations expressed by the concept of Caesarism; but rather as a matter of shifting class configurations, the result of which had been to "autonomize" the French state. However, to say that it is classes not "masses" that are the key to the French conundrum would not be totally accurate. When Marx turned to discuss the relationship between Louis Bonaparte and the *peasantry*, the familiar negative "mass" images emerge once more in all their virulence, a point to which I will have occasion to return.

In what follows, I shall concentrate on Marx's own accounts of the Bonapartist phenomenon, mostly employing for the sake of textual fidelity his own terminology and concepts to do so. The consequence of such a narrow focus is the omission of a number of areas and issues that, though important in their own right, would require more than I am here able to deliver. Notably, I will address neither Engels's theory of Bismarckian Bonapartism and the "exceptional" state,[105] nor the quite radical departures from Marx's own pronouncements on Bonapartism by later Marxist theorists, notably Trotsky, whose heterodox arguments were particularly fertile and imaginative.[106] My task, though strictly and artificially circumscribed, is challenging enough, mainly because the stylistic character of Marx's own formulations—simultaneously journalistic, historical, theoretical, and polemical—lends his ideas a mercurial quality that resists neat encapsulation. Emphases are apt to change both within particular articles, as well as between them, according to the level of analysis Marx chooses, the episode he elects to consider, and the targets of his critique or lampoon. Moreover, as Napoleon III's regime changed, so Marx's interpretation to some extent changed with it, though the transition of the regime from "dictatorship" to the increased liberalization in the 1860s was to the best of my knowledge never theoretically integrated into Marx's account of the Second Empire.[107] What people often refer to as Marx's theory of Bonapartism (a term he did not actually often use) is one that only deals with the period 1848–1861 in any detail or with any conceptual sophistication; the comments on the Second Empire in *The Civil War in France* (1871) for the most part recapitulate and reinforce the conclusions he reached almost twenty years earlier. Nonetheless, Marx's inquiries into the Second Empire during the fifties are more sustained, and integrate journalism with theoretical analysis more complexly, than those of any other thinker of the day. They also offer, in a number of respects, a major alternative to notions of Caesarism then flourishing. For these reasons, it is important to examine his work in some detail.

The Dominant Classes

Marx argued that a signal feature of French society in the period between the Restoration and 1851 was the weakness of industrial capital relative to both landed capital—dominant under the Bourbon "Legitimist" monarchy of Charles X (1815–30)—and finance capital, whose representatives directed state power under the Orleanist constitutional monarchy of Louis Philippe (1830–1848) and who, in addition, had constituted the most politically influential "fraction" of the bourgeoisie under the February Republic (Marx 1973a:46; 1973b:165).[108] These capitalist fractions coexisted in a far from harmonious condition; collisions between them were frequent and systemic. Notably, while high finance benefited from state indebtedness,[109] industrial (manufacturing) capital suffered because of it. The failure of the government to balance its revenue with its expenditure resulted in increased taxation. Increased taxation, by inflating production costs and lowering consumption capacity, resulted in lower profits. It was precisely the resentment generated by this kind of situation, Marx tells us, that motivated the industrial bourgeoisie to challenge the July monarchy of Louis Philippe, the regime that was the very incarnation of finance capital's economic and political hegemony (Marx 1973a:36–41, 110–11).[110]

Yet if financial and industrial capitals were divided among themselves over which of them was to rule the French polity, they were agreed on the essential point: the proletariat had to be exterminated as a political force. It was this determination that cemented the interests of property together. And it was the *Republic* that provided the conditions for the (albeit uneven) collective rule of capital. The means of representation for the "unity" of financial, landed, and industrial fractions was the Party of Order, an alliance of Bourbons and Orleanists, under the direction of the agents of finance. Yet this coalescence of capitals was not to last. Within two-and-a-half years of its foundation, the Republic lay in ruins. In a spectacular example of political decomposition, the Party of Order had broken up into its original components; the specter of competing dynastic claims had been resurrected; and a legitimation crisis was in full swing. By allowing the Republic to be destroyed, the conditions of bourgeois rule as a whole were destroyed (Marx 1973b:215–22). How had the French social formation arrived at this state of affairs?

Marx argued that the coup against the Republic was made possible, first, by crises within the ruling class, and, second—and ironically—by the destruction of the very political forces capital itself had sought to annihilate: the proletariat and petty bourgeoisie. I will be examining the defeat of the proletariat and the petty bourgeoisie in the next section. It suffices here only to note Marx's argument that the elimination of their political organizations, together with the severe curtailment of their strength in civil society, had two dire consequences for the shape of the Republic and thus for the basis of bourgeois rule. On the other hand, it removed key sources of resistance to state encroachment; on the other hand, by inviting the state to intervene in the suppression of the subordinate classes, the bourgeoisie encouraged the state's imperiousness and immeasurably strengthened its grip over polity and society alike (Marx 1973a:139; 1973b:186; 1974:208). The problem for the Party of Order was that while it certainly mistrusted state ambition and interference, it at the same time required a strong and interventionist state to keep subaltern groups in check. Impaled on the horns of its own dilemma, the Party of Order was forced to oversee a drastic erosion of its own power, and left to witness a series of episodes—the dissolution of the National Guard, the ousting of the Barrot-Falloux ministry, and the dismissal of Nicolas Changarnier, the anti-Bonapartist general—that heralded capital's own subsequent (if temporary) marginalization. Three crises within the Party of Order itself were of particular importance during the short life of the Republic; each of them hastened the coup and contributed to its success. First, the Party of Order was publicly discredited when it connived in the expulsion of members of the Montagne (the petty bourgeoisie's parliamentary representatives) who had sought to impeach Bonaparte for the unconstitutional use of his powers. From then onwards, no one could take seriously its own claims to parliamentary immunity, and its right to rebel when menaced by Louis Bonaparte (Marx 1973b:181). Second, a particularly serious crisis of representation became evident as legitimists and Orleanists not only once again became recognisable as distinct and separate entities, their parliamentary fusion broken, but also underwent within each fraction a new decomposition (Marx 1973b:218–19). To make matters worse, the Party of Order was deserted by both financial and industrial capitals who, interpreting the struggles between executive and legislature as disturbances to stability and order, nervously came to hanker after the repression of their onetime political proxies by the president of the Republic (Marx 1973b:221–4). Third, the haemorrhages of credibility and representation were aggravated by the trade crisis of 1851. Though economic in origin,[111] the causes of the trade crisis were construed by the bourgeoisie not as a product of capitalist relations but rather attributed "to purely political causes, to the struggle between the legislature and the executive" (Marx 1973b:225). The economic problems, compounded by fear of popular tumult, threw the extraparliamentary bourgeoisie into frenzy and panic, hammering home the conclusion: "Rather an end with terror than a terror without end" (Marx 1973b:228). The consequence was the "Cossack republic." With the victory "of force without words over the force of words," the bourgeoisie had shown just how well they understood the limits of parliamentary discussion (Marx 1973b:235–36).

The Subordinate Classes

The economic immaturity of industrial capital in France was of significance not only to capital itself. It also had serious consequences for the proletariat's capacity successfully to stage the insurrection of June 1848, and, later, to resist the Bonapartist "dictatorship": a weak industrial bourgeoisie results in a weak working class. As Marx explained:

> In general, the development of the industrial proletariat is conditioned by the development of the industrial bourgeoisie. Only under the rule of the bourgeoisie does it begin to exist on a broad national basis, which elevates its revolution to a national one; only under the rule of the bourgeoisie does it create the modern means of production, which also become the means of its revolutionary liberation. It is only the rule of the bourgeoisie which serves to tear up the material roots of feudal society and level the ground, thus creating the only possible conditions for a proletarian revolution.[112](Marx 1973a:46–47)

Industrial capital represents the most progressive of all capital fractions because its consolidation and extension signifies the growing simplification of the class structure. But in France, the "struggle against capital in its highly developed modern form—at its crucial point, the struggle of the industrial wage-labourer against the industrial bourgeois—is...a partial phenomenon" (Marx 1973a:46). The industrial proletariat of Paris may be strong enough to exert its power and demonstrate its revolutionary élan at a time of emergency; but outside the capital city, the proletariat, "crowded together in separate and dispersed industrial centres...is almost submerged by the predominance of peasant farmers and petty bourgeois" (Marx 1973a:46). Moreover, while the proletariat had been a key factor in the February Revolution, its success was both partial and pyrrhic. It was partial because its intervention had to a large extent taken place under the ideological and political leadership of sections of the bourgeoisie. And it was pyrrhic because by "dictating the republic to the Provisional Government, and through the Provisional Government to the whole of France, the proletariat immediately came into the foreground as an independent party; but at the same time it challenged the whole of bourgeois France to enter the lists against it" (Marx 1973a:43). In June 1848, the working class was defeated on the street by an alliance of disaffected petty bourgeoisie (forming the bulk of the National Guard),[113] the lumpenproletariat, mobilized in twenty-four battalions of Mobile

Guards,[114] and the army. Simultaneously, its members in the Assembly were prosecuted and outlawed (Marx 1973b:154). Associated with the general decline in the political energy of members of the working class was the trend towards "doctrinaire experiments" such as Proudhonist exchange banks, the growth of parochial craft unionism, and the emergence of a reformist leadership. It soon became clear that "for the time being, the historical process would again have to go forward *over* their heads" (Marx 1973b:194).

It would also have to proceed without the petty-bourgeoisie, both extraparliamentary and within the National Assembly. Marx's depiction of this class between June 1848 and Louis Bonaparte's coup d'état is one of growing alienation from, and hostility to, the Republic. Not only did it find itself increasingly threatened with bankruptcy; it also found its parliamentary representation in the Montagne (led by Alexandre Ledru-Rollin) outmaneuvered and marginalized. But it was on the streets that the petty bourgeoisie's power was to be finally broken. The immediate cause of its undoing was a series of clashes between the Montagne and the president, Louis Bonaparte. The dispute culminated in the tabling of a bill of impeachment against the president and his ministry for their part in sanctioning the bombardment of Rome. After the bill had been rejected by the Assembly on June 12, 1849, a demonstration the following day provided the Party of Order and the executive with a golden opportunity to rid themselves of this social irritant. The petty bourgeoisie was met with force and convincingly routed. In the aftermath it became obvious that the menacing arm that had proved so effective against the proletariat a year earlier had itself been cut off.

The liquidation of the proletariat and petty bourgeoisie as political forces removed two bastions of resistance to the Bonapartist *putsch* that was to come. But not all members of the subordinate classes opposed Louis Napoleon, and, notoriously, one major subordinate class supported him. Marx's discussion of the small-holding peasantry in *The Eighteenth Brumaire* makes plain that the relationship between that class and a Bonapartist-type state is simultaneously structural and idiosyncratic.

> By its very nature, small peasant property is suitable to serve as the foundation of an all-powerful and innumerable bureaucracy. It creates a uniform level of relationships and persons over the whole surface of the land. Hence it also allows a uniformity of intervention from a supreme centre into all points of this uniform

mass. It annihilates the aristocratic intermediate levels between the mass of the people and the state power. On all sides, therefore, it calls forth the direct interference of this state power and the interposition of its organs without mediation. (Marx 1973b:243)

At the same time, Marx points to a more specific relationship between the peasantry and Louis Bonaparte. The peasantry, particularly its small-holding section, had recognized something of its own physiognomy when, in December 1848, it had voted en bloc for Louis as president of the Republic.[115] Marx interprets this phenomenon as the victory of an image—"For the peasants Napoleon was not a person but a program" (Marx 1973a:72)[116]—and of a fantasy: "The nephew's obsession was realized, because it coincided with the obsession of the most numerous class of the French people" (Marx 1973b:239). Napoleon I had reinforced the tendency towards small peasant property that had attended the decline and then collapse of the feudal estates. In Louis Bonaparte, Marx claims, the peasants imagined a veritable reincarnation had taken place that would save them from the burden of taxation and mortgage. In addition, Bonaparte-worship was conditioned by the life experience induced by peasant small-holding. In a renowned passage (1973b:238–39), Marx argues that the isolation of the small peasant proprietor; the low division of labor typical of his small-holding, which permits little application of science and little diversity of skills; the segmental self-sufficiency of peasant life; and the productive and ecological stumbling blocks to political organization, were all factors that impeded representation through parliament or direct intervention via a revolutionary Convention. Having no institutionalized mode of influence on the body politic, it was natural that the peasants should vote for Bonaparte to represent them: "They cannot represent themselves; they must be represented."[117] On the other hand, no class showed better the fraudulent character of the "Napoleonic ideas," all of which *"are ideas of the undeveloped small-holding in its heyday"* (Marx 1973b:244, emphasis in the original). Stripped of their pseudo-heroic patina, the ideas represented the "enslavement and poverty" of the peasant small-holding, the "strong and unrestricted government" required to keep the peasants in order, the rule of bureaucrats, priests, and army officers lording it over them (Marx 1973b:240–43). Marx was sure that the development of capitalism was in the process of revealing Napoleonic ideology for the chimera it was, and that the natural ally of the peasant was not an emperor, but the proletariat. In the meantime there was no denying how injurious peasant support for Louis Bonaparte had been.

Marx's scathing description of the small-holding peasant is so well known among historians and social scientists, that there is no need to labor our commentary on it with extensive quotation. Even so, it is important to underline the point that, for all the novelty of his class analysis, Marx reverted to a depiction of the Bonaparte-peasant relationship that recapitulated in all essentials a key motif of the Caesarism debate. In both *The Class Struggles in France* and *The Eighteenth Brumaire*, the small-holding peasant family is a constant object of ridicule by Marx. It constitutes "the great mass of the French nation...formed by the simple addition of isomorphous magnitudes, much as potatoes in a sack form a sack of potatoes." Marx's use of the word "mass" here is deliberate for, as he goes on to say, there is a very real sense in which the small peasant proprietors do not actually constitute a "class" at all. "In so far as these small peasant proprietors are merely connected on a local basis, and the identity of their interests fails to produce a feeling of community, they do not form a class. They are therefore incapable of asserting their class interest in their own name, whether through a parliament or through a convention." Or as Marx also puts it: "The small peasant proprietors form an immense mass [*eine ungeheure Masse*], the members of which live in the same situation but do not enter into manifold relationships with each other" (Marx 1973b:239, 238 = Marx 1969:198).[118] The "Napoleonic ideas" represent the quintessence of peasant idiocy and decline. "They are only the hallucinations of [the small-holding's] death agony, words made into phrases, spirits made into ghosts." And in this death agony also lie the portents of the destruction of the Bonapartist state: as the small-holding degenerates so too does the "state structure erected upon it" (Marx 1973b:244).

The derision Marx levelled against the small-holding peasant is noteworthy for at least two reasons. First, while Marx mostly (though not invariably) acquitted the urban proletariat from the charge of Caesarism and passive acclamation, he retained nonetheless the conceptual linkage between Louis Bonaparte and a dangerous or ridiculous "mass." Marx's originality lay not in evicting this concept from his analysis of Louis Bonaparte, but in transferring it to a different social entity: from the urban proletariat (who appear only temporarily to lose their agency)[119] to the smallholding peasantry. Again and again,

Marx stresses the symbiosis of the peasantry and Louis Bonaparte; and just as often he presents it as one of reciprocal absurdity.

Second, even where Marx does speak of the peasantry as in some sense a class, it is evident to him that it "represents barbarism within civilization" (Marx 1973a:72). In good measure, this attitude derives from Marx's attitude towards property more generally. From the standpoint of Jeffersonian and other republican traditions, the small-holding unit was envisaged as a locus of freedom and responsibility, something to be valued not abhorred. For Marx, in contrast, it is the sure sign of economic decrepitude. The good society will emerge only after a class with nothing has confronted a class with everything. It transpires, then, that in the tribunal of History the small-holding peasant stands accused not only of being a political failure for supporting Louis Bonaparte, but of constituting an impediment to social progress,[120] an offense to "civilization" itself.[121]

The Bonapartist State: Precursors, Continuities, Ruptures

Marx declared in *The Civil War in France* that the Second Empire "was the only form of government possible at a time when the bourgeoisie had already lost, and the working class had not yet acquired, the faculty of ruling the nation" ([1871] 1974:208). But if mode of production and social formation conditions eventuated in such a situation, so too did a long process of state centralization. Marx breaks down the career of state centralization into four discernible and cumulative historical phases: the emergence of the absolutist state; the Great Revolution of 1789 and the rule of Napoleon I; the Bourbon and Orleanist monarchies; the parliamentary Republic installed in February 1848 (1973b:237–38). The Bonapartist state was less a pathological break with the past, than a continuation of the steady accretion of power that had accompanied French life for over a century. Moreover, continuity was also evident between the character of the Republican constitution drafted in the period of the Constituent National Assembly (May 4, 1848 to May 28, 1849) and the regime that toppled it. The political relevance of the constitution lay in the antagonism it created between two relatively independent sources of authority, namely the National Assembly and the President.[122] The former, elected by universal manhood suffrage, controlled the bulk of the lawmaking process, and was empowered with the ultimate decisions on issues of "war, peace and commercial treaties" and "the right of amnesty." The latter, also elected by universal manhood suffrage was endowed "with all the attributes of royal power, with the authority to appoint and dismiss his ministers independently of the National Assembly, with all the instruments of executive power in his hands, and finally with the right of appointment to every post....He has the whole of the armed forces behind him" (Marx 1973b:160–61). The consequence of this constitutional bifurcation, Marx argued, was the creation for the president of an independent popular base that immensely amplified his personal authority. Indeed, the Republican constitution provided

> for its own abolition by having the President elected by the direct suffrage of all Frenchman. Whereas in the case of the National Assembly the votes of France are divided among its seven hundred and fifty members, they are here, on the contrary, concentrated on *one* individual. While each individual deputy represents only this or that party, this or that town...*he*, the President, is the elect of the nation, and the act of electing him is the great trump which the sovereign people plays once every four years. The elected National Assembly stands in a metaphysical relation to the nation, but the elected President stands in a personal relation to it....Unlike the Assembly, he possesses a kind of divine right; he is there by the grace of the people. (Marx 1973b:161–62)

Yet if Bonaparte's coup grew almost organically from the Republican constitution it superseded, and if it epitomized both a continuation and a consummation of a statism deeply ingrained within French society since at least the eighteenth century, this did not exhaust its significance. Though many elements of "Bonapartism" were by no means original to the 1850s, their recombination and exaggeration did mark something of a rupture with earlier political forms. In essence, Bonapartism represented a new "form" rather than a new "type" of state (Poulantzas [1968] 1973:147–53). The Bonapartist regime, in other words, was clearly a capitalist "type" of state insofar as it encouraged commodity production and functioned broadly within the institutional separation of economic and political relations characteristic of capitalist society. However this capitalist "type" of state had undergone, Marx makes plain, a distinctive mutation.

- Hence, within the state as a whole, changes became evident both in the social composition of its personnel—a massive influx of lumpen-proletarian and clerical elements followed the coup—and in the regression of many state offices into private hands (Marx 1973b:243, 247; Marx [1856] 1980:617)..

- In addition, the relationship of the state apparatuses to each other experienced, under Bonapartism, a major realignment. Again, the antecedents of this realignment lay in the Republic itself that had by turns witnessed the removal of the Party of Order's ministries, its loss of control over the army, (evidenced in the dismissal of Changarnier) and over the president. However, what became particularly evident after the coup of December 2, 1851 was the enhanced role of the bureaucracy (Marx 1973b:243) and the military in the new state; "instead of *society* conquering a new content for itself," Marx protested, "it only seems that the *state* has returned to its most ancient form, the unashamedly simple rule of the military sabre and the clerical cowl" (Marx 1973b:149; cf. 184, 244, and Marx 1974:208). Marx wrote these lines in 1852, and thus shortly after the coup had occurred. By 1858 he was even more emphatic on the centrality of the military arm of state to the regime of Louis Bonaparte. Louis Bonaparte's early victory was to be explained, Marx said, "by the mutual prostration of the antagonist parties" on the one hand, and "the coincidence of his coup d'état with the entrance of the commercial world upon a period of prosperity" on the other. But now France, like other European capitalist countries, was engulfed by a severe economic crisis, and classes that had either supported Bonaparte for reasons of expediency, or acquiesced in his coup, were now eager to get rid of him. So, too, had been Felice Orsini, the Italian revolutionary, though his attempt to assassinate Bonaparte on January 14, 1858 had been bungled. With that pretext, and in response to growing disquiet at home, Napoleon III resorted to imperial decree: on January 27 he divided France into five military districts—"military pashalics" Marx called them—under the command of five marshals, revealing clearly enough that "pretorian rule" had come to France (Marx [1858] 1986c:453, 457). Increasingly, military rule seemed to be absorbing other ministries of state. France had become "the home of Pretorians only" (Marx [1858] 1986d:464). Granted, Marx acknowledges, that all French regimes since the Great Revolution "rested," that is depended, on the army. Yet

if in all the bygone epochs the ruling class, the ascendency of which corresponded to a specific development of French society, rested its *ultima ratio* against its adversaries upon the army, it was nevertheless a specific social interest that predominated. Under the second Empire the interest of the army itself is to predominate. The army is no longer to maintain the rule of one part of the people over another part of the people. The army is to maintain its own rule, personated [sic] by its own dynasty, over the French people in general....It is to represent the *State* in antagonism to *society*. (Marx 1986d:465)

Marx went on to say that such a reliance on the military, which had become to all intents and purposes autonomous, posed great dangers to Bonaparte: "In proclaiming himself the chief of the Pretorians, he declares every Pretorian chief his competitor."[123] However, Bonaparte had no choice. "He knows that the different parties have recovered from their paralysis, and that the material basis of his stock-jobbing regime has been blown up by the commercial earthquake. Consequently, he is not only preparing for war against French society, but loudly proclaiming the fact"[124] (Marx: 1986d:465–66).

• And change is also evident in the relationship between state and economy—though Marx changed his mind about what, exactly, this entailed. In Marx's writings of the fifties, the Bonapartist state is typically portrayed as a disruptive factor in the capitalist economy: hence Bonaparte "brings the whole bourgeois economy into confusion, violates everything that seemed inviolable to the revolution of 1848, makes some tolerant of revolution and others desirous of revolution, creates anarchy itself in the name of order" (1973b:248–49). Similarly, Marx argues that the shambles imposed on the French financial system through corruption and warmongering, mean that "Louis Napoleon can never more be the demigod of the Bourse and the Bourgeois. He rules henceforth by the sword alone"[125] (Marx [1871] 1974:208). Later, however, reflecting on the entire life of the Second Empire, Marx appears to have come to a different view, for now he says that "under its sway, bourgeois society, freed from political cares, attained a development unexpected even by itself. Its industry and commerce expanded to colossal dimensions"[126] (Marx [1871] 1974:208).

* * *

Marx and Engels did not expect the Second Empire to survive as long as it did. At various junctures during the fifties, they expected the small-holding peasantry, burdened with new taxation and driven increasingly into pauperism, to lose its enthusiasm for the "Napoleonic idea"; the peasants' interests were, they contended, ever more in "opposition to capital" and increasingly congruent with those of the urban proletariat (Marx 1973b:242–3). Moreover, the bourgeoisie's eclipse as a political factor, could only be temporary. True, Bonaparte "is only where he is because he has broken the political power of this middle class, and breaks it again daily. He therefore sees himself as the opponent of the political and literary power of the middle class. But by protecting its material power he recreates its political power." (Marx 1973b:245). In addition, Bonaparte's claim to represent all social classes, and his failure to do so, would ultimately promote their consolidated enmity against him. For years, Marx waited for at least one of these prognostications to be vindicated. In the end, however, it was not a class alliance, or even a *putsch* by his own generals, that brought Napoleon to his knees but a war with a European neighbour. In 1870, Prussian, not Parisian, pretorians, destroyed the nephew utterly at Sedan just as, in 1815, they had helped vanquish his uncle at Waterloo. History had repeated itself: farcically, for Otto von Bismarck and the Prussian crown; tragically, for Napoleon III and the Communards of Paris who briefly replaced him.

Conclusion

Marx's extensive and multidimensional treatment of Louis Bonaparte was unique and provocative. Its class analysis shifted the center of gravity away from questions of political legitimacy—*no* capitalist state could be legitimate, just more or less exploitative—to those of class relations. The proletariat were envisaged not as a red menace, or as an instrument to reestablish order, but as the progressive and revolutionary agent of a History that had temporarily stalled. Though Marx on occasion resorts to analogy with the Rome of the Emperors, the moral lexicon of Caesar and Caesarism is largely peripheral to his investigations. He had no more reason to revile Caesar than he had to praise him. Despite this, Marx remained in obvious ways a man of his time. The "masses," as we have just seen, did not vanish from his analysis, but appeared transmogrified in the French small-holding peasant, the pedestal of Napoleonism. The classical republican *virtù*, and the support for mixed or balanced constitutions, found no revival in a political analysis and vision which was so fundamentally opposed to them. If Marx still spoke the language of "usurpation" and "despotism," then these terms were already sounding remote from the world he sought to unmask and to transform. They would become more remote still in the work of the man who is the primary subject of the next two chapters and who has so often been seen, rightly, as Marx's chief theoretical rival. But between Marx and Max Weber lay major changes in the political structure of Europe that invited a commensurate transformation in the analysis of "Caesarism" itself. Marx wrote mostly in an age that had yet to witness the consolidation of the modern political party; academic sociology was in its infancy; the contrast between vernacular and specialist knowledge remained fluid and mutually informative. The age that followed was gradually to reveal a different kind of politics from the one that Marx had known, and different tools for its analysis.

Notes

1. I have followed the English translation in omitting Nietzsche's many emphases.
2. On the symmetry of Alexander, Caesar, and Napoleon as "world-historical individuals," see G.W.F. Hegel ([1830–31] 1956:31); on Napoleon as a "successor" of Alexander and Caesar, see Stendhal ([1839] 1971:27). On Charlemagne and Napoleon, see F. Guizot (1887: vol. II 182–86) whose comparison comes in one of a series of lectures he delivered at the Old Sorbonne between 1828–30. On Cromwell and Napoleon, see Lord Macaulay's "Hallam's Constitutional History" (originally published in *The Edinburgh Review* in September 1828; 1913:1–83, at 53–54). For Macaulay, Napoleon is one of a select band of men, which includes Caesar as well as Cromwell, "who have founded monarchies on the ruins of republican constitutions."
    Two twentieth-century analyses of the Caesar-Napoleon congruity are Ferrero ([1904] 1933:11–12), for whom the men "are the two most complete and most instructive examples" of "(r)evolutionary usurpation," an "historical experiment...the course of which is always everywhere the same, as if it followed a constant law ," (on the stages of this historical law see 12–13); and Franklin L.Ford (1970:169, 187). To Ford the comparison of Napoleon with Caesar is irresistible: "the successful and eloquent general, quick to smash all republican obstacles in the way of his own drive to power, but then anxious to give the state and society a formal structure which would restrain other ambitious men from aspiring to his high place" (187).
3. I am drawing on Napoleon's St. Helena *Mémoires* ([1823] 1986), as dictated to the members of staff who had accompanied him into exile between 1815 and his death in 1821. Quotations come from pp. 361–79.
4. Napoleon's egoism is proverbial. "My axiom is: France before everything" (from a letter of 1810). "Remember always that, in whatever position my policy and interests of my Empire may place you, your first duties are to me, your second duties to France" (to his nephew Louis Bonaparte, 1810). "Bah! The main thing is one's self" (Napoleon in conversation, 1817). These and other gems can be found in Herold (1955:179, 7).
5. According to Correlli Barnett (1978:68).
6. Alexander the Great and Hannibal were other "great captains" of antique warfare that Napoleon admired. See extracts in Herold (1955:224–26).

7. The quotation can be found in M.A. Le Normand, *The Historical and Secret Memoirs of the Empress Josephine*, vol. I (1895:250). At Josephine's incredulity Napoleon reminded her tartly "You know I am the idol of the French; everywhere I am hailed as a guardian god" (251).

8. Napoleon continued: "You would have to show the world how Caesar would have been its benefactor, how everything would have turned out quite differently if he had been given time to carry out his magnificent plans." Goethe's conversation with Napoleon was recorded by F. von Müller on October 2, 1808: Luke and Pick (eds.) (1966:72).

   Though improving on Voltaire's dramatically meagre *La mort de César* ([1733] 1964) would not have been a great feat for the German polymath, Goethe never did write the tragedy Napoleon had requested. A useful collection of Goethe's writings on antiquity can be found in Grumach (1949, 2 vols.). On Caesar in particular, see Grumach (1949 I:55–57), and the fragment reproduced in Goethe (1985:123). For an analysis of Goethe's interpretation of Caesar, see Gundelfinger (= Gundolf 1904:112–19).

9. Cited in Geyl ([1949] 1965:352). Geyl takes this quotation from Louis Madelin. According to the latter, Napoleon "was fed on Rome. Many years before he brought Caesar back to life, he made an impassioned study of Livy, Tacitus, and Plutarch and of all the works which the eighteenth century had produced on the subject of Rome."

10. Napoleon often compared his achievements with those of Diocletian: Geyl ([1949] 1965:261, 352).

11. Cited in J. McManners's "Napoleon," in his *Lectures on European History 1789–1914* (1966:75–91, at 87). Cf. 90.

    The text was published anonymously and was circulated by Lucien Bonaparte, Napoleon's brother. As propaganda, it was a blunder: its monarchical and dynastic pretensions were premature at this stage of the Consulate and Lucien Bonaparte, then Minister of the Interior, was replaced on November 12 by Jean-Antoine Chaptal (Bergeron [1972] 1981:14, 73).

12. See Groh (1972:738–39 on Constant and Vollgraff; 741–43 on Heine; 754 on Bauer).

13. In a gloss on Cicero, Benjamin Constant sought to distinguish republican patriotism from the modern educated Frenchman's more cosmopolitan sense of country. For Cicero, losing "one's country was to lose one's wife, children, friends, all affections, and nearly all communication and social enjoyment. The age of that sort of patriotism is over; what we love now in our country, as in our liberty, is the property of whatever we possess, our security, the possibility of rest, activity, glory, a thousand sorts of happiness. *The word fatherland reminds us more of the whole of these goods than of the topographical notion of a specific country.* When we are deprived of them at home, we go and seek them beyond it" (Constant [1814] 1988:141, n. 1, my emphasis). Cf. Voltaire: "What is love of country? An amalgam of self-love and prejudice, in which the good of society becomes the greatest of virtues. It is important for the vague term, *the public*, to make a deep impression ([1752] 1994:218).

14. The book from which this passage is taken—*Des circonstances actuelles qui peuvent terminer la Révolution et des principes qui doivent fonder la République en France*—was composed in 1799 but only published in 1906. I have used Morroe Berger's translation of the passages.

15. Constant acknowledged two kinds of legitimacy: "one positive, which derives from free election"—he was thinking particulary of the accession of William III in 1688—"the other tacit, which rests upon heredity; and I shall add that heredity

is legitimate because the habits it generates and the advantages it grants render it the national will." However, even in the case of William III, there was an hereditary element that "consecrated" his rule—namely, that William was "the closest relative of the king" whom the English deposed. The revolution that installed William had "nothing in common with usurpation" since it entailed an "election" that was both free and rested on the "ancient dignity" of the House of Orange. Where such an hereditary element is lacking, "positive" legitimacy can become spurious because it is easily "counterfeited"—as it was both by Cromwell and by Napoleon, both of whom sought to surround themselves with the panoply of royal pomp ([1814] 1988:158–59, 167).

16. On the influence of classicism, M. Stürmer (1977b:102–18, at 106–7). Stürmer reminds us that the symbol of the laurel crown was pressed onto coins of the First Empire.

17. A year previously, Louis Bonaparte had published the similarly titled *Des Idées Napoléoniennes* that, while linking Napoleon and Caesar, also protested: "I consider as a misfortune, the fatal tendency which we in France have always manifested, to copy the institutions of foreign nations, with a view to their adoption among ourselves. Under the Republic we were Romans…Shall we, then, never be ourselves?" (Louis Bonaparte [1839] 1856b I:96–97). The claim that Caesar and Napoleon found themselves in similar situations can be found on 35–6.

Both of these texts were translated into English as early as 1852. They were republished in 1972 by the New York based publisher Howard Fertig. See Louis Bonaparte ([1839,1840] 1972) vols. I and II. I have modified the translations in several places.

18. In the same year as Louis Bonaparte's essay was published (1840), a medal was minted in Paris to commemorate the reburial of his uncle in the Invalides. Around the periphery of one side of the medal are the names of four famous battles: Arcola (November 1796), Marengo (June 1800), Jena (October 1806), Eylau (February 1807). In the center is a picture of Napoleon—wearing a laurel crown. (The medal is reproduced in Barnett 1978:214.)

19. Twenty-five years later, Louis Bonaparte reaffirmed the point. In the preface to his *Histoire de Jules César* (1865:vi), Louis outlines the main aim of his book: to prove that "when Providence raises up men the likes of Caesar, Charlemagne, Napoleon, it is to trace out to peoples the path they ought to follow, to stamp with the seal of their genius a new era, and to accomplish in a few years the labour of several centuries."

20. Groh remarks that Tocqueville's achievement consisted in being the first to develop a sociology of Caesarism that refused at the same time to use the term, so convinced was he that old ideas were no longer adequate to convey the uniqueness of modern political forms. "Bonapartism" and "Napoleonism" were also avoided because their associations with France belied the universality of the thing at issue, that is a "specifically totalitarian democracy with a sovereign dictator at its head" (Groh 1972:746).

21. In a scintillating reconstruction of the moral and political climate that followed Louis's coup, Croce explicitly adapted Tacitus's earlier rendition of the *ruere in servitium*. France witnessed "acclamations, flattery, voluntary servitude, perjury, the rapid conversions of heated democrats—which would have been comic if they had not been humiliating—mental restrictions, compromises, and fears and terrors and desertion of friends and cowardly denunciations, insensibility to the violation of justice and to daily wrongs, the pretence of not seeing and not knowing, in order to silence the pangs of conscience, what everyone saw and knew perfectly

well, ignorance concerning the conduct of public affairs with accompanying and ceaseless whispering of scandals, supine applause for every statement or assertion coming from above and at the same time incredulity for all news of an official character; and, in the midst of this general timidity, the boldness of the bold in taking fortune by storm, the readiness to seize private advantages or to satisfy private hates under the semblance of political zeal, without anyone's daring to oppose or to protest—all those things, in short, which, when they were practiced even by men to whom society does not refuse its esteem, caused the novelist who described those times to exclaim: 'What *canaille*, these respectable people!'" ([1931] 1934:202). Composed during the dark years of Italian fascism, these lines were drawing a parallel within a parallel.

22. Somewhat later, as the repression intensified, Tocqueville offered a more local and more recent parallel. In a letter to Henry Reeve of January 9, 1852 he remarked: "Indeed, one has to go back to the Committee of Public Safety and the Terror to find anything analogous in our history to what we are seeing now" (Tocqueville 1985:283).

23. Linguistically, the word also depended on the prior development of the "ism" suffix (from the Greek *ismos*). "Originally it referred to actions which are at the same time denoted by the cognate suffix *izein* making a verb; the suffix *istes* denoting a person active in the appropriate *ismos*." In time, however, this "ism" formation came "to denote not so much the action in progress (as it did in the Greek words like *ostracismos* and *baptismos*) as principles of action or intentions. In this meaning it makes the word to which it is attached understood far beyond the country of its birth, the more so because in most cases the root of the word, like this suffix, is of classical origin" (Koebner and Schmidt 1965:xiv). The authors also note that the "ism" suffix "developed in two directions": the first, designated an ideology of a specific group of people (e.g., liberalism, socialism, communism); while the second "added a note of derogation to the words to which it is attached"—a fate to which "Caesarism" would largely succumb.

Also, see Groh (1972:726), who makes the point that "Caesarism" and "Bonapartism" were not social-constitutional concepts pointing in a certain political direction—like "liberalism" or "socialism"—but were more often treated as concepts of domination.

24. The *Grand Larousse de la langue française*, vol. I (1971:652), pins it down firmly to 1850 and the pen of M.A. Romieu. It defines "Césarisme" as the "method of government of Julius Caesar" and "by extension, the form of government which is very authoritarian, in which a single person unites all the forms of power, but this is however founded upon popular consent." This was not Romieu's own definition of Caesarism, as we shall see below.

Two pioneering essays by Arnaldo Momigliano (1956:231; 1962:369) also suggested that the word was coined in France by Romieu.

25. *Meyers Enzyklopädisches Lexikon*, vol. V (1972:364) defining "Caesarism" as "a description for a technique of rule (*Herrschaftstechnik*) characterised by the uniting of political power in the hands of one man, legitimation through plebiscite and sham-democratic institutions, as well as by the organising of support for the regime through armed force and through a staff of officials," claims that the term emerged (in Germany?) "between 1800 and 1830." Nonetheless, no examples of usage are supplied, suggesting that this is little more than a conjecture.

26. "Only the power of the Church can secure justice and freedom in the storms which threaten us. All those who strive for a non-religious state and who therefore stamp upon everything religious....[and] who always babble about freedom and progress, deserve nothing better than that the iron hand of a military dictatorship

swing the shattered pieces of the Shepherd's staff like a whip across their backs. And so it will happen...The state needs the Church and the time will come when it will plead for help; however the Church can manage without the help of the state as it now is and will inevitably develop in its absolutism, which must absorb even the very last of the Church's remaining rights. We are heading for a time of a new Caesarism; thank God that at least the old Church has never submitted to Caesarism and has always been victorious in its fight against it" (Böhmer, in Janssen 1868:278–79). Groh (1972:744) dates this comment at 1847 but examination of the Janssen source suggests that 1846, or even 1845, is the more likely date.

27. As "Caesarism, or the Necessity of the Rule of the Sword, Represented by Historical Examples from the time of Caesar to the Present Day" (Groh 1972:749).

28. The *Oxford English Dictionary* (1971:315) makes the additional point that "Caesar" is "generally held to be the earliest Latin word adopted in Teutonic, where it gave Gothic 'kaisar.'" The Old English form of the word was lost in the Middle English period. "It was replaced in ME by keiser, cayser, kaiser, from Norse and Continental Teutonic, which has in its turn become obsolete, except as an alien term for the German emperor, and been replaced by the Latin or French form. See KASER, KAISER. Another form of the word is the word Tsar or Czar."

29. This is a particularly useful and interesting source. However, given the historical referent of the term "Caesarism," it is surprising that we still have no analysis in Italian (or indeed in French) to match Dieter Groh's extensive contribution (1972) to the *Geschichtliche Grundbegriffe*. Much work remains to be done to trace the historical trajectory of the term in Italy, a task that is conspicuously not attempted in the otherwise impressive *Dizionario di politica*, edited by Norberto Bobbio and his collaborators. The slim entry on "Cesarismo" by Carlo Guarnieri (1983:155–57) concentrates on Gramsci's employment of the term, and aside from a reference to Marx, has very little to say about nineteenth-century usage.

30. Cf. Gramsci ([1951] 1966:189).

31. Groh (1972:735, 748, 759–60).

32. Details in Groh (1972: 754–55, 762; cf. 727, 752, 765).

33. Arnaldo Momigliano (1962:369) believed this might be the first usage of "Cäsarismus" in German—or at least that no one had found an earlier one. Thanks to Dieter Groh, we now know that the term was used as early as 1846. (The English translation of Buckhardt's *The Age of Constantine the Great* omits the footnote to Romieu, but does include a reference to Caesarism in the main text:see Burckhardt [1949:44]).

Burckhardt returned to the term, albeit in a different context, in November 1867. To students attending his lectures on the French Revolutionary epoch, delivered at the University of Basel, he declared confidently that Napoleon Bonaparte "is the most instructive type of Caesarism. He is, at the same time, the savior of the new French society and a world conqueror" (Burckhardt 1959:212). Also, see 34 where the Swiss historian refers to Julius Caesar as "the greatest of mortals."

34. Ironically, part of the self-same campaign that led Max Weber later to remark that Gladstone's "grand demagogy" had showed that "a Caesarist-plebiscitarian element in politics—the dictator of the battlefield of elections—had appeared on the plain" (Weber [1919] 1948a:106).

35. Conservative critics of Disraeli also adopted the language of "imperialism" to attack him, though this did not mean that the baby had to be thrown out with the bathwater. A case in point is Lord Carnarvon's distinction—the subject of an Edinburgh address in November 1878—between false Imperialism and genuine Imperialism. As Koebner and Schmidt (1964:153–54) summarize the matter, "False

imperialism was Caesarism, personal rule, a second-hand copy of Continental despotism. Its benefits were short-lived, its teachings false. It was the belief in mere bulk of territory and in the multiplication of subjects...False Imperialism was militarism and vast standing armies, a spectacle presented by the Continent whose great empires cast their colossal shadow over the smaller states; it was reckless intrigue and reckless expenditure..." Conversely, authentic Imperialism—the British non-Disraelian model—was ultimately pacific and aimed at serving the interests of those in its orbit. The charge of Disraelian Caesarism is also explored in Thornton ([1959] 1985:30–31).

British Toryism continued to attract the Caesarist epithet. In 1904, Augustine Birrell, president of the National Liberal Federation, meditated on the future of a country under a Tory Government in the following way: it was a future "in which no true Liberal could breathe, a future of Imperialism, of Caesarism, of Empire, of expansion abroad in places where no white man can live, of military conscription at home, of false ideals of national greatness and of national honour" (quoted in Thornton:105).

On other references to Caesar, and comparisons and contrasts between the Roman and the British Empire, see Betts (1971).

36. This is not to say that all who used the term "Caesarism" saw it as a global phenomenon: Walter Bagehot, for instance, saw it as peculiarly French. We return to him presently.

37. Bamberger's comment, which continues with the words "and God only knows what thousands of people imagine it to be," is quoted by Otto Ladendorf (1906:41). See also F.W. Rüstow (1879:3) who remarks that "in recent political literature, especially in the daily press, we often encounter the terms 'Caesarism' and 'Parliamentarism' which are always used in a certain opposition to one another."

38. In the preface to the second edition of the book, Romieu remarks somewhat testily that his treatise has "been judged severely, especially by those who only knew the title of it...It has been very little read although much commented on" (Romieu 1850:i).

39. Romieu (1850:75). For other biographical details see also 57 (Romieu tells us here that he was a member of the National Guard in June 1848), and 112–18 (where he volunteers the information that his experience includes three prefectures and a two week hunting session with the Prince de Joinville, the third son of Louis Philippe).

40. "We know the marvels of faith! In every subject Faith applies herself—religion, royalty, glory, honour, love, the flag—everywhere she is poetry; everywhere she transports man beyond his terrestrial sphere and shows him a fabulous universe full of intoxicating harmonies...we know the failings of reason...she has one hundred answers which mutually contradict and condemn one another" (Romieu: 197–98). Cf. Donoso Cortés: "The doctrinal intolerance of the Church has saved the world from chaos. Her doctrinal intolerance has placed beyond question political, domestic, social, and religious, truths—primitive and holy truths, which are not subject to discussion, because they are the foundation of all discussions." Liberalism, meanwhile, is that school that "never says, 'I affirm', or, 'I deny', and which ever says, 'I distinguish'. The supreme interest of that school is in preventing the arrival of the day of radical negations or of sovereign affirmations; and that it may not arrive, it confounds by means of discussion all notions, and propagates scepticism, knowing as it does, that a people which perpetually hears in the mouth of its sophists the pro and the contra of everything, ends by not knowing which side to take..." ([1851] 1879:42, 174–75). For a twentieth century

analysis of the issue which itself has become something of a classic, see Carl Schmitt ([1922] 1985:56–66).

41. See 24 on the "fight between two principles which, since Luther, are disputing the world: freedom and authority."

42. Romieu is especially scornful of thinkers like Montesquieu and Voltaire (and their followers even more) who, he claims erroneously, believed the model of the English constitution could be universally grafted (12). However, he does concede that constitutional ideas served as moderating influence in the midst of revolutionary turmoil.

43. Romieu (93) remarks that the bourgeoisie themselves are now disillusioned with the liberalism they once so zealously advocated.

44. Romieu took up this theme again in *Le spectre rouge de 1852* that predicted, in lurid terms, the destruction of bourgeois power. In the coming duel between chaos and order, that is, between "le délire furieux des masses et la discipline vigoureuse de l'armée," the bourgeoisie would find themselves utterly smashed (Romieu 1851:68, and passim).
    The reference to 1852 is an allusion to May 1852 the date in which elections were due to take place for the presidential office and for members of the legislative assembly.

45. For a similar, though less qualified, statement, see 29. It is on this page that the reader will find the first mention of "Césarisme" in the book, when Romieu says that "the simultaneous study of the present and the past has given me this belief, that there is a moment of extreme civilisation among peoples, where the obligatory issue is Caesarism."

46. For his misgivings about the use of the term "emperor," see 33–34.

47. Violence is also a major theme of Maistre's *St. Petersburg Dialogues*, but it is "war," not "force" that Maistre focuses on, and in a manner that is even more eschatological than anything found in Romieu. On the "universal law of the violent destruction of living beings," and on war "as divine," see Maistre ([1821] 1993:217–18).

48. I have here, as in several other places, omitted Romieu's emphases.

49. Romieu divides the age of the Caesars into three periods: from Augustus' Principate to the murder of Pertinax; from Didius Julianus to Diocletian; and from Diocletian onwards—Romieu tells us when this age begins but not when it ends (42–46).

50. The military theme is also a commonplace of discussions about Caesarism. We shall see it referred to in various parts of this book.

51. Burke described the first Revolutionary government (the National Constituent Assembly, July 1789–September 1791) as "illegitimate and usurped" against which another revolution "would of course be perfectly justifiable, if not absolutely necessary" ([1790] 1968:147).

52. In the composition, Napoleon is seen fabulously dressed in the raiment of imperial splendor, wearing a laurel crown while also holding the traditional crown of the French monarchy. The painting is reproduced in Barnett (1978: 90–91).

53. There was another plebiscite in 1802 to confirm Napoleon's position of Consul for life. As with the other two cases, the "figures are truly overwhelming and wholly unbelievable" 3,600,000 for, 8,374 against: Gay 1993:566, n.34.

54. Chateaubriand's *Mémoires d'outre-tombe* (Memoirs Beyond the Grave) contains an analysis of Napoleon that is one of the jewels of nineteenth century antiautocratic literature. Chateaubriand fully acknowledges Napoleon's ability to establish order and his *administrative* "greatness"—the extraordinary effects of the Council of State and the "Napoleonic code" which the First Consul and Emperor presided over. What he derides is Napoleon's *political* deeds and legacy. Dismiss-

ing the tendency of his day "to transform the Emperor into a Roman of the early days of the Aventine," Chateaubriand depicts Napoleon as man of unceasing and demonic energy—"he threw himself upon the world and shook it"—who accustomed French society to "passive obedience," and even "slavery": the "despotism which Bonaparte left in the air will close in upon us like a fortress." Moreover, since his death Napoleon had become reincarnated in a legend even more overbearing than his actual presence: "How could a free government come into being, when he has corrupted the principle of freedom in men's hearts? No legitimate power can now drive the usurping spectre from the mind of man: soldier and citizen, Republican and Monarchist, rich and poor alike place busts and portraits of Napoleon in their homes...the sometime vanquished are in agreement with the sometime victors; one cannot take a single step in Italy without coming across him: one cannot enter Germany without meeting him, for in that country the young generation which rejected him has gone" (1965:325–35; also 294, 298).

55. The reciprocity of the process is central to Richter's thesis. As he says: "the political vocabulary required categories both for legitimacy and illegitimacy. Persuasion entailed dissuasion; dissuasion in turn entailed denying, neutralizing, redefining, or redescribing competing regimes and principles. In such a situation, political theorists had to master more than the one set of terms they themselves preferred. For despite their differences they could not ignore the audiences to which they addressed themselves. Unless polemicists took notice of those concepts favoured by their opponents, they could not successfully attack them" (Richter 1982:187).

56. An important part of Richter's argument is to show how political discourse has consequences for political behavior. One might compare this with Quentin Skinner's contention (1978:xiii) that "in recovering the terms of the normative vocabulary available to any given agent for the description of his political behavior, we are at the same time indicating one of the constraints upon his behavior itself. This suggests that, in order to explain why such as agent acts as he does, we are bound to make some reference to this vocabulary, since it evidently figures as one of the determinants of his action."

57. I assume that Richter bases this date on *Robert* (1966:510) which cites P.-L. Courier's using the term "bonapartisme" in a "Pétition aux Chambres" of December 10 of that year. However, the O.E.D. (1971:245) quotes a usage from Jefferson, dated 1815, who speaks of "Bonaparteism." The best one can say, then, is that 1816 was the first record we have of the word's use *in France*.

58. This echoes Hegel's remark in *The Philosophy of History* ([1830–31] 1956:313) that "in all periods of the world a political revolution is sanctioned in men's opinions, when it repeats itself...By repetition that which at first appeared merely a matter of chance and contingency, becomes a real and ratified existence."

59. Richter (1982:199–200). Guizot construed Napoleon's regime as the exemplar of modern "democratic despotism," compared his rule with that of the Roman emperors, and claimed that the implementation of the theory of popular sovereignty issued logically in the domination of one man.

60. This two volume work was originally composed between 1852–54. Proudhon was writing of the Roman Caesars, not Napoleon III. But this kind of language was easily transferrable, not least by Proudhon himself: see Proudhon (1969:165,192) from correspondence penned in 1852 and 1861 respectively.

61. Hugo does not use the term Caesarism in *Napoléon le Petit*, but he does emphasize that the coup was illegal: see ([1852] n.d. 1:101–189), and, for a longer version, his *Histoire d'un crime* (begun in 1852 but not published until 1877). The former contains a number of sardonic comparisons between Julius Caesar and

Louis Bonaparte, but it is the concepts "dictator" and "despot" that the novelist falls back on. For Hugo, Louis is a combination of both, backed up by a spy-network (Hugo [1852], n.d. 1:74–75).
English translations of both essays can be found in *The Works of Victor Hugo*, vol. VIII (n.d).

62. Most of Tönnies' discussion of Caesarism, however, relates not to a military leader but to the office of the British prime minister. Suffice it to note Tönnies' observations of the "similarities between the British and ancient Roman empires," a parallel he discerns in both title ("the name Prime Minister reminds one of the Principate") and in the formidable extent of the Premier's powers to change laws, initiate taxation and generally harness state power to his own ends: Tönnies (1917:50).
    Max Weber also described the British prime minister as "Caesarist," as we shall see in the next chapter.

63. Richter (1982:191) adds that "Burke gave no name to such a situation, nor did he cite any previous instances, despite the Roman examples as well known to him as to Maistre. Rather it was the novelty of the situation he stressed." On Constant, Maistre and Bonald, see 191–93. For Dieter Groh (1972:738) Constant's ideas are "perhaps the first worked-out theory of Caesarism."
    Sometimes the search for the "intellectual foundations of Caesarism" takes on an air of unreality, as when Hasso Hofmann (1977:93) speaks of "the Caesarist model of Thomas Hobbes and his successors."

64. Though, as with Caesarism, sometimes necessary. Stendhal's *Life of Napoleon*, written in 1817–18 as a refutation of Madame de Staël's portrait of the First Consul in her *Considérations*, defended the "military despotism" that was installed by the Eighteenth Brumaire. Without it "France would have had in 1800 the events of 1814, or else the Terror" (1956:35; cf. 37).

65. Even where Bonapartism is criticized by conservative thinkers, this need not mean that "Caesarism" is similarly condemned: the trick is to distinguish between them. For instance, Leopold von Gerlach, the champion of legitimism, had little taste for Louis Bonaparte, a man who, like his uncle, Gerlach argues, represents revolution in its distilled form and with it "perjury and treachery." If Gerlach shared the project of conservatives everywhere to smash liberalism and socialism, this did not mean that he wanted a Napoleon to do it. At the same time Gerlach did not equate Bonapartism with Caesarism. "Bonapartism," he insisted, "is not absolutism, not even Caesarism; the former may found itself on a *jus divinum*, as in Russia and in the East, and therefore does not affect those who do not recognise this *jus divinum*, for whom, in fact, it does not exist...Caesarism is the arrogation of an *imperium* in a lawful republic and is justified by urgent necessity; to a Bonaparte, however, whether he like it or no, the Revolution—that is, the sovereignty of the people—represents an internal, and in any conflict or exigency also an external, legal title'" (in Bismarck 1898 I:206).
    On the intellectual relationship of Gerlach and Bismarck, see Gollwitzer (1952:28–31). For Gollwitzer, the correspondence that passed between these men in 1857 constitutes "the classical example of the argument between legitimist policy and *Realpolitik*."
    On the concept of Caesarism in conservative Swiss social and political thought, see Meyer (1975). Meyer, whose book came to my attention too late to consider it here, considers in detail the work of Philipp Anton von Segesser, Heinrich Gelzer, Johann Jacob Bachofen and Jacob Burckhardt.

66. On the generally derogatory German use of the term "Caesarism," at least in its relation to the rule of Napoleon III, see Gollwitzer (1952: 46, 55, 58). On those

people (mentioned in the main text) who were more positive in their estimation of the "Caesarism" of Napoleon III or who felt ambivalently about it, see 31 (Radowitz, Riehl), 32 (Manteuffel, Quehl), 41 (Segesser), 45 (Heine), 47–50 (Fröbel), 51–52 (Hillebrand), 53–54 (Mundt), 73 (Schweitzer). (Gollwitzer also remarks that there were some people in Germany, and they were not necessarily conservatives, who imagined that Caesarism might be of use in the service of German nationalism and *Realpolitik*:62–7).

67. This is a particularly valuable lexicographical source, quoting Proudhon and J. Simon ("Caesarism is democracy without liberty"), and which, while dilating on Napoleon Bonaparte, carefully avoids mention of Napoleon III. However, the author remarks: "Without entering for the moment into the discussion of the various judgements that have been made about it, we declare here that, in our view, absolute power, whatever name one gives it, and by whatever means it is established, is irrevocably condemned by philosophy and history alike, by law and also by reason; it is a form which belongs to barbaric times, which may well be born again in times of crisis, but like a sort of political monstrosity has nothing to do with the conditions of life and can only stop for the moment the march of progress" (Larousse 1867:812).

68. The remainder of this paragraph relies heavily on Turner 1986.

69. On Merivale's comparison of the French Second Empire with the Augustan Principate, see Turner (1986:591–92).

70. The relationship between Caesar-appreciation and "social imperialism"—the ideology that, eschewing partisanship, "regarded politics as a matter of achieving rational, efficient administration that addressed truly national rather than particularistic interests and problems"—is documented in Turner (1986:593–95). The *locus classicus* of this ideology as applied to Caesar is W.W. Fowler's *Julius Caesar and the Foundation of the Roman Imperial System* ([1891] 1904).

71. I deal with aspects of the German case in chapters 3 and 4.

72. For details of the British debate, see the analysis in Gay (1993:274–82).

73. The phrase belongs to John Stuart Mill—no theorist of Caesarism—but Mill had a more catholic understanding of the "masses" than most of his contemporaries. "Masses" meant the sway of "collective mediocrity" in both public life and personal relations, the supremacy of "public opinion." Masses do not take their views "from dignitaries in Church or State, from ostensible leaders, or from books," but on the contrary, "from men like themselves, addressing them or speaking in their name, on the spur of the moment, through the newspapers." However, when one asks who this "mass" is, Mill is categorical that it embraces more than the working or poorer class: in England it is chiefly the "middle class" that he is referring to, in America "the whole white population" (Mill [1859] 1971:314).

74. In the same article, Bagehot compares Napoleons I and III with Julius Caesar "the first instance of a democratic despot" who "overthrew an aristocracy...by the help of the people, of the unorganised people." Moreover, whereas the old monarchies of feudal origin claimed obedience from the people on the grounds of duty, "Louis Napoleon is a Benthamite despot. He is for the 'greatest happiness of the greatest number.' He says, 'I am where I am, because I know better than anyone else what is good for the French people, and they know that I know better.' He is not the Lord's anointed; he is the people's agent" (Bagehot [1865] 1968aIV: 111).

75. The numbers in brackets that follow are my own insertion.

76. Bagehot also asserts (157) that the army is "the great physical basis of Caesarism."

77. Bagehot (157) also contrasts Caesarism to "our own system of parliamentary omnipotence." In an earlier essay on "The American Constitution at the Present Crisis," Bagehot had made clear just where this omnipotence resided: "the dif-

fused respectable higher middle-class…Our security against tyranny is the reason-
ableness, the respectable cultivation, the business-like moderation of this governing class itself" (Bagehot [1861] 1968c IV:301).
78. Ferrand's book opens with a quotation from Michelet: "Quelle est la première
partie de la politique? L'éducation. Quelle est la seconde? L'éducation. Quelle est
la troisième? L'éducation" (Ferrand 1904:1).
79. Bismarck once contended that, without "the restraining influence of the propertied
class," a state would be destroyed by "the unreasoning masses." Even so, order
would soon reassert itself because it corresponds to a need the masses feel keenly:
"if they do not recognise this need a priori, they always realise it eventually after
manifold arguments ad hominem and in order to purchase order from a dictatorship and Caesarism they cheerfully sacrifice that justifiable amount of freedom
which ought to be maintained, and which the political society of Europe can
endure without ill-health" (Bismarck 1898:II 65–66).
80. These comments, it is true, do not derive from Treitschke's chapter on Caesarism,
but they do bear an indirect relationship to it since Caesarism, we are informed, is
the archetype of "democratic tyranny."
81. The contrast persisted for some time. As Mazzini observed ([1847] 1908b:102)
"The union of the democratic principle with representative government is an
entirely modern fact, which throws out of court all precedents that might be
appealed to." The whole essay from which these lines are drawn contains a
revealing mid-century European snapshot of the meanings and types of "democracy" then extant.
82. "Napoleon is the supreme head (chef) of state; the elected of the people; the
representative of the nation. In his public acts, the Emperor always gloried [in the
fact] that he owed everything to the French people alone," etc. (Louis Bonaparte
[1839] 1856 I:102).
83. David Hume, an important figure for both Madison and Hamilton, had employed
the Roman example to make a somewhat similar point. In "That Politics May Be
Reduced To A Science" ([1741–2] 1953:13), Hume stated: "The constitution of
the Roman republic gave the whole legislative power to the people, without
allowing a negative voice either to the nobility of consuls. This unbounded power
they possessed in a collective, not in a representative body. The consequences
were: when the people, by success and conquest, had become very numerous and
had spread themselves to a great distance from the capital, the city tribes, though
the most contemptible, carried almost every vote; they were, therefore, most
cajoled by everyone that affected popularity; they were supported in idleness by
the general distribution of corn and by particular bribes which they received from
almost every candidate. By this means they became every day more licentious,
and the Campus Martius was a perpetual scene of tumult and sedition; armed
slaves were introduced among these rascally citizens, so that the whole government fell into anarchy, and the greatest happiness which the Romans could look
for was the despotic power of the Caesars. Such are the effects of democracy
without a representative."
84. For an interpretation of Marx's thought as a rupture with the antique tradition
more generally, see Hannah Arendt ([1954] 1993:17–40).
85. On the three major varieties of "republicanism" in France between 1848 and
1851—utopian republicanism (epitomized by Alphonse de Lamartine), "red republicanism," and the republicanism of the notables—see Zeldin ([1973] 1979:120–
39), who remarks "Republicanism thus represented three contradictory things: a
belief in an ideal government which could not exist, a popular opposition to all

government, and a new establishment party, accepting responsibility, honours and compromise" (130–31).

86. The expressions in quotation come from a letter of Engels to Eduard Bernstein, dated August 27, 1883 (Marx and Engels [1955] 1975:342–43). Engels adds that just as the successful struggle by the bourgeoisie against feudalism could only take place under a constitutional monarchy (as distinct from an absolute monarchy), so a decisive resolution of the struggle by the proletariat against the bourgeoisie "can only be fought out in a republic."

87. I am greatly simplifying Bellamy's more nuanced and wide-ranging discussion of the variants of Third Republic republicanisms.

88. There is a resonance here with a pre-1848 French usage of "republican" which evoked "militarism, the passion for glory and foreign adventures" and of which Louis Bonaparte (before 1851) was considered to be a proponent. For details on Bonapartism as a "variety of republicanism" see Zeldin ([1973] 1979:144).

89. This was also a charge levelled by Catholic critics at "state socialism," a tendency, it was claimed, to which the Third Republic was clearly succumbing. The connection between state-socialism and Caesarism, participants at the Catholic Jurists' Congress of 1884 made plain, was that both entailed the worship of the state (either construed as a collective set of institutions or as embodied in a single person); both promoted the centralization of power; both, in consequence, invaded the private domain and sought to control the minds of children through secular education; and both failed in sum to recognize the proper distinction between the obligations due to fellow humans and those due to God. See respectively the comments of l'abbé Crozat and of Mgr. de Kernaeret, in *Congrès de Jurisconsultes Catholiques* (1885:19–33, 33–39).

The view that "socialism must inevitably end in Caesarism" was a notion expressed by Joseph Conrad (1927 I:84) in a letter to Spiridion Kliszczewski of December 19, 1885, though by Caesarism Conrad meant "a militarism despotism." (Cf. Groh 1972:749, 754 on the equation of Caesarism with communism.) Later, however, Conrad would offer a different definition in his novel *Nostromo* ([1904] 1963:335). He has Pedrito Montero say "that the highest expression of democracy was Caesarism: the imperial rule based upon the direct popular vote. Caesarism was conservative. It was strong. It recognized the legitimate needs of democracy which requires orders, titles, and distinctions. They would be showered upon deserving men. Caesarism was peace. It was progressive. It secured the prosperity of a country."

Sociologists among my readers might also wish to recall the slash-and-burn Introduction by George E.G. Catlin to the 1938 translation of *The Rules of Sociological Method*, which comes close to accusing Emile Durkheim—one of the Third Republic's chief advocates—of Caesarist tendencies. Catlin interprets Durkheim's theory of religion, his wish to promote "a purely lay education," and his notion of the *conscience collective* as inducements to state leviathanism. Linking Durkheim with Sorel, and Sorel with Mussolini, Catlin remarks: "By his ill-considered and scientifically pretentious psycho-mysticism Durkheim has contributed to give the colour of justification to the new religion of the altar of *divus Augustus* and to the neopagan philosophy of Caesar-worship" (Durkheim [1895] 1938:xxviii). Also xxxv-vi on Durkheim's contribution to "popular dictatorship."

90. Disappointment with the masses was a perennial theme. Of many examples, suffice it to consider the letter written by Proudhon in August 1851, cited by George Woodcock ([1956] 1987:166–67): "Using Barbès as an example, [Proudhon] went on to show that the most popular leaders were those who best typified popular myths and ideals, and that such men were in reality the led rather than the leaders.

'It is remarkable on the other hand,' he added in a tone of personal sadness, 'that the more a man gives proof of judgment, of perspicacity, of the progressive spirit and the faculty of understanding, the more he loses his ascendancy over the masses, to whom thought is repugnant and who go only by instinct'." Much later, Emma Goldman would utter an even more bitter assessment. For Goldman, the failure of the American people to defend liberty against their government's depredations was a clear sign of the victory of the "mass spirit." ."..the majority cannot reason, it has no judgment. Lacking utterly in originality and moral courage, the majority has always placed its destiny in the hands of others...Without ambition or initiative, the compact mass hates nothing so much as innovation. It has always opposed, condemned, and hounded the innovator, the pioneer or a new truth" (Goldman [1917] 1969:69–70).

91. And this must be the referent of Medvedev's discussion, for a comparison of the "dictatorship of the proletariat" with the "dictatorships" of the Late Republic— those of Sulla and Caesar—would be to equate the revolutionary party with tyranny or monarchy.

92. I am here simply glossing Carl Schmitt's fundamental distinction between "commissarial" and "sovereign" dictatorships. See Schmitt ([1928] 1978: especially 1–79, 97–152).

93. This is not to deny, of course, that "citizen" was a common form of address among Marxist and other revolutionaries. However its interchangeability with "brother"—a term denoting kinship solidarity rather than citizen equality—reveals its very limited republican substance. On "Citizen Marx," see Engels ([1850] 1978:353–69). On "brothers," Marx and Engels ([1850] 1978:371). Also Antonio Gramsci, in a passage (1919) celebrating the factory councils. "The factory council is the model of the proletarian State. All the problems which are inherent in the organization of the proletarian State, are inherent in the organization of the Council. In the one and in the other the concept of citizen decays, and is replaced by the concept of comrade; collaboration to produce well and usefully develops solidarity, multiplies the bonds of affection and brotherhood" (cited in Bellamy 1987:118). On Gramsci's view of a postcapitalist order as "the disappearance of political society and the coming of a regulated society," see Bellamy (1987:138–40).

94. Those doubtful of the consequences of such a view may wish to consult A.J. Polan's fine analysis of Lenin's political theory. As Polan shows, a fundamental distinction between the American revolutionaries of the eighteenth century and the Bolsheviks of the early twentieth concerned their attitude to the rule of law. Lenin saw the task of the vanguard party and of the Revolution to destroy extant legal forms and established public norms that were believed to be irredeemably bourgeois and oppressive. Authority became lodged in the act of Revolution itself. "Those who were not instrumental in making the revolution, or more precisely in leading it, are de facto deprived of the credentials it bestows. If the appeal is to the authority of the revolution, the Mensheviks have no right to dispute policy with the Bolsheviks in the new Soviet Union." In contrast, the "American Revolution was made in the name of established legal conventions, and not against them; the Revolution was against what were interpreted as attempts to impose a tyranny upon a previously free society. Few creators of modern states have been able to draw upon such clear and incontrovertible lineages of legitimacy, deriving from a 'free contract' arrived at in a territory previously without government."

The results of each revolution suggest that "in the period of transition from revolution to democracy, it is an incalculable benefit and safeguard that some elements and sources of traditional legitimate authority continue to exist as a counter to the totalizing ambitions of the revolutionary mood" (Polan 1984:116, 122).

95. Revolutionary syndicalism represents a more complex case, as Christopher Lasch has pointed out (1991:304–16). Georges Sorel's defence of the military virtues of heroism and glory, his belief in proprietorship, and his sense of social entropy, have many resemblances with antique republicanism. See Sorel ([1906] 1950), which also contains as appendix 3 a defense of Lenin. On the capitalist democracies as "Carthage" and the proletarian soviet republics as "Rome," see 285.

96. Writing for the *Allgemeine Deutsche Arbeiterzeitung*, in December 1864, a Marxist journalist quoted by Dieter Groh (1972:760) remarked that while he and the people he represented were "fighting for full political and civil rights for the workers and for the universal franchise" they were nonetheless "mindful that only education can really liberate; we don't want this precious right in the hands of the uneducated masses to be used as a lever in the setting up of a Caesarship hostile to liberty." On Caesarism's dissemination across the political spectrum as a political term see 726,732.

97. Cf. Eduard Bernstein's comment that "Universal suffrage in Germany could serve Bismarck temporarily as a tool, but finally it compelled Bismarck to serve it as a tool" (Bernstein [1899] 1961:144).

98. This comes across forcefully in Marx and Engels' amusing, but very tendentious, account in the *Manifesto* of extant socialist and communist literature: Marx and Engels ([1848] 1973:87–97). See also the illuminating remarks in the preface to the English edition in which Engels explains why, when the *Manifesto* was written, "we could not have called it a 'Socialist' manifesto:" Marx and Engels (1973:64–65).

99. On Louis Bonaparte's "socialism," and its reception by other socialists, see Thompson (1955:68, 233–40), and Draper (1977:439–44). Also see Marx's *New York Daily Tribune* articles of June 21 (first published on June 7 in *The People's Paper*) and of June 24, 1856 on the "Imperial Socialism" and "Bonapartist socialism" of the *Crédit Mobilier* (Marx 1986a:11, 1986b:15).

Walter Bagehot was also interested in the *Crédit Mobilier* and traced its ascendancy in part to Louis Napoleon's "socialism." On Louis Napoleon as a "free spender" rather than a "free trader," and on his taste for public works, monuments, and "immense expenditure in employing labour," see Bagehot ([1857] 1978:343–44).

100. Three important studies are Rubel (1960), Wippermann (1983), and especially Draper (1977, vol. I), from whose excellent account I have often borrowed.

101. This formulation has itself been criticized on Marxian grounds by Geoffrey de Ste. Croix (1981:64).

102. I have amended the translation very slightly. In German, the last sentence reads: "Bei so gänzlicher Verschiedenheit zwischen den materiellen, ökonomischen Bedingungen des antiken und des modernen Klassenkampfs können auch seine politischen Ausgeburten nicht mehr miteinander gemein haben als der Erzbischof von Canterbury mit dem Hohenpriester Samuel" (Marx 1968a:359–60). (The noun "Ausgeburt" suggests something potentially fiendish or fantastic).

103. Draper also interprets the statement in the *Manifesto* about the class struggle either leading to "a revolutionary reconstitution of society at large, or...the common ruin of the contending classes" ([1848] 1973:68) as an allusion to Rome. "In the *Manifesto*, Marx and Engels assumed everyone was aware of the great example in the past of 'the common ruin of the contending classes.' It was the disintegration without revolution of the society of the Roman Empire, an example which weighed heavily on all political thought and its terminology."

However Draper laments the fact that while Marx and Engels had various things to say about the economic disintegration of the Roman Empire, they said very little about the "*political* forms in which the Roman state" collapsed (Draper 1977:466).

The reference in the main text to "military despotism, the rule of the Caesars" is attributed in Marx's and Engels's *Collected Works* (1980, 16:120) to the pen of Engels alone. Draper believes the article to have been jointly written, and I follow his guidance.

104. With some bitterness, Marx quoted a report of *The Economist* (December 27, 1851) that "was already screaming of the betrayal committed by the 'masses' of ignorant, untrained, and stupid *proletaires*' against 'the skill, knowledge, discipline, mental influence, intellectual resources and moral weight of the middle and upper ranks'. The stupid, ignorant and vulgar mass was nothing other than the bourgeoisie itself" (Marx 1973b:225); cf. 241 on the bourgeoisie "now exclaiming over the stupidity of the masses, *the vile multitude*" (emphasis in the original).

105. On Engels's contributions, see Draper (1977:410–27) and the literature cited there. The most sophisticated later Marxist treatment of the exceptional state was offered by Nicos Poulantzas ([1970] 1974:313–35; [1975] 1976:90–126).

106. See Trotsky's *History of the Russian Revolution* ([1932–33] 1977:663–68) on Kerensky; and *The Revolution Betrayed* ([1937] 1972: 277–79) on the "Stalin regime" as "a variation of Bonapartism—a Bonapartism of a new type not before seen in history." Also pertinent are the articles collected in Trotsky (1975): chapters 8, 11, 12, 19, 23, and 24. Trotsky's brilliant analyses of the rise of fascism deploy "Bonapartism" as a key concept, bending it to make sense of events as they unfolded: thus while in January 1932 Trotsky implied that the Brüning government was Bonapartist (1975:126), by September 1932 he had changed his mind: "In its time, we designated the Brüning government as *Bonapartism*...that is, as a regime of military-police dictatorship....Were we to be exact, we should have to make a rectification of our old designation:the Brüning government was a pre-Bonapartist government. Brüning was only a precursor. In a perfected form, Bonapartism came upon the scene in the Papen-Schleicher government" (1975: 262–63, emphasis in original).

Trotsky's interpretation of "Bonapartism" diverged from Marx's own statements on the origins and evolution of the French Second Empire in a number of ways. For instance, in Trotsky's view, Bonapartism had emerged in Germany because Germany was the nation with "the most advanced capitalist system in the conditions of the European impasse" ([1932] 1975: 110); for Marx, to the contrary, it was France's relative social and economic immaturity that explained the rise of Louis Bonaparte. Or again: according to Trotsky, Bonapartism in Germany preceded both working class collapse ([1932] 1975:133) and a massive political backlash from the petty bourgeoisie ([1932] 1975:251–57). Marx's analysis was very different: under "Bonapartism" the proletarian organizations were entirely smashed, while the "Bonapartist" regime of Napoleon III *followed* the defeat of the petty bourgeoisie.

Trotsky also used the term "Caesarism" on a number of occasions (e.g., [1937] 1972:277–79; cf.[1932] 1975:255), but of all the "classical" Marxists, it was Gramsci who developed the concept most systematically within a Marxist framework.

107. On this matter see Dülffer (1976:109–28), at 111.

108. "The German '*Fraktion*' has the primary meaning of a parliamentary party, but

Marx also uses it for sections of a class that are the basis of different political parties" (Fernbach 1973:11).

109. Marx pointed to a special economic affinity between financial and large landed capitals based on their mutual interest in speculation. "The combination of large landed property and high finance is in general a *normal fact*, as evidenced by England, and even Austria" (1973a:110), emphasis in the original.

110. Marx's description is unabashedly instrumentalist in formulation: "the financial aristocracy made the laws, controlled the state administration, exercised authority in all public institutions and controlled public opinion by actual events and through the press." (Marx 1973a:39).

111. Marx explains the trade crisis as a manifestation of capitalist overproduction (1973b: 226). See E. Mandel (1962:345–59) for a helpful description of the Marxist theory of capitalist economic cycles. (Overproduction is construed as one "moment" of economic rotation. Thus, economic recovery: boom and prosperity: overproduction and slump: crisis and depression: economic recovery: etc).

112. Marx's model of economic maturity was England. Though French industry and the French bourgeoisie were "more highly developed" and "more revolutionary" than their Continental counterparts, they were economically weak when measured against the English case (Marx 1973a:46, 111).

113. "No one had fought with more fanaticism in the June days for the salvation of property and the restoration of credit than the Parisian petty bourgeoisie—café and restaurant proprietors, *marchands de vins*, small traders, shopkeepers, craftsmen, etc. The shopkeeper had gathered his strength and marched on the barricade in order to restore the flow of business from the street into the shop" (Marx 1973a:65).

114. Marx's definition of the lumpenproletariat can be found in Marx (1973b:197). On the lumpenproletariat and youth, see Marx (1973a:52–53).

115. V.M. Perez-Diaz (1978:46–47), ingeniously, if not totally persuasively, argues that Marx is here offering "a 'peasant variant' of a theory of the fetishism of the state...[A] 'subject' (the peasant class) projects or transfers its 'essence' (its political resources or power) on to an alien object (the state, or one state institution, the president). And, in so doing, this subject becomes powerless, to the point not only of losing actual control of the object, but also of losing the consciousness of having produced this object in the first place."

116. Cf. Wellington's comment on Napoleon I: "Napoleon was not a personality, but a principle," cited in F. Markham (1963:257).

117. "The state power does not hover in mid-air. Bonaparte represents a class, indeed he represents the most numerous class of French society, the small peasant proprietors" (emphasis omitted). Marx went on to qualify this statement with the remark that: "the Bonaparte dynasty represents the conservative, not the revolutionary peasant: the peasant who wants to consolidate the condition of his social existence, the smallholding, not the peasant who strikes out beyond it" (Marx 1973b:238, 240).

118. Marx argues that in *another sense* the small holding peasants do form a class (though this is not the sense he emphasizes in his discussion of the Bonaparte-peasant relationship): "In so far as millions of families live under economic conditions of existence that separate their mode of life, their interests and their cultural formation from those of the other classes and bring them into conflict with those classes, they form a class" (Marx 1973b:239).

The peasants are also described in class terms in Marx (1973a:72–73), though with the tone of derision unchanged. They re-emerge as "the large mass of

producers [*große Masse der Produzenten*] not directly involved in the struggle between capital and labour" in Marx (1968b:337 = Marx 1974:208).
119. See Marx (1973b:154,194).
120. The economic situation of the peasants in France appears to be similar to that of conditions obtaining under "primitive accumulation." Compare Marx (1973b:241–43) with the comments in *Capital* I: 873,876, 877–95 (Marx [1867] 1976).
121. For a socialist defence (albeit heavily qualified) of the small farmer, see Bernstein's critical comments on Karl Kautsky, in Bernstein ([1899] 1961:134–36).
122. A detailed analysis of the Constitution can also be found in Marx ([1851] 1978:567–80). Writing six months before Louis Bonaparte's coup, Marx wrote that "The game of Napoleon, is, first to play off the People against the middle-class. Then to play off the middle-class against the People and to use the army against them both. The future is pregnant with great events, and the present of France is one of the most interesting studies history affords" (580). (This article was first published in the radical Chartist news-sheet "Notes to the People," no. 7, June 14, 1851. It was probably translated into English by Engels: see Marx [1978:702, n.408].)
123. That Napoleon III was gradually becoming the prisoner of the army he relied on was a common theme of Marx at this time. Thus "At the same rate that France grows impatient of the yoke of the army, the army waxes bolder in its purpose of yoking Bonaparte. After the 10th of December [1848: the date Louis was elected President of the Second Republic], Bonaparte could flatter himself that he was the elect of the peasantry, that is, the mass of the French nation. Since the [assassination] attempt of the 14th January, he knows that he is at the mercy of the army. Having been compelled to avow that he rules through the army, it is quite natural that the latter should seek to rule through him" (Marx [1858] 1986e:482). Also, on "the substitution of the rule *of* the army for rule *by* the army" (Marx [1858] 1986f:568).
124. On the position of the army under the Second Empire, see T. Zeldin (1979:154). For Zeldin the Second Empire was not "a militaristic regime, for the army did not run the country." On just who did, see the same author's excellent *The Political System of Napoleon III* (1958).
    The military adventurism of the Second Empire was also noted by Marx on various occasions, but it was Engels who tended to address it more systematically. See for instance, his 1891 introduction to *The Civil War in France*, and his 1895 introduction to *The Class Struggles in France*, in Marx and Engels (1968: 251 and 647–48 respectively). Engels here alludes to the Second Empire's campaigns in Crimea (1854–55), its wars against China (1856–58, 1860), its expeditions against Syria (1860–61) and Mexico (1862–67), and its disastrous confrontation with Prussia in 1870.
125. Elsewhere Marx observed that "The financial fraud system could only be converted into a prosaic finance system by eliminating corruption as a general means of government; by reducing the army and navy to a peace footing, and therefore by *abandoning the Napoleonic character* of the present regime; finally, by complete renunciation of the plan followed hitherto of binding a part of the middle class and of the city proletariat to the existing government by means of great government construction projects and other public works" (Marx [1861] 1984:83–84, emphasis in the original).
126. On the political economy of "Bonapartism," see chapter 5 of R. Magraw (1983).

3

Bismarck and the Crisis of German Politics: Max Weber and His Contemporaries I

Weber's Importance and Complexity

Although Max Weber's reputation has assumed immense proportions since the Second World War, during his own lifetime (1864–1920) it was actually quite modest and circumscribed. Modern scholarship portrays Weber as a rather isolated figure, deeply impressive to the circle that knew him well, respected by those outside of it who came in contact with his work or with him personally, but in no way a commanding influence on intellectual discussion of the day (Fogt 1977; Käsler [1979] 1988:197–210). A sustained analysis of Weber's thinking on Caesarism cannot, then, be justified in terms of the ferment of discussion it provoked among members of his own generation. Instead it is to our own epoch that we must look to understand its significance. As Alasdair MacIntyre ([1981] 1985:109) has observed, "the contemporary vision of the world is predominantly, although not perhaps always in detail, Weberian...for in our culture we know of no organized movement towards power which is not bureaucratic and managerial in mode and we know of no justifications for authority which are not Weberian in form."

The remark is obviously (and deliberately) a simplification, but its main point is warranted: Weber developed a way of thinking about the world, and bequeathed a conceptual and lexical framework to do this thinking, which has proved extraordinarily durable. It has done so in part because of its "influence," but largely because of its remarkable synchronicity with modern social and political conditions. Coming to

165

grips with Weber's analysis of authority and its "justifications" thus brings us face to face with our own justifications—with both their pathos and vapidity. But how were these justifications actually formed, and what redescription of older ideas was required to form them?

Weber's work is of preeminent importance for this study because it enables us to see the growth of a language in which older political notions were gradually and fatefully reshaped. In particular, a close analysis of the German thinker's investigations furnishes a unique vantage point from which to glimpse the transformation of the Caesarism debate from its nineteenth-century origins to its twentieth-century expressions, and the further emaciation of the republican idea this development entailed. Weber, like Marx, was a man whose ideas crystallized the most acute tensions of his age. But like Marx too, he was a bold and prodigiously gifted innovator. Any satisfactory examination of his contribution to social and political thought has to convey these twin aspects; it must, in other words, seek both to locate Weber's work in contemporary debates and show how he subscribed to or, more usually, deviated from them. However, such a task is complicated, at least so far as the Caesarism question itself is concerned, by the fact that Weber addressed that question in two overlapping, but nonetheless analytically distinct, contexts.

First, Weber employs the term Caesarism in his early correspondence, his political journalism, and his public lectures to attack systematically the legacy of Otto von Bismarck, the great architect of the German Second Empire. In these directly political interventions, Caesarism is portrayed as a deeply damaging and crippling phenomenon; accordingly, the tone Weber adopts is one of regret and denigration. Bismarckian Caesarism, in brief, is adduced as evidence of Germany's failure to modernize its institutions along the parliamentary lines so successfully established in the Anglophone world. However, once Weber sketches his own alternative to the Bismarckian state we see that it is not Caesarism per se that he is rejecting. On the contrary, Caesarism—now presented in the guise of modern plebiscitary leadership, situated within a vibrant parliamentary structure—is considered by Weber to be the political secret of the remarkable imperial and civil successes of Britain and America, achievements Weber urged his German compatriots to emulate. Here, then, Caesarism is treated affirmatively, with the voice of recommendation, or even simply in the spirit of resigned realism.

It transpires from this first general context of Weberian analysis, that Caesarism (in one modality or another) is the inevitable accompaniment to electoral democracy, the inescapable corollary of modern party politics. The point is not to get rid of Caesarism as such—a project that would be both quixotic and dangerous—but to cultivate its most politically energetic and expeditious form. Nineteenth-century debates around Caesarism, as we saw in the last chapter, had been polarized between those for and against it. Positive or negative attributions were nothing new. What was highly unusual about Weber's account was its discriminating and flexible character. All the same, it is a second depiction of Caesarism that shows the greatest shift from nineteenth-century preoccupations.

The narrative context in this case is Weber's didactic, sociological writings, more especially the "ideal-type" analysis that he sought to adumbrate and apply in the sociology of religion and, more critically for our purposes, in the various drafts of work from 1911 onwards that would come to comprise the posthumously published *Economy and Society* (Weber [1922] 1978b).[1] In this more pointedly academic context, a setting in which Weber seeks to develop categories for social scientific investigation, Caesarism emerges as neither positive nor negative, ascriptions that share the common feature of being highly charged and ethically resonant. Instead, it takes its place as a relatively minor *technical* term in the vocabulary and classification of "legitimate domination," a treatment that purports to be nothing more than descriptive and analytical. Simultaneously, the perplexing inflections surrounding the question of "domination" recede and are deflated by redefining the concept to embrace any form of obedience provided it is voluntarily accepted by those within its sphere of jurisdiction; in effect, "legitimate domination" is a pleonasm. Melvin Richter is thus quite right to contrast the highly sanitized notion of Caesarism that one finds redescribed in Weber's *sociology* with the earlier nineteenth-century emphasis on Caesarism's arbitrary and despotic qualities.[2] More than this, Caesarism is not only redefined in a way that would have appeared oxymoronic or downright contradictory to a previous generation of thinkers; it is also reformulated in such a way as to render it less visible, *and thereby less problematic*, a strategy that also helps explain why the concept has received so little explicit attention among Weber scholars. For in successive versions of Weber's sociology of legitimate domination, Caesarism becomes translated into, and interchangeable with, the jargon of "plebiscitary leadership" and "plebiscitary leader democracy," at the same time as it becomes absorbed into the concept of charisma. And it is "charisma," not Caesarism, for which Weber is today remembered; charisma that has spawned thousands of studies and interpretations; charisma that has seeped into lay discussion.

Of course the diminutive stature of "Caesarism" when measured against "charisma" is understandable and, to a large extent, is also rightly conceived—*if* one focuses on Weber's sociological work alone. Charisma, after all, is the term Weber defines precisely and at length in a number of prominent, and now famous texts; it is finely tuned to his purposes, explicitly set to work and elaborated upon in his sociology of religion and domination, self-consciously stamped with his authority. By contrast, "Caesarism" as a specific term is largely absent from the sociological texts, and even in the political writings is never defined systematically. It did not have to be since the term was part of a political vernacular Weber shared with his contemporaries. Even so, there is a sense in which "Caesarism" as a leadership concept has much more claim on our attention than hitherto it has received. For it was "Caesarism" that Weber used first and continued to use from early maturity to the end of his life—it thus has a career continuity lacking in its partner term; Caesarism, which far more than the word he adopted from Rudolf Sohm and the Bible, connects Weber to a storehouse of nineteenth-century arguments and preoccupations; Caesarism, the word with which Weber issued his censure of Bismarck, lacerated the literati, and theorized about key aspects of modern democracy; Caesarism, a choice of vocabulary that once more, if unwittingly, pits Weber against Marx.[3]

I shall seek to explain the asymmetry of Weber's treatment of charisma and Caesarism in the next chapter when I turn to examine more closely the German thinker's sociological analyses of legitimacy. There I will also clarify a problem that emerges whenever one attempts a firm distinction between Weber's "political" and "sociological" writings. This chapter, however, is concerned to unravel Weber's notions of Caesarism as they appear in his analysis of Bismarck, the American and British parliamentary system, and the potential position of a German Reich president. I begin with some observations on Weber's intellectual background: specifically the interest in antiquity he shared with many other major European thinkers, and that provided one conduit to the Caesarism debate of his day.

Weber as a Student of Antiquity

During the nineteenth century, as in many centuries that had preceded it, a classical, humanistic education retained a prominence it has long since lost. Comparisons of modernity with antiquity were part of the very fabric of political reasoning, and the main characters of the Roman Republic's final drama, for instance, were well known. It was in just such a cultural milieu that Weber himself was thoroughly schooled. At the age of thirteen (1877) he had already written an essay on the "Roman Imperial Period from Constantine to the Migration of Nations," while by fourteen-and-a-half Max was confident enough to settle on Homer ("I like him best of all the writers I have ever read"), pronounce derogatively on Virgil (the *Aeneid* "seeks to arouse a certain suspense, but one hardly feels it, or, if one does, it is not a pleasant sensation"), patronize Herodotus (who though a credulous and thus "not a completely reliable historian" nonetheless "makes very pleasant reading"), write off Livy ("a bad critic" who was certainly not as hard working as Herodotus) and inveigh against Cicero, for whom Weber reveals a particular dislike. Cicero's "first Catilinarian oration and his vacillating and unstable policies in general do not impress me at all," and the consul's shortsighted behavior in failing to remove Catiline from the Roman scene also earns the young scholar's castigation: "For if he had arrested and strangled Catiline at the proper time and had nipped Mallius's preparations in the bud, the Roman state would have been spared the tremendous, bloody battle of Pistoria in which so many thousands died in a civil war" (Marianne Weber [1926] 1988:50–54 = Weber 1936:9–14).[4]

These precocious adolescent jottings were lent immeasurably greater depth and content by Weber's university studies first at Heidelberg (spring 1882–autumn 1883) and then at Berlin and Göttingen (autumn 1884–late winter 1886).[5] Jurisprudence was his chosen "major" but the prodigious appetite for knowledge that Weber possessed, whetted by the interdisciplinary opportunities afforded by the German university system, ensured the student a thoroughly omnivorous diet of political economy, theology, philosophy, and, of course, history. In this environment Weber was able to attend Immanuel Bekker's Heidelberg classes in Roman Law and take advantage, while resident in Berlin, of Mommsen's lectures (Marianne Weber 1988:65, 96). And from that time onwards Weber's intellectual development would be punctuated with analyses of the ancient world and reflections on it.[6] Key texts include: Weber's *Habilitation* thesis, "Roman Agrarian History in Its Bearing on Public and Private Law" published in 1891; the 1896 lecture on "The Social Causes of the Decay of Ancient Civilisation;" the 1897 and 1909 versions of "Agrarian Relations in Antiquity"; the article of 1904 entitled "The Argument about the Character of the Old German Social Constitution in the German Literature of the Last Decade"; and the many sections on the ancient world that can be found in Weber's *The City*, which though composed around 1911–13 only first appeared posthumously in 1921.

An assessment of Weber's scholarship in this area is beyond my competence but it is worth noting that those best equipped to judge the matter have often been enthusiastic in their praise of Weber's classical erudition. M.I. Finley (1977:318) hails the "Roman Agrarian History" a "brilliant piece of historical research." "Epoch making" is how Arnaldo Momigliano (1977:435) describes the lecture on the demise of ancient civilization. According to Alfred Heuss, the "Agrarian Relations" essays are "the most original, daring and persuasive analysis ever made of the economic and social development of antiquity...the area in which Weber's judgement, especially in the details, was most sovereign and surefooted" (cited in Roth 1977:766). Even so severe a critic of Weber's theoretical approach to history and society as Geoffrey de Ste. Croix (who observes that Weber's grasp of Greek history is inferior to his understanding of Roman) is happy to acknowledge that the 1896 lecture is "very interesting" (1981:85).[7] All these comments are impressive testimonials best left to those with specialist knowledge in classical studies and ancient history; the same caveat applies to the debate concerning the relative importance for Weber's intellectual development of such luminaries as Theodor Mommsen, August Meitzen, Carl Julius Beloch, and Eduard Meyer.[8] For our purposes it will suffice to consider Weber's relationship to a figure who recorded for posterity his own sour judgment on "Caesareanism" in a work that Weber would have been certain to know intimately: the man was Theodor Mommsen (1817–1903) who as well as being the foremost ancient historian of his age was also a friend of the Weber family; the work in question, his *History of Rome* ([1854–6] 1911), the masterpiece completed while Mommsen was still in his thirties.[9]

Unlike Jacob Burckhardt, who accepted the utility of the term Caesarism without any visible reluctance, the stance of Mommsen was downright hostile. A liberal who welcomed German unification, but who became a staunch critic of Bismarck's authoritarian domestic policy, Mommsen combined the strongest admiration for Julius Caesar with the deepest suspicion of all would-be modern imitators. Caesar, "the first ruler over the whole domain of Romano-Hellenic civilisation" was a monarch, no doubt about it, in fact his state was an "absolute military monarchy" (Mommsen 1911:424, 440). But if Caesar was a monarch, he never "resorted to outrages such as that of the eighteenth Brumaire," was "never seized with the giddiness of the tyrant" (Mommsen 1911:429). Caesar had begun his career not as a warlord but as a demagogue.[10] The very embodiment of "republican ideals," (Mommsen 1911:430), Caesar was the leader of the popular party, the culmination of the democratic project launched by Gaius Gracchus; Caesar, the man who "displayed the bitterest, even personal, hatred to the aristocracy" and "retained unchanged the essential ideas of Roman democracy, viz. alleviation of the burdens of debtors, transmarine colonisation, gradual equalisation of the difference of rights among the classes belonging to the state, emancipation of the executive power from the senate." Indeed:

> his monarchy was so little at variance with democracy, that democracy on the contrary only attained its completion and fulfilment by means of that monarchy. For this monarchy was not the Oriental despotism of divine right, but a monarchy such as Gaius Gracchus wished to found, such as Pericles and Cromwell founded— the representation of the nation by the man in whom it puts supreme and unlimited confidence.[11] (Mommsen 1911: 438–39)

The impact of Mommsen's depiction of Caesar on contemporary opinion was profound and instantaneous. The *History of Rome*'s brilliant stylistic qualities—W. Warde Fowler (1920:259) joined many others in judging it "the greatest feat of German literature in the middle of the nineteenth century"—ensured it a wide public readership (it was soon available in English, French, Italian, and Russian translations), while Mommsen's meticulous scholarship, combined with his many inflammatory verdicts about Caesar's opponents,[12] guaranteed that no historian of the late Republic could henceforth ignore it. Even those like Eduard Meyer who later taxed the *Römische Geschichte* for its failure to understand the true importance of Pompey or the Principate of Augustus, and for its completely unreal construction of a man fully aware of his destiny, conceded Mommsen's immense authority: everyone who followed, however vigorous they might fight his interpretation, was still dependent on the details and categories of Mommsen's "magnificent" portrayal (Meyer [1918] 1978:324–25).[13]

Mommsen's *laudatio* to Caesar, however, did not extend to the contemporary concept and phenomenon of "Caesarianism" (*Caesarianismus*), a point he was at pains to make clear after some had construed the first (1854–56) edition of his work as a panegyric to modern despotism. Mommsen's championship of Caesar had arisen in the aftermath of the defeat of German liberalism in 1848. The corrupt and reactionary senatorial oligarchy of Rome, the subject of Caesar's attack, were, in Mommsen's allegory, the ancient analogue of the Prussian squirearchy and state he so detested, and that he saw as the great impediment to the liberalization and modernization of Germany. Caesar represented the combination of passion and realism, of leadership and democratic conviction, that Germany so sorely needed. None of this was code for the approval of Caesarism or Bonapartism as those terms were commonly construed.[14] Indeed, both the concept and the phenomenon of Caesarianism are specifically castigated by the German writer. The *concept* of "Caesarianism" Mommsen criticizes for its clumsy and vulgar use of analogy[15] because although it "is true that the history of past centuries ought to be the instructress of the present," it is patently crude to theorize "as if one could simply by turning over the leaves discover the conjunctures of the present in the records of the past, and collect from these the symptoms for a political diagnosis and the specifics for a prescription" (Mommsen 1911:439). Similarly inappropriate is the *phenomenon* of Caesarism, if this means an attempt to ape Caesar's type of rule in present-day European conditions:

> Caesar's work was necessary and salutary, not because it was or could be fraught with blessing in itself, but because—with the national organisation of antiquity, which was based on slavery and was utterly a stranger to republican-constitutional representation, and in presence of the legitimate civic constitution which in the course of five hundred years had ripened into oligarchic absolutism—absolute military monarchy was the copestone logically necessary and the least of evils. (Mommsen 1911:440)

In contrast, where "Caesareanism" appears "under other conditions of development, it is at once a caricature and a usurpation." Europe of Mommsen's day was not a slave-owning society in which an enlightened "absolute military monarchy" was "the least of evils." It was an increasingly capitalist, urban, and industrial society that required its own distinctive constitutional, liberal-democratic state. The attempt to graft onto the modern age a type of rule that belonged organically to another epoch, was hence a monstrous mockery of a great man, a fundamental misunderstanding of history itself, and a dangerous rationalization for modern autocracy.[16]

Mommsen's personality—his "soul of fire," in Friedrich Gundolf's memorable words ([1926] 1968:327)[17]—evinces some striking parallels with Max Weber's.[18] Both men had strong liberal and patriotic instincts; both possessed intimidating intellects;[19] both displayed integrity and courage in the political stands they adopted (Mommsen, as well as losing his chair in civil law at the University of Leipzig for his part in the May 1849 Saxony uprising, came within a whisker of being sent to prison for his radical activities there); both were staunch critics of Bismarck though at the same time appreciative of the latter's role in German unification; and both recoiled from the sycophancy and submission that bowed so many other members of the middle class in the *Kaiserreich*. Friedrich Naumann was right to say, in his affectionate obituary tribute to Mommsen, that the latter "never became a *Geheimrat*"[20] (privy councillor), a comment that hints at more than the simple fact that the historian never attained ministerial office;[21] Naumann meant, surely, that Mommsen was not the sort of man to allow his political sting to be drawn. Mommsen remained a bourgeois rebel, a defiant champion of his liberal creed—in 1882 an election speech led him to be charged for an alleged slander of Bismarck; he was tried and acquitted—a man "who wished to be a citizen" in a state that was, alas, only willing to tolerate subjects.[22] Finally, both agreed on the supreme qualities necessary for the able political leader: devotion to a cause, married to a sober appraisal of historical possibility and of the uniqueness of contemporary conditions.

Yet with respect to the issue of Caesarism itself the differences between Mommsen and Weber are more obvious than the similarities. If Mommsen cautioned against such terms, Weber seemed happy enough to use them, not only with an informality that must have alarmed his teacher but even, without qualification, in ancient historical settings.[23] And what about the phenomenon that Caesarism is supposed to have denoted? Here also one finds discrepancies. In Weber's discussion of Bismarck, Caesarism is deemed a bad thing; conversely, where Caesarism is envisaged as the natural corollary of the extension of the franchise, Weber's tone is resigned, indeed, where invidious contrasts are being drawn between the German and British parliamentary systems, benedictory. Finally, if one interprets Weber's Reich president proposals as those of Caesarism in code, we are there faced with nothing less than urgent recommendation. To show how Weber handled and developed these themes is the task of the next three sections.

The "Caesarism" of Bismarck[24]

A.J.P. Taylor (1967:22) has observed nicely that people "live after their own deaths in the minds of others." He might have added that there are some people whose longevity is assured through more than human recollection or the documentary evidence that testifies to their existence: these individuals live on in the institutions they have fashioned, the pulse of their influence evident long after they have been removed from office or have exhaled their last breath.

Such a person was Otto von Bismarck. As consummate political strategist, and the prime and directing author of the Second Empire's constitution, Bismarck engaged himself in that most formative and momentous of political endeavors: the act of shaping "the lives of citizens by designing the structure or 'dwelling' which they and their posterity will inhabit" (Wolin 1981:401). It was a founding act whose significance was not lost on Max Weber, at any rate as he later reflected on it. For Weber, the achievement of German unification had been a demonstrably necessary geopolitical task to pursue, and Bismarck's role in that process cause for profound national gratitude. What appalled Weber from his late teens onwards, however, was Bismarck's management of the subsequent "peace,"[25] the grievous injuries inflicted on the fledgling Reich in both domestic and foreign arenas by a regime Weber construed to be so self-serving and short-sighted as to mistake the interests of a great power with the survival of a totally anachronistic and irresponsible system of governance. Worse still, that system proved eminently capable of enduring in the absence of its original architect, thus underscoring the need to restructure it in fundamental ways.

When Weber refers to Bismarck, the charge of "Caesarism" is never far away and the word is invariably inflected with animus. Three features of Bismarck's statecraft in particular comprise its Caesarist and reprehensible character. In the first place, there was Bismarck's own variety of populism, particularly his initiative in introducing, or, to be exact, reintroducing[26] universal manhood suffrage, now extended to encompass the whole of the Reich. Reflecting on the implications for the German polity of the 1884 Reichstag election, the young Max Weber penned a revealing letter to his uncle and confidant Hermann Baumgarten. Of course, given the National Liberals' rightward shift under Johannes Miquel at the eleventh hour of the campaign and the failure of a union with the German Free Conservatives to materialize, "the pathetic result" for the forces of liberalism "was predictable." "Interesting," on the other hand, was the success of the Social Democrats in increasing their proportion of the votes cast from 6.1 (1881) to 9.7 percent and as a consequence doubling their seats in the National Parliament from twelve to twenty-four:[27] evidently Bismarck's antisocialist legislation had failed to turn the tide of their support. After then remarking that a case could conceivably be constructed to support the antisocialist laws on the grounds that Social Democratic agitation threatened to bring about a general curtailment of civil liberties by the state—better the few repressed than the many[28]—Weber delivers his indictment: "The capital mistake seems to be the Greek gift of Bismarckian Caesarism, universal suffrage, which is sheer murder of equal rights for all in the true sense of the word."[29]

Marianne Weber interprets this statement not as an objection to the institution of universal manhood suffrage per se but as evidence of Weber's distrust of the motives behind its implementation and timing: Weber, she tells us, disapproved of the rhetoric of political equality "apparently because it was Bismarck's original plan to use universal suffrage in the Reich to keep liberalism in check" (1988:118). There is probably something in this explanation, though exactly how much is hard to determine accurately. Certainly the twenty-year-old Weber, already remarkably politically astute, would have recognized that Bismarck's establishment of universal manhood suffrage had above all a partisan objective: to outflank liberalism by creating a mass constituency for conservatism, so confident was the Junker that "in moments of decision the masses will always stand by the King."[30] Quite possibly too Weber would not have shared, in 1884, his uncle's uncompromising repudiation of universal manhood suffrage in principle: Baumgarten was convinced that the institution would end in socialism and the hegemony of a Catholic clergy. (He had declaimed to a distinguished fellow liberal, a little over three and a half years before the

Weber letter referred to above, that Bismarck "has...bestowed on us the curse of universal manhood suffrage, which admittedly he knows how to manipulate as a truly Caesarian demagogue but which must cause the greatest disaster in the hands of his successors").[31] But even if it could be demonstrated that Weber in the mid-1880s agreed with his uncle's total opposition, it could also be shown that such an agreement must have been exceedingly short lived. In 1892, writing for *Die Christliche Welt*, Weber's contempt for what he construed to be the ill-informed paranoia of those who harboured the "superstition that dark and secret powers are at work in the laboring class" is symptomatic of his own less alarmist attitude towards the consequence of mass suffrage; while by the Freiburg Inaugural lecture (May 1895) Weber's acceptance of the electoral presence of the proletariat is clear (it is their political "immaturity" and "philistinism" that he decries, not their electoral position and rights in the Reich) as, again, is his scorn for those who continue to be obsessed with the red peril.[32] And of course during the Great War Weber was robust in demanding that all remaining impediments to the suffrage in Prussia be removed, outraged that the men who had fought for the fatherland might otherwise return to find themselves in the lowest of the Prussian three class system.[33] In fact it is in one of his wartime articles ("Suffrage and Democracy in Germany," originally published in December 1917) that Weber provides us with the best clue of his thinking about Bismarck's reintroduction and geographical extension of universal manhood suffrage (though naturally one cannot be sure that this was Weber's thinking at the time of his letter to Baumgarten). What Weber questions here is not the wisdom or necessity of affording the mass of the male population the right to vote, but rather the rapidity with which the process was inaugurated. Weber seems to have thought that the ideals of national parliamentary cooperation and responsibility would have been better served through a gradualist, evolutionary approach to political democratization, say, on English lines; particularly, through a process that would have first embraced the economically and socially privileged and the political educated, only later ushering in the masses onto the political stage (Weber [1917] =1958:233–34).[34] However, this was not to be, and the interests of the nation as Weber perceived them were sacrificed to Bismarck's Caesarism.

Bismarck's attempt at electoral manipulation formed only one part of his populist strategy and any full analysis of Bismarck's career would need to consider among other things, his habit of dissolving the Reichstag when it refused to do his bidding, and appealing instead over its head to the voters—as in 1878 (when the assassination attempt on the emperor gave him the perfect opportunity to put the National Liberals in their place and come down like an avalanche on the growing socialist movement) and 1887 (when he determined to bully parliament into accepting his Appropriations Bill); his management of anti-Catholic feeling in the early-to-mid 1870s; and his part in the introduction of the famous social insurance legislation enacted in stages throughout virtually the whole period of his chancellorship. Weber actually refers to some of these events, and to others I have not mentioned here, in "Parliament and Government in a Reconstructed Germany" ([1917–1918] 1978a:1388–90 = 1958:303–6). But they largely fall under the wider rubric of Bismarck's "demagogy," whereas the term "Caesarism" is reserved more narrowly to capture a specific feature of the populist package—Bismarck's role in the establishment of universal male suffrage.

The second aspect of Bismarck's "Caesarism" to earn Max Weber's rebuke is quite closely related to the first. It concerns the chancellor's towering stature and the shadow it cast over the Second Empire, enthralling supporters, intimidating opponents and, subsequently, awing the epigones. Writing just over two decades after Bismarck's death, Weber put the matter thus:

> The present condition of our parliamentary life is a legacy of Prince Bismarck's long domination and of the nation's attitude toward him since the last decade of his chancellorship. This attitude has no parallel in the reaction of any other great people toward a statesman of such stature. Nowhere else in the world has even the most unrestrained adulation of a politician made a proud nation sacrifice its substantive convictions so completely. (Weber 1978a:1385 = 1958:299)

These comments are at first bound to strike us as hyperbolic, permissible no doubt in the context of a polemic but surely straining the credulity of the social scientist trained to be dubious of heroic conceptions of culture and society. Yet there is sufficient evidence to demonstrate that from the inception of his first Reich chancellorship onwards Bismarck came to be the object of an extraordinarily resilient and pervasive personality cult, the effects of which were as far-reaching as they were to prove ultimately damaging. Bismarck's actual deeds only partially explain the elevation he enjoyed. Just as important was the historical setting in which the man became hero, namely a Reich newly forged and vigorously particularist in its social structure and in its political and cultural temperament: discounting Prussia, twenty-four governments composed the empire, many of which remained hostile to Prussia's hegemony and extremely jealous of traditions (including confessional ones) and prerogatives they were determined to preserve. The new empire, bereft of its own identity and lacking the collective symbols through which its unity might be affirmed,[35] found in Bismarck its personal surrogate—this is the plausible thesis advanced by Gordon Craig. And Craig shows how across the whole spectrum of German culture of the 1870s and 1880s and beyond—for instance, in the historical work of Treitschke, in the paintings of Böcklin, Lenbach, and Anselm Feuerbach, in the stories of Heyse, and at the beginning of the twentieth century, in the sculpture of Begas, Lederer, and Schaudt—the Bismarck myth grew, compensatory apotheosis of an uncertain Empire seeking political and emotional coherence.[36] While the attempt to transform Emperor William I "into a popularly accepted founding father of a united Germany" was somewhat of a failure, within a single year "of Bismarck's death in 1898, 470 municipalities had decided to erect 'Bismarck columns'" (Hobsbawm 1983a:264).

Max Weber's own attitude towards Bismarck the person and Bismarck the legend are best treated separately. The Bismarck legend he quite simply detested. Bismarck the icon, "Bismarck *sans phrase*" (Marianne Weber 1988:118) he denounced not just as an intellectual capitulation but as a distortion of Bismarck's achievement by men who, in seeking to emulate his example, simultaneously misrepresented it through concentrating exclusively on "the admixture of violence and cunning, the seeming or actual brutality of his political approach" (Weber 1978a:1385 = 1958:299).[37] Weber's attitude to the man, however, was more complex. As I hinted at the beginning of this section, Weber found much in Bismarck to admire: Weber appreciated the chancellor's political adroitness and intellectual sophistication (his mental acuity, Weber would say, was often lost on admirers and detractors alike), respected the sheer lack of humbug that accompanied his power politics. At the same time, Bismarck's ambition, his monomania and the political excesses it encouraged, had left the nation with the deepest scars. For Bismarck had bequeathed to his successors "a nation without any political sophistication, far below the level which in this regard it had reached twenty years before [i.e., in 1870];"[38] "a nation without any political will of its own, accustomed to the idea that the great statesman at the helm would make the necessary political decisions"; "a nation accustomed to fatalistic sufferance of all decisions made in the name of 'monarchic government,' because he had misused monarchic sentiments as a cover for his power interests in the struggle of the parties"; "a nation unprepared to look critically at the qualification of those who settled down in his empty chair." Furthermore:

> The great statesman did not leave behind any political tradition. He neither attracted nor even suffered independent political minds, not to speak of strong political personalities. On top of all this, it was the nation's misfortune that he harboured...intense mistrust toward all even vaguely possible successors ....A completely powerless parliament was the purely negative result of his tremendous prestige.[39] (Weber 1978a:1392=1958: 307–8)

Weber's censorious attitude, deeply felt and powerful as it is, has to be treated with some care in a study part of whose aim is to clarify political nomenclature; one cannot simply assume that every article on the above list of condemnation amounts to a specifically "Caesarist" attribute. Instead it is necessary to examine other statements by Weber to confirm what was, and what was not, distinctly Caesarist about Bismarck's rule. Undoubtedly one trait that was Caesarist was Bismarck's capacity to leave his nation "without any political will of its own, accustomed to the idea that the great statesman at the helm would make the necessary political decisions," because Weber mentions just this characteristic in the Freiburg Inaugural and invokes the image of Caesar to illustrate his point. In that lecture, which Ernst Nolte ([1963] 1969:558) once described as abounding "in phrases which, in meaning and sometimes even formulation, could have appeared in *Mein Kampf*'(!), and which Wolfgang J. Mommsen, in his first, great book on Weber depicted with perfect accuracy as a "beacon of German imperialism,"[40] Weber pondered the qualification of the middle class to govern Germany, and concluded that "the bourgeois classes, as repositories of the *power*-interests of the nation, seem to be withering, and there is still no sign that the workers have begun to mature so that they can take their place" (Weber 1980:446 = 1958:23). Weber's diagnosis was, in fact, all the more gloomy in that the explanation he offered for the political immaturity of his own class cited causes that no amount of wishful thinking could reverse: "The explanation lies in its unpolitical past, in the fact that one cannot make up in a decade for a missing century of political education, and that the domination of a great man is not always an appropriate instrument for such a process" (Weber 1980:445 = 1958:22; cf. Weber 1978a:1420 = 1958:343).

Bismarck—"the great man" to whom Weber is so obviously referring, "that Caesar-like figure hewn out of quite other than bourgeois timber" (Weber 1980:444 = 1958:20–21), architect of German unification and de facto ruler of the German Empire until his "departure" from office in 1890, "the all-powerful physician to whom we have entrusted everything" as Weber's favorite uncle had once bleated[41]— was no longer in charge when Weber spoke these words, even if his scheming continued unabated. But his deeds and example had stamped their indelible imprint on an impressionable Reich to such a degree that the middle class (at least this is Weber's thesis) accustomed to a prostrate position before a Titan, had lost the will, perhaps even the ability, to get off its knees: "One section of the haute bourgeoisie longs all too shamelessly for the coming of a new Caesar, who will protect them in two directions: from beneath against the rising masses of the people, from above against the socio-political impulses they suspect the German dynasties of harbouring" (Weber 1980:445 = 1958:21).[42] There had been a time when Bismarck had been compelled to force "his Caesarism" on a "reluctant bourgeoisie";[43] then, increasingly terrorized by their own insecurity, they had come to accept willingly their own subaltern status within the Reich, reconciled to a regime "half 'Caesarist,' half 'patriarchal'" (Weber [1898] 1971:31) whose existence was severely detrimental to the nation's political education.[44]

When, many years later, Weber returned to the relationship between Bismarck and the bourgeoisie his treatment was noticeably different, at least in emphasis. Musing, in "Parliament and Germany," on what he called the "Reichstag's prime period," by which he meant the prime period of German liberalism,[45] the bourgeoisie's political *leadership* is dealt with sympathetically and respectfully, in sharp contrast to the hectoring the bourgeois *class* had received in the earlier Freiburg lecture. These leaders, predominantly National Liberal in affiliation, had been candid enough to admit Bismarck's "tremendous intellectual superiority" without thereby abdicating their political responsibility. For while Weber recalled hearing liberal bigwig guests of his parents

opining that "they would consider Caesarism—government by a genius—the best political organisation for Germany, if there would always be a new Bismarck" (Weber 1978a:1387 = 1958:302–3), the
point of this reminiscence is to insist that these same people were fully
aware of the impossibility of such an outcome. They had therefore
attempted to secure a strong parliamentary and party system capable
of "attracting great political talents," and capable of providing political stability and continuity. Moreover, many of the most vibrant Reich
institutions, such as the office of the imperial chancellor, and the most
imaginative innovations, such as the creation of the *Reichsbank* and
the unification of the civil code, had been born of liberal parliamentary initiatives (Weber 1978a:1387–88 = 1958:302–3). That they failed
to wrest power from the Bismarck system, in which they were also
enmeshed, was due to more than the anachronistic aspects of their
economic and social policy: it was ultimately because Bismarck himself had successfully stymied every attempt to involve parliament in
government. Evidently, then, Weber did not believe that the
bourgeoisie's political immaturity was due to its political leaders.[46] On
the contrary, history had vindicated the National Liberals' sense of
political foreboding, a fact Weber sought to ram home to those whom
he saw as the far less percipient members of the contemporary middle
class: "a Caesarist figure like Bismarck," and a "Caesarist regime"
like his (Weber 1978a:1452, 1413 = 1958:382, 335) were rare occur-
rences—"At best, a genius appears once in several centuries" (Weber
1978a:1387 = 1958:301)—and it was time the nation grew up and
threw off a political system ripe not for a Bismarckian epiphany, but
fertile only for a posturing literati, an histrionic Kaiser intoxicated by
his own vanity, and an arthritic parliamentarianism constitutionally
destitute of the capacity to exercise real power and responsible leadership.

   I come now to the third reproach that Weber levelled against
Bismarck's "Caesarism," one that focused on its illegitimacy. We might
recall Weber's earlier comment that Bismarck "misused monarchic
sentiments as a cover for his power interests in the struggle of the
parties." Or, if that statement is not explicit enough in binding together
the elements of Bismarckian governance, illegitimacy and Caesarism,
then consider Weber's comment that "one of the worst legacies of
Bismarck's rule has been the fact that he considered it necessary to
seek cover for his Caesarist regime *behind the legitimacy of the mon-*

arch" (Weber 1978a:1413 = 1958:335),[47] a remark that seems to make the affinity sufficiently transparent.

The observation that Caesarism involves an illegitimate form of rule was, as we saw in the previous chapter, hardly an original insight. By Weber's day, however, it was possible to delineate it not only in relation to the two Napoleons but Bismarck also. What was the connection between these men and their regimes? We are given some clues in a tricky passage in "Parliament and Government." Because of the importance of this passage, notable for the plethora of references to Caesarism it contains, I propose to quote it at some length. The context of Weber's discussion is the issue of "the relationship between democracy and parliamentarism:"

> Active mass democratization means that the political leader is no longer proclaimed a candidate because he has proved himself in a circle of *honoratiores*, then becoming a leader because of his parliamentary accomplishments, but that he gains the trust and the faith of the masses in him and his power with the means of *mass* demagogy. In substance, this means a shift toward the *Caesarist* mode of selection. Indeed, every democracy tends in this direction. After all, the specifically Caesarist technique is the plebiscite. It is not an ordinary vote or election, but a profession of faith in the calling of him who demands these acclamations. The Caesarist leader rises either in a military fashion, as a military dictator like Napoleon I, who had his position affirmed through a plebiscite; or he rises in the bourgeois fashion: through plebiscitary affirmation, acquiesced in by the army, of a claim to power on the part of a non-military politician, such as Napoleon III. Both avenues are as antagonistic to the parliamentary principle as they are (of course) to the legitimism of the hereditary monarchy. Every kind of direct *popular election* of the supreme ruler and, beyond that, every kind of political power that rests on the confidence of the masses and not of parliament—this includes also the position of a popular military hero like Hindenburg—lies on the road to these 'pure' forms of Caesarist acclamation. In particular, this is true of the position of the President of the United States, whose superiority over parliament derives from his (formally) democratic nomination and election. The hopes that a Caesarist figure like Bismarck attached to universal suffrage and the manner of his antiparliamentary demagogy also point in the same direction, although they were adapted, in formulation and phraseology, to the given legitimist conditions of his ministerial position. The circumstances of Bismarck's departure from office demonstrate the manner in which hereditary legitimism reacts against these Caesarist powers. Every parliamentary democracy eagerly seeks to eliminate, as dangerous to parliament's power, the plebiscitary methods of leadership selection.[48] (Weber 1978a:1451–52=1958:381–82)

From this historical dissertation we learn at least something about the genus of Caesarism, modelled on the Napoleonic experience, and its Bismarckian species. The genus of Caesarism that the account suggests might be represented thus:

a. Mode of selection (i.e., leadership route): military *or* civil ("bourgeois")
b. Mode of acclamation: plebiscitary
c. Relation to parliament: antagonistic
d. Relation to hereditary legitimism: antagonistic
e. Conditions of existence: political democratization.

And what of Bismarck? Glossing somewhat, his mode of selection is "civil" (he is called on by his monarch to become minister president, and though a strategist is not a general);[49] his mode of acclamation is plebiscitary (albeit in the most loose and most unsatisfying of senses—historians will wince at Weber's procrustean tendencies): he is a "demagogue" who leads from the front and who is willing and able to dissolve parliament and appeal to the people for support of his policies;[50] his relation to parliament is antagonistic, particularly when it will not succumb to his commands (at which point Bismarck countenances coups d'état);[51] his relation to the Hohenzollerns is uneasy in that despite constitutional authority ultimately residing in the Emperor, it is Bismarck himself, ostensible agent of the sovereign, who de facto rules the Reich (a situation Wilhelm II would eventually rudely correct);[52] and, finally, his political orchestration takes place within a society that, though far from socially democratic, sanctions universal manhood suffrage.

So it is that Bismarck can be reckoned, in Weber's account, the embodiment of a Caesarist ruler. I shall be returning to the wider issue of Caesarism, parliament, and democracy in the next section and so shall say nothing more about those matters here. However, and somewhat in anticipation, it is worth remarking on an ambiguity of Weber's treatment concerning the question of Caesarist illegitimacy. In *Economy and Society*, though not only there, Weber deals with the two Bonapartes under the rubric of charisma, and also presents the idea of Caesarism as a sociological subtype of his famous leadership concept. Charisma happens to be one of Weber's trinity of *legitimate* domination, so the question arises as to how it is possible for Caesarism to be designated as illegitimate in one context (the discussion of the Bonapartes in "Parliament and Government") and yet, tacitly related to charismatic legitimacy in another?[53] The answer is simply that Weber is using the concept of legitimacy to mean different things. Caesarism is *il*legitimate only in the constitutional sense that it is a type of rule devoid of a hereditary, dynastic foundation. A Bourbon, Habsburg, or Hohenzollern monarch could never be labelled "Caesarist,"[54] nor could any other monarchy of venerable lineage. By contrast Caesarism necessarily assumes the stamp of legitimacy if we look at it from Weber's *sociological* angle: here it is legitimate to the extent that it elicits from a group of people, who believes in the moral authority of the Caesarist leader's mission, their voluntary compliance: Weber says as much in his remark that "active mass democratisation means that the political leader...gains the trust and the faith of the masses in him" and so on.

* * *

Bismarck was not the only person to be called "Caesarist" by Weber—the two Bonapartes (as we have just seen), Pericles, Cleon, Gladstone, Ferdinand Lassalle, and David Lloyd George were all to enjoy that dubious honour[55]—but, in the end, it is the Iron Chancellor who supremely holds this title. No one, not even the Bonapartes, is referred to as Caesarist more often than he, though I am not concerned here with the question of how far the regimes of the Bonapartes and the governance of Bismarck were in fact comparable political formations.[56] Instead I now turn to the second, and much more positive way that Weber interpreted modern Caesarism.

Caesarism and Parliamentary Democracy

Weber's critique of Bismarck drew on an established nineteenth-century tradition in which Caesarism was deplored as harmful and threatening. That tradition, however, also often insisted on a quite sharp distinction between parliamentary forms of representation and "democracy," a term that for most of the nineteenth century still carried menacing associations. For the modern reader, this distinction is likely to appear somewhat strange since we have become habituated to a notion of "parliamentary democracy" that, in an earlier epoch, would have been considered to elide two very different, probably incompatible, political phenomena. On the one hand, "democracy" conjured up mob rule or, later, a mass electorate dangerously capable of ceding power to a Caesarist demagogue. On the other, educated people were well aware that representative assemblies of privileged orders and classes had in Europe long existed without any trace of extensive, popular involvement; depending on their nationality such people might have thought of the Spanish Cortes, the French Estates General, the

German Landtag, the Polish Sejm, the Swedish Riksdag, the Serbian Sabor, or the British parliament itself as examples of predemocratic institutions.[57]

In contrast, Max Weber's view anticipated, just as it helped imperceptibly to shape, the modern position. He acknowledged that "Parliamentarisation and democratisation are not necessarily interdependent, but often opposed to one another." Where he differed from most of his liberal and conservative predecessors, however, and from a number of his German contemporaries on both the political left and right as well, was in his conviction that parliament was an irreplaceable political mechanism for securing, and medium for expressing, the consent of the governed; that the "existence and formal power position of the parliaments [were] not threatened by democratic suffrage" (Weber 1978a:1442–3 = 1958:371); and that the institutions of parliament and democracy were in principle capable of functioning symbiotically—indeed were already so functioning in the United States and Great Britain to their enormous national benefit.[58] If government in Germany had failed in recent decades this was not due to the influence of parliamentary democracy so much as the result of national institutional pathologies that had rendered parliament an impotent talking shop repugnant to men of will, ability, and responsibility; such a state of affairs constitutional change might remedy, Weber declared. Moreover, instead of defensively denying that democracy results in Caesarism, Weber stridently reaffirmed the equation, simultaneously imparting to it his own peculiar twist. Caesarism offered Germany an opportunity for its own political revitalization, Weber insisted, provided it assumed forms analogous to those of the British prime minister or the American president, and eschewed the Bismarckian example. The point was not to bemoan Caesarism but to learn how to cultivate it; not to reject it *in toto*, but to mobilize its possibilities for national leadership and mass containment, while at the same time ensuring, through its insertion into a vibrant, watchful parliamentary electoral system, that the Caesarist leadership was deterred from making inroads into fundamental civil liberties. In addition, it would remain ultimately accountable to the voting public who might, or might not, choose to reelect it. In such a way did the overwhelmingly negative association of Caesarism with Bismarck's governance *coincide* with a much more constructive view of Caesarism within a vibrant parliamentary-democratic system.

This, in any event, was Weber's standpoint as he articulated it during the Great War. Underlying it was an historical analysis of the rise of democracy and its implications for the parliamentary system to which I now must turn.

* * *

Though Weber sometimes depicted modern democracy as a product of the French Revolution and its aftermath, his discussion of Caesarism was concerned with a much more specific process: the extension of the suffrage to the little-propertied and to the working class. Politically, democracy "means simply that no formal inequality of political rights exists between the individual classes of the population" (Weber [1918] 1972:194 = 1924a:494)[59] and of course the supreme expression of political inequality is the prohibition on the general right to vote. The movement towards universal suffrage, conversely, signalled the gradual removal of this prohibition, an emancipatory process of the most fateful moment because in conjunction with its realization emerged an institution without which contemporary parliamentary Caesarism, as Weber depicts it, is impossible to imagine: the modern mass party system.

The rise of the modern mass party was by no means a smooth and effortless ascent for in its path stood the so-called "notable" form of party organization, founded upon an exclusive franchise and characteristic of the bourgeoisie's early parliamentary development, the vested interests and style of life of which could be counted on stubbornly to resist the new vulgarity. Since Weber's contrast between these two modes of party organization is quite well known it will be dealt with here only briefly; furthermore, though Weber did actually trace the evolution of the notables in a number of countries including his own (their far from vestigial influence on the Germany of his day confirmed his worst fears about the Reich's political backwardness) I shall confine my comments almost exclusively to the English case: this is done for reasons of economy but also because it was always to England that Weber looked for the paradigmatic case of the notable system's rise and fall, as well as for the classic example more generally of the route to political modernity by whose benchmark the rest of Europe might best properly be measured and evaluated.

The halcyon days of the English notables (or *honoratiores*) stretched approximately from the eighteenth to the mid-nineteenth century, the notables themselves being a status-group of bourgeois patricians, that is, of gentlemen of private wealth—rich farmers, rentiers, and lawyers, for instance—respected in their communities as people of substance, and equipped with the material means and inner disposition to live "for" politics. Reflecting the limited public sphere to which the notables addressed themselves, their politics was fundamentally that of class nepotism. On the one hand, it was they who, composing and controlling the party committees and the elite clubs of the local, privileged middle class, selected those parliamentary candidates whom it was thought would most competently and assiduously represent notable class, family, and ideological interests; on the other hand, successful candidates themselves could be expected to hail from notable circles. As for the everyday practice of politics, the notable system functioned on an essentially ad hoc and decentralized basis. Outside parliament, the parties consisted of relatively loose and malleable affiliations, bound together by issues of provincial mutual concern as well as by tribal cultural identities. Lacking a paid, regular, professional officialdom, party administration was dispensed predominantly by amateurs, offering their services for the most part gratis: what motivated this primitive organization to do its work was not pecuniary compensation so much as the glamour and prestige that political involvement was felt to bestow on its agents, itself a striking index, a modern person might be led to suppose, of the notable system's antiquity. Inside parliament, meanwhile, the elected notables would congregate in their respective parties but usually in a flexible manner, expected to toe the party "line" but nonetheless capable of exerting their independence where, say, local issue or religious conviction might seem to demand it: in short, the member retained, as MP, a degree of autonomy rare in the lobby-whipped modern House of Commons. Finally, under the notable system, there was no question but that parliament itself was the definitive locus of political authority and of political patronage: it was *within* parliament that a member's advancement was decided, a career contingent not upon his demagogic or plebiscitary qualities but upon parliamentary skill and the support of the party leader (Weber 1970a:100–2 = 1958:518–20; 1978b:290–92 = 1964:215–17).

It was precisely this configuration of amateur local party politics and parliamentary sovereignty that was shattered by "the advent of *plebiscitarian* democracy" by, that is, the democratization of the suffrage. The modern mass parties are the consequence, "the children of democracy, of mass franchise, of the necessity to woo and organise the masses, and develop the utmost unity of direction and the strictest discipline" (Weber 1970a:102–3 = 1958:520–21). And it is the mass party system that at one and the same time underpins and depends upon the Caesarist leader.

The extension of the suffrage had a number of consequences for the structure of the party system, all of which transformed it fundamentally. The bureaucratization that "inevitably accompanies modern *mass* democracy" (Weber 1978b:983 = 1964:723)[60]—"inevitably" because the realization of the formal demand for political equality necessarily generates a state apparatus charged with the administration of that achievement—is mightily reinforced by the related bureaucratization of the party system itself. The latter in turn squeezes out by stages the notables' influence on local politics that now succumbs to the salaried, career party officials and the highly disciplined professional politicians whom they serve. "The rule of notables and guidance by members of parliament ceases. 'Professional' politicians *outside* the parliaments take the organisation in hand" (Weber 1970a:102 = 1958:520). The party machine is born: that electoral engine organized around the extraparliamentary caucus (already established in the U.S. by the 1840s, developed in Britain towards the end of the 1860s), primed and regulated by its characteristic figure, "the American boss and the English election agent," dedicated fulltime to the activity of grooming the demagogic candidate and of winning elections. To this end a number of conditions must be secured: party coffers must receive the steady flow of subscriptions, contributions, and affiliation fees necessary to run a campaign and pay the staff; newspapers, advertising bureaus and schools must be established to propagate the party wisdom and to train political agitators in the skills of public speaking and persuasion; and, of course the electors themselves must be mobilized and corralled into the polling booths so to translate their preferences into votes (Weber 1978a:1443–45 = 1958:372–74). Without a doubt the machine's job is a formidable one; but under conditions of democratized suffrage it must be done, and done efficiently if the party is to monopolize the highest offices of state and be in a position to provide the sinecures and benefices its members crave.

The paradox of this political democratization is, for Weber, unmistakeable. Formally, power is vested in the party membership, the active among whom fashion and superintend policy at conference that parliamentary representatives then ostensibly execute; more distantly it might be said that parliament carries out the will of the people at large. But the reality is very different, since effective power is concentrated in a manner that scoffs at all notions of substantive participatory democracy. In the first place, "power rests in the hands of those who, within the organisation, handle the work *continuously*"— that is to say the machine's bureaucracy and its head—and those who provide the organization with financial backing and personal assistance (Weber 1970a:103 = 1958:520). It is invariably a hard core of professionals that drafts the party program, plans tactics, and selects candidates, even in the most professedly democratic parties. As for the voters the parties seek to attract, they "exert influence only to the extent that programmes and candidates are adapted and selected according to their chances of receiving electoral support" (Weber 1978a:1396 = 1958:312). In the second place, and at the apex of the power pyramid, this machine itself, willingly or in the last resort, falls into line behind a leader whose demagogic ability to attain the highest parliamentary office will ensure its own continued existence or growth. In effect, the machine becomes the leader's personal clientele, following him out of a fluid combination of inspired devotion to his unique qualities and calculated want-satisfaction. Taking the English case Weber declares:

> the parties are forced by the "Caesarist" feature of mass democracy to submit to men with political temperament and talent as soon as these prove that they can win the confidence of the masses. The chance for a potential leader to get to the top is a function, as it turns out time and again, of the parties' *power chances*. Neither the parties' Caesarist character and mass demagogy nor their bureaucratization and stereotyped public image are in themselves a rigid barrier for the rise of leaders. Especially the well organised parties that really want to exercise state power must *subordinate* themselves to those who hold the confidence of the masses, *if* they are men with leadership abilities.[61] (Weber 1978a:1459=1858:391)

But of course it is not only the party machine that must subordinate itself to the person who holds "the confidence of the masses"; the parliamentary deputies of the demagogue's party must also do so. For in a party "oriented toward sharing governmental power and responsibility" every member knows

> that the survival of the party and of all the interests which bind him to it depends upon its subordination to qualified leaders. Nowhere in the world, not even in

England, can the parliamentary body as such govern and determine policies. The broad mass of deputies functions *only* as a following for the leader or the cabinet who form the government, and it blindly follows them *as long as* they are successful. *This is the way it should be.* Political action is always determined by the "principle of small numbers," that means, the superior political maneuverability of small leading groups. In *mass states* this impact of Caesarism is ineradicable.[62] (Weber 1978a:1414 = 1958:336)

Inexorably, then, the mass vote cedes power to the officialdom of the party machine, while the machine and the back-benchers are themselves beholden to the party leader. Everything turns on the ability of that leader to capture the imagination of the masses, as Gladstone showed himself so brilliantly capable of doing. In this case, the machine's victory over the notables was due to "the fascination of Gladstone's 'grand' demagogy, the firm belief of the masses in the ethical substance of his policy, and above all, their belief in the ethical character of his personality. It soon became obvious that a Caesarist plebiscitarian element in politics—the dictator of the battlefield of elections—had appeared on the plain" (Weber 1970a:106 = 1958:523).[63] However, Weber continued, while the masses are crucial in a "democratized" society as the means through which leaders are acclaimed, and in this most limited of senses "selected," their political functions are more or less exhausted with the exercise of that acclamatory imprimatur and its threatened withdrawal. Even their "choice" of leader is to a large extent foisted upon them since "it is not the politically passive 'mass' that produces the leader from its midst, but the political leader [who] recruits his following and wins the mass through 'demagogy'"(Weber 1978a:1457 = 1958:389).[64] Mass politics, it thus appears, is democratic in name only, "apparently democratic" (Weber 1970a:105 = 1958:523), but not really so. That "the great political decisions, even and especially in a democracy, are unavoidably made by a few men" (Weber 1978a:1452 = 1958:383),[65] Weber accepted as the most elementary datum that only the intellectually dogmatic could fail to acknowledge. The mass suffrage, the modern party machine, and parliament, hence, were for Weber all locked into the same system of political domination. All three institutions provided the conditions of existence of the Caesarist figure; all three submitted, in their different ways, to his regime.

*   *   *

So far we have seen that, in the new post-"notable" situation, the party machine, emotionally and materially dependent on the leader it serves, organizes the masses to deliver their vote at election times. The status and autonomy of the ordinary parliamentary deputy suffers a corresponding degradation. By contrast to an earlier era of politics, the MP becomes little more than lobby-fodder, a minion dangling on the string of the party leader's preferment and success. It is a scenario that might lead one to conclude that parliament's role is confined exclusively to that of providing party leaders with a loyal retinue, and it is undeniable that this emphasis is often paramount in Weber's descriptions of modern democracy. But in other places, especially where Weber is attempting to convince his contemporaries of the dangerously outmoded character of the German parliament as measured against its British counterpart, the accent is quite different. For then it is part of Weber's argument that a parliament armed with the constitutional powers necessary to engage in "positive" politics, to engage that is in the responsible exercise of real power, might function as an indispensable means of Caesarist selection and control. Clearly, then, as Weber explains it, modern parliament has a twin aspect: though the individual deputy may to a large extent be diminished by the party leader's prominence, the *institutions* afforded by a strong parliament are able to perform functions of Caesarist processing and monitoring that make it far from redundant. On the contrary, if responsible Caesarism is to be achieved, a parliament engaging in "positive" politics is absolutely vital for the nation's well being. What I shall do now is explore more fully both sides of parliament's position, namely, its disabilities and capacities. In the process it will become clearer what is specifically "Caesarist" as opposed to just vaguely dictatorial about the modern heads of state in Britain and the U.S., the national examples that fascinated Weber and to which he constantly returned.

With the coming of the democratized suffrage, Weber tells us, the mediatory and representative integrity of parliament becomes doubly enfeebled. On the one hand, the hero-worshipping propensity of the masses finds its target in the person, the party leader, who knows best how to appeal to emotion and credulity; on the other hand, it is to the people at large that this leader must periodically report for endorsement for dismissal. Crucially then, the power-base of the demagogue lies in the country at large, not parliament first and foremost; and it is above parliament he stands when in government as a "plebiscitarian dictator" (Weber 1970a:107 = 1958:524). Ostrogorski ([1902] 1970), on whose account of plebiscitary politics Weber leans heavily in *Politics as a Vocation*,[66] described this effective circumvention of parliament in the following way:

> Raised above the levelled crowd of M.P.s, the leaders now lean directly on the great mass of voters, whose feelings of loyalty go straight to the leaders over the heads of the Members...Always requiring to look up to some one, the English voter naturally transfers to the great leader the respect and devotion which he no longer has the opportunity or need of bestowing on the Member for the division. Here, again, the "intermediate ranks" to which Montesquieu refers are done away with or obliterated, the door being open to a sort of popular Caesarism, with which the great chief of the party has become invested. No doubt the highly magnetic personalities of Mr. Gladstone and Lord Beaconsfield have powerfully contributed to set up the Caesarean supremacy of the leaders, but it was sufficiently developed by the situation which I have just described to enable their successors, who lacked the gift of impressing the popular imagination, to obtain the usufruct of this power over the masses. This being so, the elections have assumed the character of personal plebiscites, each constituency voting not so much for this or that candidate as for Mr. Gladstone or against Lord Beaconsfield or Lord Salisbury.[67] (Ostrogorski 1970 I:608)

Ostrogorski deplored many aspects of this state of affairs, and Robert Michels was highly contemptuous of it: "In the history of party life," he would say, "it is undeniable that the democratic system is reduced, in ultimate analysis, to the right of the masses, at stated intervals to choose masters to whom in the interim they owe unconditional obedience" (Michels 1959:222).[68] Weber's position, in contrast, was far more resigned to a situation it was impossible to change in any fundamental way. "Caesarism," Weber abbreviates in "Suffrage and Democracy" *is* "the election of the leader" (1958:279) and under modern conditions it cannot be evaded. Moreover, Weber applies this perspective not only to the election of national leaders such as the British prime minister and the American president, but equally to the election of leaders of much smaller political units such as the American city mayor. As Weber puts it: "in the broadest sense of the word," Caesarism means "the direct popular election of the head of state or head of the city, as in the United States and some of their large councils" (Weber 1958:277). Further, the designation "Caesarism" implies for Weber something more than direct election: it also suggests a certain kind of recruitment and executive stance—in a word, administration—in which the leader himself independently appoints his officials, selecting them "freely and personally without regard to tradition or to any other impediments" and ruling over them as "the unrestrained master" (Weber 1978b:961 = 1964:707). Evidently, in this discussion of "Caesarist" administration Weber was thinking primarily of the American scene with its spoils system—Weber (1970a:108 = 1958:526) describes the president ("elected by plebiscite") as "the chief of office-patronage"[69]— for he would have known perfectly well that, in Britain, civil service career continuity obtains for all but the very highest departmental posts. So what is it, then, that British and American practices share that permits them to be placed under a Caesarist rubric?[70]

Like his American counterparts, the British Prime Minister owes his tenure, status, and power to the devotion of the masses; he is their "free trustee," and though not technically (constitutionally) directly elected to the highest office of state is actually so elected in all but form: in voting for the individual candidates who compose his party, the masses, Weber argues, are essentially and in effect voting for the leader at the party's head, for it is he who inspires them and he whom they wish to see govern. The parliamentary candidates are, thus, mere vehicles of the electorate, a means by which that electorate affirms a commitment to the person who towers over his colleagues as their chief.[71] Second, like his American counterparts too, the premier's mass base affords him great autonomy in relation to both the machine that serves him and the parliament at whose head he stands. While in a "democratized hereditary" monarchical system such as Britain's the "Caesarist-plebiscitarian element is always much attenuated," particularly when contrasted to "the President of the United States, whose superiority over parliament derives from his (formally) democratic nomination and election," it is certainly "not absent," a conclusion Weber sought to illustrate with the example of Lloyd George. Lloyd George's position during the Great War, Weber maintained, was "based *not* at all on the confidence of parliament and its parties, but on that of the masses in the country and of the army in the field. Parliament acquiesces (with considerable reluctance)" (Weber 1978a:1452 = 1958:382–83).[72] Finally, Weber construed the American and British political systems to be similar in the extent of the enormous powers of patronage invested in their leaders (Weber 1970:106–8 = 1958:523–26).

Hence, parliament's mediatory and representative role vis-a-vis the electorate is to a large extent effectively short-circuited by the modern

Caesarist leader towards whom parliament feels understandably ambivalent. On the one hand, "every parliamentary democracy eagerly
seeks to eliminate, as dangerous to parliament's power, the plebiscitary
methods of leadership selection" (Weber 1978a:1452 = 1958:382) that
inevitably prove corrosive to the power and standing of the assembly.
Yet on the other hand, since the fate of the ordinary member is inextricably tied to the fortunes and popularity of the leader, the former has a
sort of perverse interest in his or her own continued subservience.
However, Weber's conclusion is not that parliament per se is a body
without function or relevance. Assuredly, to the extent that it resembles
the case of the German Second Empire, and is constitutionally reduced
to a mere talking shop; stripped of all powers save that of the legislative veto; politically displaced by the authoritarian state bureaucracy
that makes all the crucial decisions in domestic and foreign policy;
and is hence "excluded from positive participation in the direction of
political affairs"[73]; it will be little more than a "mere drag-chain, an
assembly of impotent fault-finders and know-it-alls" (Weber
1978a:1408 = 1958:327–28). Indeed the constitutional arrangements
of the *Kaiserreich* more or less ensured that those people with the
instinct for power and the capacity for independent judgment were
funnelled by "negative selection" into vocations other than the parliamentary one, aware that all that awaited them in the chamber was
frustration and emasculation. Essentially, the parliamentary system in
Germany had been organized in such a manner as to guarantee its
enervation. Subject to unofficial, often hidden, patronage by the bureaucracy and by big business; capable of little more than posturing
intransigence and irresponsibility in which ideological party purity
(the SPD) or fear about the material consequences for their position
(notably, the Catholic Center) became a substitute for compromise and
real power; and deprived of the minimum material facilities—crucially, an office and staff—to do the job properly, it was little wonder
that parliament functioned merely as the purveyor of negative, token
politics.[74] One still had Caesarism, but it was of the Bismarckian type.
But parliament need not be restricted to this subaltern role, and the
Caesarism it coexists with and promotes need not be of this debilitating kind.

It has been said that "Weber's theory of Parliamentary government
was an attempt to secure the advantages of the Caesarist leader without the disadvantages associated with Bismarck's rule," (Beetham

1985:238) and those advantages were no more obvious than in a strong, positive parliamentary system like Britain's. There, parliament was not only able to discharge those general functions that make the institution "indispensable in the electoral democracies"—operating as "an organ of public control of the officials and of really 'public' administration, as a means for the elimination of unfit top officials, as a locus for establishing the budget and for reaching compromises among parties" (Weber 1978a:1457 = 1958:388).[75] It was also in a position to produce the responsible Caesarist figure from its midst, his personality forged in the heat of party struggle, his political metal tested by his colleagues and proven on the floor of the House (and not just at the hustings), his native wit and ambition supplemented by an education derived from the stringent standards demanded in the parliamentary committee. Naturally, the Caesarist British leader is by definition a demagogue. What matters to Weber is that, unlike Bismarck, he can be given rein *and* controlled as well, and that the system of which he is part promotes in him a sense of realism and responsibility. Weber wrote:

> Today political (and military) leaders no longer wield the sword but resort to quite prosaic sound waves and ink drops: written and spoken *words*. What matters is that intelligence and knowledge, strong will and sober experience determine these words, whether they be commands or campaign speeches, diplomatic notes or official statements in parliament. (Weber 1978a:1419–20 = 1958:342)

In its turn, a strong parliamentary system in the British mould provided the conditions most conducive to such effective political leadership. Notably, it furnished "a suitable political proving ground of the politicians wooing the confidence of the masses," while lessening the possibility that leaders would be selected on merely "emotional" grounds (Weber 1978a:1452, 1459 = 1958:383, 391). In addition, a parliament equipped with real power was able to supervise the Caesarist leader once installed as head of the executive, monitoring his activities[76] within the chamber, and, by extension, helping to publicize them in the constituencies and through the media. These functions of parliament are critical if the leader is going to respect "established constitutional arrangements," Weber acknowledged (1978a:1459 = 1958:391).

Equally, a vibrant parliament is organized to ensure the political system's continuity in the event of a period in which "no one appears to hold the confidence of the masses to a fairly general degree," and in the event of a problem of leadership succession. As Weber puts it, "everywhere the problem of succession has been the Achilles heel of purely Caesarist domination. The rise, neutralisation and elimination of a Caesarist leader occur most easily without the danger of a domestic catastrophe when the effective co-domination of powerful representative bodies preserves the political continuity and the constitutional guarantees of civil order" (Weber 1978a:1457 = 1958:389).[77]

Parliament thus contributes to responsible Caesarism when it is able to stand as the guardian of civil liberties—a host of rights that the Caesarist leader, left entirely to his own devices, might otherwise imperiously seek to dismantle—and when it is able to ensure "the peaceful elimination of the Caesarist dictator once he has lost the trust of the masses" (Weber 1978a:1452 = 1958:383).

Such were the advantages that accrued, Weber argued, to a virile, as distinct from a token, parliamentary system. They constituted not only a sum of constitutional mechanisms to empower political dynamism at home, and the pursuit of an imperialist policy abroad,[78] but also a set of conditions in which genuine statesmen, rather than bureaucrats and placemen, could find a home. For the character of political leaders was inseparable from the institutional structures that allowed them expression. A token parliament encouraged token leaders; it succoured opportunism and ideological posturing. A strong parliament, by contrast, conduced to the selection and enculturation of those "three preeminent qualities" (besides the obligatory will to power) that Weber believed "decisive" for the politician worthy of his vocation: "passionate devotion to a 'cause,' to the god or demon who is its overlord" combined with realism; "a feeling of responsibility" for the results of one's actions; and "a sense of proportion," ("the decisive psychological quality of the politician"), a sense, that is, of "distance to things and men," the ability of the politician "to let realities work upon him with inner concentration and calmness." Of course this ideal combination of qualities, whose essence is perspective and inner discipline ("that firm taming of the soul") is not an exclusive property of any person or any system; in any case, it is a rare individual who will prove able to bear the tensions it imposes on him. But there are some political systems that crush potential, and others that call it forth. The ideal leader in a "democratic" society will have gained his spurs in the latter type; he will be in a position "to put his hand on the wheel of history,"[79] complemented by a parliamentary structure that will be there to watch the wheel's direction and ensure that, in extremis, it can be stopped before flattening all in its path.

* * *

As a general description of the way things actually run in liberal-democratic polities, Weber's account is still immensely illuminating. However, Weber offered more to his German contemporaries than sober political analysis or the injunction to face hard facts. Simultaneously, he was recommending a model of Caesarism deeply congruent with his own values. Operating within a robust parliamentary framework, Caesarism promised not only to make Germany a modern world power in which national greatness would be balanced with civil liberty. It also afforded the necessary scope for those supremely willful and gifted individuals to realize their values in history. This conflation of normative and descriptive elements in Weber's account is by no means a trivial issue. Because the model Weber examines is the same one that he wishes to see imitated, there is no substantial attempt to criticize it, or to think about a more expansive sense of politics and democracy. On the contrary, Weber's readers are essentially invited to make a choice between a Caesarism that is debilitating—the Bismarckian variety and its bungling continuation in the "personal rule" of Wilhelm II—and a Caesarism of energetic and productive disposition typical of Britain and America. The point is that we get some sort of Caesarism either way.

That there is something claustrophobic about such an alternative will be evident to anyone whose conception of politics and its compass is less restrictive than Weber's. We will see in the next chapter how his diagnosis rested on an account of mass behavior, and a definition of politics itself, that made such exclusivity all but inescapable. Moreover, while it is no *criticism* of Weber's work to emphasize its distance from the republican tradition—it makes little sense to evaluate his work on the grounds of a tradition on which he did not stand— it remains historically pertinent for this book to do so, particularly since Weber's relationship to that tradition has recently been underlined by one of his most sophisticated interpreters (Hennis 1988:196– 97). In fact, it is Weber's divergence from republicanism, rather than his connection to it, that is striking. The contrast goes way beyond the positive connotations that now attach to a name that for republicans conjured up the most heinous aspects of political corruption. Nor should the heroic cast assumed by the Caesarist leader in Weber's work be thought comparable to the republican quest for glory. The parliamentary Caesarist leader is Weber's political answer not simply to Germany's travails, but to a crisis of liberalism more generally. That crisis—absent from the republican experience—arose from a combination of circumstances whose main legacy was the squeeze on human initiative attendant on the growth of massive public and private bureaucracies. Modern people, Weber noted, were implicated in organizations that were procrustean in nature, typically demanding order, routine, and standardization from their incumbents. Long gone was the "practical, world-shaping individualism that had characterised the bourgeoisie in its period of ascendancy" (Beetham 1989:321). Responsible Caesarism, with its combination of discipline and autonomous leadership, offered the best bet for a world that was becoming increasingly rigid, conformist, and philistine. If Caesarism involved "demagogy," then so be it; that was a price well worth paying to stave off bureaucratic stultification.

In contrast, wherever republicans had invoked "demagogy" they had normally done so either as an insult or as a warning. Classical and other republicans may not have been radical democrats, but nor did they envisage politics as a largely acclamatory process in which a passive and incredulous mass endorsed a charismatic figure; nor was "dictatorship" envisaged as a normal mode of political leadership. The "devotion" or "sacrifice" (*Hingabe*) inspired in the followers of the Caesarist leader, Weber argued, is for the *person* of that leader as he seeks singularly to project and realise his values. Republicans, on the other hand, were more likely to see service and duty owed first and foremost to the polity itself. Leaders were glorious and entitled to respect to the degree that they exemplified, and sacrificed themselves to, the greater interest of the commonwealth. Political self-governance enshrined a collective sense of liberty; it did not harbor the Weberian view that there is something admirable about individual autonomy as such, particularly as the locus of value-creation.

I have been careful to say that a contrast of Weber with republican traditions is not thereby a criticism of his political views. The times that Weber lived in raised urgent questions and challenges that republican thought was ill-equipped to face: above all, the rapid expansion of a modern proletariat, "mass" electoral democracy, bureaucracy, and the emergence of a modern great power geopolitical system. I am more concerned to trace the impoverishment of republicanism, than to tax the greatest German "liberal" of his age for not subscribing to it. Yet the nagging problem remains that since Weber's description of Anglophone Caesarism is simultaneously a personal endorsement of that model as a political template, it generates no normative criteria or analytical resources with which it might be evaluated. Moreover, it is historically noteworthy to recall that the fragility of Weber's "solution" to the crisis of German politics—Caesarism within a sturdy parliamentary system—became evident when, after the First World War, he felt compelled to abandon its equilibrium of civil liberty and command, and argue instead for a largely plebiscitarian remedy for Germany's plight. We cannot be sure that Weber was wrong to reason the way he did when we consider the situation he faced after the First World War. What we can say with some certainty, however, is that Weber's super-plebiscitary strategy failed to secure either order *or* liberty in Germany. Weber's reasoning, its background, and its relationship to Caesarism are examined next.

The Reich President

In the period during and immediately after the First World War, Weber's political interventions reached their crescendo.[80] There was much to fill the liberal nationalist with anger and foreboding: the highly publicized rantings of an intemperate emperor unrestrained by the national parliament, the irresponsibility of pan-German agitation, the unrealistic expectations that cleaved to the demands for unlimited submarine warfare, the machinations of the Supreme Command, the Russian Revolution and the Brest-Litovsk debacle, and, of course, the great defeat itself and its aftermath—Wilson's humiliating cat-and-mouse diplomacy, naval mutiny at Kiel and at other ports in north Germany, insurrection in Berlin and Bavaria. Faced with all of this Weber had not hesitated to ventilate his opinions with a frankness that impressed most who knew of them. But Weber's sphere of action was limited. As a scholar by vocation he was obliged to engage in politics through the media intellectuals customarily use: the public lecture, the congress speech and report, the memorandum to persons of influence, the newspaper article (in November-December 1918 he was actually living in Frankfurt as the political advisor for the *Frankfurter Zeitung*) with the intention of moulding informed opinion in conformity with his own. He could only hope that policymakers would listen to his arguments and be persuaded by their logic. But in December 1918, and thus a good five months before the presentation of allied peace conditions that the German delegation at Versailles would eventually be compelled to accept, Weber was given the opportunity to do more than air his political preference for Germany's constitutional future in the ebullient atmosphere of a public debating hall or in the columns of a prestigious daily paper. At the instigation of Hugo Preuss (the secretary of state for the interior), Weber was invited to join the committee charged with the responsibility for drafting what would become known as the Weimar Constitution:[81] at last the man of letters might become truly a man of palpable political influence. The committee's deliberations and conclusions, as we shall see, were not wholly to disappoint him. Even after six drafts of the constitution, the last two conditioned by heated discussion on the floor of the National Parliament, the final product endorsed on July 31, 1919, would carry a recognizably Weberian stamp.

Directly preceding and following his cloistered involvement in Preuss's committee, Weber wrote a series of constitutionally oriented articles in which he publicly campaigned for a plebiscitarian Reich president. These texts need to be situated in the overall development of Weber's thought for they mark a major reappraisal of the conditions he thought most likely to produce effective political leadership in the German situation.

During the latter part of the war, Weber had argued that a vigorous parliamentary democracy of the British type was the model system for Germany to adopt if it were to produce the leaders of energetic intelligence necessary for national reconstruction. Weber's argument was examined at length in the previous section. His postwar writings, in contrast, entertain few hopes that parliamentary government could furnish the political conditions imperative for dynamic leadership in Germany. On the contrary, Weber now insisted that the "necessity for a leader to provide decisive political direction and a focus for national unity could now only be met by divorcing him from Parliament and giving him a separate power base in a direct presidential election" (Beetham 1985:232).[82] Weber, in effect, had given up on the German parliament as a recruiting ground for national leadership. The reasons for what would prove to be an irrevocable disenchantment are the reverse side of the coin that impelled Weber to argue for a Reich president elected not by Parliament (as happened, to Weber's great consternation, on February 11, 1919, when Friedrich Ebert was exalted to the Republic's highest executive office) but by the people as a whole. The rest of this section is devoted to a summary of Weber's argument and its relationship to Caesarism. Two published sources are especially pertinent for understanding Weber's constitutional change of heart: first, the series of articles printed originally in the *Frankfurter Zeitung* during November and the first week of December 1918, then issued by the same paper's publishing house as a pamphlet entitled "Germany's Future Constitution" in January 1919;[83] second, the piece for the *Berliner Börsenzeitung* of February 25, 1919 simply dubbed "The Reich President."[84] In these texts Weber specifies a number of reasons why "it is essential that the future President of the Reich be elected directly by the people" (Weber 1986:128 = 1958:486).

To begin with, only a president so chosen would be able to affirm the identity and the unity of the infant Republic in the teeth of those divisive interests that threatened to asphyxiate it at birth. Of these divisive forces, consider first the particularism arising from Germany's federal make-up. In the near future, Weber claimed, the *Bundesrat* (Federal Council)[85] "will rise again" and with its resurrection the demands of the Republic's constituent states (dominated by Prussia) will come to be elevated above the national interest. The power of the *Reichstag* will decrease correspondingly—especially its capacity to select and promote national leaders (Weber 1970a:113–14 = 1958:532; Weber 1986:128, 131 = 1958:486, 488–89).[86] Consider also the quite literal provincialism of regionally based parties that will continue to fragment the political process in Germany. And, relatedly, consider the danger posed for a weakened Germany by proportional representation. Such an electoral system, Weber declared, is guaranteed in postwar German conditions to transport the quest for economic advancement directly into the political arena. Where interest groups constrain political parties to place the former's preferred candidates at the head of the party list, parliament will become

> a body within which those personalities who care nothing for national politics set the tone, and who, in the nature of things, will rather act according to an "imperative" mandate from those with particular economic interests. It will be a parliament of philistines—incapable of being in any sense a place where political leaders are selected.[87] (Weber 1986:130 =1958:487–88)

Such a parliament could not be expected to cultivate greatness and should not, concomitantly, be in a position to decide who will reach the president's office. Only a president elected directly by the citizenry, that is, elected "in a plebiscitarian way and not by parliament," can become "the safety-valve of the demand for leadership."[88] Only through a "headship of state which indubitably rests on the will of the whole people without intermediaries" (Weber 1986:128 = 1958:486) can the prospect of centrifugal politics be averted.

The second reason Weber campaigned for a Reich president elected by the whole people hinged on his assessment of Germany's economic plight. Economic restructuring, including a dose of "socialization," would be essential for Germany's postwar financial and manufacturing recovery. It was vital that such transformation be endowed with the authority and legitimacy that a president chosen in Weber's preferred manner alone could provide.[89] The president, Weber editorialized, should be no parliamentary manikin, no mere figurehead, but actually just the opposite: a democratic dictator helping to create the conditions in which fundamental change would be possible. It was a point he levelled at the Social Democrats, claiming that his prescription for the nation's sickness was analogous to their view of the dictatorship of the proletariat: "let the Social Democrats remember that the much-discussed 'dictatorship' of the masses does indeed require the 'dictator,' chosen by them, to whom they subject themselves just as long as he retains their confidence" (Weber 1986:129 = 1958:487).[90] Without a president elected by the *demos*, symbolizing the unity of the nation, and acting accordingly "the reconstruction of our economy, on whatever foundation, is impossible" (Weber 1986:129 = 1958:487) was Weber's grim conclusion.

Third, Weber envisaged in a plebiscitarian president the institutional prerequisite, though not the guarantee, of strong, creative, *personal* leadership. Bound to parliament in the selection of government ministers, the president would nonetheless remain free to formulate his own initiatives, and as the focus and representative of millions "would often be superior to the respective party majority in parliament, all the more superior the longer his period of office" (Weber 1958:458). Recent elections had shown, Weber declared, that the German parliamentary party response to a strong personality was overwhelmingly negative, manifesting a combination of plain "very petty-bourgeois hostility...to leaders," and fierce resistance among entrenched party veterans to the specter of "socialization" (Weber 1970a:114 = 1958:532; 1958:458).[91] Parliament could thus not be expected to supply the leaders Germany so urgently needed. The alternative was clear:

> Previously, in the authoritarian state, it was necessary to advocate the increase of the power of the parliamentary majority, so that eventually the significance and thus the standing of parliament would be enhanced. Today the situation is that all constitutional plans have fallen victim to an almost blind faith in the infallibility and omnipotence of the majority—not the majority of the people but of the parliamentarians, which is the opposite, but equally undemocratic, extreme. We must restrict the power of the popularly elected President as always....But let him be given firm ground under his feet by means of the popular election. Otherwise every time there is a parliamentary crisis—and where there are four or five parties involved these will not be infrequent—the whole edifice of the Reich will totter (Weber 1986:131 = 1958:488).

Weber acknowledged that a popular election of the head of state could conceivably in the future lead to the reestablishment of a dynasty. However, because the monarchical system had been so profoundly discredited by the war and its outcome, he thought such a prospect remote (Weber 1958:458). A far greater and more pressing problem, on the other hand, concerned the dearth of those "outstanding political leaders who can influence the masses," a problem consequential upon "our long inner impotence" (Weber 1958:458).[92] Commanding personalities with insight, will and vigor do not appear overnight. Moreover Weber was certain that a parliamentary election of the Reich president, say, on the model of the French Third Republic, or a rotating presidential system analogous to the Swiss collegial case (Weber 1958:460–61) would only aggravate an already dire situation. Both options were incompatible with firm, coherent, and creative leadership because both (but especially the latter) militated against that ingredient that Weber returned to again and again: "the responsible *personality*."[93]

Weber understood well enough that there would be a range of political interests repelled by his ideas; he knew that a species of parliamentarian would be "loath to make the sacrifice of self-denial required to allow the choosing of the highest organ of the Reich" to pass out of its hands. But, he warned:

> it must happen, and the movement in that direction is unrelenting. Let not democracy put this weapon of agitation against parliament into the hands of its enemies. Just as those monarchs who limited their own power at the right time in favour of

parliamentary representation were not only acting in the noblest but also in the shrewdest fashion, so may parliament voluntarily recognise the Magna Carta of democracy, the right to the direct election of the leader. If the ministers remain strictly bound to its confidence, parliament will not have cause to regret this. For the great movement of democratic party life which develops alongside these popular elections will benefit parliament as well. A President elected by means of particular constellations and coalitions of parties is politically a dead man when these constellations shift. A popularly elected President as head of the executive, head of office patronage, and perhaps possessor of a delaying veto and of the authority to dissolve parliament and to call referenda, is the guarantor of true democracy, which means not feeble surrender to cliques, but subjection to leaders chosen by the people themselves.[94]

* * *

Though Max Weber's brother Alfred would later write with regret to (an unsympathetic) Theodor Heuss of his brother's "disturbing" Reich president proposals, describing them as a lamentable "slide into romanticism,"[95] the person who was the object of this solicitude had shown, in December 1918, no little satisfaction about the Preuss proceedings in general and his role in them in particular. A letter penned to Marianne the day after the commission's work had been concluded, though in the interregnum before the first draft had been composed, positively oozes self-congratulation: "All right, the Reich constitution is ready in principle, and it is *very* similar to my proposals" (Marianne Weber 1988:640).[96] And sure enough the Constitution, when it eventually came into force on August 14, 1919 undeniably enshrined a number of Weber's preferences. Wolfgang Mommsen (1984:355) has described Weber's participation in the constitutional committee ("the delivery room of the Weimar constitution") as "his greatest hour" though, as Mommsen also reveals, one should be careful not to exaggerate Weber's influence and success. A number of Weber's proposals concerning the Reich president's standing were in fact either amended or rejected both in the committee itself, where other voices prevailed, and in the legislative process that followed. Crucially, a liberal conception of "balance of powers," which owed much to the influence of Robert Redslob and found support in Preuss, displaced the more Caesarist projections of Max Weber; the political independence of the Reich president for which Weber had pressed so insistently was accordingly quite extensively curtailed.[97] Nonetheless Weberian residues were still discernible in the final draft of the constitution, particularly as it related to aspects of the president's powers.

First, the demand for the president to be elected by the totality of eligible German citizens (male and female) became enshrined as Article 41 of the Weimar Constitution.[98] Second, the duration of the president's tenure of office was fixed at seven years—another of Weber's recommendations.[99] And third, Weber's proposal that the president be invested with the powers to initiate elections and referendums, so as to enable decisive action in the event of party deadlock, was also realized in the Weimar Constitution's final draft.[100]

The subsequent career of the Reich president proposals need not concern us here;[101] nor is it necessary to rehearse the debates concerning the historical relationship of Weber to fascism. We do know that Weber took little interest in the notorious Article 48 (which facilitated the suspension of all the major civil liberties),[102] and such nonchalance is revealing in its own way. Then again, the significance of the draconian Article for subsequent events has probably been exaggerated. The president could not, under the constitution, be an absolute dictator (nor did Weber want him to be). The third paragraph of Article 48 actually invested in parliament a sanction compelling the president to withdraw his emergency measures if the *Reichstag* so requested; while other articles also allowed for presidential constraint.[103] Besides, over-preoccupation with Article 48 may divert attention from other aspects of the Constitution that, though having nothing to do with the president as such, arguably had a more serious impact on later history. For instance, it is Hannsjoachim Koch's contention (1984:269–70, 298, 306–9) that Article 76, which stipulated that the constitution could be altered by a bill with at least two-thirds *Reichstag* support, was the really decisive instrument in establishing the Third Reich.

The impact of Weber's ideas on later developments can only be a subject of speculation. Much easier to establish, on the other hand, are the "Caesarist" elements of Weber's proposals (though the term itself is not actually employed in the texts on the Reich president I have been summarizing thus far). The president, we have seen, is to be a leader of robust personal authority, "supported by the revolutionary legitimacy of popular election" elected "without intermediaries" (1958:457).[104] Moreover, the president's powers to dissolve parliament and resort to referendums display the familiar "Caesarist" mechanism of legitimation.[105] He is also a "dictator," an expression Weber elsewhere employs in relation to the Caesarist leader.[106]

So it was that the earlier synthesis Weber had proposed between leader and parliament crumbled under the duress of post-war German conditions. The hopes Weber had attached to a vigorous parliamentary system in Germany lay momentarily suspended. His death in June 1920 meant there was no time left to revive them.

Conclusion

Carlo Antoni would later remark that Weber's attempt to introduce an "anglicised, constitutional brand of Caesarism" in a country that lacked the ethical-religious traditions and the parliamentary experience to nourish it was "more than a sociological paradox; it was an historical error" (Antoni [1940] 1959:133–34). This may be true, but then again any major reform, at any time and in any country, might be subject to much the same kind of objection. The more serious point is not whether Weber was wrong to try and encourage the adoption of "constitutional Caesarism" in a country not yet ready for it, but whether there was something problematic in the model itself. How was it possible, in other words, for Weber so quickly to jettison his arguments for a vigorous parliamentary system in favor of a "plebiscitary" presidential model that so evidently seemed to undercut its powers? The answer may well lie in Weber's broader view of modern democracy. Since Weber was convinced that modern "democracy" *meant* the subjection of the masses to leaders chosen by them, he was inescapably pushed towards an authoritarian solution to Germany's problems once his view of parliament had soured. Weber (1958:458) did suggest the referendum as a means of disposing of a tyrannical president, subject to a determinate majority agreement of the *Reichstag*. "We must ensure," he would also say, "that whenever the President of the Reich attempts to tamper with the laws or to govern autocratically, he sees the 'noose and gallows' before his eyes." He added: "we must restrict the power of the popularly elected President as always, and ensure that he can intervene in the machinery of the Reich only in case of temporarily insoluble crises (by suspensory veto, and by calling upon civil service ministries) and in other circumstances only by calling a referendum," (Weber 1986:129, 131 = 1958:487, 488.) However, the restrictions on the president are only vaguely defined and since Weber had manifestly little confidence in either parliament or the people as a locus of political potency or acumen, the sanctions he does suggest carry very little credibility. Parliament, he had argued, would stymie any initiative that impeded its own particular interests; while the "masses" who are to be given the final role in deciding who is to rule over them are an entity of the most curious agency. Weber, as we have seen, has consistently portrayed them as credulous and emotional, yet here they are becoming the arbiters of a supreme leader and of a nation's destiny. As Moses Finley (1985:96–97) once observed: "How do the people who are incapable of judging the issues on their merits nevertheless choose in the contest for leadership a victor whose political program then turns out to be the best?" The very Caesarism that Weber had scathingly denounced in his critique of Bismarck—autocratic, demagogic governance with a token parliament to check it— thus threatened to be reintroduced in a revised form.

In Weber's defence it might be said that the historical conditions then obtaining made such an intellectual position plausible. Germany was in crisis. Energetic and independent leadership was necessary for reconstruction and to confront the "foes," in Carl Schmitt's sense, of the new Republic. The lack of a democratic culture, on this account, meant that Weber could not look to the "masses" for the Republic's reinvigoration. But the point is that Weber could not look to a "democratic," let alone a "republican," culture in any event, since he believed it to be a misnomer, a rhetoric for what in practice amounted to a new kind of elite formation. As we now turn from Weber's political writings to his sociological "ideal-types," we shall see that his limited conception of public involvement in politics, of self-governing liberty, was not simply conjunctural but structural in character. Weber always insisted, of course, that such types were simply heuristic tools, mere instruments to be discarded when they lost their use. That they have prevailed so long says something, to be sure, about their utility, but also something about the political culture that continues to find them illuminating.

Notes

1. The English translation of *Economy and Society* was originally published in 1968 in a three-volume hardback edition. All the references to *Economy and Society* that follow are taken from the 1978 unexpurgated paperback version in two volumes.
2. This I take to be the main point of Richter's contrast between Weber and Tocqueville that, despite Lawrence Scaff's criticisms (Scaff 1983:133–35), appears to me well founded. Richter does not, however, examine Weber's critique of Bismarck. Had he done so, he would have seen that Weber can use "Caesarism" in a fashion that is damning.

3. Another way of putting this is to employ a distinction of Charles Camic and say that "Caesarism" is a "background" rather than a "foreground" concept in Weber's sociology (though not, as I have remarked, in his political discourse). An examination of such a background concept enables us to identify the "developmental process" that occurs in an author's work as a whole, and measure changes in its "underlying conceptual structure" (Camic 1986:1042–43).

4. The quotations derive from a letter Weber wrote to his elder cousin Fritz Baumgarten on 9 September 1878. In the letter to Fritz of 25 October 1878 we learn of Max's familiarity with T. Mommsen's *History of Rome* (see below).

5. Interrupted by spells of military service, though even here, despite the mind-numbing monotony and exhaustion of barrack life, he still found time for Gibbon: see Marianne Weber (1988:72).

6. In the introduction to *Economy and Society* Guenther Roth reminds us that "From the beginning of his academic career Weber addressed himself to two broad historical questions: the origins and nature of (1) capitalism in Antiquity, the Middle Ages and modern times, (2) political domination and social stratification in the three ages" (Weber 1978:xl).

7. See also the appreciative comments in Perry Anderson (1974:20, n.3).

8. It is Momigliano's thesis, for instance, that by 1897 Weber had broken with the influence of both Meitzen and Mommsen and had become engaged in a dialogue with Meyer, "one of the few German historians who was independent of Mommsen." Meyer, Momigliano contends, not only helped shift the focus of Weber's interest from land to city but also, through Meyer's emphasis on social and economic history, provided Weber with a "point of reference in his progressive liberation from Mommsen's juridical approach and in the extension of his historical interests from the Middle Ages and Rome to Greece and, ultimately, the Near East" (Momigliano 1977:435).

The importance of Meyer for Weber's work on the sociology of religion is emphasized by Tenbruck (1987).

9. W.P. Dickson's four-volume English translation, which I am using here, was first published in London between 1862–67. All references that follow are to volume 4 of the 1911 edition.

10. "According to his original plan, he had intended to reach his goal, like Pericles and Gaius Gracchus, without force of arms, and over an eighteen year period he had as leader of the popular party moved exclusively amid political plans and intrigues until, reluctantly convinced of the necessity for military support, and already forty years of age, he headed an army. It was natural that he should even afterwards remain still more statesman than general..." (Mommsen 1911:427). I have amended slightly the translation.

11. This quote crisply indicates the divergence between Mommsen's notion of "republicanism" and its classical predecessors for whom the Gracchi and Cromwell were diabolical figures. Mommsen also believed that Cromwell, who "transformed himself from a leader of [the] opposition into a military chief and democratic king" was "in his development as well as in the objects which he aimed at and the results which he achieved of all statesmen perhaps the most akin to Caesar" (Mommsen 1911:427–28). Mommsen's acidic depiction of Cato and Cicero—"republican" heroes—is mentioned below.

12. Cato is "a fool," notable for his "perversity" and "spurious phrases," even though he dies honourably; Cicero is a "statesman without insight, opinion, or purpose," never becoming politically anything more "than a short-sighted egotist." Where Cicero "exhibited the appearance of action, the questions to which his action

applied had, as a rule, just reached their solution," etc. (Mommsen 1911: 422–23, 574).

13. Meyer thought that Ferrero's *Grandezza e Decadenza di Roma* (1904) had made the opposite mistake to Mommsen's work in seeing Caesar as "a mere toy of events" (Meyer 1978:329).

14. A concise statement of Mommsen's somewhat ambivalent position towards Napoleon III—the two had met in 1863—can be found in Gollwitzer ([1952] 1987:385–86). Napoleon III was one of Mommsen's greatest admirers. On their relationship see Momigliano (1956:237–38).

15. The same general objection, incidentally, that Marx in *Capital* III levelled at Mommsen himself ("who discovers the capitalist mode of production in every monetary economy"). See Marx ([1894] 1981:923; cf. 444, n.46). Mommsen's use of words like "democracy" in the Roman context, and his frequent attempts to provide analogies between antique and modern conditions, have often been criticized as strained and historically inappropriate.

16. Mommsen cannot have been here alluding to Bismarck since in 1857, when these lines on "Caesarianism" were first added, Bismarck's star was not yet in the ascendant; that constellation would have to wait for the years following Bismarck's appointment as Prussian prime minister (minister president) in September 1862.

17. The same expression was used by W. Warde Fowler (1920:259) in his affectionate sketch of the great historian.

18. Mommsen's esteem for his protégé is recorded in the famous exchange between them on the occasion of the young scholar's doctoral defence. Details in Marianne Weber (1988:113–14).

19. The author of the entry on Mommsen in the *Encyclopedia Britannica* (15th ed.) remarks, ironically, that Mommsen's academic critics responded to his own autocratic brand of scholarship with the charge of "Caesarism."

20. First published in *Die Hilfe* (1903, no.45) but more conveniently located in F. Naumann, *Werke*, vol. 5, pp. 325–27, at 325. And Naumann added, "He was the voice of principle...the voice of...the people in the middle of Caesarism," 326.

21. Mommsen served as a deputy in the Prussian *Landtag* in the years 1873–79, and in the Empire's *Reichstag* in 1881–84.

22. The words come from Mommsen (1952:71).

23. Weber uses the term, vaguely, in the 1897 and 1909 versions of *Agrarverhältnisse im Altertum* (Agrarian Relations in Antiquity). See, respectively, Weber (1897:1–18, at 12), and Weber (1924b:1–288, at 242, 253). R.I. Frank has translated the latter, expanded version of the essay as *The Agrarian Sociology of Ancient Civilisations* (Weber 1976:35–386). (The references to Caesarism can be found on 322, 335). Weber deploys the term loosely to refer to the social conditions of Caesar's support: for example those relating to the decline of the peasantry and the growth of a proletarian army.

24. An earlier version of this section appeared as Baehr (1988).

25. Anthony Giddens (1972:10) has gone so far as to claim that Weber's ambivalent attitude towards Bismarck "lies at the origin of the whole of his political writings."

26. Universal manhood suffrage had suffered a checkered career in Prussia. Established in April 1848 only to be superseded in May 1849 by the notorious three class system, itself a product of reaction, Bismarck had made the institution a central plank of the North German Confederation constitution, ratified in April 1867.

27. The figures can be found in table 4 of Koch (1984: 384–85).
28. The context suggests that this would not be a case to which Weber himself would subscribe.
29. Letter to H. Baumgarten, dated November 8, 1884, in Weber (1936:139–48, at 143). There is a slightly different translation in Marianne Weber (1988:118) with an added emphasis that is absent in *Jugendbriefe*. To the best of my knowledge, this is the first occasion in Weber's work that "charisma" (the Greek "gift": cf. 1 Corinthians 1:4–9) is linked to Caesarism.
    Weber reaffirmed the link in his own mind between universal suffrage and Caesarism in "Parliament and Government in a Reconstructed Germany" (1918), a revised and extended version of articles published in the *Frankfurter Zeitung* in May and June 1917. See his comments on "the hopes that a Caesarist figure like Bismarck attached to universal suffrage." In Weber (1978a:1452 = 1958:382).
30. Quoted in Erich Eyck ([1950] 1968:116).
31. Hermann Baumgarten to Heinrich von Sybel, March 29, 1881, in Bramsted and Melhuish (1978:561–62, at 561). Wolfgang Mommsen, commenting on Baumgarten's influence on Weber, points to the "astounding similarity in direction, temperament, and critical focus" of the former's views "with Weber's later comments about Bismarck, William II, and the political immaturity of the nation," and Mommsen also notes that Weber "came to share Baumgarten's opinion of the Caesarist-demagogic character of Bismarck's policies" (Mommsen [1959] 1984:6, n. 22, 7). Cf. Weber's letter to Baumgarten of April 30, 1888, in Weber (1936, 292–302 at 300).
    Baumgarten's prophecy of "disaster" was, from the liberal standpoint, partially realized by 1912: in the election of that year one in every three Germans who cast their ballot voted socialist, and though the SPD were denied an overall parliamentary majority they had become nonetheless the single largest party in the *Reichstag*: see Carr (1979:191).
32. The remark in *Christian World* is quoted in Mommsen (1984:20). On the Freiburg lecture see Weber's comment "The danger does *not* lie with the masses, as is believed by people who stare as if hypnotised at the depths of society" (Weber [1895] 1980:446–47 = 1958:23, emphasis in original).
33. See Weber (1958:235), and the parallel discussion in Weber (1978a 1382–83 = 1958:296).
34. Also Weber (1978a 1442 = 1958:370–71).
35. "Germany had no national flag until 1892, and no national hymn until after the First World War; and the choice of the day of the victory at Sedan as the national holiday was widely opposed. Even in the matter of national monuments, the Germans had their troubles. The Teutoburger Wald monument (1875) and the Niederwald 'Germania' monument (1885) celebrated events so remote in time as to have little sentimental importance for the new Reich," Craig (1981:58); cf. Mosse (1971:175–76). The controversy that surrounded the 1913 centenary "celebrations" is another indication of the absence of agreed-upon national symbols: see, on the controversy, G.Eley (1976:284–85).
36. Craig (1981: 58–60). Also Hofmann (1977:96) who informs us that Bismarck himself consciously exploited the constitutional idea of (his monarch's) *emperorship* to promote national centralization and a German sense of unity.
    Weber's perception of Bismarck was anticipated in 1879 by Gustav Freytag, the novelist, whom Craig quotes (60) as saying: "We are still going to suffer a long time from the circumstances that the political strength of the nation has, for one and a half decades, been personified in one man. And, along with all the

good fortune and progress of this age, we are going to have to bear the damage that attaches itself to this kind of domination by a single individual."

37. Weber's rather nebulous target is a section of the "political literati which entered public life from about 1878 on." He tells us that from 1878 this group represented the dominant tendency of "political literati" opinion.

38. The interpolation is by Guenther Roth. Roth's translation, on which I mostly rely, renders the English equivalents of *"Cäsarismus," "cäsarisch,"* and *"cäsaristisch"* with a small "c." To conform to the practice I have adopted up to now, I propose to use in all cases the capital letter (e.g., Caesarism and Caesarist rather than caesarism and caesarist).

39. I have omitted Weber's many emphases. Weber also says here that the "intellectual level" of the parliament Bismarck left behind him "was depressed," an opinion contested by James J. Sheehan (1968–69:511–28, esp. 527, n.47). On the other hand, Weber's point (1978a: 1388 = 1958:303) that "Bismarck did not tolerate any autonomous power—neither within the ministries nor within parliament" has received authoritative documentation by J.C.G. Röhl. On the fascinating minutiae relating to how Bismarck attempted comprehensively to rule over his Prussian ministers and state (Reich) secretaries, see Röhl (1967:20–26).

40. Nolte goes on to insist, however, that Weber is wrongly seen as an intellectual precursor of fascism. On Weber's imperialism, see Mommsen (1984:137), and on Weber's "liberal imperialism" more generally, 68–90, 205–7, 210–11 and passim.

41. In another letter to Sybel, this one dated July 21, 1880: see Bramsted and Melhuish (eds.) (1978:559).

42. Over two decades earlier, Engels had already commented at some length on the political weakness of the bourgeoisie in Prussia, and the backwardness of German capitalism, though he had deployed the category of "Bonapartism" rather than "Caesarism" to do so. On the "comparatively young and extremely cowardly bourgeoisie," and the Prussian "Bonapartist monarchy" to which it was subordinated, see Engels ([1872–3] 1988:363), an article in which he also writes of "pseudo-constitutionalism." The expression was revived and expanded on by Weber in his analysis of the Russian Revolution of 1905–6 (Weber [1906] 1995b).

See also Engels's 1870 preface to the second edition of "The Peasant War in Germany" on the predicament of the National Liberals who "have been left in the lurch by those who stand behind them, by the mass of the bourgeoisie. This mass does not *want* to rule. It still has 1848 in its bones" (Engels [1870] 1968a:237). Compare with Engels ([1884] 1968b:578–79) on the "Bismarck nation: here capitalists and workers are balanced against each other and equally cheated for the benefit of the impoverished Prussian cabbage junkers."

43. As Weber later remarked in "Suffrage and Democracy in Germany" (1958:233).

44. Weber's unflattering description of the bourgeoisie has had a significant influence on the development of the theory of the German *Sonderweg*, a favorite theme among historians and sociologists of Germany. The *Sonderweg* (literally, "special way") has a number of variants but revolves around the core idea that German history was exceptional in not experiencing an authentic bourgeois revolution, this supposed authenticity being measured against a British or French model. The theory is the subject of an interesting though repetitive critique by Geoff Eley in his essay "The British Model and the German Road: Rethinking the Course of German History before 1914," in D. Blackbourn and G. Eley (1984:39–155).

45. The National Liberals were unceremoniously ditched by Bismarck in 1879, by which date he had already begun the makings of a new political alignment of conservative parties and the (Catholic) Center founded on the policy of economic protectionism.
46. Note, however, the telescoping of causality that occurs between the Freiburg lecture and "Parliament and Government." In the former, Germany's travails are attributed to "a missing century of political education"; in the latter they are adduced to the "legacy of Prince Bismarck." The ambivalence actually seems to have been present as early as 1894, on which see Mommsen (1984:86).
47. Emphasis in German original. Also Weber (1978a: 1452 = 1958:382): "The circumstances of Bismarck's departure from office demonstrate the manner in which hereditary legitimism reacts against...Caesarist powers." and Weber (1978b:986 = 1964:726), where "legitimate" and "Caesarist" political power are presented as antinomies.
   Weber had also implied a similar antithesis between Caesarism and legitimacy as early as January 3, 1891 in the course of more correspondence with Hermann Baumgarten. Weber remarked that after Bismarck's resignation on March 20, 1890, five days after a stormy confrontation with Wilhelm II over parliamentary and foreign affairs, "one could make the most interesting observations on his previous admirers, from the opportunists (*Strebernaturen*) who had discovered shortly afterwards that Bismarck basically 'had not grasped his time,' to some eager disciples of Treitschke, young historians, who declared that they would only very reluctantly tip their hats before the emperor after he had covered the tribe of the Hohenzollern with the 'ignominy of ungratefulness and petty ambition' like nobody before him. The latter were not able to contradict our response that now it would become clear that, as we have always claimed, their ostensible monarchistic loyalty had been nothing else than hidden Caesarism" (Weber 1936:327–28).
48. I have retained all the emphases of the German original. On Bismarck's "low estimation of legitimacy" and the manner in which the "'Bonapartist' character of Bismarckian politics is concealed by the monarchist, traditional cloak of the royal servant and imperial chancellor, by the heritage of the conservative Junkers" see Gollwitzer (1952:65–66). Also Stürmer (1977b:115) who quotes Ranke's crisp judgment of Bismarck: "Indispensable for the state, but intolerable for the dynasties" (1877).
49. In fact Bismarck is consistently having to assert the civil arm of government to restrain military enthusiasm and encroachment, as after the battles of Königgrätz and Sedan, and again during the Bulgarian crisis of 1887: details in Craig (1981:2–7, 31–33, 133–34).
50. See the earlier discussion of Bismarck's populism.
51. Bismarck's *Staatsstreichpläne* (coup d'état plans) were prosecuted in the early spring of 1890 when the old pugilist felt the parliamentary ground collapsing beneath him, and as he also witnessed a new Kaiser attempting to assert his own personal rule. However, as later events were to show, scheming of this sort was endemic to the whole Wilhelmine system and, thus, far transcended Bismarck's designs: the plans were resurrected, for instance, by Count Philipp Eulenburg in the summer of 1894 and by Wilhelm II himself in the winter of 1896–97. On all this Röhl (1967: 50–55, 110–17, 217–22) is excellent.
52. One of Bismarck's objectives in planning his coup against the *Reichstag* was actually to increase Wilhelm's dependency on him.
53. For instance, and under the characterization of *Führerdemokratie*, Weber (1978b:268–69, 1126 = 1964:199–200, 846).

54. Though polemically speaking he might be so called: Weber does refer to Wilhelm II as "Bonapartist" (if one wishes to equate that charge with "Caesarist") and also calls him a "Caesar," though Weber may well be punning here on the German word "Kaiser." See, respectively, statements to Hermann Baumgarten of December 31, 1889 and January 3, 1891, in Weber (1936:323, 328).

W.J. Mommsen points out that, for Weber, strong *parliamentary* monarchical systems (like Britain's) had an important advantage over modern "republics": the former were able to function as a check against Caesarism of the militarist variety. A parliamentary monarchical system, Mommsen paraphrases, was in Weber's opinion "the only institutional form of government capable of neutralising the constant desire of the military to expand its power from the military into the political realm" (Mommsen 1984:289). On other reasons for Weber's support for parliamentary monarchy, due less to "royalist sentiments" and more to "technical considerations about the best form of government" see Mommsen (1984: 289–91); and for Mommsen's instructive comments on the Weberian perception of the Reich president as an "elected monarch" (the expression the American anti-federalists had used in horror), see 251, 342–43 (especially the remarks on the Reich president's office as "a parliamentary electoral monarchy on a Caesarist basis"), 344, 353; cf. 385.

55. Pericles, Cleon, and Lassalle (Weber 1978b:1130 = 1964:849); Gladstone (Weber 1970a:106 = 1958:523–24); Lloyd George (Weber 1978a:1452 = 1958:383). Weber also likened Trotsky to a Caesar, on which see Mommsen (1984: 279, n.333).

56. A superb analysis is Allan Mitchell's (1977) devastating critique of "Bonapartism as a Model for Bismarckian Politics." For an attempt, of which Mitchell is highly critical, to employ Caesarism in this context, see Stürmer (1977a) and, for much greater detail, Stürmer (1974), especially 322–33 on Bismarck as a "Caesaristic statesman." Stürmer's position is defended and elaborated upon by Gay (1993:252–65, 628–29).

Other historians have been much less critical of the Bonapartist analogy than Mitchell. See, for example, Eyck (1968: 116–17) according to whom Bismarck's "practical model was Napoleon III, whose government was sustained by the masses and opposed by a portion of the educated middle class; Napoleon had introduced universal suffrage to get rid of the Second Republic and had been successful in that. Bismarck was confident that he would be able to achieve the same success." (Eyck is also interesting on the relationship between Lassalle and Bismarck); G. Eley, in Blackbourn and Eley (1984: 150–51), who takes issue with Mitchell (on Eley's assessment of the concept of Caesarism see his *Reshaping the German Right* 1980:206 ff.); H.-U Wehler (1970 esp. 122–23, 140, 142); M. Kitchen (1976) where the notion undergoes an unapologetic elastication ("The characteristic form of government in Germany from Bismarck to Hitler was…bonapartism," 10; cf. 11–24); E. Crankshaw (1981:233–34) who endorses Engels's letter to Marx of 13 April 1866 portraying the Bismarck regime as a "Bonapartist semi-dictatorship"; and A.J.P. Taylor (1945:138).

57. On the variety of predemocratic assemblies see A.R. Myers 1975.

The conflation of "parliament" and "democracy" still grates in the ears of some: "I slightly bridle when the word 'democracy' is applied to the United Kingdom. Instead of that I say, 'we are a Parliamentary nation.' If you…put us into the jar labelled 'Democracy,' I can't complain: I can only tell you that you have understood very little about the United Kingdom." Enoch Powell, interviewed in *The Guardian*, June 15, 1982 and cited in A. Barnett 1982:24.

58. Weber thus reminded his readers that Great Britain, for all its much-vaunted political democratization, managed to retain a parliamentary system capable of bringing "a quarter of mankind under the rule of a minute but politically prudent minority." Germany, by contrast, "now fights for her life against an army in which Africans, Ghurkas and all kinds of other barbarians from the most forsaken corners of the world stand poised at the frontiers ready to devastate our country" (Weber 1978a:1420, 1382 = 1958: 343, 295).

Weber's Anglophilia, and in particular his debt to British Puritan and liberal traditions, is nicely explored and contextualized by Roth (1993).

59. Weber also speaks from time to time of the social, as well as the political dimension of democracy, but only the latter concerns me in the discussion that follows. Suffice it to note Weber's observation that formal political equality is perfectly compatible with "the growth of a raw plutocracy," a juxtaposition nowhere better seen than in the U.S. (1970b:392 = 1958:272).

On the social dimension of democracy as "the levelling of social distinctions," and as "the growth of mass literacy and the popular press," see Beetham (1985:103).

60. See also Weber (1978a:1446 = 1958:375).

61. Emphases as in the German original.

62. I have slightly modified the translation and restored all the original emphases. On the "law of the small number," see also Weber (1978b:952 = 1964:700).

63. It is worth comparing this account of Gladstone as an orator with that given by Walter Bagehot in an article he wrote for *The Economist* of November 4, 1871 (Bagehot 1968d:461–64), and entitled "Mr. Gladstone and the People." To Bagehot, Gladstone's speech at Greenwich marked "a new era in English politics, " heralding "the time when it will be one of the most important qualifications of a prime minister to exert a direct control over the masses—when the ability to reach them, not as his views may be filtered through an intermediate class of political teachers and writers, but *directly* by the vitality of his own mind, will give a vast advantage in the political race to any statesman." And Bagehot goes on to say that so greatly has this speech enhanced the government's previously flagging position that "if Parliament were to meet again tomorrow, Mr. Gladstone's position would be quite changed. It would be at once felt by all his discontented allies as well by (sic) his party foes that Mr. Gladstone's direct command over the people is still immense,—that the result of an appeal to the people by him against a divided and hostile Parliament would very probably end in his full reinstatement in power, with as large a majority as ever." (As things turned out, Gladstone actually lost the election of 1874.)

Bagehot, unlike Weber, did not go so far as to claim that the position of Gladstone was tantamount to that of a "dictator" but by the early twentieth century the portrayal of the British prime minister as one was fairly common. It could be found in the writings of such people as A.L. Lowell, M. Ostrogorski, Sidney Low, and J.A. Hobson; and was by no means unknown within Germany itself. Otto Hintze, in an article first published in 1908, was one such person to have observed that, in England, "the parliamentary ministry is developing further and further into a popular dictatorship of the Prime Minister" (Hintze 1975:266); while Tönnies (1917:52) could confidently declare: "the Prime Minister of England has a great future, and this future is Caesaristic."

See also the instructive discussion in Birch (1964:72–81).

64. On electoral passivity see also Weber (1970a:99 = 1958:517).

65. Compare with Weber (1978a: 1421, 1439–40 = 1958: 344, 368).

66. As Weber was the first to acknowledge (1970a:104 = 1958:522).
    The extent of Ostrogorski's impact on Weber's theory of party organization has been questioned by Lawrence Scaff (1980–1: 1279, n.11). Scaff concludes instead, on the basis of his close study of the correspondence between Weber and Michels that spanned the years of their friendship (1906–15), that James Bryce's influence was "primary." The argument is plausible, particularly since Weber does not mention Ostrogorski in the correspondence with Michels. Yet so far as the term "Caesarism" is concerned—at least as Weber formulates it in the parliamentary democratic context—Weber's usage is much closer to Ostrogorski's than Bryce's for whom Caesarism essentially denotes "military despotism" in an older nineteenth-century sense that was recapitulated in Germany by Wilhelm Roscher, to whom we shall have occasion to return (Bryce [1888] 1927:623). Moreover, while Ostrogorski himself invoked Bryce on various occasions where the two thinkers shared a common opinion (e.g., Ostrogorski [1970 II:567] on the "fatalism of the multitude"), Bryce in his turn contributed the preface to *Democracy and the Organization of Political Parties*. This suggests that an attempt to untangle Bryce's influence on Weber from Ostrogorski's is no simple matter.
    Bryce's conviction that a military tyranny was extremely unlikely in America can be interestingly compared with Benjamin Disraeli's reflections on England. Writing under the pseudonym of Vivian Grey, Disraeli remarked (1833:11–12): "It seems to be impossible for a military leader to practice upon the passions of an insular people, to whom he can promise no conquests. If it be urged that a military despotism has already been erected in this country, I remind the respondent of the different state of society in England at present to what it was in the time of Cromwell. It appears to me that the manufacturing districts alone, which, in a moment, would supply masses of population and abundance of arms, are a sufficient security against the imposition of a military despotism."
67. Reasons adduced by Ostrogorski to explain the loss of prestige suffered by the ordinary M.P. included the caucus system, "which undermines the voter's respect for the M.P."; advances in techniques of communication and information that put the voter in immediate contact with the leader and make the backbencher that much more individually dispensable; and a general process of enlightenment the effect of which is to make the voter more aware of the power he commands over his representative in the electoral market place.
68. See also Michels (1959:333–38) on the Caesarist character of referendums.
69. And even in the American case the reference to an "unrestrained master" is an exaggeration. The overstatement is partially explained by Weber's wish to employ the word Caesarism to encompass military as well as civil relationships of super- and subordination, a point to which I return in the next chapter.
70. Naturally I am not suggesting that this is the only rubric under which Weber discusses these practices. In the analysis of "Representation," in *Economy and Society* (1978a:294–96 = 1964:219–21), for instance, Weber is explicit in distinguishing between (a) "parliamentary cabinet government" of the British type, and (b) "constitutional government," of which the United States is paradigmatic, particularly in combining "an elective presidency" with a "representative parliament." Weber adds for good measure that the American system is typified by a combination of "plebiscitarian" and "representative" elements. But the point remains that, whatever their peculiar features, all modern "democratic" systems are, for Weber, "Caesarist" in some shape or form. Weber's ideal-types elaborate on and, under a sociological redescription, partly camouflage this fact, but do not refute it.

For a more subtle analysis and critique of Weber's view of American politics than I am here able to give, see Guenther Roth (1985).

71. One is reminded here of Sidney Low, according to whom "it is the Premier who has been nominated by the choice of the people, as expressed at a general election. His associates in office, or in the leadership of the Opposition, may or may not count; a few of them do, most of them do not. Bismarck once said that the issue at a general election in Germany was *für oder gegen Bismarck.* And something of the sort is often true at a general election in England. It has been for or against Mr. Gladstone, Lord Salisbury, or Mr. Balfour, or some other eminent statesman who stands at the head of a party. When the plebiscite has been declared in favour of the successful leader, he is "sent for" by the Sovereign, to whom he has been in fact "sent" by the electorate" (Low 1904:156–57, emphases omitted). On 158 Low likens the "amount of authority" exercised by men such as Pitt, Peel, Palmerston (all figures who *preceded* the real expansion of the franchise in 1867) Disraeli and Gladstone to that of a "dictator"—his precise words are that such figures "may come near to being" dictators.

   For one of the great modern statements on prime ministerial power, see R.H.S. Crossman's (1963) "Introduction" to Bagehot's *The English Constitution,* esp. 51–53 comparing the British and American cabinet systems. For a vigorously dissenting view that reveals the obstacles to which prime ministerial governance is subject, see Ferdinand Mount (1992:134–46). (Lord Hailsham's 1976 Dimbleby Lecture, which caused quite a stir at the time of its delivery, extended the idea of dictatorship to the whole House of Commons. However, since the author quickly establishes that the House is itself dominated and directed by the prime minister's office, the analysis he presents is far less original than he supposed it to be.)

72. Consider also Weber's comment that "In the United States, equal suffrage has resulted time and again in the election, as lord mayor, of a popular trustee who was largely free to create his own municipal administration. The English parliamentary system equally tends towards the development of such Caesarist features. The prime minister gains an increasingly dominant position toward parliament, out of which he has come" (Weber 1978a:1415 = 1958:337).

73. Weber (1978a:1408 = 1956:327–28).

74. Weber (1978a:1413, 1429–30 = 1958:334, 355); Weber (1970a:111–12 = 1958:530).

   My account only skims the surface of the very detailed analysis Weber provides in "Parliament and Government," and "Politics as a Vocation." On the constitutional liabilities of the Second Empire that militated against a vibrant German parliament, see Weber (1978a:1423 = 1958:347 [on Article 27]), and, more importantly, Weber (1978a: 1410–16, 1425, 1431 = 1958:330–38, 350, 357 [on Article 9]).

75. Also Weber (1978a:1454 = 1958:385), on parliament's irreplaceability as "the agency for enforcing the public control of administration, for determining the budget...for deliberating and passing laws," emphases omitted.

76. "Monitoring" his activities, but not determining them: "Weber by no means shared the view that parliament, as a free decision-making body, should prescribe policy for government, being in principle an executive committee delegated from its ranks. Weber's notion of political leadership was...diametrically opposed to this notion. In his view the leading politician ought not to be the executive organ of the will of the parliamentary majority but something qualitatively different: a leader" (Mommsen 1984:397).

77. On continuity, see also Weber (1978a: 1452, 1459 = 1958:383, 391).
78. On this issue contrast Mommsen (1984:79, 172, 321–22, 395–96) with Beetham (1985:119–50).
79. All of the above quotations are from 1970a:115 = 1958:533–4; a number of emphases have been omitted.
80. An earlier version of this section appeared as Baehr (1989).
81. The background of Preuss's own appointment as convening chairman can be found in G. Schulz (1963: I:123–24). Also, 125–28 where, somewhat tendentiously, Preuss's "dogmatic" romantic-idealist constitutional conceptions are contrasted with Weber's more "empirical," rationalist approach.
82. While David Beetham believes the postwar writings "substantially revised" Weber's earlier (1917) views on the leadership question, Wolfgang Mommsen points to an element of continuity: "Weber permitted the leading politician a plebiscitary-charismatic precedence vis-a-vis his party as well as parliament, as early as 1917–18" (Mommsen 184, n.170; cf. xv, 186, 187, 364, chapter 10). Nonetheless Mommsen himself seems actually to come quite close to Beetham's position when Mommsen says (340) that "In 1917, the implicit restriction of the power of parliament in favour of rule by a charismatic leader was not yet fully manifest; in 1918–19 it became central."

    This is also the place to record my great indebtedness to Mommsen's and Beetham's books which remain the preeminent contributions to the study of Weber's political thought.
83. "Deutschlands Künftige Staatsform," reprinted in Weber (1958:436–71).
84. "Der Reichspräsident," also reprinted in Weber (1958: 486–89); translated by G.C. Wells as "The Reich President," (Weber 1986:128–32). The article was also printed in two other papers at around the same time: the *Heidelberger Zeitung* of 27 February and the *Königsberger Hartungsche Zeitung* of 15 March, details in Martin Riesebrodt 1981.

    The impact of Weber's Reich president proposals is put into context by Mommsen. The thrust of constitutional reformist thought in the years before the fall of the Hohenzollerns was in the direction of a constitutional parliamentary monarchy based on English practice, an idea much in line with Weber's own wartime writings. But with the collapse of the dynasty there was at first no clear idea about what a *republican* constitution—in the modern sense of this term— should look like. Mommsen remarks (1984:346) that "For this reason, Max Weber's powerful conception of a plebiscitary Reich president as head of the executive and the guarantor of Reich unity, with a Reich parliament supporting him, aroused great respect and interest." The distinction between this "republican" constitution and the principles animating its classical forbears will become evident as this section unfolds.
85. Under the Weimar Constitution this body was transmuted into the so-called Committee of States: see Koch (1984:264).
86. Though Weber remained a committed federalist, he nonetheless believed that the new German state would require a compensatory element to provide a factor of cohesion. In particular, Prussia could be counted on to remain a pressing problem for the Reich since Berlin would not be easily reconciled to the loss of its hegemonic position in Germany as a whole. Weber believed that the breaking-up of Prussia into regional states as a means of stemming its power was impractical. Instead he preferred the idea of "counterweights in *constitutional law* against the *actual* predominance of Prussia," (1958: 450), emphasis in original. The office of Reich president can, I think, be construed as such a counterweight to Prussia, as well as to federalism more generally.

On the connection between Weber's federalism and plebiscitarianism, see Mommsen (1984:334–40).

87. In "Germany's Future Constitution" Weber says that proportional representation is tolerable "in *normal* times," that is, in a period of relative social peace, but its overall effect is to weaken "unified political leadership"—something crucially needed to overcome Germany's current social travails. He adds, "Applied to government formation, a proportional system would be the radical opposite of any dictatorship. That will be differently judged according to one's economic, social and political views": Weber (1958:462), I have omitted a number of emphases). Also Weber (1970a: 114 = 1958: 532): "...in its present from, proportional representation is a typical phenomenon of leaderless democracy," and Weber (1978a: 1443 = 1958: 372) on coalition government.

88. Weber (1970a:114 = 1958:532). Also Weber (1958:457): "A Reich President supported by the revolutionary legitimacy of popular election, who would stand opposite the Reich corporate bodies in his *own* right, would have an incomparably greater authority than one who was parliamentarily elected." Emphasis in original. (Wolfgang Mommsen [1963:310] interprets the phrase "revolutionary legitimacy" as code for charismatic legitimacy. We could just as well say "Caesarist.")

89. Weber (1958: 457, 462, 486). For Weber, this "socialization"—state-intervention to kick-start a stalled capitalist economy—had nothing to do with socialism though, as Beetham remarks, Weber probably used the term to attract the attention of Social Democratic sceptics: see Beetham (1985: 248, n.80). Also Mommsen (1984: 298–300, esp. 299–300).

One finds an echo of the resort to a directly elected executive as a strategy for political and economic transformation in an essay by the leader of the erstwhile British Social Democratic Party: "There is no doubt that if there was the slightest chance of bringing it about, the quickest way of changing the total political configuration would be to make a change as radical as General de Gaulle did with the Fourth Republic—elect the Prime Minister directly, though retaining the monarch as head of state, while leaning further than France did towards the US system with its federal structure and explicit separation of power between the executive and the legislature. But this is wishful, escapist thinking. Britain would have to be at or on the cliff of economic disaster before such a radical shift could have even a chance of implementation," David Owen (1984:178). Max Weber, one may surmise, felt Germany had not just reached this "cliff edge" but had actually gone over it.

90. That the Reich president's office entailed a form of dictatorship was also well understood by Preuss himself. Referring in 1924 to the far-reaching powers vested in the president under Article 48 of the Weimar Constitution, Preuss stated that his preference was "to preserve as much scope as possible for the constitutional dictatorship." He added portentously: "The chances are that it will be needed even more than before." Carl Schmitt was another person who saw the president as a dictator. On all this see A. Dorpalen (1964:169–700, and the appendix to Schmitt ([1928] 1978:215–59). Cf. Weber's parallel discussion of dictatorship in 1978b:278 = 1964:206–7.

91. Weber stresses that it is entrenched politicians who are resisting leadership— and they are the dominant voice in parliament—not party politicians in general. For the latter, "popular election [of the Reich president] creates a change in the form of selection for official patronage"; it does not curtail official patronage, the oxygen of the ambitious deputy, as such.

92. I have omitted the emphasis in the original.

93. Weber (1958:461), emphasis in the original; cf. Weber (1978b:278–79 = 1964:206–7). Cf. Mommsen (1984:341) who comments on Weber's debt to the U.S. presidential model: "The Reich President, supported by plebiscitary legitimacy like the American president, ought to constitute the head of the executive, unlike the situation in the French republic, whose chief of state was limited to purely representative functions and where the executive authority was the exclusive province of a cabinet responsible to parliament." Nonetheless, as Mommsen notes, the Weberian Reich president departs from the American presidential model in a number of ways; for instance, in the German case, the president was not to be given the power to freely appoint his political staff.

It is also of some historical interest to note Weber's imitation of a phrase then extant that likened the Reich president to an "elected monarch" (Weber in correspondence to Ludo Moritz Hartmann, Austrian envoy in Berlin, January 3, 1919, in Mommsen (1984: 299–300, n. 65, and 342–44). The reader will recall from chapter 1 that the idea of an "elected monarch" was attacked with especial ferocity by anti-federalist writers; and that the American constitution-makers at Philadelphia were expressly concerned to *dilute* the plebiscitary content of the presidential office.

94. Weber (1986:132 = 1958:489). Weber's definition of "true democracy" in this last sentence is profitably compared with his famous remarks to Erich Ludendorff recorded in Marianne Weber (1988: 653).

95. Cited in Eduard Baumgarten's collection of extracts and documents, *Max Weber: Werk und Person* (1964:550). Alfred's letter to his president is dated April 11, 1958, but since the former died shortly after the letter was sent, Heuss never wrote a formal reply. He did, however, allude to the letter in his memoirs only to rebut Alfred's charge: Max Weber's goal, Heuss insisted, had been the pragmatic one of constitutional-political flexibility (551).

96. The remark caused one indignant commentator to retort: "What amazing presumption! A few intelligent, learned, and experienced people meet and believe they can decide upon the principles of a constitution which is meant to be the political framework for sixty millions. It is true that Preuss only received drafting instructions, but considering the fact that his first draft was already in print on January the 3rd [1919], it is probably correct to say that never has a constitution been drafted so quickly" J.P. Mayer ([1944] 1956:99).

97. On Redslob's proposals and his influence, see Mommsen (1984:348–52). On how Weber's Caesarist proposals for the Reich president were quite radically qualified by the committee and, in parliament, by the Social Democrats, see, respectively, 353–54, 376–78.

98. The Constitution is reprinted in R. Schuster (ed.), *Deutsche Verfassungen* (1978:99–131). For Article 41 (which contains the added stipulation that eligibility applies to all who are thirty-five or over) see 107. The word "Reich," which sits rather uncomfortably with the promulgation of a republic, was retained in the Constitutional terminology. (Thus: "Das Deutsche Reich ist eine Republik," from Article 1, which also declares that sovereignty resides in the people).

99. Compare Weber (1958:458) with Art. 43, para. 1 = Schuster (1978:107). The first draft of the Constitution had suggested a ten year period: see Koch (1984:266).

100. Though not quite in the form he had originally intended. See Mommsen (1984:368–69, 376–77). Also compare Weber (1958:457) with Art. 25 and Art. 74, para. 3, in Schuster (1978:104, 112).

101. It is Mommsen's view (1984:381–82) that although Weber's Reich president proposals were, constitutionally, "only partially implemented...Weber's *theory*...had a great deal of impact" later. "The efforts during the Weimar period to build up the power of the presidency at the cost of the rights and responsibilities of the Reichstag relied significantly upon Weber's theory of plebiscitary-charismatic rule. During the 1920s it gained in influence and contributed significantly to the theoretical legitimization of the praxis of presidential government" (my emphasis).

102. Mommsen (1984:377–78). Article 48 entitled the Reich president to "suspend the seven most important basic rights, if he considered it necessary, namely liberty of the individual (Art. 114), inviolability of one's home (Art. 115), secrecy of one's mail (Art. 117), freedom of opinion (Art. 118), freedom of assembly (Art. 123), freedom of association (Art. 124) and the right to property (Art.153)." Between "1919 and the end of 1932, 233 pieces of emergency legislation were enacted" under these and related provisions (Koch 1984:306–7).

103. See especially Art. 43, para. 2 (on suspension) and Art. 59 (on impeachment), in Schuster (1978:107, 109 respectively).

104. Also Weber (1978a:1452 = 1958:382): "Every kind of direct popular election of the supreme ruler and, beyond that, every kind of political power that rests on the confidence of the masses and not of parliament...lies on the road to these [the reference is to Napoleon I and III] "pure" forms of Caesarist acclamation." (I have omitted Weber's emphasis in the German original.)

105. A contrast between Weber and J.A. Hobson on this issue is instructive. For Weber, the plebiscite-referendum is expeditious in its place—as a method of endorsement of decisions that have been made elsewhere—but is a disaster if extended to the wider sphere of *legislation*. His arguments against the plebiscite, wherever it is conceived as an instrument of "direct democracy," are various. The plebiscite, he objected, is inadequate for the technical reasons that it only lends itself to dichotomous Yes-No alternatives, thus affording no means of thrashing-out the party compromises that are required in a state composed of multiple values and interests; that it is ill-equipped to deal with the complicated calculations and procedures entailed in fixing the budget or drafting a law; that, unlike a parliamentary vote of no-confidence, it provides no method of ensuring the resignation of incompetent persons: the plebiscite is not constructed to specify the reasons for the decision it arrives at, nor is there a mechanism open to it for replacing those who are no longer trusted by more responsible and competent representatives. In addition, Weber continued, the plebiscite is useless as a mode of selection of trained officials and as a watchdog of their performance; while, where the plebiscite is used to *elect* officials, the technical qualifications of the latter for office are rarely a consideration. Weber also claimed that the sheer magnitude of political effort entailed in constant plebiscites eventually results in the apathy or lassitude of the voters, and, accordingly, their manipulation by well organized interest-groups (Weber 1978a:1455–57 = 1958:386–88). Crucially, where the plebiscite-referendum is employed ostensibly to maximise popular participation, the effect is not only to weaken "the autonomous role of the party leader" (Weber 1978a:1456 = 1958:387)—but also to encourage stasis. According to Weber, the referendum on laws "has an effect which is *politically* exactly the *opposite* to a plebiscitary presidential election. For, according to all experience, it is a thoroughly *conservative* political means: a strong hindrance to the rapid advance of legislation" (Weber 1958:462).
      J.A. Hobson's view was very different. The great advocate of New Liberal-

ism envisaged referendums as a means of collectively involving the citizenry in the decisions that most affected them. Their role was not to be one of mere ratification; instead "direct democratic control" was to supplement representative government. Hobson hoped that an increase in referendums, conjoined with other reforms (particularly the introduction of proportional representation, and the destruction of the House of Lords' power of veto) would engender a vibrant body politic—its parts relating to one another through consultation and participation—armed to resist and reduce what he referred to as "Cabinet autocracy," a state of affairs in which a few people held in their hands the governance of the country. That state of affairs "might easily lead to Caesarism, where a magnetic party leader either succeeded in capturing the imagination of the populace or in engineering a supremacy among competing politicians" (Hobson (1909:12), a possibility Hobson was keen to see stymied. Hobson, like Weber, recognized the conservative possibilities of referendums but believed this was a price worth paying when balanced against their democratic benefits. He wished to see the referendum implanted as a normal organ of democratic political rule; Weber on the other hand, confined its worth to exceptional situations and its utility to the statecraft of exceptional leaders.

106. Weber (1970a:106 = 1958:523); cf. Weber (1978b:268 = 1964: 199). It is thus perfectly appropriate for Eduard Baumgarten (1964:549) to entitle his own short section on Weber's constitutional proposals: "Der Reichspräsident: cäsaristische Demokratie," and for Wolfgang Mommsen (1984:340, 343–44, 353, 366) to agree on an identical equation. See also the extended analysis of Weber and Carl Schmitt by Luisa Mangoni (1979:37–52).

In Weber's *sociological* writings, the president chosen by plebiscite is described under the rubric of "charisma," to which I turn in the next chapter. See Weber (1978b:219 = 1964:162); Weber (1922:552).

4

From German Politics to Universal Sociology: Max Weber and His Contemporaries II

The Emergence of Weberian Sociology

After his precarious recovery in 1902 from the emotional breakdown that had struck him a few years earlier, Weber began a series of "methodological" investigations that laid the groundwork of the sociology for which he would later become celebrated. The 1904 essay, "'Objectivity' in social science and social policy" (Weber 1949), to take the most relevant case, contains Weber's first major statement on the "ideal-type" approach that would be extended, in 1913, to encompass the "Categories of Interpretive Sociology" (Weber 1981). Sandwiched between these dates is Weber's role in the founding of the German Sociological Society in January 1909, and his withdrawal from the Society four years later when it failed to adopt doctrinal positions compatible with his own. Still, whatever Weber's frustrations with the Society, and however ambivalent he felt about "this confounded science,"[1] he continued to pursue and deepen his interest in sociology until his death in 1920. The cardinal testament to this interest is *Economy and Society*, "a mixture of several torsos" written between 1911 and 1920 that stands as the very exemplification of Weberian sociology.[2]

Weber was always keen to insist that "scientific" work, of which his sociology was part, was distinctive from political engagement in a number of ways. Respectively, each possessed its own characteristic emphasis (explanation, intervention), its own criterion of validation (verisimilitude, effectiveness), and each addressed a different audience or the same audience in different roles (the scholar specialist, the citizen) through specific media (typically, the technical book and periodical, the newspaper, the public address). In practice, this meant appreciating the contrasting logics governing social science and political partisanship. Whereas partisanship, or what today we would call social advocacy, tends to make research ancillary and subordinate to a political program, scientific research proper is experimental, independent, and skeptical, not propagandist. Because these distinctions are ones that Weber returned to persistently and emphatically,[3] they cannot simply be ignored or evaded if we are to take his expressed intentions seriously. Yet, needless to say, the issue is not so easily settled.

That the difference between the political and the scientific or scholarly writings is constantly being confounded in reality is nowhere more evident than in the work of Weber himself. Thus while the pugnacious "Parliament and Government in a Reconstructed Germany" (1917–1918) is a clear example of the former and part I of *Economy and Society* (written between 1918 and 1920) with its stark formalism an example of the latter, where is one to place a document like "Politics as a Vocation" (1919)? As we know it in its published form (for it began life as a lecture delivered in Munich on January 28, 1919), academic and political elements sit in the closest proximity; we witness Weber as sociology teacher (the outline of the three types of legitimate domination, the summary of the principal ideas of M. Ostrogorski, etc.), as critic (of the German parliamentary system, of those who espouse absolutist ethical principles), as advocate and partisan (of a president of the Reich elected by the whole people), and as prophet of "polar night." And the status of "Politics as a Vocation" is hardly tangential for this study since it contains one of Weber's most important discussions of Caesarism.[4]

So what are we to conclude from this attempt at narrative discrimination? On the one hand, the unavoidable artificiality of conceptual distinctions is not a reason to avoid employing them. It is only grounds to treat their formulation with care and with sensitivity, and, in the last analysis, it is not implausible to admit of the different tasks, emphases, and idioms of academic-scientific and political work. That being so, it is incumbent on us to treat Weber's writings mindful of the tasks for which they were intended: hence the division of his work on Caesarism into two separate chapters of this book. In the previous chapter, I focused on Caesarism in relation to Weber's adversarial and propagandist interventions intended to shape state policy. In this much shorter one, I turn to discuss the concept as it was framed within those more deliberately scholarly treatises concerned with the sociology of domination.

On the other hand, we should not be deterred from seeking systematic relationships *between* texts and genres wherever it appears to be relevant and historically credible to do so. Much of what I am here calling Weber's political writings were composed during the same period in which he was constructing the categories of Weberian sociology. Quite often, one sees evidence of ideas formulated in a political context being reformulated in a sociological one; just as often, conversely, a sociological investigation or train of thought will help inform his political judgments. Short of narrative schizophrenia, this is exactly what one would expect. In consequence, I shall have no hesitation in drawing on both kinds of text where the subject matter seems to invite it. Moreover, we also have to avoid operating with an artificially restricted notion of "politics" and the "political." As Sheldon Wolin (1981) has cogently argued, Weber's "scientific" work encompassed both. The *"politics"* of Weber's program for the human sciences consisted in strategic and tactical arguments intended to defeat "rival theoretical claims." Equally, Weber's program was *"political"* in its attempt to constitute a new discursive domain: to establish, that is, a framework or template of concepts, methodological procedures and protocols that would win acceptance by other practitioners and be imitated in subsequent inquiry. Once established, the political aspects of theory tend to become muted because naturalized—until, that is, the founder's colonization of theoretical space is challenged successfully from other points of view.[5]

Weber's work, it is true, has been challenged from the beginning, though how successfully is a matter of opinion. What appears indubitable is its extraordinary influence on sociological investigation, and its uncanny foreshadowing of the kind of society in which we now live; to that extent, its concepts have helped determine, though obviously far less than they have anticipated, the way modern intellectuals and other educated people have come to think about the social world. The point has some significance for the topic of this book. During the nineteenth and early twentieth century, Caesarism was a particularly vibrant term and concept in the vernacular of political discussion.

Today it is largely forgotten, and even in specialist usage finds only a marginal place in political and sociological theory. While it would be pointless to lament this state of affairs, it remains pertinent to understand how we have reached it; how, in other words, a once hotly contested notion, passionately argued about and debated, faded into something arcane and peripheral. Changes in social and political relations are clearly the key to this transformation. But language itself is part of these relations. The way we think about the possibilities and the alternatives open—or closed—to us; the values we happen to embrace and fight for—or deem hopelessly outmoded; the descriptions we employ to make sense of ourselves, our fellow citizens, and our epoch; all this is mediated through the terms, metaphors, and stories that are publicly available. The importance of Weber's sociology for this book lies in his contribution to a new language in which an older term and debate—Caesarism—is drained of its previous normative content to become a mere shadow of its former self, a minor element in a universalistic typology of domination. In the process, the nature of democracy and legitimacy are themselves quite radically redescribed. To examine this metamorphosis is the key concern of what follows. I begin, however, with two earlier attempts to construct a systematic and didactic theory of Caesarism. This exercise will help us see not only the residual connections of these authors to an older classical tradition, but also the marked extent to which Weber broke with that tradition in the creation of Weberian sociology.

Competing Typologies

The two authors who merit our attention are the organicist thinker and social reformer Albert Schäffle—Weber described his *Bau und Leben des sozialen Körpers* ([1875–76] 1896) as a "brilliant work"[6]— and the historical economist Wilhelm Roscher[7] whom Weber subjected to a merciless methodological critique in an article first published in 1903, nine years after Roscher's death. (As far as I am aware, Weber never developed a commensurately sustained critique of Roscher's political writings, though he does mention in passing the *locus classicus* of Roscher's theory of Caesarism in the article mentioned above).[8] Common to the historical perspective of Schäffle and Roscher was a broadly cyclical, Aristotelian-Polybian view of political transformation, and a related interest in the conditions of legitimate rule. Each politico-constitutional structure or stage—monarchy, aristocracy, democracy—had its season; each had its immanent principle of emergence and principle of decline. "Caesarism" formed a subtype of the triad.

Let me deal first with Schäffle's very abbreviated account. He prefaces his specific remarks on Caesarism with a quotation from Aristotle in which the latter describes how "kingship" (or what Schäffle [1896 II:486] calls "legitimate monarchy,")[9] becomes debased from within, a victim of either dissension between members of the ruling dynasty or of the ambition of a king determined to expand his power beyond its lawful boundaries, or of both.[10] As kingship disintegrates, Schäffle glosses, society is thrown into crisis: the eventual result is tyranny or, what is just another word for the same thing, "Caesarism," "the product of a long and tiring battle between aristocrats and democrats, the rich and the poor. Out of the anarchy of civil war comes as the 'saviour of society' and democratic at the same time, the ancient Greek tyranny, the Roman imperator system, modern Caesarship."

The tyrant's power base, Schäffle continues, rests on a combination of brute force and popular incitement as he protects his position, on the one hand, by the deployment of a mercenary army,[11] bodyguards and "praetorians" and, on the other, by a divide-and-rule policy in which the poor are pitted against the educated and propertied classes. More generally:

> In a superb manner, and as if he had portrayed the most modern Napoleonism, Aristotle draws the basic characteristics of a policy by which alone the tyranny can survive. Its arts are: imitation of genuine monarchy; condemnation, destruction, slander, criminal pursuit of all brilliant independent men; attraction of all the weak characters amongst the rich and noble; corruption in every shape and form; repression of associations and open discussion; the stirring-up of estates, classes and friendships; enormous public extravagance, the feeding and entertaining of the mob; instigation of wars in order to divert internal opposition; police terror and a system of informers. (Schäffle 1896 II:486)

Thus, in Schäffle's schema, Caesarism is portrayed as identical to tyranny. Its origins lie in the internal collapse of kingship; its rule is simultaneously divisive, despotic, and bellicose; its connection to democracy tenuous; its recent manifestation "the most modern Napoleonism," by which Schäffle meant the rule of Napoleon III.[12]

Wilhelm Roscher, in his *Politik* (1892) agreed with Schäffle that Napoleon III (and his uncle even more so) was a prime example of the

Caesarist phenomenon, and that "tyranny" was a suitable term with which to designate it. In other respects, however, Roscher begged to differ. Not only does he define Caesarism with more precision as a "military tyranny" (Roscher 1892:588), he also pivots his theory on the argument that Caesarism arises out of conditions in which *democracy*[13] (as opposed to kingship) has degenerated into chaos; that is to say where rich and poor live in a state of mutual hatred, where the rivalry of demagogues and the parties they lead has become increasingly irresponsible, where the masses have become utterly capricious, and where the educated suspect that the extant system allows too much freedom. As a consequence, people in general long for order, for stability at any cost, and no group is better placed to satisfy this yearning than the military. This fact, says Roscher (echoing a long line of previous thinkers) is made explicable by the consideration that in periods of tumult and convulsion it is the army and its commander that provide the only source of social anchorage. Furthermore, the military virtues such as courage and obedience, the ones that are in a sense politically primordial, survive the common decadence, enabling those who possess these virtues to rise to a position of almost natural superiority. Caesarism, therefore, is a product of a society on the wane, just as it is that society's coup de grâce.

The mass of the people, moreover, are entirely unsentimental about Caesarism. They submit to it not out of love, but because in a situation where the "best" have withdrawn from the political arena, and where confusion reigns, the attitude emerges "that it is better to be oppressed by one lion, rather than ten wolves, a hundred jackals or even a thousand rats," a conviction, Roscher insists, that is the very driving force of Caesarism. For the sake of an end to "anarchy," people quite instrumentally trade their liberty for Caesarism, "the graveyard of general bondage." The tyrant, who once in power assumes a monarchical guise, is conscious of the people's pragmatism and the taste this realization leaves in his mouth is invariably bitter. Aware that he has become their choice not by winning hearts and minds but as the lesser of two evils, aware also that he lacks that halo of legitimacy and may even in fact be hated, the tyrant becomes ever more suspicious and his rule increasingly severe. Thus the monarchy that emanates from democracy's crisis "is as a rule despotic" (Roscher 1892:589–90).

The regimes and persons that Roscher happens to call Caesarist are enormously varied (in contrast to Romieu, incidentally, Julius Caesar is among the men so labelled) and his general discussion manysided. For my purposes, though, it will suffice to expand on what he has to say about Caesarism's relationship to democracy and on what he believed to issue from that relationship.

Two of Roscher's observations are of special pertinence. The first regards his contention that democracy paves the way for Caesarism, not only because of the turmoil that issues from its death throes, but because democracy's tendency to centralize, a consequence in turn of its equalitarian, "levelling" aspect, has removed potential loci of resistance to the tyrant from status groups of various sorts. Moreover, as a consequence of democracy's obsession with novelty and because of its agnostic mood more generally, old values that might have figured to restrain the tyrant, together with old religious and moral truths that might have guided the masses, have eroded. Hence democratic centralization and banality serve as both prelude and preparation for the Caesarist takeover.

Roscher's second observation turns on the peculiarities of the Caesarist leader's administration once installed in power. Essentially, Caesarism in power is a heteroclite formation because the strong egalitarian current it inherits from democracy is in constant tension with the monarchical system it also seeks to build. This accounts both for the strengths of Caesarism and its disabilities. As an example of the former, consider what Roscher refers to as Caesarism's "Janus-faced" nature, that is to say, its combination of monarchical and democratic governance, that enables the Caesarist ruler to encompass, and claim to represent, the most diverse social interests. Napoleon I is offered in illustration. Here was someone who attempted with some success to appeal to everyone across the political spectrum of his day from the old-guard nobility, at one extreme, to disenchanted Jacobins at the other. Thus Napoleon flaunted himself as a traditionalist—one of his first acts on becoming emperor was to abolish the celebration of Louis XVI's execution—while simultaneously claiming that if he occupied a lofty position this was because he was the living embodiment of the sovereign people (Roscher 1892:590–91, 600).

And what of Caesarism's disabilities? They are many. There is the onus on the leader who exists in an egalitarian culture to prove through public displays—acts of war, dazzling diplomacy, patronage of the arts—his right to occupy a position of superiority. There is the perplexing uncertainty that attends the tyrant daily: should his powers fail him and expectations of success be dashed his rule will be short lived, a predicament that reminds us of charisma's fate in similar circumstances. There is the impossibility of secure abdication, of a quiet and dignified retirement because the Caesarist leader must always fear the revenge of those whose hatred he has earned; besides, to his successor he will forever remain a potential source of competition (Roscher 1892:592–93, 603–6). Other disabilities could also be mentioned but ultimately they all boil down to this: the Caesarist leader is plagued by insoluble problems of legitimation. His constant need to prove himself attests to this insecurity. His striving to found a dynasty, his wish to confer on his progeny or chosen successor some modicum of respectability, rarely succeeds, and when it does, rarely succeeds for long. His political edifice, tarred by its violent origins, is in the last analysis an artificial juxtaposition of elements that can never possess the solidity, the vibrancy, of something organic. And while, like Edmund in *King Lear*, he may live in hope that "the base shall top the legitimate," that "now gods stand up for bastards!" (1.2:20–3), his hope will be to no avail if his subjects do not stand up for the bastard as well.

Let me conclude this exposition by providing one of Roscher's own examples to illustrate the contrast between Caesarism's inevitable discomfiture, and the far more relaxed demeanor afforded to the occupant of a hereditary monarchy. One of the paradoxes of Caesarism, Roscher says, is its military weakness. True, it rises to power through the achievements of a commander of the armed forces. But precisely because so much of its stature is focused on its military qualities, the Caesarist leader must always beware the general more able than himself. The emperor Domitian, for instance, recalled Agricola in 84 AD after the latter's victories in Britain, in order to let him languish at court, and later had him poisoned at a time when imperial defeats in foreign places might have commended such a man to the people.[14] By contrast it is said about Wilhelm I that when, in October 1870, one of his generals requested an extra division of troops, the Kaiser replied that it was up to Field Marshal Helmuth von Moltke, chief of the Prussian general staff, to decide; as for Wilhelm's own protection it was sufficient that he be left in control of his personal guards. Roscher cites this incident as a testament to the confidence and security a legitimate, hereditary monarch can enjoy who need not be afraid of even his most brilliant commander. An analogous response by the Caesarist leader would have placed him in the utmost peril and for that reason is unthinkable (Roscher 1892:608).

* * *

The accounts of Roscher and Schäffle clearly belong to an older tradition of political theory. The resonances not just of Aristotle and Polybius, but of Benjamin Constant and the mainstream nineteenth-century debate on Caesarism examined in a previous chapter, are numerous. It has long been recognized that Weber's own typology of legitimate domination broke with this tradition in several ways. Notably, while Weber shared the ambition of many of his peers to build global and comprehensive taxonomies, he jettisoned the organicist model, and the phase-teleology it entailed, typical of their endeavors.[15] However, the contrasts go much deeper than this, a point that is worth clarifying before we proceed any further.[16] This clarification, drawing on both Weber's political and sociological writings, in part recapitulates, in part anticipates, what is to follow.

Like Roscher, though in contrast with Schäffle, Weber views Caesarism as intrinsically connected to democracy: "every democracy" tends "toward the Caesarist mode of selection" (1979a:1451 = 1958:381–2). However, this Caesarism is not cancerous for the democratic body politic, heralding its protracted or imminent demise into military tyranny (*pace* Roscher) but the natural complement of mass democracy's existence. On Weber's account, furthermore, Caesarist domination is a normal, not a crisis, form of rule; a state in which the civil, as distinct from the military, arm of government is the dominant one; and a political formation in which civil liberties (entirely obliterated in Schäffle's and Roscher's versions of Caesarism) are capable of preservation by a robust parliament equipped with real constitutional power.

Schäffle and Roscher, like Auguste Romieu and most other thinkers in the mainstream of the nineteenth-century debate, depicted Caesarism as an essentially "illegitimate" political system. For Weber, by contrast, Caesarism may be deemed legitimate, sociologically speaking, to the extent that people living under its jurisdiction believe in its authority and voluntarily comply with its orders. Hence, the normative, condemnatory connotation of illegitimacy is erased from Weber's forensic (praise or disapprobation he deems inappropriate in a scientific discussion); the dynastic component considered irrelevant as the sociological criterion of legitimacy; and the rule of force (first arrestingly asserted by Romieu, endorsed in modified form in the theories of

Schäffle and Roscher) conceptually subordinated to the rule of consent: the Caesarist leader's fate in the modern mass suffrage party system is dependent, both initially and ultimately, on his ability to inspire devotion to his person and, secondarily, to the policies he is capable of executing.

Caesarism: The Sociological Redescription

In the previous chapter I showed that Weber's political writings were the source of a uniquely mercurial and dynamic theory of Caesarism. According to the context and purpose of Weber's arguments, "Caesarism" functioned variously as an instrument of criticism, endorsement, and recommendation. The uses Weber found for the concept may have been diverse—that is part of their originality—but they were at least quite salient. By contrast, Caesarism's place in Weber's sociology is far harder to discern and track. This is essentially because in the switch from one idiom to another, Caesarism is overtaken by two narrative developments that render it opaque. First, "Caesarism" in Weber's sociology is increasingly displaced by a set of cognate expressions with which it becomes more or less interchangeable; the new terminology includes: "plebiscitary rulership/domination" (*plebiszitäre Herrschaft*),[17] "leadership democracy with a 'machine,'" "plebiscitarian leadership,"[18] "leader-democracy,"[19] and "plebiscitarian leader-democracy."[20] Second, Caesarism, and this new terminology as a whole, is demoted to a subtype of Weber's master concept of charisma. I turn now to show how this transformation occurs.

That "Caesarism," or "plebiscitary rulership," or "leader-democracy," is a variant of charisma is a fact swiftly established: Weber is explicit about the matter in *Economy and Society*[21] and, with more brevity, in a piece written in 1913 as the introduction to the series "The Economic Ethic of the World Religions."[22] But if Caesarism is indeed a modality of charisma, of what sort exactly? The answer to this question is delphic and calls for some close textual analysis.

Compare for instance the discussion of charisma in "Politics as a Vocation," with those portions from the analyses of "legitimate domination/authority" in *Economy and Society* where charisma receives systematic and (in two cases) sustained examination, to wit: chapter XIV of part II composed in 1913 and called "Charisma and its Transformation"; the bit on charisma from the posthumously published "The Three Pure Types of Legitimate Domination" (Weber [1922] 1964) composed around 1918;[23] and sections iv, v, and vii, chapter III of part I, probably drafted around 1919. The overlap between what I shall feel free henceforth to call the 1913, 1918 and 1919 treatments of charisma in *Economy and Society* is considerable though differences are evident too in length—the 1913 treatment is a little more than twice as long as its 1919 counterpart, while both dwarf the 1918 version—and in substance: for instance, the 1919 discussion expressly develops the "anti-authoritarian" aspect of Weber's idea of charisma that is muted in the 1913 analysis and only briefly mentioned in the 1918 draft.

In "Politics as a Vocation" Weber's argument is straightforward enough. Having sketched the general character of charisma, and observed that it "has emerged in all places and in all historical epochs" Weber adds:

> Most importantly in the past, it has emerged in the two figures of the magician and the prophet on the one hand, and in the elected war lord, the gang leader and the *condotierre* on the other hand. *Political* leadership in the form of the free "demagogue" who grew from the soil of the city state is of greater concern to us; like the city state, the demagogue is peculiar to the Occident and especially to Mediterranean culture. Furthermore political leadership in the form of the parliamentary "party leader" has grown on the soil of the constitutional state, which is also indigenous only to the Occident.[24]

These comments suggest a universal, tripartite division of charisma into religious, military, and political dimensions; its political manifestation in the shape of the city-state demagogue and the parliamentary party leader, however, is unique to the West. Still, a little earlier in the same essay Weber had presented us with what was more akin to a bifurcation of his concept: we read there of charismatic domination "as exercised by the prophet or—in the field of politics—by the elected war lord, the plebiscitarian ruler, the great demagogue, or the political party leader" (Weber 1970a:79 = 1958:495). But whether charisma is tripartite or dualistic, it seems clear that Caesarism is a component of its political guise. True, the word "Caesarism" is missing from both these contexts, but it emerges explicitly when Weber subsequently cites Gladstone's "'grand' demagogy" and its success in wooing the mass vote, as irrefutable evidence that a "Caesarist plebiscitary element" had transformed the prime minister into a "plebiscitarian dictator" who "stands above Parliament."[25] However, while Weber's discussion of Caesarism and plebiscitarianism in "Politics as a Vocation" is direct and transparent, in *Economy and Society* it is much more tortuous. Once again "plebiscitary domination" is portrayed as a type of Occidental, political charisma; only this time it is the paradoxical nature of the phenomenon that Weber now chooses to emphasize. To understand the nature of this paradox it is necessary to consider briefly what Weber considered charisma, in its most pristine manifestation, to be.

Pure or "genuine" charisma, Weber maintained, is doubly extraordinary: its bearer is "treated as endowed with supernatural, superhuman, or at least specifically exceptional powers or qualities" (Weber 1978b:241 = 1964:178); its lifeblood, at least initially, is a psychological condition of human excitement, enthusiasm, or distress that may or may not be related to a wider social crisis. In the intense personal devotion to the master that it inspires, and its irreverence for tradition and legality for their own sake, "charismatic belief revolutionises men 'from within' and shapes material and social conditions according to its revolutionary will" (Weber 1978b:1116 = 1964:836). Nonetheless, the fealty of both close associates and the rank and file is neither unconditional nor uncritical. The leader must bring forth the requisite material and emotional satisfactions to keep the following committed to his mission. Charisma, to retain its spell over heart and mind, must continually display its powers. Should triumphs succumb to disaster and the promised well-being for all believers fail to come about, the leader will find himself deserted, ridiculed, and, worst of all, ordinary. In the final analysis, therefore, the charismatic figure is the captive of others' devotion. When that devotion turns to indifference or hostility, the gift of grace vaporises (Weber 1978b:242, 1114 = 1964:179, 834–35).

Though the ability to perform miracles of various kinds is, thus, a condition of charisma's longevity, it is not the ground of its claim to legitimacy. This rests upon the "conception that it is the duty of those subject to charismatic authority to recognise its genuineness and to act accordingly." It is this moral imperative, this demand of allegiance on behalf of a leader convinced that he is the vessel of some deity or of providence that constitutes charisma's "authoritarian principle" of legitimacy (Weber 1978b:242, 266 = 1964:179, 198.) By contrast *plebiszitäre Herrschaft* (Caesarism, etc.) reflects a situation in which charisma has strayed such a long way down the road of rationalization that the premises of its original claim to legitimacy have been inverted; in other words, charismatic legitimacy is subjected "to an anti-authoritarian interpretation" (Weber 1978b:266 = 1964:198; Weber 1964:558). Instead of the leader's authority being founded upon a mission that the following, to the extent that it recognizes him, is duty-bound to acknowledge (charisma in its purest revelation), legitimacy is now *formally* derived from the will of the following itself, whom the charismatic (political) leader professes to embody. Legitimacy in this way assumes a "democratic" coloration.[26] As Weber remarks:

> The personally legitimated charismatic leader becomes leader by the grace of those who follow him since the latter are formally free to elect and even to depose him—just as the loss of charisma and its efficacy had involved the loss of genuine legitimacy. Now he is the freely elected leader. Correspondingly, the recognition of charismatic decrees and judicial decisions on the part of the community shifts to the belief that the group has a right to enact, recognise or repeal[27] laws, according to its own free will, both in general and for an individual case.[28] (Weber 1978b:267 = 1964:198)

Any reader who takes these lines literally will conclude that the core meaning of charisma has been changed in them. The leader who once led by virtue of his own qualities to which the masses (or a section of them) submitted in awe, has become reduced to a mere cipher of popular sovereignty. How it is possible for Weber to argue that the "democratic" leader is, despite his apparent abasement, a *charismatic* figure? The answer becomes apparent once we understand Weber's view of the election and the plebiscite, and his related perception of the *demos* that exercises them.

Although great play is made in *Economy and Society* of the distinction between an election and a plebiscite, in the end it amounts substantively to very little. The plebiscite, Weber explains, is an acclamatory technique peculiar to democracy; through it voters give expression of their endorsement of a leader of policy.[29] A plebiscite, strictly speaking, is not politically identical to an "election" if by that word we are implying "a real choice between candidates" (Weber 1978b:1129 = 1964:848). Rather, a plebiscite "is the first or the renewed recognition of a pretender as a personally qualified, charismatic ruler; an example of the latter case is the French plebiscite of 1870."[30] And yet there is, the previous comments notwithstanding, an essential link between the plebiscite and election after all,[31] a connection that becomes plain when Weber describes the social and semantic provenance of the latter. Originally, the election was an acknowledgement

by a following—faced with the problems of charismatic succession—
of the grace of a charismatic aspirant. There was only one "right"
choice of, say, a feudal king; to choose "wrongly" was tantamount to a
sacrilegious error. And the majority principle had absolutely nothing
to do with this "election" process since "a minority, no matter how
small, might be right in its recognition of genuine charisma, just as the
largest majority might be in error" (Weber 1978a:1126 = 1964:846;
Weber 1964:557–8) a dilemma that spawned in the case of the papacy
the practice of unanimous election. Weber adds here that the kind of
election he has just described is not one "in the modern sense of a
presidential or parliamentary election" (Weber 1978b:1126 = 1964:845)
but this is an observation that requires some care in its interpretation.
For it is clear that in one key respect the older and modern senses of
election *are* similar where the issue of charismatic leadership is concerned: both are essentially practices of acclamation, affirmations of
the master's mission. With that endorsement, the key purpose of the
demos in the "election"—and the plebiscite—is exhausted.[32]

But why is it exhausted? Weber scholars have variously traced
Weber's theory of charismatic leadership to a compound of sources,
both characterological and doctrinal: the "aristocratic" pathos of
Nietzsche's *Übermenschen*, Kantian individualism, early Protestantism are often mentioned. However, every theory of political leadership
supposes not only some notion of those who wield authority and command, but also a sense of the agency and the capacities of the led. Not
until we uncover *this* side of the theory, I now want to suggest, are we
able to understand the deepest antidemocratic implications of Weber's
line of argument. The point will bear some elaboration.

The "Irrationality" of the Masses

The nineteenth-century debate on Caesarism, as I described it in
chapter 2, was characterized by two fundamental motifs. The first
turned on the lack of "legitimacy" of Caesarism, a concern that could
itself be rendered in various ways: the end of tradition, the attack on
God, the dread of political "usurpation" or "despotism." Weber's sociological framework conceptually swept away such concerns when it
redefined "legitimacy" to mean either a report on the nature of people's
beliefs about a power relationship, or a series of "legitimations"—
traditional, rational-legal, charismatic—projected by those in power.

In both cases, the older strains of legitimacy became *sociologically* irrelevant. On the one hand, belief in the rightness of an authority claim now becomes sufficient grounds for its legitimacy *irrespective of its content.* On the other, legitimacy itself appears to dissolve into claims that the powerful make about themselves and their ability to persuade others of their right to rule. More than this, Weber defined "domination" or "rulership" (*Herrschaft*) in such a way as to make it exceedingly difficult to untangle from "legitimacy" or "legitimations." It is true that, as a kind of "power"—"the authoritarian power of command"—domination comprises a relationship between ruler and ruled, between those who command and obey. But Weber adds that, in his sense, domination[33] means "the situation in which the manifested will (command) of the ruler or rulers is meant to influence the conduct of one or more others (the ruled) and actually does influence it in such a way that their conduct to a socially relevant degree occurs as if the ruled had made the content of the command the maxim of their conduct for its very own sake." Or, in other words, the "merely external fact of the order being obeyed is not sufficient to signify domination in our sense; we cannot overlook the meaning of the fact that the command is accepted as a 'valid' norm." (Weber 1978b:946 = 1964:695).[34]

The second theme of the older Caesarism debate concerned the political character of the "masses." The majority of commentators believed these masses to be demonstrably unfit to participate in the political process, either because of their lack of education or because there was something about the social nature of "masses" as such that made them politically irrational. Weber developed a variant of the latter position. Of itself, this would be noteworthy but, given nineteenth-century attitudes, conventions, and theories of crowd psychology, not especially remarkable. Articulated to Weber's concept of legitimacy, however, it has major theoretical consequences. For if legitimacy rests in the final analysis on the beliefs of the governed; and if the governed themselves are in the main an irrational mass; *then no rational democratic politics is possible in modern society.* As in Weber's political writings, Caesarism or "plebiscitary leadership" is, again, inevitable in one form or another; but this time Weber's conclusion is predicated on more than a conjunctural analysis of his times, on more, in other words, than the arguments of a citizen concerned to demonstrate what political arrangements would be best for his country; it is inscribed within the very structure of his theory of social relationships. That conclusion may be startling, but it is not hard to find evidence for it.

Weber's commitment to "democracy" was always heavily qualified by the view that extensive public participation in politics—the Machiavellian ideal—was an impossibility in densely populated, technologically complex, and socially heterogeneous nation-states. In part this conviction derived from his study of modern political parties that seemed amply to corroborate the "law of the small number"—Weber's variation on Robert Michels's iron law of oligarchy. But there was another part to Weber's thinking that must be grasped if we are to comprehend his position. This concerns his understanding of the social psychology of the "mass" or "masses," terms that are used by Weber in different, though complementary and overlapping, senses. First is the idea of mass as a simple social aggregate that in its very amorphousness cuts across all other social divisions (of class, status, occupation, etc). This is the mass "as such," "irrespective of the social strata which it comprises in any given case" (Weber 1978a:1459 = 1958:392). In this sense, all persons, whatever their level of intelligence, their disposition, or their social background are potentially or in fact members of a mass. As a designation for some indeterminate body of people, "mass" may be devoid of any notion of assembly—as revealed in such expressions as the "mass" of the electorate or "mass administration" (Weber 1978b:285, 951 = 1964:212, 700).

Second, a mass suggests what Gustave Le Bon ([1895] 1960:23–24) once dubbed a "psychological crowd" by which he meant a combination of people the density of which engenders a sort of collective personality. Broadly speaking, a crowd is a distinct sort of mass in that it involves some spatial location, some social intercourse, some congregation. Typically, crowds are heterogeneous in composition, and our contact with fellow crowd members is brief and unarticulated by formal relations of authority. The study of how our membership in a crowd affects our conduct is the subject matter of "crowd psychology" that may or may not be approached in the Le Bonnian mode (Weber 1978b:23 = 1964:175).

Finally, "mass" may shade into notion of "the masses" or "the mob" (Guenther Roth's translation of *Strassenherrschaft*)[35] evoking a variety of allusions. One theme is simply subordinate groups or classes. Another is specific groups within subordinate classes that have resisted political integration or whose behavior exposes a breakdown in the structure of political integration: that is to say, groups that remain politically unorganized and undisciplined by professional politicians or trade union leaders. Mass in the sense of mob refers particularly to those among the unpropertied whose insurgent, spontaneous street activity, notably characteristic of "neo-Latin forms of life," makes them dangerously amenable to the demagogue of, say, syndicalist predilection.[36]

Weber's references to mass and masses are, thus, varied and complex. Yet common to all his depictions is a theme that binds them together in a broadly coherent framework and that is the key to understanding why, for Weber, "democratic" politics is synonymous with oligarchy. According to Weber, the mass is handicapped by an inherent and crippling disability: it is "irrational." By this term Weber typically means behavior that is myopic, amorphous, imitative, but especially "emotional," (the term he most often uses to characterize mass behavior) oscillating between passivity and explosive spontaneity, and causally determined rather than meaningfully oriented.[37] What is particularly problematic about such a view is not the concepts of "masses" or "mob" in themselves, notions that with analytical care may be justifiably imputed in some circumstances to collective behavior. Nor need one deny that, under some description, and under some conditions, mass conduct can be irrational, even if to describe it as such today usually attracts the ire of historians and social scientists. The really serious problem is that, on Weber's account, there is no way to distinguish mass behavior from any other kind of collective action; indeed, given Weber's methodological individualism the very idea of collective "action" is strictly speaking a misnomer. Similarly, Weber fails sociologically to disaggregate emotional "mass" intrusions into political life from collective civic interventions or social movements. Indeed, with the reduction of a public to a mass, Weber is left with a definition of politics itself as "any kind of autonomous *leadership*" (Weber 1958:493 = 1970a:77). Since masses are evidently destitute of all characteristics that could make them "autonomous,"[38] it follows that self-governing liberty on an extended scale, and the taxing responsibilities that go with it, is a *categorical and stipulative* impossibility within Weber's schema. As Weber put it:

...one must always remember that the term "democratisation" can be misleading. The *demos* itself, in the sense of a shapeless mass, never "governs" larger associations, but rather is governed. What changes is only the way in which the executive leaders are selected and the measure of influence which the *demos*, or better, which social circles from its midst are able to exert upon the content and the direction of administrative activities by means of "public opinion." "Democratisation," in the sense here intended, does not necessarily mean an increasingly active share of the subjects in government. This may be a result of democratisation, but it is not necessarily the case.[39]

So it is that though the legitimacy of "plebiscitary democracy" is "*formally* derived from the will of the governed" (Weber 1978b:268 = 1964:199) and in that sense "anti-authoritarian," the leader in fact remains the source of devotion and duty—and thus authoritarian after all. All talk of popular sovereignty is an empty slogan.[40] Modern democracy or "plebiscitary domination" is "anti-authoritarian" only in its "claim" to legitimacy, rather than its substance, and that claim only tells us how the charismatic democratic leader, and the society of which he is a part, justifies his mission, as opposed to why people actually support him. As with all other kinds of charisma, the democratic leader wins allegiances on the basis of what he does, or on the basis of what people perceive him to do, or on the basis of what they perceive he is capable of doing; in short, because of his powers and their actual or potential realization. Insofar as a democratic leader can prove his ability and win a devoted constituency through extraordinary feats, his domination is thus essentially charismatic and authoritarian, never mind the pious phrases concerning mass participation that surround it.

To sum up: Weber's sociological remodelling of Caesarism as "plebiscitary domination" and other cognate expressions depicts it as a social relationship involving a modern variant of charisma—Occidental, political, demagogic—founded on the democratization of the suffrage and its corollary, the mass party system, in which the masses vote for the person they find most exemplary. Caesarism—or "plebiscitary domination"—is anti-authoritarian in rhetoric, but acclamatory in practice. A plebiscitary model of politics in some shape or form is inevitable under modern conditions, not only because of the character of party politics but also because of the nature of the masses. Where nineteenth-century critics of Caesarism feared or regretted such a situation, Weber accepted it as a fact of life. But there was still one twist left in his argument.

Most previous thinkers examined in this book had sought to distinguish the military, command mode of governance typical of Caesarism, from the kind of politics in which law and representation are respected and form the bedrock of political life. Weber also often followed such a distinction, notably in his defense of parliament against Bismarck's constitutional system. But in other places, particularly where the question of "democracy" is at issue, and where Weber seeks to expose what he considers to be the sociological truth behind the ideological veil, he extends his categorical framework of "plebiscitary domination" to incorporate both military and civilian relationships. For example, in a passage from *Economy and Society* (1978b:961–62 = 1964:707) on the means by which elected mayors of some American cities have effected their reforms "in a 'Caesarist' fashion," he goes on to observe:

> Viewed technically, as an organised form of domination, the efficiency of "Caesarism," which often grows out of democracy, rests in general upon the position of the "Caesar" as a free trustee of the masses (of the army or of the citizenry), who is unfettered by tradition. The "Caesar" is thus the unrestrained master of a body of highly qualified military officers and officials whom he selects freely and personally without regard to tradition or to any other impediments. Such "rule of the personal genius," however, stands in conflict with the formally "democratic" principle of a generally elected officialdom.

Again, in discussing *plebiszitäre Herrschaft* Weber informs his readers that while its "most common examples are the modern party leaders," it "is always present in cases where the chief feels himself to be acting on behalf of the masses and is indeed recognised by them. Both the Napoleons are classical examples, in spite of the fact that legitimation by plebiscite took place only after they seized power by force" (Weber 1978b:267 = 1964:198, emphasis omitted). The meaning of "Caesarism" here seems to be uncommonly strained since one would think that "modern party leaders" like Gladstone or Lloyd George embodied a form of rule fundamentally different from that of the two Bonapartes who "seized power by force." What can the "Caesarian domination of military parvenus"[41] have in common with the likes of these British statesmen?

Considered from the perspective of Weber's universalistic ideal-type approach, three features appear fundamental. First, the party leaders (or city mayors) of the modern day represent a continuation, a rationalization, of a process of political democratization presaged by Cromwell, by the leaders of the French Revolution, and by the Bonapartes. Second, the military and civilian power relationships that fall under the rubric of Caesarism can be typified as rhetorically "anti-authoritarian" and plebiscitary: both systems derive "the legitimacy of authority from the confidence of the ruled, even though the voluntary nature of such confidence is only formal or fictitious" (Weber 1978b:267 = 1964:198); both also conflict to a greater or lesser extent with crown or parliament. Third, Caesarism, be it military or incarnated in the form of the modern party leader is akin to a kind of "dictatorship." We have seen Weber use this term in a number of contexts already including Gladstone's leadership of the Liberal party, and the office of the German Reich president; his perception of democratic dictatorship was also doubtless sharpened by the behavior of Allied leaders during the First World War.[42] That military rule and Caesarism sprang out of democracy was not of course a new idea; for generations thinkers had condemned democracy precisely for that reason. That, under modern conditions, military rule and the rule of civilians are—in some fundamental respects—mirror images of each other was a rather different notion.[43] Again, the "anti-authoritarian" claims of plebiscitary domination had been exposed as a charade.

Charisma and Caesarism Revisited: Their Systematic Relationship Considered and a Problem Addressed

Up to this point I have sought to show how Caesarism is doubly redescribed in Weber's sociology. From being a prominent term in the political writings devoted to Bismarck and the Anglophone alternative to the constitutional arrangements of the *Kaiserreich*, "Caesarism" is first reformulated under the lexicon of "plebiscitary domination," and simultaneously absorbed within the general concept of charisma. To meet the possible objection that I have been quoting Weber selectively and prejudicially, I now want to show in a more systematic way how and why this transformation occurred. My starting point is the observation that Weber's work as a whole reveals a clear textual asymmetry in his discussion of Caesarism and charisma. In what I have been calling the "political" writings, Caesarism is Weber's preferred term for political leadership and charisma a word rarely employed. Conversely, in the academic-sociological treatises, charisma is paramount and obtrusive, while Caesarism is demoted as a *term* to virtual insignificance. Why is this? A satisfactory answer to this puzzle, I suggest, depends on a scrutiny of four kinds of linguistic relationship that it will be the job of the rest of this section to elucidate.

Charisma in the Sociological and Political Writings

Although "charisma" made a brief appearance towards the end of *The Protestant Ethic and the Spirit of Capitalism* ([1905] 1930)[44], it was not until around 1913 that the concept really came to prominence in Weber's sociology, a position it would retain to the end. In its first formulation, David Beetham (1989:321) reminds us, "charisma itself is a gift possessed by all believers; in Weber's later sociology it becomes a special attribute of leadership. In like manner the individualism that was a general characteristic of the 'heroic age of capitalism,' as Weber terms it, becomes in the bureaucratic age a special quality of heroes."[45] Insofar as the term appears at all in what I am referring to as the political writings, it merely serves the function of repeating, summarizing, or reinforcing what Weber has said at much greater length, and with much greater sophistication, in his sociological texts. Indeed, the only usages of the term "charisma" in the political writings known to me come from the pages of "Politics as a Vocation,"[46] a document that, as I indicated earlier, enjoys a special position in the Weberian corpus because it so evidently straddles a number of idioms.

The Relationship between Charisma and Caesarism in the Sociological Writings

In the sociological writings such as *Economy and Society* and the studies of the world religions, charisma is Weber's most salient term to describe individual leadership, the ardor and sense of duty it inspires on behalf of the following, and the routinization of wonder. Caesarism, on the other hand, is Lilliputian by comparison, and is explicitly mentioned as a word only rarely.[47] Furthermore, if one concentrates on the chapters specifically devoted to the analysis of charisma in *Economy and Society* it becomes clear that while "Caesarism" emerges twice in the 1913 draft of the typology of legitimate domination,[48] it is completely absent from its 1918 and 1919 counterparts; in those cases, "Caesarism" has been entirely expunged by the cognate expressions *Führer-Demokratie*, *plebiszitäre Führerdemokratie*, and *plebiszitäre Herrschaft*.[49] These words, and Caesarism itself in the 1913 version (in which the one reference to *plebiszitäre Herrschaft* is specifically linked to "Caesarism")[50] possess little independent status in the sociological texts; as Weber explains them, they seem to be mere derivatives or adjuncts of the master term charisma. Accordingly, they share the most significant properties of charisma, even in contexts where charisma is not specifically mentioned. Thus, in Weber's chapter on bureaucracy in part II of *Economy and Society* we are informed that "Caesarism" amounts to the "'rule of the personal genius,'" "who is unfettered by tradition" (Weber 1978b:961–62 = 1964:707) a comment that reminds us of the qualities possessed by the bearer of the gift of grace.

The Relationship between Charisma in the Sociological Writings and Caesarism in the Political Writings

In the political writings, too, Caesarism is projected in such a way as to remind us constantly of what Weber says about charisma in his sociological discussions: we are told of Caesarism's succession problem;[51] a number of men named Caesarist also appear as embodiments of charisma in Weber's formal sociology, for instance Gladstone,[52] Napoleons I and III,[53] and Pericles;[54] Caesarism, like charisma, is depicted as a highly personalized form of domination resting on mass emotionality;[55] and both are designated acclamatory.[56] However, contrasts are also in evidence. First, Caesarism is overwhelmingly Weber's favored leadership term in the political writings; indeed, with the exception of "Politics as a Vocation," "charisma" is never mentioned in them. Second, the theme of illegitimacy, which arises in the political texts that deal with Caesarism, is an issue of no real substance in the context of charisma. Moreover, even where Weber raises the question of Caesarism's illegitimacy in *Economy and Society*, he does so only in the most casual way.[57] Third, while Weber's wartime polemics against Bismarck repeatedly castigate him as Caesarist, Bismarck is the one figure conspicuously excluded from Weber's list of charismatic personages. The only vague allusion to charisma in Bismarck's case is the reference to his "rule of genius", an expression Weber also uses of the charismatic Napoleon I[58] and which in both the sociological and political works is said to characterize Caesarism also.[59]

The Relationship between Caesarism in the Sociological Writings and Caesarism in the Political Writings, and Some Questions Answered

The most prominent aspect of this relationship has already been considered: Caesarism, the term that Weber uses as early as November

1884, and continues to use until virtually the end of his life in his political writings has, by 1919, become supplanted in the sociological-academic texts (never of great prominence there in any case) both by the terminology of *plebiszitäre Herrschaft* and its correlates, and simultaneously digested as an idea into the wider notion of charisma. How, then, is one to explain this discrepancy between Caesarism's relatively high standing in the political writings, and its inferior status in the sociological ones? What happened to make Caesarism dematerialize in the 1918 and 1919 versions of the three types of legitimate domination? Why, if Caesarism had become redundant as a sociological term, should Weber have chosen to retain its services as a political foil? Why, if charisma is Weber's preferred sociological terms for the leader-follower bond is its employment, outside the sociological texts, restricted to "Politics as a Vocation?"

The absence of "Caesarism" from the 1918 and 1919 typologies of legitimate domination has to be put, I suggest, in a methodological context. Weber's objective in the sociological writings was not simply to inform his specialist audience about the social character of the world but also to provide it with a model of how social information should be processed and presented. For him, sociology was to eschew value judgment and be scientific in Weber's understanding of that term: dispassionate in its formulations; saturated in empirical knowledge; modest in its claims and its conclusions; driven by that demonic passion to learn yet able to discipline that passion once the choice of subject matter for research had been decided on so to prohibit *parti pris*; and generally prudent and controlled. That Weber often breached his own rules is well known, but not the point here. What is the point is Weber's sociological design, clearly apparent in part I of *Economy and Society*, the "Conceptual Exposition" (*Soziologische Kategorienlehre*),[60] the part that also contains the 1919 version of the analysis of charisma; for in that part Weber marks out, as nowhere else in his work,[61] the ground of sociology as a discipline and the methodological approach it should adopt. Part I is the closest Weber ever got to articulating a manifesto for sociology, and under the turgidity of its prose and its interminable model-building pulsed a crusading purpose. Admittedly, as manifestos go, it is at times reticent and even self-deprecatory. Does Weber not disclaim, in the preface to chapter 1, methodological novelty for the terms and concepts he is about to use in that chapter and by extension in the whole of part I? Does he not declare

that he has simplified his language in order to make it more comprehensible and accessible? Yet while the modesty of the first remark is
undermined by the sentence that immediately follows it ("The
method...attempts only—[!]—to formulate what all empirical sociology really means when it deals with the same problems"), the second
stands qualified by Weber's own concession that his account may
seem "pedantic," that "the most precise formulation cannot always be
reconciled with a form which can readily be popularised. In such cases
the latter aim has had to be sacrificed" (Weber 1978b:3 = 1964:3).

Now Caesarism, being a word so protean and politically combus-
tible, was not the sort of term suitable for a project like *Economy and
Society*, part I, which required instead a more anodyne language to do
the sort of work Weber wished it to perform. Moreover, Caesarism's
unsuitability as a technical term might also have been compounded by
the fact of its inclusion nonetheless in other "textbooks" with scientific aspirations (Roscher's *Politik*; Schäffle's *Bau und Leben*) that
Weber would have been compelled to rebut in conformity with his
professed goal of formulating "what all empirical sociology really
means when it deals with the same problems." Sometimes a word or
distinction is so fundamental that Weber cannot avoid confronting
opposing formulations, as he does with Rudolf Stammler's concept of
"order," Georg Friedrich Knapp's notion of money, or, indirectly, with
Marx's category of class. In other cases, Weber is able to bypass
extended critique through coining or adapting notions such as
plebiszitäre Herrschaft or "leader democracy" and its equivalents, expressions less anachronistic and pejorative than "Caesarism," and more
specifically honed to the modern conditions it is the sociologist's task
to investigate.

The virtue of *charisma* as a term, meanwhile, was that it was a
word with which few people at that time, sociologists included, would
have been acquainted. Affording ample scope for sociological definition and elaboration, it provided Weber with both a blank check, and a
route of escape from the unruly preconceptions tenanted in the house
of Caesarism. Naturally, this was not charisma's only merit.
"Caesarism" was invariably linked to the political realm: the council
or state. Its orbit of meaning was hence commensurately circumscribed,
a restriction that could only be reinforced by the marriage of the term
to a particular historical person or group of persons. By dint of this
semantic confinement, Caesarism could never have furnished the more

general, more abstract, tool Weber required to theorize his third mode of domination. His ideal-type trinity needed a concept that could accommodate all that was known as Caesarism but much more besides. And this was to be charisma's role. Charisma could be made to traverse a vast territory of devotional relationships, from state leadership over a mass of people at one extreme, to the artistic leadership exercised over an aesthetic coterie at the other; it thus possessed the versatility lacking in "Caesarism" to bestride universal forms and local situations. Moreover, the religious dimension of leadership, mostly absent from "Caesarism," in fact often squarely opposed to it, could be conveyed generously in a term like charisma that, through its Biblical origins, came equipped with its own numinousness.

"Charisma," then, presented itself as an attractive alternative to "Caesarism" because it was not bowed down under the weight of previous controversy; because it allowed elbow room, as Weber saw it, for scientific formulation; and because it was capable of encapsulating the plurality of relationships between leaders and followers that Weber was keen to depict. Insofar as Weber wrote as a founder of sociology, engaged in the formative process of creating a comparative discipline free from value judgments, it is natural that Caesarism is, in his sociology, generally demoted as too polemical and too narrow a term for his technical purposes. Equally, it is significant that in the 1919 *Kategorienlehre* (and the 1918 section on "The Three Pure Types of Legitimate Domination"), where Weber is setting out the lexicon and basic concepts of sociology, Caesarism disappears altogether as a word, supplanted by the vocabulary of *plebiszitäre Herrschaft*, and absorbed into charisma. By contrast, insofar as Weber wrote as a liberal-nationalist partisan, as a person determined to take a stand in public affairs, it is just as natural that Caesarism, a common term in the political vernacular of his day, should have been retained, and charisma—esoteric as it then was—omitted from discussion. It figures, too, that a piece like "Politics as a Vocation," simultaneously pedagogical and polemical in intention, should have employed virtually the whole gamut of terms considered in this chapter—Caesarism, charisma, plebiscitary democracy, plebiscitary domination/rulership, leader-democracy—which in other texts are quite rigorously separated.

This reconstruction of Weber's reasoning is, of course, hypothetical. What is beyond doubt is that in Weber's *sociology* Caesarism suffers a double eclipse. Not only is a once highly charged idea placed under a new and sanitized vocabulary; it also virtually disappears into a concept—charisma—that now becomes, in some shape or form, the source of all authority. Caesarism's previous overtones of illegitimacy and oppressiveness are accordingly erased in a sociology aspiring to global application.

Conclusion

No other analysis of Caesarism in the nineteenth and the twentieth century was more complex, more transitional, more Janus-faced, as Wilhelm Roscher might have put it, than Weber's. On the one hand, it looked back to an older tradition in which demagogy and populism were viewed with distrust and dismay. This is how, in the main, Weber depicts the effects of Bismarck's governance on the German state. On the other hand, it anticipated and served to delineate a view of democracy as little more than an acclamatory process, a competition between leaders or elites for the popular vote. Such are the implications of Weber's defense of the British parliamentary system, his championing of a plebiscitarian Reich president for the postwar German Republic, and his sociological treatises on the nature of domination and democracy. The concept of Caesarism is correspondingly subject to an unprecedented volatility: damned *and* exonerated in the political writings, depending on the context; erased through the invention of a new sociological language that can no longer speak its name. That such theoretical turbulence reflected major social and political changes is obvious. We have already seen that some of the very best minds of the nineteenth and early twentieth century understood clearly enough that new times required new concepts and that modernity had spawned developments—industrial capitalism and mass democracy among them—about which classical and later republican thought was mostly silent. At the same time, the republican idea waned because of a lack of commitment to its fundamental values: political *virtù*, a balanced constitution, self-governing liberty. On this at least, the consensus between Weberian "competitive elite" liberalism[62] and classical Marxism was clear. For both, the republican ideal of a responsible community of citizens, each having his salutary role to play in the *res publica* was absurd, and gave way to plebiscitary or vanguardist models of rule. The notion that politics is an activity valuable *sui generis*—a space for human creativity and accommodation in pursuit of diverse public goals—was also artificially circumscribed or flatly rejected. For liberals like Weber, the notion of oligarchy was no longer to be understood, as it had been for classical republicans, as a tendency to be resisted in political relations, or even a stage in a political cycle that will itself be superseded, but as an iron and universal law. Similarly, political democracy under modern conditions was now considered to be sham: little more than a rhetorical device of party managers, or a fraudulent "hegemonic" instrument employed to win consent and continue the uninterrupted business of bourgeois rule. Such ideologies of constriction did more than express existing realities. By legitimating the evisceration of citizenship, they helped shape and reproduce them.

Notes

1. From a letter to Franz Eulenburg, October 10, 1910, quoted in Scaff (1989:140). See also the remarks of Wolf Lepenies ([1985] 1988:244–47), and Keith Tribe (1989:1).
2. The expression in quotation marks comes from Wolfgang Mommsen (1974:15). It refers to the various layers and drafts that comprise *Economy and Society*. More on this later.
3. Their most persuasive and moving formulation can be found in "Science as a Vocation" ([1919] 1970b).
4. The fact that *Economy and Society* itself contains a theory of politics (Collins 1986:2–3) is no objection to the distinction previously made. From a Weberian standpoint, a theory of politics is concerned with causal explanation, rather than with partisan advocacy, and is thus subject to the same protocols that govern any other area open to scientific analysis.
5. For a more extended discussion, see Baehr and O'Brien (1994:19–28).
6. Weber (1978b:14 = 1964:11). On Schäffle as a social reformer, and on his ideas regarding workers' insurance in particular, see H.J. Braun (1983:51–60, esp. 55–56).
7. A. Oncken has admirably summarised the various branches of Roscher's scholarship in R.H. Inglis Palgrave (ed.), volume III (1908:323–27). On Weber's relationship to the German *Nationalökonomie* tradition, see Tribe (1989).
8. Weber, *Roscher and Knies: The Logical Problems of Historical Economics* (1975:227, n.69) = "Roscher und Knies und die logischen Probleme der historischen Nationalökonomie" in Weber (1951:1–145, at 28, n.4). The reference is to Roscher's *Politik. Geschichtliche Naturlehre der Monarchie, Aristokratie und Demokratie* (1892), a consolidation and extension of articles written over the previous decade.
9. According to Aristotle, "tyranny" is a wrongful form of monarchy, "kingship" a rightful one; the former is a deviation from the latter: Aristotle (1962:115–16, 135–38).
10. Schäffle (1896:486); cf. Aristotle (223–24) who adds a third cause of decline: "Those who inherit may be persons of no account, whom it is hard to respect; and though the power they possess is royal, not tyrannical, they may abuse their position."

11. "A king's bodyguard is made up of citizens, a tyrant's of foreign mercenaries," Aristotle (1962:218).

12. Schäffle (1896 II:487) says that Napoleon III could have been the model for Aristotle's depiction of tyranny in *The Politics* "V, c.9" (he must mean Book V, chapter 11) since "faked plebiscites, an army of praetorians, corruption, police censoring of the press, the adventures from Mexico to China, the European wars, well paid but servile deputies, civil servants, jailing, deportation, assassination, incarceration of 30,000 political opponents and the like" are all "characteristics of tyranny."

  Lewis Namier would later offer a similar formulation, though emphasizing, much more than Schäffle, the pseudo-democratic dimension of "plebiscitarian Caesarism." According to Namier, Caesarism's "direct appeal to the masses" intrinsically involved "demagogical slogans; disregard of legality in spite of a professed guardianship of law and order; contempt of political parties and the parliamentary system, of the educated classes and their values; blandishments and vague, contradictory promises for all and sundry; militarism: gigantic blatant displays and shady corruption. *Panem et circenses* once more—and at the end of the road, disaster." For Namier, "Napoleon III and Boulanger were to be the plagiarists, shadowy and counterfeit, of Napoleon I; and Mussolini and Hitler were to be unconscious reproducers of the methods of Napoleon III," (1958:54–55).

13. Cf. Aristotle 1962:201; "In earlier times a change from democracy to tyranny took place whenever popular leader and military leader were one person."

14. The classic account is in Tacitus (1948).

15. See the section on "Combinations of the Different Types of Authority" in Weber (1978b:262–66 = 1974:195–97). Also, the discussion in Mommsen (1974:74–75).

16. David Beetham (1978:177, n. 1) has remarked that "The discussion of Caesarism in, for example, W. Roscher's *Politik* bears many similarities to Weber." I shall seek to show that the divergences are more telling.

17. Weber (1978b:267, 1126 = 1964:198, 846).

18. Both expressions can be found in Weber (1970a:113 = 1958: 532).

19. Weber (1978b:268, 269 = 1964: 199). See also Weber (1964: 558).

20. This expression—*plebiszitäre Führerdemokratie*—is especially favored by Wolfgang Mommsen (1963), at least to judge by the frequency with which it appears (over a dozen times) in one of his most cited articles on Weber's theory of leadership. The effect on the unsuspecting reader of this repetition, reinforced by Mommsen's habit of invariably placing either part or all of the expression in quotation marks, is to assume that Weber himself chose often to employ it, but I have only been able to locate one written occasion in Weber's published work that he does so, that is, Weber (1964:199) (rendered in the English translation simply as "plebiscitary democracy": Weber [1978b:269]).

21. Weber (1978b:266–68, 1126, 1129 = 1964:198–99, 846, 849).

22. Weber ([1916] 1970c 267–301 at 295–96 = 1920 I:237–75, at 268–69).

23. I follow the dating of composition suggested in Mommsen (1974:16–17).

  The 1918 "Three pure types of legitimate domination" found its way into part II of the fourth edition of *Wirtschaft und Gesellschaft*. It is omitted from the English translation of *Economy and Society*.

24. Weber (1970a:80 = 1958:496); cf. Weber (1964:556).

25. Weber (1970a:106–7 = 1958:523–24). One should add that though "demagogy" is a necessary element of Caesarism, it is not to be equated with it. The prime case of a non-Caesarist demagogue, Weber claimed, was the modern journalist (1970a:96

= 1958:513). Similarly, although Weber adopts a phraseology that appears to compound demagogy and *charisma*—as in his references to "charisma of the spirit and the tongue" (the context is Periclean democracy) or to "the 'charisma of rhetoric'" (the context is modern electioneering)—the ideas remain analytically distinct. See, respectively, Weber (1978b:1126 = 1964:846), Weber (1978b:1129 = 1964:849).

    On the concepts of "demagogy" and "charisma" in Weber's writings see also Walter Struve (1973:142).

26. Weber (1978b:267 = 1964:198) maintains that *plebiszitäre Herrschaft* is a transitional mode of law-making between the charismatic and rational-legal types, if anyone can make sense of that.

27. "Appeal" as the translation of *abschaffen* is presumably a misprint.

28. I have omitted the emphases.

29. On nondemocratic acclamation see Weber (1978b:1126 = 1964:846).

30. Weber (1978b:1126 = 1964:846). Cf. Weber (1978b:1129 = 1964:848: "We are not at all dealing with an election, of course, when voting for a political ruler has a plebiscitary and hence charismatic character") and Weber (1978a:1451 = 1958:392) where Weber remarks that "the specifically Caesarist technique is the plebiscite. It is not an ordinary vote or election, but a profession of faith in the calling of him who demands these acclamations").

31. See their compounding in Weber (1970a:108 = 1958: 525–26: "That the plebiscitarian "machine" has developed so early in America is due to the fact that there, and there alone, the executive—this is what mattered—the chief of office-patronage, was a President elected by plebiscite."

32. It is notable that Weber (1978b:1128 = 1964:847) construes "a system of direct democracy" as the antithesis of a charismatic leadership structure.

33. I am excluding Weber's discussion of domination as it relates to economic interests. On this, see Weber (1978b:941–46 = 1964:691–95).

34. For critical observations on Weber's theory, see Beetham (1991:6–14, 23–25); and Parkin (1982:74–80).

35. Literally, "the rule of the street": Weber (1978a:1460 = 1958:392).

36. Weber (1978a:1460–61 = 1958:392–93); Weber (1970d:394–95 = 1958:274). Here as elsewhere there are strong Le Bonnian overtones: see Le Bon (1960:39, 54) on Latin crowds. (Le Bon's *Psychologie des foules* was published in a German translation—*Psychologie der Massen*—in 1908.)

    It is also possible that Weber borrowed Le Bon's concept of "prestige" to fashion the notion of "charisma;" the similarities are legion. For Le Bon, "prestige" is "a sort of domination exercised on our mind by an individual, a work, or an idea. This domination entirely paralyses our critical faculty, and fills our soul with astonishment and respect." "Prestige," moreover, is not an isolated property but "the mainspring of all authority," (Le Bon 1960:130)—a remark that reminds one of Talcott Parsons's ([1937] 1949:665) comment that "Weber's fullest treatment of legitimacy leaves no doubt that there is no *legitimate* order without a charismatic element."

    In addition, Le Bon divided "prestige" into two parts: "acquired" or "artificial"—an idea redolent of Weber's analysis of charisma's routinization—and "personal," "a faculty independent of all titles, of all [institutionalised] authority, and possessed by a small number or persons whom it enables to exercise a veritably magnetic fascination on those around them, although they are socially their equals, and lack all ordinary means of domination ....The great leaders of crowds such as Buddha, Jesus, Muhammad, Joan of Arc, and Napoleon, have possessed this form of prestige in a high degree, and to this endowment is more particularly due the position they attained" (131–33). Le Bon's paradigmatic case of personal prestige is Napoleon I (133–36) but he has earlier compared Napoleon with Julius Caesar (69). In fact, "The type of hero dear to crowds will always have the semblance of a Caesar. His insignia attracts them, his authority overawes them, and his sword instils them with fear" (54–55).

Weber does, in one place, present charisma and prestige as synonyms (Weber 1964:556) while in another place he makes the point that "in general, it should be kept clearly in mind that the basis of every authority, and correspondingly of every kind of willingness to obey, is a *belief*, a belief by virtue of which persons exercising authority are lent 'prestige'" (Weber 1978b:263 = 1964:195; I have omitted a number of emphases). Yet "belief" was typically not a strong enough term for Weber when he wished to depict charismatic domination. As Beetham (1985:247, n.65) remarks: "The term Weber uses to describe the attitude of those subject to charismatic authority is not 'Glaube' (belief), as in the other types of legitimacy, but the more emotional 'Hingabe' (devotion)."

37. The following statements illustrate Weber's position:
(a) "The 'mass' as such (irrespective of the social strata that it comprises in any given case) thinks only in short-run terms. For it is, as every experience teaches, always exposed to direct, purely emotional and irrational influence...A cool and clear mind—and successful politics, especially democratic politics depends, after all, on that—prevails in responsible decision-making the more, 1) the smaller the number of decision-makers is, and 2) the clearer the responsibilities are to each of them and those whom they lead" (Weber 1978a:1459–60 = 1958:392).
(b) "Completely irrational...is the unorganized 'mass'—the democracy of the streets" (Weber 1978a:1460 = 1958:392).
(c) "It is not the politically passive 'mass' that produces the leader from its midst, but the political leader [who] recruits his following and wins the mass through 'demagogy'" (Weber 1978a:1457 = 1958:389). On electoral "passivity" also Weber (1970a:99 = 1958: 517).
38. For an alternative account of masses, see Arendt ([1951] 1979:305–64, and the discussion in Canovan (1992:40–42, 53–55). Also, on mass and masses, Williams ([1958] 1963:287–300), and Briggs (1979).
39. Weber (1978b:984–85 = 1964:724–25). Again, while few will take exception to the claim that the "*demos*...in the sense of a shapeless mass, never governs," Weber's remark hints that "shapeless" *is what the demos of necessity is* (he offers us no other "sense" of *demos* in this context; "in the sense of" can be taken to mean "in my sense"). Consequently, with the equation of *demos* with "shapeless mass," a self-governing republic is unthinkable. Or, as Mommsen (1984:395–96) notes: "Weber made no attempt to save even the ideal core of the classical democratic theory under the conditions of modern mass democracy. He replaced the postulate of the free self-determination of the people, that, since Rousseau, had bestowed a special dignity on the democratic idea, with the principle of a *formally* free choice of leaders. The ordinary citizens were no longer supposed to actively participate as responsible individuals in the creation of political community life ....The democratic constitutional state was perceived essentially as a technical organisation for the purpose of training political leaders and enabling them to rise to power and to rule."
40. We have already seen Weber describe democratic government as a sort of "dictatorship": for example 1970a:106–7 = 1958:523–24.
41. Weber (1970e:370), for which there is no German equivalent. The statement

quoted comes from a lecture delivered by Weber in 1905 to the St. Louis Congress of Arts and Science.

42. See Weber's comments in 1958:278 on the manner in which the highest democratic executive office transmuted, in the First World War, into "a political military dictatorship," emphasis omitted. Cf. Weber (1978a:1452 = 1958:383).

43. The "military" aspects of dictatorship, and their Roman precedent, are also addressed explicitly in *Economy and Society* (1978b:1125 = 844–45): "The designation of a *dictator* in the field, during military exigencies that called for an extraordinary man, remained for a long time a characteristic remnant of the old pure type of charismatic selection. The *princeps* emerged from the army's acclamation of the victorious hero as *imperator*; the *lex de imperio* did not make him the ruler, rather it acknowledged him as the rightful pretender." See also Weber's remarks on "plebiscitary democracy" in which:"The leader (demagogue) rules by virtue of the devotion and trust that his political followers have in him *personally*. In the first instance his power extends only over those recruited to his following, but if they can hand over the government to him he controls the whole polity. The type is best illustrated by the dictators who emerged in the revolutions of the ancient world and of modern times: the Hellenic *aisymnetai*, tyrants and demagogues; in Rome Gracchus and his successors; in the Italian city states the *capitani del popolo* and mayors; and certain types of political leaders in the German cities such as emerged in the democratic dictatorship of Zürich. In modern states the best examples are the dictatorship of Cromwell, and the leaders of the French Revolution and of the First and Second Empire. Wherever attempts have been made to legitimise this kind of exercise of power, legitimacy has been sought in recognition by the sovereign people through a plebiscite. The leader's personal administrative staff is recruited in a charismatic form usually from able people of humble origin. In Cromwell's case, religious qualifications were taken into account. In that of Robespierre along with personal dependability also certain 'ethical' qualities. Napoleon was concerned only with personal ability and adaptability to the needs of his imperial 'rule of genius'" (Weber 1978b:268 = 1964:199).

44. Weber (1930:178 = 1920 I:200). Weber also speaks of Caesarism in this essay, with an obvious reference to Bismarck: commending "the relative immunity of formerly Puritan peoples to Caesarism, and, in general, the subjectively free attitude of the English to their great statesmen" Weber contrasts that state of affairs to "many things which we have experienced since 1878 in Germany positively and negatively." In England "there is a greater willingness to give the great man his due, but...a repudiation of all hysterical idolisation of him and of the naive idea that political obedience could be owed to anyone out of gratitude alone," (224–25, n. 30 = 1920 I:99, continuation of 98, n.1. [I have amended slightly Talcott Parsons's translation]).

On the use of the concept of charisma around 1913 see part II of *Economy and Society* (1111–57 = 1964:700–2). Weber also includes the trinity of charismatic, traditional and legal modes of domination in the "Introduction" to the series of essays entitled "The Economic Ethic of the World Religions, Comparative Essays in the Sociology of Religion." Though the "Introduction" and the first essay of "The Economic Ethic" series (on Confucianism, which also contains important sections on charisma) were both written in 1913, both had to wait until 1916 for publication in the *Archiv für Sozialwissenschaft und Sozialpolitik*. On their references to charisma see Weber (1970c:295–96 = 1920 I: 268–69), and Weber, (1951a:30–42, 119–29, et cetera = 1920 I:310–25, 408–17, et cetera).

45. Elsewhere, Beetham observes that while in the Freiburg Inaugural the leadership

that Weber desires is "presented in terms of leadership by a class—hopefully the bourgeoisie—and is dependent upon their achieving a wider political and national outlook as a class...political leadership in Weber's later writings is presented as leadership by an individual, within a context of political institutions and on the basis of a political relationship with a mass electorate." Beetham traces this transformation in Weber's thinking to the latter's realization that the bourgeoisie, and every other modern class, were "too closely bound to a particular economic function and outlook to be capable of wider political achievement which went beyond that of class interest...Hence, the need for a distinctively political elite or leadership to counteract the dominance of class and economic factors" (Beetham 1985:216–17).

46. See Weber (1970a:79–80, 106, 113, 124 = 1958:495–96, 524, 532, 543). Arthur Mitzman (1970:247–48) implies erroneously that the term charisma is employed in "Suffrage and Democracy in Germany" (1917). References to "Caesarism," on the other hand, occur three times in that text, viz, 1958:233, 277, 279.

47. As in Weber (1978b: 961, 986, 1126, 1130 = 1964: 707, 726, 846, 849); and Weber (1970c:296 = 1920 I:269). Also Weber (1970e: 370). If "Politics as a Vocation" is included in the category of sociological/academic writings, see Weber (1970a:106 = 1958:523).

48. Respectively, Weber (1978b:1126, 1130 = 1964: 846, 849).

49. Weber (1964:558), and Weber (1964:198–99 = 1978b:267–69).

50. Weber (1978b:1126 = 1964:846).

51. Weber (1978a:1457 = 1958:389).

52. Compare Weber (1970a:106 = 1958:524), with Weber (1978b:1132 = 1964:851).

53. Compare Weber (1978a:1451–52 = 1958:382), with Weber (1978b:244, 266–70, 1126, 1149 = 1964:181, 198–201, 846, 867). Also, Weber (1964:556).

54. Actually called a "demagogue" in Weber (1970a:96 = 1958:513), called "Caesarist" and demagogic in Weber (1978b:1130 = 1958:849). Also, Weber (1964:556).

55. Compare Weber (1970a:106–7 = 1958: 524–25) with, *inter alia*, Weber (1978b: 269, 1117, 1130 = 1964:199–200, 837, 849).

56. Compare Weber (1978a:1451 = 1958:382) with Weber (1978b:1127 = 1964:847).

57. Twice: Weber (1978b:986, 1130 = 1964:726, 849).

58. On Napoleon see Weber (1978b: 244, 268 = 1964:181, 199); on Bismarck, Weber (1978a:1387 = 1958:302).

59. See, respectively, Weber (1978b:961–62 = 1964:707), and Weber (1978a:1387 = 1958:302).

60. Part I was written between 1918–20, part II between 1910–14: see Roth's "Introduction" to Weber (1978b: c, lxv, respectively).

61. The importance of the earlier *Über einige Kategorien der verstehenden Soziologie* (1913), Weber (1951b:427–74 = 1981:151–80) is not in dispute here, but that text is not anything as comprehensive as the *Soziologische Kategorienlehre*. More importantly, though it has a little to say about the meaning of legitimacy and domination, it has absolutely nothing to say about the types of legitimate domination.

62. "Competitive elitism" is well discussed in David Held (1987:143–85).

5

Caesarism in Twentieth-Century Political and Sociological Thought

Modern Times

By the time of Weber's death in 1920, the Caesarism debate had already lost the considerable vitality it had enjoyed in the nineteenth century. Thereafter, with some notable exceptions, "Caesarism" became increasingly remote from public discussion, a once vibrant and visceral term giving way inexorably to specialist usage in political theory and sociology. To be sure, the popular novel, the theater, the cinema, and the study of literature all served to keep Caesar's name alive during the remainder of the twentieth century. And Caesar proved a durable allegorical resource, too, in the hands of artists and intellectuals concerned to illuminate contemporary events and crises. During the dark years of fascism and National Socialism, in particular, the Roman dictator offered novel symbolic opportunities both for propagandists of the new regimes and their enemies, a point to which I will return.

Moreover, it is obviously important not to treat a complex and traumatic century as if it were monolithic. Between 1918 and 1945, an interest in Greece and Rome remained lively among self-improving readers to an extent that could catch even contemporaries off guard. Nobody, for instance, appears to have been more "astonished" than H.G. Wells and his publisher at the "extraordinary reception" and "enormous sale" that greeted the many editions of his *Outline of History* (1920), volume 1 of which is largely devoted to the prehistoric and ancient world.[1] In addition, analogies with antiquity remained common right through the years of the Depression, the New Deal, and the Second World War. Since 1945, by contrast, the reception of Caesar in particular, and antiquity in general, has been markedly weaker than in any other period sketched in this book. I will be told that historians of antiquity have continued to probe, in fact more abundantly than ever before, the nature of Caesar and his times. Yet such scholarly productivity cannot conceal the limited nature of its consumption, even in the academy itself. Today, most students of the human sciences are expected to know next to nothing about Graeco-Roman civilization, a presumption that would have seemed incredible to our forebears less than a hundred years ago. Since I have already considered some of the implications of this fading of the Graeco-Roman world, I will not belabor the matter here. Instead I have another issue to tackle.

Up to this point, my principal interest has been to examine the significance of Caesar and Caesarism as indices of cultural and political change. I have sought to delineate various constructions of the man and of the concept, and to draw out their implications, rather than evaluate in any detail their veracity or utility. In particular, I have wanted to trace their relationship to the enfeeblement of republicanism and the emergence of a plebiscitarian view of modern politics. From such a standpoint Caesar*ism* is best seen as part of a cultural and political code, an understanding of which can clarify a little-known chapter in the history of European thought. To approach it in such a manner remains my firm preference, but such a stance has one obvious limitation: it remains silent on the actual nature of Julius Caesar's rule, the ostensible referent of so much of the discussion. I thus propose to end this study, as I begun it, by returning to antiquity itself. I shall ask not how Caesarism was perceived by later generations, nor shall I be concerned about its significance for the history of republicanism. Rather my focus will be on the Caesar phenomenon during its own time. However, I must first review the most important post-Weberian accounts with which my own will later be contrasted. What follows in no way claims to be exhaustive; we still await a thorough analysis of Caesar and Caesarism in the twentieth century. I do not pretend to provide it here.

Classical Residues: Spengler, His Legacy, and American Caesarism

After the end of the First World War, the concept of Caesarism briefly found a new and expanded audience in Germany, and soon all over Europe, with the publication of Oswald Spengler's *Decline of the West* ([1918, 1922] 1926, 1928).[2] Though now widely considered a period piece of postwar despondency and apocalyptic irrationalism, it caused something of a sensation at the time of its publication, and turned Spengler into an instant celebrity. The great theme of those volumes was a reworking of an older distinction between "culture" and "civilization."[3] Culture, Spengler argued, represented an organic totality that moved through a number of phases from creativity and vibrancy at one extreme to the beginnings of decrepitude at the other, at which point "civilization" emerges. To an Anglophone audience, "civilization" carries associations of grandeur and nobility, but its key characteristics to Spengler are artificiality, mechanical process, vulgarity, pragmatism, agnosticism, urban gargantuanism, soullessness, and the dissolution of property (originally rooted in the natural conditions of life) into mobile monetary transactions. Spengler's eightfold division of "cultures" and the details of their fate need not concern us[4] except to say that he saw Rome as the "civilization" that followed Greece's final cultural eclipse, and that he saw the modern West as analogous to the Roman period. Politically, Caesarism expressed that extreme degeneration of civilization in which democracy, initially a worthy intellectual aspiration, had become by turns subject to the manipulation of party managers, to financial corruption, and thence to the despotism of the one ruler. Caesarism breaks the rule of money and intellect and returns the world to war, primitivism and "formlessness." "Caesarism grows on the soil of Democracy"—particularly the emergence of "masses" equipped with the right to vote but always "an object for a subject"—yet "its roots thread deeply into the underground of blood tradition." Soon, as always before, a new phase will overthrow the last vestiges of money-managed democracy (the "more nearly universal a franchise is, the less becomes the power of the electorate"), will reassert the primeval "powers of the blood" that have remained dormant under the rationalism of the Megalopolis, and will witness the "purely political will-to-order of the Caesars" (Spengler 1928 II:431–35, 455–65; I have omitted many emphases.)

It seemed as if Auguste Romieu had come back from the grave and switched national allegiances. The great parallel had returned with a vengeance.[5] And while Spengler might attack Mommsen's and Nietzsche's theories of classicism alike, he was convinced that "there is no better place than Classical antiquity to learn how matters really stand in the world," and just as certain that while Germany would "never again produce a Goethe" it would find "a Caesar" (Spengler [1921] 1967:149,154). From the standpoint of the late twentieth century, Spengler's cyclical philosophy of history, and his notion of Caesarism, appear like relics of a bygone age. But although his influence in Germany had largely evaporated by the time of his death in 1936—his last work, *The Hour of Decision* ([1933] 1934) was suppressed by the Nazis three months after its publication—it was quite soon to enjoy a recrudescence. During the 1940s and 1950s, the work of writers such as Arnold Toynbee, Pitirim A. Sorokin, Alfred L. Kroeber, and Philip Bagby, sought to reinvigorate the comparative study of civilizations in a manner which in ambition, and sometimes even in formulation, rivalled Spengler's *Decline*.[6] And in 1958, a book appeared that would even seek to extend Spengler's argument about Caesarism. The book in question was *The Coming Caesars* by Amaury de Riencourt; its argument was as follows.

The Western world is on the brink of Caesarism, the culmination of a long process of social evolution and biocyclical development in which American civilization has triumphed over European culture.[7] This triumph is not one of conquest; nor is it the replacement of one society by another. Rather European culture and American civilization represent different phases of the *same* society, broadly approximating youthful vigor and old age respectively. American civilization is the supersession of an earlier European culture, but both belong to an identical human social stock. The "human society" that constitutes the Western world is "an entity in its own right, endowed with a life of its own, a collective life greater and far more lasting than the lives of the separate individuals who belong to it: it is a spiritual organism" (Riencourt 1958:9–10). As such it is "compelled to follow certain biological laws throughout its historical development: it is born, grows, blooms, decays, and eventually dies" (Riencourt 1958: 9–10; cf. 349). By tracing the operation of these laws we can interpret the past, judge the present and predict the future.

That these biological laws are no figment of the author's imagination is made evident by historical reflection. This reveals that the cycle the Western world has been undergoing since the Middle Ages is a direct equivalent of a previous evolutionary rotation: "Superimposing the thousand years of Greek culture that started in Homeric days with the thousand years of European culture that started at the dawn of the Gothic age, we can roughly estimate out present historical position" (11). And the estimate is ominous. Europe is in irreversible economic, moral and political decline, its youthful vitality all but spent; American power and influence is inexorably on the rise: "The twentieth century is the dramatic watershed separating the culture behind us from the civilization that lies ahead" (11). As that civilization becomes increasingly ossified, Caesarism is the result: the concentration of Western power in the office and person of the chief executive.

Since the key terms of the above analysis are culture, civilization, and Caesarism, let me now examine them a little more closely, concentrating on the unit that Riencourt himself deals with at some length, the "human society" of America and Western Europe.

Culture:

> predominates in young societies awakening to life, grows like a young organism endowed with exuberant vitality, and represents a new world outlook. It implies original creation of new values, of new religious symbols and artistic styles, of new intellectual and spiritual structures, new sciences, new legislation, new moral codes. It emphasises the individual rather than society, original creation rather than preservation and duplication, prototypes rather than mass production, an aesthetic outlook on life rather than an ethical one. Culture is essentially trail-blazing (10).

Civilization, by contrast,

> represents the crystallization on a gigantic scale of the preceding culture's deepest and greatest thoughts and styles, living on the petrified stock forms created by the parent culture, basically uncreative, culturally sterile, but efficient in its mass organisation, practical and ethical, spreading over large surfaces of the globe, finally ending in a universal state under the sway of a Caesarian ruler: India's Asoka, China's Shih Huang-ti, Egypt's Thutmose III, Babylon's Hammurabi, preColumbian Peru's Inca Roka, Mexico's Aztec emperor Itzcoatl, Islam's Turkish sultans, and Rome's Caesars who organised under their personal rules the universal societies toward which all the higher cultures tend when they pass into civilizations (10).

In a previous cycle, ancient Greece constituted the Mediterranean world's epoch of culture, Rome the epoch of civilization; in the current cycle the New Greece is Europe, while the New Rome, master of all it touches, is the United States of America. Signs of the decline of European culture were plainly apparent as far back as the Renaissance, signs of the rise of the new civilization tangible in the European Puritan communities that first landed on the Eastern seaboard during the seventeenth century. Shades marking transitional stages between waning Europeanism and American ascendancy are many and complex. But in the twentieth century, particularly after the Second World War, American civilization has really come into its own, stark and devoid of complicating Cultural admixtures. Its civilization is identical to that of Rome in the latter years of the Republic: democratic, equalitarian, impersonal, standardized, urban, philistine, unitary, conservative and behavioristically minded, pragmatic, hero-worshipping, effeminate;[8] and the consequence of these civilized traits is also more than likely to parallel Rome's experience: America is soon to witness its own Caesars. Why is this?

Riencourt offers two major reasons—"internal" (domestic) and international—to account for the approaching American Caesarism, which he depicts as an organic accretion of power condensed in the office of the president. In the first place, American civilization, like all previous civilizations, is democratic in social structure and egalitarian in moral temper, suspicious of all aristocracies, even those of talent. Internally, American civilization is a mass, anonymous, mediocre society, and yet just because of these properties Americans constantly seek psychological compensation in a father figure who is able to relate directly, and in a personalized manner, to ordinary people. A political assembly such as the Congress is completely unable to provide a collective substitute for this psychological craving since an assembly "is after all only a reproduction in miniature of [the people's] own faults and weaknesses." Besides, "the larger the masses, the more they display *feminine* traits by emphasising emotional reactions rather than rational judgment. They instinctively tend to look for masculine leadership as a compensation—the leadership they can find in a strong man" (329).[9]

At the same time, the growth of democratic civilization brings with it "the development of imperial expansion, military might, and foreign commitments" which all "increase the power of the American Executive" (329). Before Riencourt, H.G. Wells (1961:382) had also noted that the "*princeps* was really like an American wartime president", but Wells had then gone on to enumerate the important differences: the Roman *princeps* was "elected not for four years but for life; he was able to appoint senators instead of being restrained by an elected senate;" he was also *pontifex maximus,* chief of the sacrificial priests, a function unknown in Washington."[10] Riencourt doubtless knew these differences but was apparently not impressed by them. Wars and foreign crises, he argued, naturally enhance the powers of the president against the Congress, while the president's position as commander in chief of the armed forces, his dominant position, mediated by his agents, in NATO, and so on, all make him virtually omnipotent.

Riencourt is willing to acknowledge that a number of American presidents—for instance, Ulysses S. Grant (174), Calvin Coolidge, Warren G. Harding, and Herbert Hoover (221)—found themselves subordinates to Congress; he is also aware of the constitutional provision, voted by Congress after the Second World War, stipulating that no person can be president for more than two terms. But the general trend of social development is towards Caesarism, and no weak president or constitutional amendment is going to halt or reverse that process. And it is a process: Caesarism is not the outcome of a violent revolution or a coup d'état that then installs a temporary dictator as society's overlord; nor is it the emanation of a program or doctrine. Caesarism "is a slow…unconscious development that ends in a voluntary surrender of a free people escaping from freedom to one autocratic master" (5). In America's case, Caesarism is the consummation of a development that became discernible under Andrew Jackson's term of office (146–58) when the president emerged as a veritable Roman "tribune," representing "the whole people as opposed to local and particular pressure groups and privileged minorities entrenched in legislatures, senates, and other assemblies" (78). Abraham Lincoln (166)[11] and Franklin Roosevelt (232–46)[12] confirmed the trend and strengthened it in such a manner that the president increasingly becomes "the indispensable man" (336) on whom, as a heroic personality, the nation's mood and desires are focused, and on whom the people rely to champion their interests against those of "Big Money,"—high finance and the multinational corporations (148).

Like Auguste Romieu before him, Riencourt insists that Roman Caesarism really commenced with Augustus; Julius Caesar is presented to us only as a forerunner of the imperialist-democratic system that bears his name. Similarly, past presidents of the New Rome, such as Jackson and Franklin D. Roosevelt, are also described as pre-Caesarist figures, important anticipations of total power, no doubt, but still not the real thing. The first authentic American Augustus has still yet to attain office but the path to his supremacy is even more obstacle-free than it was in Rome of the Republic. This is not only because the American tribunate resides in one person, rather than being dispersed among several as it was in the antique equivalent. It is also because "democratic equality, with its concomitant conformism and psychological socialisation, is more fully developed in the United States than it has ever been elsewhere at any time" (340). Moreover, "Caesarism in America does not have to challenge the Constitution as in Rome or engage in civil warfare and cross any fateful Rubicon. It can slip in quite naturally, discreetly, through constitutional channels" (340–41).

The future looks bleak. American Caesarism is inevitable, but our responses to it are not predetermined. We may choose to abdicate our responsibilities and allow modern Caesarism total dominion, in which case the technology of future imperialist expansion will probably end in the nuclear holocaust. Or we may act in such a way as to modify Caesarism's worst features, and attempt to harness technology for constructive purposes (12). However, we will only be truly safe from Caesarism when we manage to break the cycle in which our human species has hitherto turned. This will entail nothing less than a complete overcoming of our animal nature, and our entry "into a new 'geological' age," a feat it is difficult to imagine let alone achieve in practice.

*   *   *

The originality of Riencourt's analysis lay not in its comparison of America with Rome. Since at least the late nineteenth century this had been a familiar theme of political discussion, not least among Americans themselves as they had begun to witness their country aggressively project its power abroad.[13] Europeans too were quick to see the similarities. Seeking to explain the success in America that had greeted his *Greatness and Decline of Rome*, Guglielmo Ferrero (1909:iv-v) ventured the opinion that in "many matters the United States is nearer than Europe to Ancient Rome":

> First of all, it is a republic, as Rome was, while almost all of the European states are monarchies....Further, while all the states of Europe are bureaucratic, the United States, like Rome, has an elective administration. Many public functions which in Europe are confined to a professional bureaucracy are exercised in America as

they were in Rome, by officers elected by the people....An American understands easily the working of the old Roman State because he is a citizen of a state based on the same principle.

Americans may not have been totally reassured by a comparison with a republic that eventually collapsed into civil war and dictatorship, even though Ferrero considered Caesarism to be unlikely in America because of the plasticity and durability of her political institutions (Carter 1989:213–14). By contrast, Max Weber—who in November 1918 would remark to Friedrich Otto Crusius that "America's world rule was as inevitable as that of Rome after the Punic Wars" (Marianne Weber 1988:637)—offered a very different gloss. For Weber Caesarism was already firmly entrenched in the United States, a constitutive element of its national dynamism and geopolitical standing. Caesarism in the American context was not something to be bemoaned; it was tantamount to a particularly vibrant form of "leader-democracy." Yet most Americans who have thought about presidential Caesarism have emphasised its perversion of democratic or republican principles rather than its consummation of them.[14] Caesar and Caesarism have continued in America to be terms of disapprobation or alarm, serving to describe presidents—or aspirants to the presidency such as Ross Perot in 1992—who would eviscerate Congress or short-circuit the "deliberative democracy" of the American system.[15] Riencourt shared such views, but his distinctive contribution was to revive a flagging concept, significantly elaborate on it, and in so doing place it at the heart of a discussion about the future of the world. How might we assess his theory of presidential Caesarism?

All philosophies of history, Riencourt's included, raise peculiar difficulties for anyone who wishes to appraise them, but one difficulty is paramount: as inherently speculative constructions, in which events pose as symbols, these philosophies are not strictly speaking amenable to empirical criticism at all. Evidence that sits uncomfortably with the philosophical schema is easily rendered compatible with it by invoking a range of theoretical integrative devices. For instance, and as we have already seen, those American presidents who remained captives of Congress are simply dismissed as insignificant aberrations from the main Caesarist trend. Or consider Riencourt's belief that Americans are fundamentally of a behaviorist, empiricist mental disposition. Nothing will shake him of this conviction, even when he has to acknowledge the fundamentalist and ecstatic strain in "American" thought. As he puts it, "The fact that many native American institutions...proclaim the exact opposite [of behaviorism] means only that they are contrast-phenomena, psychological compensations for the prevailing American outlook on life" (277). With Riencourt, aspects of social reality that appear to depart from his philosophical characterizations are invariably secondary or "superficial" (280).

Moreover, in order to make evident the connections between Greece-Europe, Rome-America, Riencourt is compelled to engage in some extraordinary historical contortions. Some examples: Rome experienced "a rudimentary Industrial Revolution in the second century B.C." (171); Franklin Roosevelt's "alliance with Edward Flynn, boss of the Bronx, was comparable to Caesar's reliance on Clodius' machine against Milo's 'Tammany Hall'" (240); the "New Deal started in Rome when Caius Gracchus pushed through his *Lex Frumentaria*" (242);[16] the "north side of Rome's Forum had become the Classical world's 'Wall Street'" (244). Other judgments likely to startle the historian include the view that Rome's early imperialism was defensive and reluctant (71, 113); and that Rome was an "open" society (123). And these are not the only aspects of Riencourt's interpretation of history and of Caesarism with which the reader must contend. There is also the hyperbole: Americans "research endlessly but rarely contemplate" (278);[17] the crassness: "an increasingly feminine public opinion will look increasingly for a virile Caesar:" (289); the occasional contradiction: "hero worship and bossism are marked American features," yet Americans "have no feeling of awe or reverence for other human beings" (341). And most of all, naturally, there is the contentiousness of the main thesis itself.

Though few modern commentators have been willing to adopt Riencourt's Spenglerian philosophy of history, many have echoed his concern about presidential authority, its capacity for peremptory and authoritarian actions, its "plebiscitarian" and "imperial" features (Schlesinger 1973:247–48)—elements, it will be recalled, that during the 1780s had so agitated anti-federalist critics of the constitution drawn up at Philadelphia. The president's role in foreign policy (Draper 1991), the formidable powers assumed in wartime and economic emergency (Rossiter 1948)[18] have all been extensively studied, and in at least one case Riencourt's own analysis has been explicitly endorsed.[19] At the same time, other commentators have insisted that the president's vaunted imperium is being tested by a technological development

Riencourt did not anticipate: the transformation of political life by electronic and other media. This, it has been argued, has had two related consequences for the American presidency.

First, the presidential office is increasingly reduced to the banality of a popularity contest; presidents tend to become more concerned with their poll ratings than they do with the long term impact of their policies since the indeterminate judgment of posterity is a poor consolation for the loss of office (O'Brien 1994:46). The very demagogy that presidents are constrained to embrace—a showbiz style governed by sound bites, photo opportunities, image manipulation—does not enhance the power or authority of the presidential office, but to the contrary assimilates it to the transient fashions of the day. The politics of expediency and drift, according to this interpretation, not "Caesarism" in Riencourt's sense, is the definitive characteristic of the modern presidency (the target is invariably Bill Clinton).

Second, presidential power is constantly undermined by the pressure to act quickly to events—too quickly—because of the speed with which these events are communicated to a mass audience. As Edward Luttwak (1994:11) puts it:

> Designed in the eighteenth century, when government only had narrow responsibilities and events could move no faster than horses could gallop, the Presidency still provides only one driving seat for the entire vehicle of the US government, which must now contend with every issue and every emergency under the sun, communicated to the White House at the speed of light. That leaves US presidents with a choice between two kinds of failure: they either make too many decisions too quickly, so that quite a few are bound to be exposed as wrong a day, a week or a year later; or else they are discredited by their visible inability to keep up with the flow of events.

On such an account, then, it is the very concentration of decision making in, and visibility of, the presidential office that contributes to its weakness in an ever more complex world. The politics of vacillation, not "Caesarism," is the result, a tendency deepened by a media culture with an insatiable hunger for prurience and celebrity pornography.

The Marxist Reprise: The Gramscian Contribution

The rise of fascism in Europe during the twenties and thirties showed that America enjoyed no monopoly when it came to charges of Caesarism. Indeed, the analogy with Rome and its dictator appeared irresistible not only to critics or skeptics of the fascist movements, but also to some of their ideologues and commanding figures. Among them, the obvious case was Benito Mussolini who, rather like Napoleon Bonaparte before him, appeared both to welcome and reject the Caesar label (Seldes 1935:371–72).[20] Adolf Hitler, too, had a great admiration for the Roman Empire, though for Sparta—"the greatest race-state in history"—even more.[21] But the most explicit theoretical attempt to resurrect Caesarism within the context of the new movements came from a less likely quarter: the leader of the British Union of Fascists, Oswald Mosley. The theme of Mosley's address to the English-Speaking Union in March 1933 was the philosophical basis of the fascist creed, and the need to give it a specifically English articulation. Spengler, Mosley told his audience, was unduly "pessimistic" about social development because he had failed to see the tremendous and "progressive" implications of "modern science and mechanical development." What Spengler had to say about Caesarism, on the other hand, was of immense value. Mosley offered his own gloss:

> It is, of course, true that fascism has an historical relation to Caesarism, but the modern world differs profoundly from the forms and conditions of the ancient world. Modern organization is too vast and too complex to rest on any individual alone, however gifted. Modern Caesarism, like all things modern, is collective. The will and talent of the individual alone is replaced by the will and ability of the disciplined thousands who comprise a fascist movement. Every blackshirt is an individual cell of a collective Caesarism. The organised will of devoted masses, subject to a voluntary discipline, and inspired by the passionate ideal of national survival, replaces the will to power and a higher order of the individual superman. Nevertheless, this collective Caesarism, armed with the weapons of modern science, stands in the same historic relationship as ancient Caesarism to reaction on the one hand and to anarchy on the other. (Mosley 1968:323–24)

The genius of Spengler had been to appreciate that "whenever the world under the influence of Spartacus drifted to complete collapse and chaos, it was always...the 'fact-men' who extracted the world from the resultant chaos and gave mankind very often centuries of peace and of order in a new system and a new stability." Modern Caesarism and modern science—or in other words, "order and progress," the disciplined élan of a revolutionary movement, and the introduction of scientific method into governance—was what British fascism promised to deliver. Together such a combination would promote the evolution of "Faustian man; a civilization which could renew its youth in a persisting dynamism."[22]

However, if Mosley used Caesarism as a kind of political advertisement and slogan for the fascist cause, this did not mean that it had been definitively appropriated, in either Britain or on the Continent, as a fascist concept. Marxists, too, would find a place for it, none more imaginatively than a Sardinian who, from a prison cell in Turi, offered the assessment to which I now turn.

Antonio Gramsci's writings on Caesarism, penned between 1929 and 1935, are the most sophisticated treatment of that subject to be found within the classical Marxist tradition. Much more than fascism was encompassed by his manifold analysis.

"Caesarism," Gramsci writes (1971:219), with a clear allusion to the Marxist theory of Bonapartism:

> can be said to express a situation in which the forces in conflict balance each other in a catastrophic manner; that is to say, they balance each other in such a way that a continuation of the conflict can only terminate in their reciprocal destruction. When the progressive force A struggles with the reactionary force B, not only may A defeat B or B defeat A, but it may happen that neither A nor B defeats the other—that they bleed each other mutually and then a third force C intervenes from outside, subjugating what is left of both A and B.

Or in other words, Caesarism "always expresses the particular solution in which a great personality is entrusted with the task of 'arbitration' over a historico-political situation characterised by an equilibrium of forces heading towards catastrophe."[23] But matters are not this simple since the historical formation and significance of Caesarism vary in space and time. Notably, Caesarism can be either progressive or reactionary. "Caesarism is progressive," Gramsci remarks tautologously, "when its intervention helps the progressive force to triumph, albeit with its victory tempered by certain compromises and limitations. It is reactionary when its intervention helps the reactionary force to triumph" (219). Heroic manifestations of the former include Julius Caesar and Napoleon I; of the latter, Napoleon III and Bismarck.

So, as a first approximation,[24] Caesarism is at once "a situation" of a determinate kind, and a "solution" to that situation in which the instrument is an individual of a special stamp. Yet in the paragraph immediately following the claim that Caesarism "always expresses the particular solution in which a great personality is entrusted with the task of 'arbitration,'" Gramsci qualifies his position in a passage that would later be much quoted by his pupils:

A Caesarist solution can exist even without a Caesar, without any great, 'heroic' and representative personality. The parliamentary system has also provided a mechanism for such compromise solutions. The 'Labour' governments of MacDonald were to a certain degree solutions of this kind; and the degree of Caesarism increased when the government was formed which had MacDonald as its head and a Conservative majority. (220)

To complicate matters further still, Caesarism may also exist in "various gradations" such that, for example,

Every coalition government is a first stage of Caesarism, which either may or may not develop to more significant stages (the common opinion of course is that coalition governments, on the contrary, are the most 'solid bulwark' against Caesarism). (220)

Moreover, to the "progressive" and "reactionary" couple, Gramsci adds another dualism. Caesarism may be qualitative, that is to say so innovatory, so revolutionary that its appearance and career mark the historical transformation of one type of state into another (again, the regimes of Caesar and Napoleon I are proffered as illustrations). Or, as evident in the rule of Napoleon III and Bismarck, Caesarism may be purely quantitative, representing "only 'evolution' of the same type [of state] along unbroken lines" (222).

Overlap between the "progressive"—"reactionary" and "qualitative"—"quantitative" distinctions is discernible though never made absolutely explicit by Gramsci. Progressive Caesarism would appear to be qualitative, an inference to be drawn, first, from the fact that Gramsci refers to Caesar and Napoleon I in both cases,[25] and second from a comment to the effect that "restorations *in toto* do not exist" (220) suggesting that a qualitative leap forward[26] is never matched by a qualitative leap backward. Reactionary Caesarism—Napoleon III (though not Bismarck) is mentioned—would seem to be largely quantitative.[27]

Three more features of this analysis of Caesarism are particularly worthy of comment. To begin with, and like so many others before him, Gramsci relates Caesarism to the armed forces, construed in turn as an arm of the bureaucracy. Gramsci argues that "military influence in national life means not only the influence and weight of the military in the technical sense"—that is, the General Staff or officers pursuing their own interests as a group—"but the influence and weight of the social stratum from which the latter (especially the junior officers) mostly derives its origin" (214–15) The principal, though not exclusive, social class basis of military influence is "the medium and small rural bourgeoisie" (212) whose conditions of life—particularly its familiarity with superintending and ordering-around (for example peasant) dependents, its rentier income, its hostility to town culture and the urban bourgeoisie—all conduce to military organisation and military political solutions. The observation that military influence has a class location, "is indispensable for any really profound analysis of the specific political form usually termed Caesarism or Bonapartism—to distinguish it from other forms in which the technical military element as such predominates, in conformations perhaps still more visible and exclusive" (215). This suggests that although Caesarism can be expected to have a strong military element, it is more than a military government, a government of "'great' generals," (215) as in the Spanish case. Caesarism must be related to the class or classes that sustain it and also to a "formally organic, political and social ideology" (216).

Second, Caesarism in general, and its military element in particular, has changed as a result of transformations within the wider society. Conspicuously, post-Napoleon III Caesarism is no longer as dependent on the military as its forbears were:

> In the modern world, with its great economic-trade-union and party-political coalitions, the mechanism of the Caesarist phenomenon is very different from what it was up to the time of Napoleon III. In the period up to Napoleon III, the regular military forces or soldiers of the line were a decisive element in the advent of Caesarism, and this came about through quite precise *coups d'état*, through military actions, et cetera. In the modern world trade-union and political forces, with the limitless financial means which may be at the disposal of small groups of citizens, complicate the problem. The functionaries of the parties and economic unions can be corrupted or terrorised, without any need for military action in the grand style—of the Caesar or 18 Brumaire type. (220)

More generally, "in the modern world, Caesarist phenomena are quite different, both from those of the progressive Caesar/Napoleon I type, and from those of the Napoleon III type—although they tend towards the latter" (222). Previously, under Napoleon I for instance, the contending progressive and reactionary forces might eventually amalgamate—"albeit after a wearying and bloody process"—whereas in the contemporary era "the equilibrium with catastrophic prospects occurs not between forces which could in the last analysis fuse and unite...but between forces whose opposition is historically incurable and indeed becomes especially acute with the advent of Caesarist forms," an allusion to the struggle between bourgeoisie and proletariat. This struggle is incurable because it involves structurally incompatible and irreconcilable class interests; no rapprochement comparable to that between various fractions of property owners is historically possible (222). The contradiction between labor and capital, the inability to find a road of ultimate compromise, means that the dominant class must explore all avenues open to it to secure its position, and to exploit the weaknesses of its class enemy through state security and other measures: "this is why it has been asserted that modern Caesarism is more a police than a military system" (222).

Finally, Gramsci points out that since every dominant "social bloc" is necessarily an alliance of not always symmetrical ideologies and interests, it is always possible that one group within the bloc will desire a Caesarist solution to a political problem while another group will resist it. This, for Gramsci, was the significance of the Dreyfus affair:

> not because it led to "Caesarism," indeed precisely for the opposite reason: because it prevented the advent of a Caesarism in gestation, of a clearly reactionary nature ....[T]he Dreyfus movement...was a case in which elements of the dominant social bloc itself thwarted the Caesarism of the most reactionary part of that same bloc. And they did so by relying for support not on the peasantry and the countryside, but on the subordinate strata in the towns under the leadership of reformist socialists (though they did in fact draw support from the most advanced part of the peasantry as well). (223)

*   *   *

Gramsci's analysis is variegated and nuanced, addressing imaginatively the class location of Caesarism and some of its salient military features. But there are problems. The treatment of Caesarism is evasive and, as we have seen, lacks consistency in places. The progressive-reactionary distinction introduces into the concept of Caesarism a politically tendentious metaphysic. And Gramsci's comments on parliamentary Caesarism are another area of difficulty. What are we to make of his statements about Caesarism's relationship to party coalition and compromise? It is difficult to be sure because the truncated nature of Gramsci's remarks gives us so little to go on. We could leave it simply at that. Fortunately, however, there may be another way to assess the potential insights, or otherwise, of Gramsci's theory of "Caesarist" coalition and compromise.

During the 1980s, an explicit attempt was made by Bill Schwarz and Stuart Hall to apply the Gramscian theory of Caesarism to the British case.[28] Their concern was not to develop the theory of Caesarism in all its various mutations, but instead to advance the view that Caesarism enshrines a situation of class compromise and political coalition as a response (or "solution") to a major crisis of state, particularly a rupture of representation between social classes and their parliamentary agents. Insofar as Schwarz (1985) is concerned with Caesarism, his interest is directed at that period, 1915–1922, when British political life was dominated by a series of coalition governments, led initially by Herbert Asquith (May 1915–December 1916), but for the most part by David Lloyd George (December 1916–November 1918, November 1918–October 1922). The composition of these governments included at different times Liberals, Lloyd George Liberals, Conservatives, and members of the Labour Party whose galvanization followed the failure of the populist tariff reform movement to win over a mass antiLabour, antisocialist, constituency. The crisis of confidence that afflicted the nation's rulers in a period of accelerated social change, together with the attendant disillusionment with the instabilities that seemed to dog two-party politics in that era, were two other factors that led to the formation of coalition regimes. The details of Schwarz's historical reconstruction can be left to one side, though it is important to note that the period of coalitionism with which he is concerned is inserted into a broader context, namely, "the crisis of liberal hegemony" (Hall and Schwarz 1985): a perplexity that struck state, civil society and ideological conceptions alike from the 1880s onwards, and that paralleled the recomposition of capital, the struggle for the extension of the franchise and for women's rights, and the development of collectivist ideas and (to a lesser extent) institutions. What we need to determine is Caesarism's place in this conjuncture:

By caesarism[29] I refer to a political situation characterized by the following features: first, a protracted crisis of representation; second, the strength of opposition forces ranged against the state; third, the exhaustion of the resources for the power bloc to construct and command its own popular interventions; and fourth, the concentration of power at one point in the state. These features led Gramsci to observe that "every coalition government is the first stage of Caesarism." In such a situation the state representatives are captured by their own logic of constraining popular struggles and recomposing the apparatuses of the state internally and administratively. From this perspective comes the understanding of "various grada-

tions of caesarism" and of parliamentary caesarism without the classic hero, without the "Caesar" or "Bonaparte." (Schwarz 1985:46)

As "a political situation" Caesarism is not confined to a type of a
coalition government, even if the latter is its most tangible expression.
Caesarism can also exist as a "configuration of political forces," and
such a configuration became especially evident after the constitutional
crisis of 1910 when the nation's most authoritative political leaders
attempted to find a workable solution to their shared distress. The
1915–1922 coalitions, the fruition of earlier attempts to bridge political differences, seem to mark the culmination of Caesarism in Schwarz's
account (1985:50)[30] though this view stands in some tension with
Gramsci's own remark, slightly misquoted by Schwarz, that "every
coalition government is a first stage of Caesarism," suggesting as it
does that Caesarism's consummation is subsequent to the establishment of a coalition. Of greater clarity is the significance attributed to
the coalition period in question, and thus the importance of Caesarism
itself. For in the "long, defensive period of coalition governments"
from 1915 to 1922:

> the old party formations finally dissolved and regrouped; the syndicalist challenge
> was confronted and repelled; labour, its internationalism broken by the war, was
> constitutionalized into the alternative party of government; state intervention in the
> economy hastened the transition to monopoly forms in some sectors; and the
> system of industrial conciliation, with the state as "neutral" mediator between
> capital and labour, was fully institutionalized. (Hall and Schwarz 1985:28)

By 1922 Caesarism was on the wane; thereafter "the gradations of
Caesarism slowly decreased," only to be resurrected in the figure of
Ramsay MacDonald and his 1931–35 coalition. "This new phase of
parliamentary caesarism held until 1945 when a newly formed popular
movement generated by the war had the effect of finally breaking,
'from below,' the political logjam and completing the diffusion of
coalitionism and caesarism" (Schwarz 1985:59–60).

I shall have occasion later to comment on the Gramscian penchant
for equating coalition and compromise with Caesarism. The more pertinent observation to make at this stage is that such an equation has not
been limited to a theory of pre-1945 administrations. Far from being a
relic of Britain's past, Caesarism, on one reckoning, was thriving during the 1980s too. Its reincarnation was to be found not, as one might
have guessed, in the regime of Mrs. Thatcher—for whom an older

description of Caesarism might have actually functioned quite faithfully[31] but in the British Social Democratic Party (SDP).[32]

Writing in an article first published in the April 1981 edition of *Marxism Today*, Stuart Hall argued that the advent of the SDP represented "a significant regrouping of parliamentary forces" that the Left in Britain needed carefully to consider.[33] The SDP's "appearance as an independent force...signals a crisis and break in the system of parliamentary representation" (1983b:310). This crisis was one essentially of political and social authority; its root cause a condition in which (Hall is quoting Gramsci) "the ruling class has failed in some major political undertaking for which it has requested or forcibly extracted the consent of the broad masses."[34] The "major political undertaking" in question here was the effort to arrest Britain's industrial and economic decline, an effort to which two strategies had been devoted. The first strategy, canonized in the Harold Wilson-James Callaghan years of Labour rule, had sought to confront Britain's decline by a mixture of incomes policy, neo-Keynesianism and corporatism, a particularly unattractive statist version of socialism no longer acceptable to great constituencies of the Britain electorate. The second strategy designed to turn around the British economy was, of course, that advanced by the "radical right" itself. In its own terms, Hall acknowledges, Thatcherism has had some spectacular triumphs. It has succeeded in dampening down wage militancy and disciplining the work force through the threat of unemployment; it has steadily overseen the erosion of trade union power through legislation designed to strip the unions of their legal immunities; it has championed management's prerogative to manage; and it has begun to roll back public ownership through a program of privatization. Economic recovery itself, however, did not materialize despite a fall in the rate of inflation.

Enter the SDP. Capitalizing on a situation of growing electoral disenchantment with both Labour and Conservative parties and with two party politics more generally, the SDP was admirably placed to present itself as an authentic alternative. The image its leaders projected combined energy with emollience. Their claim to the mantle of mould-breakers of British politics and neanderthal laborism, suggested a radical stance and astringency that Thatcherism in its own way had busily been promoting. Yet unlike Thatcherism, the SDP ideologues offered themselves as healers, as conciliators, as centrists who appreciated that conviction politics must, if it is to be morally acceptable to the basic decency and good sense of the British people, commingle with the social balm only SDP policies made possible. "Toughness and tenderness"—the political elixir that Dr. David Owen would later prescribe to the British public—was thus presaged in the original SDP enterprise. However, according to Hall, the SDP agenda, when dissected, was both vacuous and derivative. It was vacuous because the SDP's talismen of "participatory democracy" and "decentralisation" were phony; behind the slogans lay no real intention, perhaps no real capacity, to mobilize the mass of the people for democracy and to confront those in power (Hall 1983b:320). And the SDP's agenda was derivative because, on inspection, its articles of faith recapitulated the older collectivist commitments of the Labour Party: managerialism, incomes policy, neo-Keynesianism, fidelity to the EEC and to NATO.

Only in the SDP's "final break with the historic Labour-trade union connection" and with "working-class politics" could it claim distinctive credentials (Hall 1983:316), but for the break to be successful the new party was compelled to build a viable political constituency of its own, a task that, at the time Hall was writing, it had yet to do. Expressed in the terminology of Gramscian theory, the SDP exemplifies a "transformist solution"—a solution embraced by "the moderate left in a period of progressive political polarisation along class lines." The function of "transformism" is "to dismantle the beginnings of popular democratic struggle, to neutralise a popular rupture, and to absorb these elements passively, into a compromise program." The result is a "'revolution' without a revolution. Passive revolution 'from above' (i.e. Parliament)" (Hall 1983b:320). Or, in other words, the SDP are the contemporary manifestation of "Caesarism," "a type of *compromise* political solution, generated from above, in conditions where the fundamental forces in conflict so nearly balance one another that neither seems able to defeat the other, or to rule and establish a durable hegemony." No great or heroic personality is required in such a situation; in a parliamentary system, a coalition will suffice. "The Social Democrats are our "little Caesars" (Hall 1983b:320–21). For Hall:

In a period when the discipline of unemployment is sending a shiver of realism through the labour movement, it may seem over-optimistic to argue that we now confront a situation of stalemate between the fundamental classes. Yet this does once more seem to be the case. Thatcherism lacks the economic space or the political clout to impose a terminal defeat on the labour movement. The working class and its allies are so deep in corporate defensive strength that they continue to provide the limit to Thatcherism despite their current state of disorganization. Irresistible force meets the immovable object. On the other hand, the labour movement lacks the organisation, strategy, programme or political will to rule. So far it has failed to act as the magnet for new social forces, thereby itself embracing new fronts of struggle and aspiration. It still shows no major sign of reversing its own long decline. Such stalemates[35] are ready-made for the appearance of grand compromise. (Hall 1983b:321)

* * *

The neo-Gramscian theory of Caesarism is open to at least two possible objections. The first is that it is implausible as an account of recent changes in Britain; the second is that it implausible in its own right. It can be argued, for instance, that by 1983—the year Hall's article was reprinted without substantive revision—the British political landscape looked very different from the Gramscian reconstruction of it. Far from the "fundamental forces" being in equilibrium[36] (if ever they were), there was now a stark asymmetry of social power. The clearest indicator of this came in June 1983 with a landslide Conservative victory in which Labour "lost one in five of its already low number of votes" and presided over a "massive defection of supporters of all classes, ages and genders."[37] The ongoing impact of the 1980 and 1982 Employment Acts that effectively outlawed secondary picketing, together with the upward climb of unemployment, also served to weaken the labor movement, and foreshadowed the crushing defeat inflicted in 1984–85 on the miners, typically regarded as its most formidable arm. Throughout this same period, the SDP, now in alliance with the Liberal Party, remained a political force to be reckoned with, garnering just over a quarter of votes cast in 1983, and over a fifth in the general election of 1987.[38] In any case, while Gramsci's original argument had addressed coalitions as governments, the SDP-Liberal Alliance to which Hall applies Gramsci's analysis was no more than an electoral pact— one which never achieved office. It is doubtful then, even in Gramscian terms, whether the analogy is an appropriate one.[39]

But there is also a structural deficiency in the Gramscian theory of Caesarism and coalitions. The assertion that "every coalition government is a first stage of Caesarism" contains not only an astonishing exaggeration; it also contains a teleological premise that fails to account for the specific nature and range of possibilities of this kind of political alliance. The teleological premise hinges on the belief that coalitions are best thought of not as enduring institutions but as indications of a political interregnum; they are staging posts between a crisis on the one hand and its resolution on the other. Coalitions are responses to crises and attempts to resolve them, exceptional strategies designed for exceptional situations. Such a perception may well be accurate with regard to a specific set of cases; what cannot be assumed, however, is that the description above admits of universal application: coalition governments are not necessarily crisis governments, nor are they necessarily heading in any direction whose goal is extrinsic to them. Thus, in the majority of European countries that have experienced coalition and minority governments since the Second World War, such an arrangement has not for the most part been a temporary, exceptional affair, an expediential response to immanent or extant catastrophe, but rather part of the normal, expected operation of the political process. One has only to examine the post-1945 history of Germany, Italy, the Scandinavian countries, Holland, and Belgium to establish the institutionalized character of coalitions in these nations—which is not to say, naturally, that coalition politics has proceeded smoothly and without drama. It is only to assert the obvious point that proportional representation, not a "crisis of hegemony," or class stalemate, is the bedrock of coalition governments. The *British* experience in which a period of extremity has been the prelude and trigger to coalition governments, in which coalitions have appeared erratically and spasmodically, cannot be construed as prototypical and, besides, the concept of coalition itself demands some disaggregation. That coalitions are not unidimensional structures is evident from Britain's own political history since 1895. As Vernon Bogdanor (1983:10–12) points out, coalition governments can be divided into (a) governments of national unity, where the majority of parties combine to tackle a situation—for example, war or economic crisis—deemed potentially perilous to nation and state; (b) alliances that figure as "a prelude to the fusion of parties;" (c) and so-called "power-sharing" coalitions—in which "two or more parties, none of which is able to gain an overall majority on its own, combine to form a majority government." In this last type of coalition the ruling parties retain their individual identity as competitors for votes and as representatives of distinct ideological and economic interests. Moreover, apart from coalition governments, there are also what Bogdanor calls "parliamentary coalitions"—for example, the 1977–78 Lib-Lab pact—where a minority government secures, subject to the requisite compromise in policy, the agreement

Figure 5.1
Coalitions and Electoral Pacts in Britain since 1895

Coalition governments: Dates of Formation and Dissolution	Prime Minister	Parties Comprising Coalition	Type of Coalition
June 1895— December 1905	Lord Salisbury, 1895–1902 A.J. Balfour, 1902–1905	Conservatives and Liberal Unionist	Prelude to fusion, achieved in 1912.
May 1915— December 1916	H.H. Asquith	Liberals, Conservatives and Labour	Wartime government of national unity
December 1916— November 1918	David Lloyd George	Lloyd George, Liberals, Conservatives and Labour	Wartime government of national unity
November 1918— October 1922	David Lloyd George	Lloyd George Liberals, and Conservatives	Attempted fusion, but dissolved by Conservatives, 1922
August 1931— May 1940	J. Ramsay MacDonald, 1931–1935; Stanley Baldwin, 1935–1937; Neville Chamberlain, 1937–1940	National Labour, Conservatives, Liberal Nationals, and until September 1932, Liberals	Attempted government of national unity. Prelude to fusion of National Labour and Liberal Nationals with Conservatives (1945 and 1966 respectively)
May 1940— May 1945	Winston Churchill	Conservatives, Labour and Liberals	Wartime government of national unity

Electorial pacts with or without coalition	Component Parties
1903: Gladstone— MacDonald Pact	Liberals, and Labour Representation Committee (later Labour Party)
1981–1987	Liberals and Social Democratic Party (SDP) Alliance

Source: V. Bogdanor, 1983:11; amended and updated.

of one or more rival parties to lend support to the administration for a determinate period—and "electoral coalitions" (such as that of the Liberal-SDP Alliance). Electoral coalitions are predicated upon an arrangement by distinct parties, designed to promote their cooperation and mutual political welfare, "providing for the mutual withdrawal of candidates so as to avoid splitting the vote" (Bogdanor 1983:5–7). Coalitions, then, are a complex and multifaceted phenomenon, as figure 5.1 indicates. To envisage them as "a first stage of Caesarism" simply fails to recognize this fact.

Caesarism and Political Sociology

Since 1945, sociology has increasingly assumed the character of a specialized and esoteric discipline, equiped with its own language and concepts. To the degree it has become academic, it has steadily lost contact with vernacular or mainstream social discussion. What this has meant in practice is that sociological writers on Caesarism, or those influenced by sociology, have tended to follow Weber in coining increasingly technical definitions of their topic, just as they have come to share the Weberian penchant for stipulative definitions and abstractions. For very different reasons, Gramsci had been driven to adopt a similar esoteric practice. Although he embraced a project of social transformation, and was no academic sociologist—indeed he often criticized the science of sociology for its tendency toward "mechanicism," for its redundancy, for its evolutionism and positivism, and taunted it as the "philosophy of non-philosophers" (1971: 222, 243–44, 426)—Gramsci was compelled by the prison censorship regime under which he labored to employ code-like formulations ("passive revolution," "social bloc," "hegemony," "organic intellectuals," "modern Prince," "war of position," "Caesarism" itself) every bit as removed from the vocabulary of ordinary citizens as their sociological counterparts have proved to be. In consequence, Gramsci, like Weber before him, helped transform Caesarism from a common term of political discussion into a highly specialized theoretical notion.

Turning now to sociology itself, consider first the treatment of Hans H. Gerth and C. Wright Mills (1954) in which Caesarism appears as a kind of "Oriental despotism,"[40] itself part of a wider taxonomy of "Democracies and Dictatorships." Gerth and Mills begin by defining Oriental despotism in general as a system of domination centred on bureaucratic, monopolistic control of the means of life, particularly irrigation complexes, and then proceed to outline two types of it of which "Sultanism" is one (bureaucratic control operating from within the structure of the harem) and "Caesarism" is the other. The sum of what they have to say about Caesarism is as follows:

> The Caesarism of Rome's empire was based upon an imperial bureaucracy of army officers and tax farmers. The Diocletian Empire is the clearest example of an imperial bureaucracy led by hereditary dynasties and punctuated by military usurpers. It was a theocracy with Caesar as god. The military order was important, as a chronic state of war was necessary to provide slaves for the economy. Public financing was shifted from taxes to services in kind. A money economy broke down as the area of domination spread, so the centre of gravity shifted inland. The rich, who provided the liturgies, fled from the cities and, going to country estates, rusticated. (Gerth and Mills 1954:210)

There are a number of problems with this exposition. The first is that Caesarism itself is nowhere actually specified: we are told not what Caesarism *is*, but rather what it was "based upon." Then there is the puzzling question about why Caesarism should be considered Oriental. Perhaps the authors are thinking about the transfer of the seat of the Empire to Byzantium (Constantinople) in 324 A.D. But not only would this development, of itself, be a weak reason for designating "Caesarism" Oriental, that transfer was inaugurated not by Diocletian, to whom they refer, but Constantine. Perhaps, even more obliquely, they are alluding to a claim made frequently in the scholarly literature on Roman antiquity, that Julius Caesar had intended, before his life was cut short by murder, to establish an Alexandrian, Hellenic monarchy, with himself as a god. However, this claim is impossible to prove and, at best, was an aspiration, not a plan fulfilled. Third, what of those periods before Diocletian,[41] notably from Augustus' Principate to the end of the Severan dynasty in the third century A.D., when Roman politics was not "punctuated by military usurpers?" Presumably this could not be "Caesarism" in Gerth and Mills' terms, even though republican institutions had ceased to function and Augustus and those who followed him were officially Caesars. Fourth, the reader is struck by the eclecticism of the account. Caesarism appears to encompass bureaucracy, militarism, theocracy, services in kind, the breakdown of a money economy, a rusticated rich, without us ever knowing how those features relate to one another. Without this knowledge we are left with a ragbag of social phenomena loosely associated with the

"Diocletian Empire," based on an interpretation of the facts that will not stand close examination.

A much richer and more sophisticated attempt to construct a social scientific concept of Caesarism was bequeathed to us by the political and legal theorist Franz Neumann in an essay written shortly before his death in September 1954.[42] In contrast to Gerth and Mills (though they are not mentioned by name) Neumann is unwilling to describe Caesarism as a "despotism:" like "tyranny," another word to which he objects, "despotism," he says, lacks precision and furthermore is "emotionally charged"; parenthetically, Neumann also mentions the oriental overtones of the word. His preferred designation for Caesarism[43] is "dictatorship" by which he understands "the rule of a person or a group of persons who arrogate to themselves and monopolise power in the state, exercising it without restraint" (Neumann 1957:233). I will say more about Neumann's concept of Caesarism presently. For the moment, however, it is important to examine more carefully the master notion of which Caesarism is but one variant: that of "dictatorship."

By defining "dictatorship" in the way that he does above, Neumann comes face to face with an anomaly arising from a tension between the original and the contemporary meaning of the word, an anomaly, one should add, that he never satisfactorily resolves. In its original Roman sense (and as Neumann was aware), a "dictatorship" was not *arrogated by* someone, but was *conferred on* him as an extraordinary, albeit perfectly legal, office: the dictatorship was a magistracy enshrined within the Republican constitution together with such other magistracies as the consulate, the praetorship, the aedileship, the quaestorship, the censorship and the tribunate, to mention only the most important.[44] The dictator's primary function (he was usually an ex-consul) was what today we would call crisis management, particularly in times of foreign war or civil strife when decisive action was required, and when the rule of one person was felt to be better adapted to deal with the emergency than the more cumbersome collegiate governmental system. The dictator was empowered with wide-ranging civil and military prerogatives.[45] For instance, he was freed from the restraints of the tribunician veto; could not be held responsible for his (legal) actions once having relinquished the office; could raise without further ado more than four legions—a right denied, in normal times, to a military commander without the express permission of the Senate;

"could convoke any of the assemblies and preside over them, and this power extended to the Senate" (Rossiter 1948:25); could issue decrees that in effect had the force of law; and generally could exercise formidable judicial rights of arrest and execution.

However, and returning now to Neumann's definition, the powers vested in the dictatorship, though wide-ranging, were hardly untrammelled, hardly exercised "without restraint." The dictator's authority was generally limited to a period of six months' duration, the regime it instituted therefore being strictly temporary. And, furthermore, the scope of the dictator's jurisdiction was constitutionally circumscribed: for example, he had no authority to interfere in civil cases and was not permitted to declare war or entitled to tamper with the constitution itself. Neumann was acquainted with these facts; indeed he specifically recognized many of them in his essay. But having done so he jettisoned the original meaning of dictatorship and, as we have seen, redefined it. His impulse to do so is understandable. Once Neumann rejected "tyranny" and "despotism" as working alternatives, he had few familiar concepts left with which to express his thoughts apart from the *modern* idea of dictatorship—which certainly does suggest "the rule of a person or a group of persons who arrogate to themselves and monopolise power in the state, exercising it without restraint." In addition, Neumann wished to emphasize the different character of the early Republican dictatorship from that of Sulla and Caesar where constitutionalism had become increasingly a sham. (The affinity between the concepts of dictatorship and *Caesar*ism is especially strong given Julius Caesar's almost constant occupation of the office from 49 to his murder in 44 B.C.). Whatever Neumman's reasoning, the result is to blur a term that was once distinct, giving some credence to Roy Medvedev's observation that:

> in current political literature and in the political practice of the last hundred years, the distinctions between the terms "dictatorship," "tyranny" and "despotism" have been eroded. Nowadays they are virtually synonymous expressions. The various regimes of Mussolini, Hitler, Salazar, Franco, Somoza, Duvalier and Stroessner are referred to not by the name of tyranny, despotism or fascism but as "dictatorships." All of these, incidentally, avoided any time limit. Some of them were transferrable by heredity from father to son, and, although the dictatorships of Hitler, Mussolini, Salazar-Caetano and Somoza did not go on forever, they came to end not because the dictator himself abdicated "on the expiry of the specified period" but because he was overthrown by war or revolution.[46] (Medvedev 1981: 41)

We can now turn to Neumann's account of "caesaristic dictatorship." Neumann depicts Caesarism as a type of dictatorship occupying a logically intermediate position in a triad. "Simple dictatorships," which he mentions first, are those in which power is exercised by an individual (for example, an absolute monarch) or group (for example, a junta or caudillo) by virtue of "absolute control of the traditional means of coercion only, that is, the army, police, bureaucracy and judiciary" (Neumann 1957:235). It is a sort of dictatorship that flourishes in countries and historical periods distinguished by minimal mass involvement in politics and low political awareness, "where politics is the affair of small cliques who compete for favors and hope to gain prestige and wealth by association with the dictator" (236). Social control exercised by the dictatorship tends to be limited, haphazard and generally rudimentary. "Totalitarian dictatorships," which Neumann describes last, are all-encompassing. Totalitarian dictatorships are not modern creations, unique to the twentieth century; according to Neumann we find instances of them in Diocletian's regime,[47] and as far back as fourth-century B.C. Sparta. But they only develop their full and fearsome potential when, as political formations in an industrial society, they are harnessed to modern technology and science. Under totalitarian government social controls are pervasive: the rule of law is undermined and eventually extinguished as a "police state" reigns unchecked; power becomes concentrated in the hands of a "monopolistic state party"; all of civil society's branches are permeated by, and brought under the supervision of this party which deliberately sets about atomizing and isolating the individual through the destruction of established social, cultural, and biological ties, and then proceeds to reintegrate him or her in a hierarchical social structure governed by the leadership principle. Essentially, then, in a totalitarian dictatorship, the line separating state from society virtually disappears as the latter suffers total politicisation—in effect the private sphere is absorbed into the state apparatuses—and loss of autonomy.[48] Germany under Nazism, and the Soviet Union following the Bolshevik takeover (though particularly the post-1928 regimes) are paradigmatic of totalitarian dictatorships.

"Caesaristic dictatorships," as distinct from the other two sorts,[49] arise in situations where an individual is "compelled to build up popular support, to secure a mass base, either for his rise to power or for the exercise of it, or for both" (236) Or in other words Caesaristic dictatorships are a contingent product of "democratic" conditions or at least conditions in which the populace is vocal and cannot be ignored. This dependence on the "masses" distances Caesarism from "simple" dictatorships where, as we saw, politics is for the most part confined to the dictator, his notables and sycophants; and Caesarism differs from totalitarianism in that the division between the private and public spheres, though under pressure, remains relatively intact. True, totalitarianism does possess a "caesaristic element," but "up to the nineteenth century at least, caesaristic dictatorship does not necessarily lead to a totalitarian system, nor is the totalitarian state necessarily the result of a genuine caesaristic movement" (243–45). In addition, "caesaristic dictatorship...as the name indicates, is always personal in form" (236); "in all caesaristic and totalitarian movements" one can witness the "the masses' identification with a leader, the hero" (253).

Aside from the intrinsic "democratic" and personal features of Caesaristic dictatorship, there are two further aspects of Neumann's discussion that are worth noting. The first concerns the sort of individuals he classified under the caesaristic rubric. As one might expect, Julius Caesar and Augustus are prominent members of the club; so too are such individuals as Cola di Rienzo, Savonarola, Cromwell, Napoleon I and III, Mussolini, Hitler, and Perón (241–43). More surprising, on the other hand, is the inclusion of a number of individuals who flourished centuries *before* the rise to power of the Caesars, notably King Agis IV, King Cleomenes III, and Pisistratus (237–38). For Neumann, then, Caesarism is a phenomenon that has existed intermittently from the sixth century B.C. to our own time, and the adjective "Caesaristic" has, accordingly, pan-historical applicability.

Second, Neumann suggests that "in terms of class relationships, the function of dictatorship may be related to three basic and recurring situations" (250):

1. Where an insurgent, disenfranchised social class is aspiring to power, influence and representation, but where the authorities of the day are doggedly resistant to these claims, Caesarism may be purely transitory if the class in question is politically mature; or Caesarism may become protracted indefinitely if that class is immature. An example of the former possibility is the dictatorship of Cromwell and Robespierre (Neumann adds that in bourgeois revolutions the new commanding class "will for various reasons demand a liberal political

system": [250]); an example of the latter is the dictatorship initiated by Lenin.

2. "The second case is the attempt of a social class threatened with decline and striving to preserve its status and power. Dictatorship may then arise as an attempt to preserve the status quo. The most striking examples are Sparta, to a lesser extent the half-hearted efforts of Napoleon I, and probably the regimes of Franco and Perón" (250).

3. The third situation concerns the attempt of "doomed" classes to reverse the existing social and economic order, "and to install a political system that would restore them to their old preeminence. This is the kernel of the German and Italian Fascist movements" (251).

*   *   *

Neumann's analysis of Caesarism was ambitious and manysided but this can be a weakness as much as a strength. Notably, there is something strained and unhistorical in the attempt to categorize such diverse figures as Pisistratus, Cola di Rienzo, and Lenin as Caesarist. Especially incongruous is the inclusion of figures who hail from epochs before Julius Caesar's own, for one might argue that Caesarism is either an exemplar of a distinct type of political formation (and Neumann accepts that Julius Caesar is the paradigmatic case[50]) or it is not. If it is an exemplar it is novel ipso facto, and backward extrapolation is anachronistic. If it is not an exemplar, then the personal nomenclature is misleading and "Caesarism" should be replaced by another name that establishes the political archetype. The concept of Caesarism is also inconsistently applied by Neumann. At one moment Caesarism is a dictatorship; at another it is an "element";[51] at yet another it is a "movement."[52] I conclude from this review of Neumann and from the authors examined in this chapter that attempts to "operationalize" Caesarism—to transform it from a vernacular term of public discussion into an analytical tool of social science—have been largely unsuccessful or implausible on various counts. Some are factually inaccurate or anachronistic; others are too general, or speculative or teleological; still others fail to bear any clear relationship to Caesar himself.

The most recent attempt to produce a political sociology of Caesarism—Philip Thody's study of the careers of Napoleon I, Napoleon III, Philippe Pétain, and Charles de Gaulle—is assuredly more sensitive to these problems than many of its predecessors were, but does not completely escape them.[53] Defining Caesarism "as the assumption of power at a moment of real or alleged national crisis by a figure owing his prestige to genuine or associated military achievements," Thody argues that "such a definition makes it a more general phenomenon than Bonapartism."[54] For unlike Bonapartism, "it does not suggest the idea that the power thus obtained can be inherited by members of the same family. Neither is it automatically discredited by the military defeats which ended the reigns of both Bonapartes." On the contrary, precisely because Caesarism "is a general phenomenon, it invites speculation about the possibility, occasionally put forward by the French themselves, that they are not really a democratic nation" (Thody 1989:15).[55] However, it is arguable that the very generality itself obscures many important differences both between the figures mentioned, and between the Julius Caesar exemplar against which they are all measured. For instance, the term itself is misleading as historical analogy. Julius Caesar took power from the civil authorities (the Senate) in 49 B.C. by force. Pétain did not, nor did de Gaulle, and some might even say the same for Napoleon Bonaparte. Caesar was a brilliant field commander, the greatest of all the *popularis* generals. No one could say this of Napoleon III or of de Gaulle. Caesar's still-flourishing career ended with his murder. The "French Caesars," by contrast, saw their rule terminated by foreign invasion or defeat at the polls. Finally, there is a constant slippage in Thody's account between a figurative and a literal rendition of expressions like "usurpation" and "coup d'état" (Thody 1989:48, 97). Only in the figurative sense could Pétain be thought of as a usurper, and in the case of de Gaulle, Thody is compelled to admit limply that his was a *"coup d'état* by proxy."

So the question is, how should one proceed? I have already stated my preference for considering Caesarism as a marker of a politico-cultural debate, rather than as a social scientific concept. Attempts to produce a social scientific account, such as in Weber's sociology,[56] have either sanitized and obliterated the dangerous connotations that Caesarism assumed in earlier times, or been liable to the many problems I have rehearsed in this Chapter. Originally, Caesarism was part of a public debate about the dangers, opportunities and pathologies of nineteenth-century politics. That debate was tied to a mode of thinking markedly influenced by the great parallel with antiquity, a mode of thinking that has probably passed for ever. Of course, the concept of "Caesarism," and the treatment of Caesar himself in the classical and later republican tradition, was *always* anachronistic, always a distortion of actual events as we now consider those events to be revealed by modern scholarship. As Gramsci (1966:190) observed, the Caesar of nineteenth-century construction was significant, not as history, but as political myth; indeed that Caesar had as little basis in historical reality as the eighteenth-century "exaltation of republican Rome as a democratic and popular" state.[57] But this did not matter so long as both concept and symbol belonged to and illuminated a public debate about the nature of politics. In most of its articulations, Caesarism was not *meant* to be taken as a scientific term to be "operationalized" and subject to scientific protocols of accuracy and verisimilitude; it was a warning, a polemical weapon, an evocation of hubris, a vehicle of political evaluation. Today Caesarism cannot be revived in common parlance, nor is there any point in wishing for it to be revived. Devoid in good measure of a classical education, aware of new problems and challenges, we are bound to feel that Caesarism is arcane and irrelevant in many respects—though perhaps not in all. Demagogy is still a problem in politics, so is manipulation and irresponsibility, so is the concentration of power, so is an ill-informed electorate. However, once we make Caesarism into a sociological notion, even if it is supposed to depict a dangerous phenomenon, we are likely to fall into the very traps that are problematic and unsatisfactory in an academic analysis—as distinct from a popular discussion. For this reason, in the reconstruction that follows I shall talk not about "Caesarism," nor the Caesar-question, but the Caesar phenomenon. The distinction may appear simply pedantic. The intention behind it is to make plain the uniqueness of the entity I am about to discuss, and to signal a refusal to absorb, "transcend," or dismiss earlier concepts or debates by the formulation of a new academic coinage purporting to show what Caesarism *really* is. The Caesar-question, which so animated republican-oriented thinkers, and the Caesarism debate of the nineteenth century, remain valuable as chapters in a political history which, barring catastrophe, will never be complete. To the degree that we see history as our living past we will want to return to these chapters as episodes in their own right, not subsume them under some overarching academic theory.

The Caesar Phenomenon in Its Time

Nature of the Social Crisis: Mobilization from Above of Agrarian and Urban Discontent

The general social crisis that shook the foundations of the Roman Republic and finally reduced it to rubble is our necessary point of departure. Only if we understand the nature of this crisis will we be able adequately to locate Caesar's conditions of possibility. In what follows all dates, unless otherwise specified, are B.C.; and the genealogical divisions demarcated conform to conventional periodisation: I shall refer to the Early Republic (509–287),[58] the Middle Republic (287–133),[59] and the Late Republic (133–31).[60]

Republican Rome collapsed from within fundamentally because its own city-state institutions proved in the long run incapable of coping with the consequences of imperial expansion.[61] Three consequences of empire building are particularly important for our subject: the growth of a proletarian army that came increasingly to look to victorious generals to reward it with booty, cash, and, crucially, land; hardship among the rural small-holders and the urban plebs; and the emergence of politically ambitious men, the so-called *populares*, who mobilized the discontent of the subordinate classes to challenge the senatorial oligarchy.

During the Early and for most of the Middle Republic, the Roman army had been composed in the main of a rustic, citizen militia, the majority of whom were small peasant farmers. In those days, excepting periods of great emergency, military service was restricted to those (sedentary) citizens who owned sufficient landed property to be registered by the census in the Roman polity's five-class system, itself internally stratified on a property basis. Men who belonged to these five "classes" were known as *assidui*, and were expected to provide arms and accoutrements commensurate with their means. The remainder of the citizenry were the *proletarii* or *capite censi* who, unable to afford martial equipment, were debarred from military service as a general rule. An exception would be a major threat to Rome which required supplementary forces to fight in its defense; in such a situation the state would recruit *proletarii* and defray the costs of their military requirements. This happened, for instance in the Second Punic War of 218–201 (the war against Hannibal).

As years passed, however, an expedient was steadily transformed into a convention. *Assidui* suffered marked depletion; *proletarii*, concomitantly, increased in number and probably formed the majority of citizens by the time of Hannibal's depredations. War—the engine of Rome's imperial might, the medium and instrument of her awesome power—inflicted a heavy toll on the small farmer. He might fall in battle, or die of disease. He might return to his farm after a long campaign overseas to find it in total disarray, fields unploughed, crops unpicked, abandoned by those charged to look after it in his absence. The farm itself might have been devastated by war and requisition, or by roaming gangs. If he was lucky enough to avoid these catastrophes, bad harvests might strike him down or drive him further into debt and dependence (he might, for example, be reduced to the status of someone's bondsman.) At the same time, the state's demand for military manpower was increasing and only the swelling ranks of rustic *proletarii* would be able to satisfy it. Provinces had to be won and garrisoned; enemies repulsed. To begin with, the Roman state responded to this situation through a formalistic fiction. By lowering the census property qualification, *proletarii* could artificially be elevated into a higher station (i.e., the fifth class, though of course they would still require military provision), a practice that has been well documented by Emilio Gabba ([1949] 1976a:1–19) in his study of census manipulations and their significance. To Gabba, the process of property qualification reductions affords a window from which to view "the stages in the [rural] proletarianisation of the Roman citizen militia"[62] and the rise "of military professionalism of which the chief characteristics may be defined as continuity of service and a mercenary outlook."[63] Marius's much-discussed contribution to the reform of the army structure must be seen in this context. Essentially, Marius stripped away the old pretences and, as consul in 107, and then again from 104 to 100 (entrusted respectively with the tasks of defeating Jugurtha and, afterwards, the Cimbri and Teutones) brazenly resorted to openly recruiting soldiers (volunteers, to boot) from the propertyless. Breaking with the farce of census casuistry, he also intensified the extent to which the army became proletarianized, and full of men of the sort described by one authority as "the younger sons of yeomen whose farms brooked no subdivision, tenants who wished to own rather than rent land, and day labourers whose work in the fields hardly sufficed for subsistence" (Brunt 1962:72). After Marius, the legions would be

solidly proletarian in composition; the conscripted would still, however, outnumber volunteers. The creation of standing armies, stationed
for long periods in the provinces was, as Matthias Gelzer (1968:9–10)
puts it, "a development with far-reaching social and political consequences":

> For the emergence of the soldier committed to serve for as long as he was fit for
> service immediately faced the state with the problem of providing for the veteran.
> According to Roman concepts this was, in the first instance, a question of provid-
> ing him with land. The generals were faced with the duty of championing this
> claim, but at the same time they gained a new and imposing *clientela*. As a result
> the figure of the victorious general acquired political power of unprecedented
> dimensions, and it is clear that the greatest danger for the [senatorial] oligarchy lay
> in the increased power that could now be won by individuals in this way.

Land distribution and land allotments were the natural demand of
those who still eked out a meagre living from the land, and of those
who had left it, voluntarily or through compulsion, to join the army.
The power of ambitious generals to enlist a personal following would
have been seriously undermined had the senatorial oligarchy, to whom
Gelzer refers, taken even the most basic precautions. The Senate could
have responded to the plight of the impoverished through a limited
distribution of public land. Or the army's loyalty to the Republic might
have been fostered by paying it "regular bounties on discharge" (Brunt
[1971] 1978:110); Augustus saw the wisdom of such a move and
acted on it. Instead, myopic and unsympathetic, Rome's ruling class
did nothing; and, with a growing sense of alienation from Republican
institutions, the rural plebs donned armor, glanced cynically at their
rulers, and hitched their fortune to the military juggernaut of the commander who seemed best placed to ease their burdens. In the final
analysis, the Republic was destroyed by soldiers composed overwhelmingly of members of the rural proletariat,[64] led by generals whose role
in mobilizing them was indispensable and, ultimately, decisive.

The second consequence of imperial expansion—rural and urban
Plebeian hardship—overlaps to some degree with the first. We have
already seen the existence of a growing rustic proletariat and the plight
faced by the small peasant farmer. But the latter's problems were
made even more grave by another development of the Middle and
Late Republic. I will turn to this now, and then venture some comments on the position of the Roman urban proletariat.

The primary source of private profit in the Middle and especially the Late Republic lay in the exploitation of the "provinces." These were conquered regions outside Italy, such as Asia (modern Turkey and Syria), Spain and northern Africa over which a (usually proconsul) governor was granted *imperium*[65]—military and jurisdictional authority with a broad discretionary remit to ensure order abroad, to protect Roman citizens resident there, to promote the development of Roman and Latin colonies,[66] and generally to add to the prestige and influence of the imperial power. The indigenous peoples of these areas, for whom the Roman state had little solicitude, paid a heavy price for being provincials; the rapacity of governors and their staffs was notorious. Verres' three year governorship of Sicily is reputed to have milked from the unfortunates in his sphere of influence assets worth ten million *denarii*; Caesar, whose reputation as a governor was never sullied by official charges of extortion, could still make enough money in his tenure in Hither Spain to repay his considerable debts (A.H.M. Jones reckons five or six million *denarii*) and have enough left over to become a rich man.[67] The wealth flowed from a variety of channels, and governors were by no means the only beneficiaries.

If governors might enrich themselves through the seizure of booty (e.g., the pillaging of temples), the sale of slaves and hostages, bribes "from foreign potentates and communities for political services" rendered (Jones 1974:117), and the like, other Roman senators, and *equites* too, could also make fabulous fortunes out of the provinces.[68] Senators might act as bankers, lending money at extortionate rates of interest to those who would otherwise default on their tax payments; *equites* also would lend money, though their revenue could be expanded in other ways as well. An important group within the *equites* was the stratum of *publicani*, usually the richest men of their order, who gained their livelihood through tax-farming (in the absence of a civil service to collect taxes the Roman state was compelled to privatise this function[69]), and through other state contracts, auctioned under censorial supervision every five years. Awarded to the highest bidder, state contracts covered mining, public works and army supplies, and profits could be vast. A significant portion of this yield would be frittered on hedonistic pursuits—luxury articles of all kinds; exotica and erotica. But as Jones (1974:121; cf. 123–24) makes clear:

> most of the recipients wished to put a part of their profits into the only permanent form of capital known to the ancient world, land. There was thus built up a great

demand for land, primarily Italian land, which was probably the most important cause of the growth of *latifundia*, at the expense of the small holdings of the peasantry.

The plight of peasant proprietors was made even more serious by a related development: the massive influx of slaves that accompanied military domination and piracy. Slaves became eminently affordable and were imported into Italy in prodigious quantities. The figures are staggering. Brunt (1978:18) conjectures that, by 28, the combined number of slaves in Italy had reached "3,000,000 as against 4,000,000 free persons." They were found various employment by their masters: in workshops, in a domestic capacity; slaves "even predominated as secretaries, accountants and doctors." But the majority of them probably ended up in the chain gangs that serviced the *latifundia* of the Late Republic. These massive estates of the wealthy gradually swallowed up the land of poorer farmers who, now also priced out of the labor market by slaves as cheap as they were plentiful, declined into ruin. Some of the dispossessed drifted into Rome; others joined the legions.

So far I have concentrated almost exclusively on the plight of the rural plebs. But what of their urban counterparts? What were their grievances and what part did they play in the Republic's downfall?

Imperial expansion was not totally without benefit for the plebs of Rome. Provincial exploitation subsidised cheap corn and public works; retail opportunities opened up as Rome became the centre of the Mediterranean world; and employment might be found in private and public building construction, in the assembly and repair of ships, or in the houses of the rich and powerful. On the other hand, the increasing use of slaves also "must have caused severe unemployment or chronic under-employment among the free poor" (Brunt 1978:38). Other causes of economic hardship are conveniently itemised by Zwi Yavetz (1969:33) who mentions "the burden of debts, the increase in the rate of interest, the housing shortage (resulting from the collapse of homes, from fires, or the flooding of the Tiber), the increase in rents, the rigorous collection of taxes, and, above all, the distress brought about by famine." To some degree, such famine was itself directly attributable to the growth of empire. Owners of *latifundia* were tempted to concentrate production in profitable viniculture (particularly grape and olive) or pasturage, thus increasing the capital city's reliance on foreign import of cereals from, say, Africa and Egypt. The significance of such imports must not be exaggerated; indigenous cultivation in the

Italian countryside was still widespread. Yet it was nonetheless mostly produced for local consumption, and where pirates interrupted trade, or military commanders blockaded Rome with fleets no longer prepared to conform to Senate authority, the results for the urban plebs could be dire.

They were not helpless. Outright rebellion was out of the question when troops remained loyal to the Senate. Riots were put down with viciousness and cruelty. But when riot proved ineffective, the plebs would resort to other means of pressure: they might stop work (if they had work) or, if they owned small shops, close them; they might shout or curse at the objects of their hatred; they might raise insulting effigies, smash statues, post up seditious proclamations at night or daub walls with graffiti (Yavetz 1969:9–21). Elections, too, could sometimes produce individuals willing to champion the people's rights; while the theater and circus—the butt of Juvenal's infamous "bread and circuses" jibe—also provided areas in which public opinion could be given expression.[70] It is nonetheless undeniable that the crowd's actions were also profoundly limited by its cultural background as well as by the structure of Roman society. Rome, though a Republic, was not a democracy and the lack of democratic practices militated against leadership from below (tribunes would invariably be, in the Late Republic, men of the propertied class). Quasi-political guilds (*collegia*) that might organize resistance were constantly subject to repression, and no urban plebeian social movement of protracted duration ever arose (though of course many plebeian demands remained more or less constant). A compact of poor urban citizens with slaves never materialized. Also of major importance was the existence in Rome (and elsewhere) of the *clientela* system that, so to speak, structurally disorganized the urban populace (Crawford 1978:36; Runciman 1983:166–7; Mann 1986:252). This system of patron-client reciprocity was deeply embedded in Roman culture and society, and was taken with great seriousness by both parties.[71] Patrons were expected to defend their clients in court, for instance, and often did so; some economic remuneration and social welfare functions might also devolve onto the patron. Clients (who were often freedmen—former slaves—morally and legally bound to their former master) would, for their part, provide the patron with a retinue, with muscle if he needed it to deal with competitors in the Forum, and with pliant instruments in the voting assemblies. According to Geoffrey de Ste. Croix (1981:342):

Even during the Republic, where political activity by the lower classes was still possible in some degree, many individuals, out of obedience to their patrons or in deference to their known attitude, must have been diverted from participating actively in political class struggle, and even induced to take part on the side of those having interests directly opposed to their own. One of the proverbs in the collection of Publilius Syrus, a late Republican, declares that "To accept a favour (*beneficium*) is to sell one's freedom."[72]

At the same time it would be a mistake to underestimate the urban plebs. They could, opportunity permitting, impose themselves effectively on a political situation[73] and were "capable of imperilling any government by actively joining a rival leader" (Yavetz 1969:73); politicians in Rome had to take account of them. Yet I suspect that most historians of antiquity would agree with one of their most distinguished colleagues when he wrote that, contrasted with the rustic army I described earlier, the urban plebs played "a subsidiary role in the Revolution" (Brunt 1978:152). Class primacy in the destruction of the Republic goes to the country folk. But the rural plebs, every bit as much as their urban class counterparts, could not make the "Revolution" alone. The influence of both subordinate classes on the Roman political and social system was indirect; they required mobilisation by class outsiders to realise their hopes for a better life. They found such leadership in generals and men who came to be called *populares* (who might also be generals themselves).[74] It is to this latter group that we must now devote our attention.

The convulsions that threatened the Republic from below were made immeasurably more dangerous for the ruling class by divisions within itself, which became ever more apparent after 133 (the year that marks Tiberius Gracchus' momentous tenure as tribune). The split between *populares* and *optimates* is a major discussion point in the literature on this period, and one is tempted simply to refer the reader to the sources. But since Julius Caesar is generally acknowledged to be the most successful and "the most consistently *popularis* of all the great leaders" (Taylor 1949:15), and since his career and regime is at the centre of my discussion in this section, I must forego a cursory treatment and deal with the topic in a little detail.

It is first necessary to make clear that the distinction between *optimates* and *populares* relates neither to class nor order. *Optimates* and *populares* came from the same economically and politically dominant landed propertied class; and were members also of the Senate and/or nobility. It is not even possible to distinguish the categories on a "fractional" basis. In addition, one must avoid the temptation to view the dissension between *optimates* and *populares* as deriving from "party" differences: in Rome of the Republic there simply was "no large-scale party organisation, no party caucus or ticket, and no fixed party line";[75] political alliances were temporary, ad hoc, and entered into for personal and family advancement; ideologically based alignments were unknown. Finally, to view *optimates* as aristocrats and *populares* as democrats would also be erroneous: both were social and political aristocrats;[76] both would have found in the equality of wealth and power the most obnoxious of situations. Rather, the opposition between *optimates* and *populares* is probably best envisaged as a conflict respectively between, on the one hand, a majority grouping within the ruling class that was determined to protect the power, dignity, and exclusivity of the Senate as a collegial body, and to ensure the preservation of the political and social status quo; and, on the other, those individuals also within the dominant class who were intent on breaking with senatorial tradition in certain respects. Members of this latter "group", which consisted of such individuals as Tiberius and Gaius Gracchus, Saturninus and Glaucia, Sulpicius Rufus, Marius Gratidianus, Catiline, Clodius, and Julius Caesar,[77] professed their commitment to agrarian and urban reform; "provided the essential leadership without which the struggles of the lower classes could hardly have emerged at all at the political level" (Ste. Croix 1981:351–52): they were greatly respected by members of the lower classes and were often worshipped after their—usually bloody—deaths as heroes of the common people; and, finding senatorial oligarchical government too constricting for their own ample personal ambition, showed themselves willing to overturn its collective hegemony. *Optimates* were thus conservatives; *populares* were radicals. And while I have spoken above of the latter as a "group," they formed one only in a typological sense: in reality, they were a series of "prominent individual politicians" as opposed to "a compact body of men having substantially the same outlook on major political issues" such as the *optimates* comprised.[78]

If one turns to the ancient sources for enlightenment on the meanings of *optimate* and *popularis*, one discovers that the terms are remarkably tendentious. Cicero's *Pro Sestio* may serve to illustrate the point. There we are instructed that the *optimates* include such people as senators, those who comply with senatorial policy, those classes from which the Senate is recruited, citizen residents of the Italian municipalities and countryside, businessmen and freedmen or, "in a few words" all those "who are neither criminal nor vicious in disposition, nor frantic, nor harassed by troubles in their households." *Optimates*, in short, are good citizens, men "who are upright, sound in mind," men whose goal is public order and the dignity and prestige of the commonwealth.[79] By contrast *populares* are those "who wished everything they did and said to be agreeable to the masses"[80] and who, evidently, were successful in their designs: Cicero states that men like the Gracchi and Saturninus were "applauded in the theatre; they obtained by votes whatever they had striven for; their names, their words, their looks, their bearing, were objects of popular affection."[81] So much the pity then that these *populares* suffered from "a sort of inborn revolutionary madness,"[82] that naturally gave offence to loyal, "serious and honourable men."[83]

This kind of description has not satisfied historians of antiquity who instead customarily describe the *populares* in terms of their program, their methods, and their rhetoric.

The program of the *populares*, enacted sporadically from 133 to Caesar's death in 44, contained a series of recurrent features that have been helpfully summarised by Ste. Croix (1981:352):

> agrarian measures of one kind or another, including above all the distribution of land to the poor or to army veterans, whether in individual lots or in the form of colonies; the supply of corn to poor citizens living at Rome, either free or at a low price (*frumentationes*); the relief of debt; and defence of the democratic elements in the constitution, such as they were, especially the privileges of the tribunes and the right of appeal (*provocatio*). All these policies were anathema to the oligarchs.

We might add to this that it was typically *populares* who championed the Italian "allies" in their struggle for the political privileges that citizenship conferred; and that it tended to be *populares* too who sought some kind of minimal protection for provincials against at least the worst abuses of senatorial and *equite* extortion.[84]

The methods employed by *populares* also distinguished them from their *optimate* opponents. *Optimates* expected that magisterial bills and decrees should first be subject to senatorial discussion and permission before they were submitted to the assemblies. Though the Senate originally and in constitutional principle was supposedly only a consultative body to which the two consuls might have recourse as they saw fit, with the evolution of the Republic it assumed through an accretion of convention ever greater authority; by the beginning of the Late Republic there was no question but that the Senate was the power-house of the Roman empire.[85] Threats to its supremacy as an organ of domination were bloodily repressed by the Senate's agents;[86] magistrates who only usually served for one year at a time, but would become by virtue of their tenure life long members of the Senate, had good reason to accept senatorial restrictions and prerogatives. *Populares* scoffed at such presumption. "None of them claimed indeed that the people at Rome, as at Athens, should control all policy and even routine administration; but they all asserted the sovereign right of the people to decide any question that might be referred to it, and rejected the *optimate* claim that the prior sanction of the Senate was required" (Brunt 1978:94). *Populares* claimed the authority of the people and, where ever possible, strove to become tribunes, an office with important rights attached to it. A tribune's person was inviolable. He had extensive powers of veto and arrest that could be used to confound or coerce other magistrate colleagues. He might intervene to secure a citizen from the clutches of a magistrate. Even more important, tribunes had powers to introduce legislation and to summon meetings (over which they were also entitled to preside) both of the plebeian assembly and of the so-called *contiones*: gatherings in which the public could, with the tribune, debate issues, candidatures and laws (extant or anticipated). In a political system in which the space of public debate was severely curtailed by legal restrictions on assembly, the power to convoke *contiones* was of especial value.[87] *Populares*, as tribunes, were in a position to exercise that power to maximum advantage. Their ideas and policies could be addressed to the people directly, thus circumventing the blocking-tactics of a fractious and obstructive Senate. And where it was constitutionally impossible for a *popularis* to become one of the ten annually chosen tribunes—a citizen of patrician birth was ineligible for the office (hence Caesar was excluded)—he would be compelled to act by proxy, a tactic to which the greatest *popularis* of all often found recourse.[88]

The foregoing paragraph has already to some degree hinted at the nature of the rhetoric employed by *populares*. The touchstone of their discourse and "fiery orations" (Taylor 1949:22) was the slavery to which the people had succumbed thanks to an oppressive clique of oligarchs. *Populares* did not champion the rights of the people to participate actively in the formulation of state policy or in the running of government; what they had in mind was "the sovereign right of the assembly to decide any matter that might be put to it, without the sanction of the Senate " (Brunt 1978:94–95). Closely identifying themselves with the people's right in this regard, *populares* emphasized the division of society and state between the *optimates*, on the one hand, and a homogenous bloc of citizens on the other. *Populares* invoked the antagonistic imagery of them-us, faction-people, and crystallized the alternative between enslavement and liberty.[89] Sometimes the legitimating principle to which *populares* appealed might just refer to "the people"; at other times "The Senate and the People" might be summoned. If anything the emotional charge of the latter was more powerful than mention of "the people" alone. For by emblematically unifying Senate and people, the *populares* could isolate even further that gang who stood outside this grand conception, accused of "oppressing the Republic and exploiting the constitution in its own interests" (Syme [1939] 1974:155).

If the sincerity of the *populares* is a matter for speculation, the consequences of their ambitions and of the reform "movement" they spearheaded are indubitable. Roman politics after the Gracchi brothers' tribunates would never be the same again. "The Gracchi exposed all the divisive forces in Roman society, and their reforms and ruin set in train the events that culminated with the fall of the Republic" (Brunt 1978:92). The Gracchi, and the *populares* that followed them, provided the essential leadership for the urban and rural discontented, and could also count on support from the Italian "allies," the provinces and, from time to time, the *equites*. Men who comprised the *populares* were of a varied sort and their individual careers are illuminating. I shall in what follows deal with only one of them, a man who in his genius and in his achievements had no peer.

* * *

In the preceding narrative I have been concerned to show how Rome's empire building resulted in a series of severe social and political crises. Agrarian hardship was one of my main themes, particularly as it translated itself into a rustic, proletarianized army demanding land on retirement, and dependent on a commander to realize that aspiration. The plight of the urban plebs also received consideration, but I observed that their role in the destruction of the Republic, was secondary to that of their rural class counterparts. I also sought to demonstrate that both urban and rural plebeian discontent was mediated, mobilized, and directed by men—tribunes and generals—who hailed from the dominant class. These leaders and reformers for whom senatorial government was too constraining for their autocratic ambition, deepened the crisis by splitting their own ruling class; the consequent dissension eventually destroyed the Republic. Caesar's career, personal style, rhetoric, and regime as the *popularis*-general *par excellence* is inexplicable without this context.

Caesar's Rhetoric and Style

For the modern student schooled in sociology or political science, there is a tremendous temptation to describe Caesar as a "populist" figure, particularly given the Latin root of this term. We should resist it. Common to all modern populisms is "some kind of exaltation of and appeal to 'the people,' and all are in one sense or another antielitist" (Canovan 1981:294);[90] in addition, all are characterized by an organizational structure in which traditional organs of authority are bypassed to establish "a direct and unmediated rapport" between leader and led (Mouzelis 1986:90). In very general terms, such remarks do have pertinence in Caesar's case; but again it is the generality that is the problem. On closer inspection there is good reason to make a distinction between a Roman *popularis* like Caesar and more modern figures to whom we refer as "populist"; we shall see why presently. In any case, Caesar was not any *popularis* or any general. He was a supreme example of both species and his genius resided in the unparalleled brilliance he brought to the combination. In what follows I shall enlarge upon Caesar's *popularis* rhetoric and style. However it is important to clarify at this juncture a possible source of confusion. "From 63," Zwi Yavetz (1969:44) observes, "there was no doubt among the wider public that Caesar had chosen the *via popularis*."[91] December 5, 63 was the date on which Caesar eloquently sought to persuade the Senate not to execute the Catilinarian conspirators, a plea that might have succeeded but for Cato's even more eloquent demand for the death sentence. (Catiline had been highly popular with the crowd.) Caesar's *popularis* allegiances and sympathies, his *popularis* credentials were evident to most from this time onwards (i.e., till his death). Caesar's *popularis regime*, on the other hand, occupies only the last few years of his life: the period of autocracy and "dictatorship" (49–44). Before that time, although Caesar is certainly considered "a friend of the people" he does not control the state, notwithstanding his election to the consulship in 60. In 60–59 he had to share dominion. By contrast, in 49, faced with a Senate that sought to strip him of his powers and that threatened his life, Caesar crossed the Rubicon, plunged Italy into civil war and, in the same year, became master of Rome. Of the military and autocratic nature of Caesar's regime I shall speak presently; his public "image," which encompassed his regime, but also preceded it, is my subject here.

At first glance Caesar appears an improbable *popularis* candidate. He came, after all, from redoubtable patrician stock, and was proud to advertise in the funeral oration he delivered for his aunt Julia (in 69) the Julians' descent from kings (the Marcii Reges) and from Venus herself. Since the Caesars were a branch of the Julians they could with justice claim "'both the sanctity of kings, who reign supreme among mortals, and the reverence due to gods, who hold even kings in their power" (Suetonius I.6 = 1980:14). Such a man with such a lineage could have become a pillar of the *optimate* establishment had he but wanted to do so. Caesar cannot therefore be assimilated to a situation of the sort described by Ernesto Laclau (1977:173) in which "a new fraction seeks to impose its hegemony but is unable to do so within the existing structure of the power bloc." This was not Caesar's position. Had Caesar been an *equite* perhaps Laclau's statement might have more explanatory force. But Caesar was of the same class and class "fraction" of the *optimates* he first pilloried and later politically destroyed. No necessary social or political obstacles barred him or most other *populares* from the highest senatorial offices. His class location did not require him to appeal directly to "the multitude," did not require an attack on the Senate's legitimacy. It is true that Caesar's family had Marian connections: Caesar's aunt Julia been the widow of the great *popularis* general. Moreover, Caesar's first wife Cornelia (she also died in 69) was the daughter of another famous *popularis* figure: Cinna. But in the shifting alliances that made up Roman Republican politics, *popularis* family associations or allegiances could readily be shed (or adopted and shed, as Pompey's career attested); and, at least up to the Catilinarian conspiracy, Caesar's career was open-ended. In any case, as already indicated, the *populares* themselves derived from the same class and rank as their *optimate* opponents.

I shall not trace step by step the career of Caesar as a *popularis*; the reader interested in that development is referred to Gelzer's book on Caesar—by common consent the most important biography of the man this century—where the subject is handsomely treated. Nor shall I here expatiate on the reasons that motivated Caesar to assume the *popularis* mantle. Personal ambition seems to have been the dominant factor, but then Caesar's intentions are of less historical significance than the consequences of his actions. It is on the latter that I shall now, albeit selectively, concentrate.

We get a vivid picture of Caesarean rhetoric from the commentaries that comprise the *Civil War*. (I use the term "rhetoric" to denote simply the art of persuasion and without the negative connotations that attach to the adjective "rhetorical." Caesar's commentaries are anything but florid and declamatory; controlled simplicity is their defining feature.)[92] The *Civil War* was not, it appears, published in Caesar's lifetime;[93] it cannot therefore be assigned causal status (as propaganda) in the explanation of his rise to power. The significance of the document lies elsewhere. What it shows is how Caesar wanted publicly to project himself and, presumably, did so project himself wherever, context allowing, political capital might thereby be acquired. Caesar's political shrewdness is legendary, his antennae renowned for their sensitivity.[94] It is therefore possible to hypothesize that the *Civil War* also reveals something important about Roman society, its receptivity to the kind of discourse in which Caesar engaged.

The *Civil War*—probably drafted by Caesar in Egypt in 47[95]— appears to exemplify the core populist motifs often rehearsed by modern political theorists. There is the claim of Caesar to be acting as the people's agent: the Senate had attempted to terminate his military command six months prematurely and haul him back to Rome "although the will of the people had been that I should be admitted as a [consular] candidate *in absentia* at the next elections."[96] The commencement of the civil war, he protests innocently to Lentulus Spinther, was not of his doing: "I did not leave my province with intent to harm anybody. I merely want to protect myself against the slanders of my enemies" and "to restore to their rightful position the tribunes of the people, who have been expelled because of their involvement in my cause."[97] Added to this theme, is another—the polarization of a corrupt, tyrannical *factio* versus the downtrodden multitude. Hence Caesar must reclaim for himself "and for the Roman people independence from the domination of a small clique."[98] But the distance of *popularis* rhetoric from its ostensible populist modern counterpart becomes evident once one examines more closely the context and content of Caesar's arguments. Strictly speaking, the doctrine of "popular sovereignty" did not exist in ancient Rome. Someone like Caesar might claim that he was acting in the people's interests, or on the basis of an authority derived (at least in part) from the people's wishes and institutions, but the relationship between *popularis* and people was asymmetrical by its very nature. Caesar, assuredly, was glad to advertise his services to the *res publica*; but he could never say, as Juan Domingo Perón did later, that he was "no more than the servant" of the people (Canovan 1981:145) for to make such a remark would have been to deny the distinction, renown, and fame that all great Romans sought through leadership and command. Significantly, most modern populist leaders have come from relatively humble backgrounds—not, as we read in Caesar's boast, from the seed of kings and gods. And in the *Civil War* it is Caesar's own dignity and position that is emphasized every bit as much, if not more, than the plight of the citizens he is defending. He says to the soldiers of the Thirteenth legion: "I ask you to defend my reputation and standing against the assaults of my enemies";[99] he declares that the Senate's mistreatment of him threatens his prestige, and prestige "has always been of prime importance to me, even outweighing life itself."[100] Lily Ross Taylor (1949:163) grasped well the deeper meaning of these and other statements:

> Caesar in his constant communications to the Senate stressed particularly his *dignitas*, a word that Syme renders 'rank, prestige and honor,' but he managed to relate his *dignitas* to the cause of the people that he was championing. Caesar's position had been guaranteed by the law of the ten tribunes passed in 52, the law that granted Caesar the privilege of standing for the consulship *in absentia*. This privilege, this *beneficium populi*, the oligarchs had, according to Caesar, taken from him. Caesar and the people were one, and, as he quotes his conversation with Lentulus, he was liberating both, *se et populum Romanum*, from the *factio paucorum*, the tyranny of the oligarchy. Caesarism meant the identification of the Roman people with Caesar.

But did it mean Caesar's identification with the Roman people? That is more doubtful. In defending his own honor, Caesar was simultaneously championing the tribunate, the legal institution most associated with the protection of the people's rights. To that extent, each were implicated in, and inseparable from, the other. He quotes the veteran Crastinus rallying his fellow soldiers at Pharsalus with the cry: "'Follow me, you who were formerly in my company, and give your general the service you have promised. Only this one battle remains; after it, he will recover his position, and we our freedom.'"[101] Caesar's position and freedom for the common person: in this order.[102] Caesar may well at this stage in his career have wished to support the tribunate as an institution in its own right, but "a state where every man is a king but no man wears a crown," as Huey Long once put it (Canovan 1981:155), is a republican sentiment for which the Late Roman Republic had not much use.

Nor is the "plebiscitarian" aspect of populism—the direct and unmediated relationship between leader and led—strictly applicable in the Roman case.[103] In the Roman Republic there were indeed *plebiscita* but their working and significance has to be properly understood. *Plebiscita* were decrees or resolutions with the force of law passed by the *concilium plebis*, an exclusively plebeian, tribal (i.e., territorially based) assembly.[104] The *concilium plebis* was a body empowered to pass laws *and* elect magistrates though, confusingly, this assembly did not monopolize sovereignty (legislative or electoral) but rather had to share it with two other main bodies:[105] the similarly tribally based *comitia tributa*, which consisted of plebeian and patrician citizens; and the *comitia centuriata*, also of mixed (plebeian and patrician) composition, but founded on timocratic criteria, that is, on the wealth one owned.[106] Notwithstanding their peculiar electoral prerogatives—each was charged with the election of specific magistrates—all three bodies voted on legislative matters in an identical manner: bills submitted to the assemblies could not be amended but had to be voted on in their entirety. (Discussion in the actual assembly place itself was also prohibited.) But here the vague similarity with modern referendums ends, since the unit of voting was not an individual person, casting a ballot that counted equally with other individual persons; the unit of voting was a collective agent—either a tribe (*concilium plebis, comitia tributa*), weighted heavily in favour of the rural populace, or a timocratic class (*comitia centuriata*) weighted heavily in favor of the richest citizens.[107] Hence the "mass," atomized plebiscitary electoral constituency of Weber's Caesarist leader is absent from the Roman scene, and the analogy of *plebiscitum* with the modern plebiscite is extremely imperfect.[108]

This is not to say that Caesar was a remote figure to his men. On the contrary, his personable style and manner were vital in solidifying the devotion of ordinary people to his person. The army, composed in the main of rustic plebs, was dedicated to him because of his fortitude and courage, his proven concern for agrarian form, evident since the two agrarian laws he had instigated during his consulship of 59, his ability to win and reward his veterans,[109] but also because of his charm: he would customarily refer to his fighting men, not as "soldiers" or "citizens"—a term he reserved for those like the men of the mutinous Tenth legion he wished to chide—but as "comrades" (Suetonius I.67, 70 = 1980:38–90). And this charm is the clue to Caesar's popularity with the urban plebs as well.

What was the secret of Caesar's capacity to so engage the mass of his contemporaries in Rome? Was it his outstanding generosity that made people warm to him? To some extent, yes: Caesar was "famous for his lavishness in bestowing bounties" (Yavetz 1969:43). On the other hand many of the nobility in the last years of the Republic, seeking to shore up support, distributed extensive largesse, yet none of them attained a public stature comparable to Caesar's. Perhaps, then, one should search for the key to Caesar's popularity in the reforms he instituted during his regime. Certainly, aspects of his policies and legislation must have endeared him to the crowd. He attended to the question of rents; he sought measures to reduce the burden of indebtedness; he resettled 80,000 of Rome's poorest citizens on colonies abroad; he attempted to create employment through public works. At the same time, however, Caesar curbed the people's electoral influence, studiously avoided an extremist stance of debt cancellation, and upheld the rights of private property holders;[110] no one is even sure of the effectiveness of his policies to combat unemployment.[111] So if Caesar's program does not adequately account for the widespread affection in which he was held, to what other explanations should we have recourse? Caesar's military prowess was legendary: his victories in Gaul enthralled the Roman populace, while his invasion of the mysterious Britain caused a sensation (Gelzer 1968:116, 131, 177). But Rome had a history of great generals and, during Caesar's lifetime, Pompey's reputation too was formidable, even if he was a failure as a *popularis*. Besides, greatness on the battlefield was no guarantee of domestic esteem: Mark Antony, for instance, was hated by the Roman plebs (Yavetz 1969:64–65, 69–70, 71–2). Or what about Caesar's ability to thrill ordinary people with spectacle? Could this make intelligible the popularity he enjoyed? It must have had some effect, yet according to the author who has made a thorough study of Caesar's "public image," "the festivities and games instituted by Caesar were impressive but not unusual. Caesar did not discover any new means of dealing with the Roman masses, he only changed the scale" (Yavetz [1979] 1983:167). Finally, one can discount as a factor of special importance Caesar's claim to divine lineage; the urban plebs were sceptical people who required acts to convince them that men were gods.

Now all the above mentioned characteristics of Caesar's public persona would have helped establish him as a great man, but they were insufficient, even in combination, to explain the singular popularity he managed to attain. Zwi Yavetz, whose interpretation I have been following, locates one quality as decisive in translating all other factors into authentic popular goodwill and devotion: an attribute Cicero would refer to (disparagingly) as *levitas popularis*.

The politician with *levitas* has the ability to mix easily with members of the class socially below him whom he treats with courtesy but never reserve. He is a people's man, unaffected with the stiff and distant formality that comes with *gravitas*. His sincerity is transparent: he cares for the people not for what he can gain from them but for what he can achieve on their behalf. In consequence he sides with the small person against the arrogance and power of the mighty. He cares for the people's needs and amusements but is careful in his bearing and carriage not to humiliate them or offend their pride and dignity.[112]

According to Yavetz, Caesar had cultivated this ability to a supreme degree, though even with him lapses were evident on occasion: his habit of dealing with correspondence during the games, for instance, was considered by onlookers to be rude. Usually, however, his image was of "a friend of the people," attentive to their sensibilities and desires. Playing on the loathing felt by the lower classes for the senatorial aristocracy, Caesar lampooned the oligarchs, humiliating them vicariously for a public that had little opportunity for such action itself. So far as the mass of the plebs was concerned, republican *libertas* meant the freedom of a gang to exploit them; the man who could strike out at this clique with impunity would be bound to win the estimation of the *plebs Romana*. Moreover, unlike his protégé Mark Antony, Caesar managed to win the affection of both army *and* plebs (Antony's brutality to the common people of Rome made him a figure of detestation); while, unlike Pompey, Caesar was not burdened down by the liability of *gravitas*.

One must be careful, it is true, not to exaggerate Caesar's popularity; it is a commonplace to observe that during the last couple of years of his life he showed signs of losing his popular touch. Caesar, for instance, acted imperiously towards the tribunes whose rights he had earlier claimed to be defending, and in so doing threatened to alienate the support of the plebs.[113] (Needless to say, the hostility of the *optimates* to Caesar was more or less constant from the trial of Catiline onwards.) His *Anticato*—a personalized attack on a man who had come to symbolise Republican virtue—looked mean and petty, and seems to have backfired. His kingly appearance could begin to look distinctly removed from the renowned *levitas* of old. Yet when all is said and done the facts seem to be that the common people were profoundly moved by Caesar's murder, eloquent testimony to the extraordinary public standing Caesar achieved and retained till (and after) the end. The conspirators' hope or belief that the people would support the tyrannicide failed completely to materialise: "the masses remained faithful to their leader."[114] When, on the day of Caesar's funeral (March 20, five days after the assassination) Caesar's body was displayed in the Forum, a wave of outrage broke through the crowd. Antony's speech was low key as opposed to inflammatory, but it did not subdue feelings of revulsion and anger. Immortalization of Caesar was practically instantaneous. Suetonius (I.85 = 1980:45) recounts that people later "raised a substantial, almost twenty-foot-high column of Numidian marble in the Forum, and inscribed on it: 'To the Father of His Country'. For a long time afterwards they used to offer sacrifices at the foot of this column, make vows there and settle disputes by oath taken in Caesar's name." Caesar's reputation was also augmented by transcendental intervention when, on the first day of games instituted by Octavian to commemorate the dead man, "a comet appeared about an hour before sunset and shone for seven days running. This was held to be Caesar's soul, elevated to Heaven."[115] Official recognition of Caesar as a god followed (in 42), though dedication of his temple would have to wait till Octavian's sixth consulship in 28 (Nock 1934:471).

Lastly, without the special popularity that clung to Caesar's name it would be impossible to understand why Octavian, the adopted son and heir of the murdered autocrat, seized on that name as avidly as he did. From the time in 44 when he accepted the inheritance and adoption,

Octavian always called himself, and was customarily known by others as, "Caesar." "He might have taken the additional name Octavianus, but never did, preferring to identify himself completely with his adoptive father" (Jones 1977:12; cf. xi, 24, 32–33). In later years, it is true, Octavian (he received the title of Augustus[116] in 27) attempted to distance himself ideologically from the revolutionary origins of his rule,[117] but initially he had shown no such ambivalence. His purpose was revenge and glory. Caesar's badge and blessing commended itself to the people and, crucially, to his adoptive father's veterans. Octavian would use both groups to promote his triumphant ascent to supreme power.

Military and Autocratic Character of the Regime

The foundation and longevity of Caesar's regime was dependent on the army he commanded. Without the support of his Gallic legions he could never have conquered Rome; without armed might to back his *popularis* pretensions he would have been utterly destroyed by Pompey. No one understood this, of course, better than Caesar himself, as one of his own remarks attests. On the field of Pharsalus, with Pompey's army in tatters, he would say of his vanquished enemies: "They brought it on themselves.They would have condemned me regardless of all my victories—me, Gaius Caesar—had I not appealed to my army for help" (Suetonius I.30 = 1980:27).[118]

Naturally, all political regimes, ancient or modern, rely in the last instance on armed force. But there are three good reasons especially to stress the military dimension in the case of the Caesar phenomenon. First, Caesar was the greatest of all the *popularis* generals and, arguably, one of the greatest generals of all time.[119] Second, Caesar—that "aspirant to autocracy based upon the sword" (Rostovtzeff [1927] 1975:148)—attained power because ultimately he was able to seize it by force, by what would later be called a military coup d'état. Within the Late Republic, the impetus for this kind of intervention was irresistible. As Michael Mann (1986:259) has remarked, the "general *had* to intervene politically. The loyalty of his troops depended on his ability to secure legislation for pensions, later in the form of land grants." Third, Caesar's regime was always overshadowed by war. In the years between 49 and 44 Caesar spent not more than sixteen months actually resident in Rome (Taylor 1949:172); the rest of the time was devoted mostly to campaigning, since even after Pompey's defeat in 48, there were major dangers in Egypt and Spain with which to contend. He met these dangers in person and, before his life was cut short, was planning another expedition, this time against the Parthians.

A docile Senate was another manifestation and prerequisite of Caesar's autocracy. Its submission would be secured by various means. Increased in size from 600 to 900 members by an influx of Caesar's adherents—mainly *equites* from the Italian towns, supplemented by a clutch of provincials[120]—the Senate could now be expected more faithfully to reflect the will of its overlord: as the Senate's number expanded so its power declined. The government of an oligarchy was replaced by that of a clique, or cabinet, with Caesar at its head; that Caesar "made his most important decisions in meetings with his reliable friends L. Cornelius Balbus, C. Oppius, C. Matius, A. Hirtius and C. Vibius Pansa was an open secret" (Yavetz 1983:172–73). Concomitantly, the Senate's input into policymaking diminished; the body that had once been the seat of government was reduced to the undignified position of talking shop and rubber stamp.[121] Nor was senatorial contumacy much in evidence. Senators grumbled at Caesar's consecutive occupation of the consulship from 46 to 44 but put up no concerted opposition—until March 44; while, in the same period, the master of Rome was lavishly decorated with Senate-dispensed honors. Gelzer's catalogue of the honours bestowed on Caesar in the autumn and early winter of 45 gives some idea of their scale and will tolerate selective quotation:

> He was granted the title of *pater patriae*, his birthday was declared a public holiday and statues of him were to be set up in all the temples of Rome and the municipalities ....The month of his birth Quinctilis received the name of Julius, and a tribe was to bear his name. His dictatorship and censorial authority...were extended for life.[122] To his honorary tribunician rights inviolability (*sacrosanctitas*) was expressly added. His son or adopted son was to be designated *pontifex maximus*, a veiled recognition of hereditary monarchy, as was also his use of the name Imperator....All the senators swore an oath that they were ready to protect his life. New officials on entering their posts had to swear to abide by the acts of his administration, and his future governmental actions were declared valid in advance....The divine image in his likeness which was carried in the circus procession was to receive a holy resting-place (*pulvinar*) like other deities, and a pediment like that on temples was to be set on his house. The new god was to be honoured as *divus* (meaning the same as *deus*) Julius in a separate temple together with Clementia. Antony was appointed his priest (*flamen*). In contrast to all other mortals, when the time came, Caesar was to be buried inside the city. (Gelzer 1968:315–17)

In such a manner did the Senate solemnise its own redundancy. Yet an obedient Senate was insufficient for Caesar; his dominion required that other nodal points of resistance be neutralized. The bulk of the *collegia* were outlawed. During the last years of the Republic these guilds and clubs had functioned as primitive electoral associations, employing intimidation where persuasion proved ineffective, and providing a *popularis* like Clodius with an organization to attack the Senate. With the dissolution of the guilds Caesar was giving notice that, under the new regime, no *popularis* competition was to be tolerated. The popular assemblies fared better. Their formal existence was never challenged, but Caesar took care that they should, wherever possible, arrive at the right decisions. He added to the arsenal of his powers the right to nominate half of the yearly magistrates (consuls excluded) and, invariably, Caesar's authority and patronage was such that "nomination" meant election would follow; it transpired that "in practice all elections degenerated more or less to formalities" (Gelzer 1968:309).

Caesar's power inside and outside the Senate seemed irresistible; his constitutional status as dictator even put him beyond the reach of the tribunes who, in any case, were mostly now his creatures. In the end he was struck down by men he believed to be his allies, if not his friends. The significance of his murder should not be exaggerated: only about sixty senators appear to have been involved in the conspiracy: they were not the vanguard of a widespread revolt, not even a majority senatorial revolt. Moreover, one should not let the bloody conclusion of Caesar's regime obscure one of its more extraordinary features, namely Caesar's own largely successful attempt to construct and then to maintain what one author has called a "superclientele" of "senators and citizens alike" (Taylor 1949:174). We have to answer the question: What enabled such a superclientele to be built and to persist as long as it did? Military force, and autocratic power (the subjects of an earlier discussion) no doubt partially explain the phenomenon; so do the interests of the parties involved. But then force and autocracy is more liable to atomise than it is to build, while the parties just mentioned were farraginous and full of faction. To account for this achievement one must look more closely at Caesar's leadership qualities.

Caesar's Syncretic Political Leadership

A remarkable aspect of Caesar as a leader was his ability—evident both in his rise to power and once the regime was established—to unify and galvanize under his direction a social alliance of forces whose interests were in many respects irreconcilable. This quality of the man and the regime has been much commented on; in an earlier chapter, we saw Wilhelm Roscher write of the "Janus faced" character of "Caesarism." Before him, Theodor Mommsen (1911:428–29) had remarked on how the sheer force of Caesar's character had "compelled the most heterogeneous natures to place themselves at his service." Perhaps this is also the germ of truth, garbled as it is, behind the tendency of Gramscians to equate Caesar with coalitions of various kinds. In modern times, however, nobody has illustrated his syncretic ability better than Zwi Yavetz in his book on Caesar's public image. As he shows, "Caesar never based his support on a single stratum of society, and he knew how to establish his personal authority by complicated manoeuvres between groups who were often opposed to one another" (1983:178). In this final part of the discussion, let me first enlarge upon the nature of Caesar's coalition, and then proceed to examine some of the skills that made it possible. My debt to Yavetz, Gelzer, and Ronald Syme will be even more obvious here that it has been throughout this entire section.

The heteroclite character of Caesar's following (in the period immediately before and during the regime) becomes clear as soon as one begins to probe its social composition. On one side we have groups from the dominant classes: financially embarrassed tribunes, consuls and other senators willing to join Caesar's *clientela* for gold bled from Gaul; young publicists, "orators and poets" sickened with the oligarchy, aligning themselves with Caesar. We witness the remnants of the Marians, ambitious and anti-*optimate*, joining Caesar's "party" (Syme 1974:62–65.) Some fifty-five nobles are among Caesar's supporters in the civil war, as compared with around forty who attached themselves to Pompey (Yavetz 1983:172). *Equites*, with bankers prominent among them, gave Caesar financial support and formed his close circle of advisers, spies, and agents: "Many of the bankers were already personal friends of Caesar: it may be presumed that he gave them guarantees against revolution." Provincials, colonists, and Italian "allies" flocked to Caesar's banner seeking a quid pro quo in the political rights, and economic opportunities, that full citizenship would bestow on them.[123]

These groups were in themselves diverse; historic snobberies, differences in rank and sometimes regional background lent them centrifugal momentum. But Caesar managed to recruit them to his cause, and make it appear that his fate and their objectives were inextricably bound together. He did not stop there. For on the other side he also procured the support of the subordinate classes, or at least major sections of them. His legions—the rural plebs in armor—were offered cash, booty, and, on retirement, land; if Caesar's generosity to his men during the Gallic campaigns gave weight to the credibility of his promises, his victory in the civil war materially confirmed the sincerity of those declarations. Equally, Caesar the *popularis* offered the urban plebs the chance, not only of a better economic existence (their grievances were considered above), but of seeing the hated aristocracy humbled. Caesar's regime did not revolutionise their conditions, nor did it destroy the elite they so detested; but it did address their most serious complaints, and made them feel that Caesar was their man.

Yet here we come to the riddle of Caesar: he was nobody's man and everyone's man (everyone's except that of the diehard Republicans, and after the war they were few). An array of skills and qualities help explain this integrative achievement. Of his *levitas* I have already spoken, a quality that commended him to ordinary folk. At the same time Caesar was careful not to alienate the propertied class. Those among them who had joined his enemies he strove publicly to forgive: Caesar's clemency was proverbial. It was also informed by practical, political calculation. The mercy he showed at Corfinium in February 49 and thereafter, reassured those nobles who had joined the oligarchy's cause but were now having second thoughts: hearing that Caesar would countenance no summary execution and that private property was being respected (i.e., not confiscated) they began to drift back to Rome. Caesar proclaimed loudly and persistently that his ultimate aim was social harmony: he would insist that "he was not fighting to annihilate his enemies, but to reconcile their differences with as little bloodshed as possible, and so to pave the way for a final pacification of a Roman world that had been convulsed by a series of violent crises" (Gelzer 1968:217). It is likely that Caesar's *clementia* derived from more than sheer cynicism; but its consequence was in most cases to bind his enemies in chains of obligation.[124] Cato saw the ensnarement that

Caesarean forgiveness entailed when he wrote: "I do not wish to be indebted to the tyrant for his illegal actions: for he is acting against the laws when he pardons men over whom he has no sovereignty as if he were their master."[125] Cato took his own life and thereby refused Caesar's *clementia*; the majority of his peers preferred to take Caesar's *clementia* and thereby save their lives and their property.

The propertied class were wooed in other ways too. The colonization program Caesar put into operation removed tens of thousands of the poorest citizens from the city of Rome, so reducing considerably the scope for popular agitation. Repression of the *collegia* would have been welcomed, while the reduction in the number of citizens eligible for the corn dole must have warmed the hearts of those, like Cicero, who viewed free grain as conducive only to the cultivation of indolence and a drain on the city purse. Even the settlement of Caesar's veterans was done with maximum sensitivity to the rights of those already living on the designated land. Confiscation was selective, for instance targeted against those among the Pompeians who had remained inveterate enemies of Caesar. Compensation was available to many of those on whose land the veterans were to dwell. Furthermore, veteran allotments were not to form a bloc that would menace nonveteran farmers already resident in the assigned region of settlement: veterans were to be spread among those established farmers in a manner supposedly consistent with social peace.[126]

Men of property had other reasons not to be alarmed at Caesar's regime. Caesar's approach to the debt and rent question was moderate; indirect taxes levied on the province of Asia remained to be farmed by the *publicani* (who also appear to have gained by the import tax on foreign goods that Caesar's administration imposed); and the opportunities for profit were generally boosted by the (temporary) end of civil war and a tamed populace in Rome.

The alliance of social forces that Caesar forged was a tremendous accomplishment. As we know, it eventually failed: the limits of Caesar's syncretism are starkly revealed by his murder. A section within the Senate remained steadfast in its Republican commitments, implacable in its opposition to "the tyrant." Caesar's *levitas* offended this group, while his contempt for senatorial authority outraged its number. But it was a small group he estranged. The truly extraordinary thing is that Caesar's integrative achievement occurred at all, and then lasted for almost six years. The accomplishment is not to be dissolved into its conditions, for while the conditions were there for a number of people to take advantage of, only Caesar managed to do so effectively. A contrast with Pompey helps illuminate the argument. Pompey was, like Caesar, a great general; like Caesar, too, he had an extensive *clientela* (Badian 1958:252–90). And he had the backing of the legitimate government during the civil war. Yet Pompey, not Caesar, was defeated, though initially Caesar's army was smaller than the one Pompey commanded. To explain both Caesar's victory and the regime he proved able to establish one would want, naturally, to invoke a range of causes. Military strategy and tactics would figure prominently in any sensible account. But one would also have to say that Pompey was a complete failure as a syncretician. Hence Cicero complained to Atticus: "Is there a more wretched spectacle than that of Caesar earning praise in the most disgusting cause (*causa*), and of Pompey earning blame in the most excellent; of Caesar being regarded as the saviour of his enemies, and Pompey as a traitor to his friends?" And about one of Pompey's speeches Cicero remarked that it was "of no comfort to the poor or interest to the rascals; the rich were not pleased and the honest men were not edified." To which Yavetz immediately appends the comment: "Caesar would not have let such an opportunity slip away. He would have obliged everyone, at least for a short time."[127]

My emphasis on the uniqueness of Caesar clearly raises the question of his historical and political relationship to Augustus. The continuity between the regimes is undeniable. Both seized power by military means (Augustus in 32). Augustus' regime (firmly installed only after the battle of Actium in 31 and enduring till Augustus' peaceful death in 14 A.D.) perpetuated and perfected the fraud of his adoptive father's administration: monarchical power, though now enormously augmented,[128] camouflaged itself with republican form. Like Caesar too, Augustus was a popular, if somewhat avuncular, figure with the ordinary Roman people: he enjoyed *levitas* and received the great honour of *tribunicia potestas*—tenureship of the tribunician power.[129] Furthermore, if anything, Augustus surpassed Caesar's ability as a syncretician: he possessed what Pliny the Younger called *humanitas* which may be rendered as the capacity to endear "oneself to the lowly while at the same time winning the affection of the eminent" (Yavetz 1969:102). Tacitus (*Annals* I.2 = 1982:32) put the matter somewhat differently but the import of his observation was the same:

He seduced the army with bonuses, and his cheap food policy was successful bait for civilians. Indeed, he attracted everybody's goodwill by the enjoyable gift of peace. Then he gradually pushed ahead and absorbed the functions of the senate, the officials, and even the law. Opposition did not exist. War or judicial murder had disposed of all men of spirit. Upper-class survivors found that slavish obedience was the way to succeed, both politically and financially. They had profited from the revolution, and so now they liked the security of the existing arrangement better than the dangerous uncertainties of the old régime. Besides, the new order was popular in the provinces. There, government by Senate and People was looked upon sceptically as a matter of sparring dignitaries and extortionate officials.

Yet between Augustus and Caesar lies a significant break.[130] This is not just because Augustus, unlike his adoptive parent, was indifferent as a military leader; Antony and Agrippa were the two commanders on whom Augustus' most fateful victories depended.[131] Nor is it only because much of Augustus' popularity with the people was essentially second-hand, derived from his being Caesar's son and heir.[132] It is primarily because though Augustus had occasional recourse to a rhetorical mode critical of the old oligarchy—the very first paragraph of his *Res Gestae Divi Augusti* ("The Achievements of the Divine Augustus") tells of how in 44 he "successfully championed the liberty of the republic when it was oppressed by the tyranny of a faction" (Brunt and Moore 1967:19)—no-one would claim that he was a *popularis*. And as for the rest of the Julian house, matters are more simple; none of them even approximate to Caesar even though they now bear officially his name.[133] Tiberius was unloved by the people despite all his attempts at ingratiation, Claudius was respected but remained aloof. Caligula and Nero were hugely popular but proved to be totally without syncretic capacity: Nero lost the support of the army leaders and the Senate, while Caligula's antics began by alienating the Senate as the price of winning popular acclaim, but then lost popularity also as his cruelty became less discriminate.

Julius Caesar's syncretic ability, his *levitas* and *clementia*, his military talent and political astuteness are all integral to the Caesar phenomenon. The social conditions of the Late Republic provided the circumstances in which his abilities could practice and play; they did not necessitate them. What some would later call "Caesarism" required, in other words, the brilliance of Caesar.

Notes

1. The quotes are from an introduction Wells wrote shortly before his death in 1946, and can be found in Wells (1961:1–10). The success of the *Outline* "revealed the existence of a new immense stratum of intelligent people in the modern community eager and ready to supply the deficiencies of school and college education."

2. The 1920s was also the decade that witnessed two major studies by Friedrich Gundolf: *Caesar. Geschichte seines Ruhms* (1924), translated into English in 1928 as *The Mantle of Caesar*; and *Caesar im neunzehnten Jahrhundert* ([1926] 1968). Gundolf was particularly interested in the cultural reception of Caesar, and his works remain a vital resource for anyone working in this area. However, he paid practically no attention to the Caesarism debate.

   Spengler and Weber publicly discussed some of the themes arising from the first volume of *The Decline of the West* in the winter of 1920 (Marianne Weber 1988:674–75). (It is the second volume of Spengler's opus, published in 1922, that contains the analysis of Caesarism.) Weber and Gundolf, a member of the Stefan George circle, were better acquainted: on their relationship, see Lepenies (1988:283–96), which also contains Gundolf's poetical tribute to Weber. Also pertinent is Rolf Hochhuth (1987:15–25, 43–45).

3. The roots and variations of this distinction are briefly explored in The Frankfurt Institute for Social Research ([1956] 1973:89–100).

4. A useful, short summary is Pierard (1982).

5. It had never really departed. Moreover, the immediate legacy of the Great War and of the Russian Revolution of 1917 prompted many writers to re-think the historic connections between antiquity and modern times. An instructive case is Herbert S. Hadley's *Rome and the World Today* ([1922] 1923) which bore the sub-title "A study, in comparison with present conditions, of the reorganization of civilization under the Roman Empire which brought to a war-torn world two hundred years of peace." Hadley quoted approvingly James Bryce's comment that "we are still very near the ancients; and have still much to learn from their writings and their institutions," and shared his view that the growing bias in education towards the natural sciences made it "all the more needful for those who value historical inquiry and the literature of the past, to do what they can to bring the old world into a definite and tangible relation with the modern times, a relation which shall be not only stimulative, but also practically helpful." Hadley's book was also notable for its thesis that among the many causes that destroyed the Roman Empire was "a scheme of economic and industrial legislation that brought all the evils, disadvantages and dangers of modern socialism with none of its possible advantages" (Hadley 1923:x–xi, 325). On "socialism" in ancient Rome and modern Russia, see also 337.

   Frank Frost Abbott, Kennedy Professor of Latin Language and Literature at Princeton, was another American author who was keen to insist that "the political and social problems which confronted Rome are those which America, England, and France face today." Among those problems to which the reader is referred are the "color and labor questions," "voting and elections," "paternalism," the "political boss," and "pensions, bonuses and militarism" (Abbott 1923:138–63). Abbott's book appeared in the "Our Debt to Greece and Rome" series.

6. The ground is well covered by H. Stuart Hughes ([1952] 1962:137–51, 176–87).

These thinkers had many criticisms to make of Spengler, but the point is that they could not ignore the scale, purpose and method of his enterprise as they sought to construct and define their own. As so often, "influence" is a much wider concept than emulation.

7. Riencourt (357) remarks that not only Spengler, but Nietzsche, Thomas Mann, and John Stuart Mill adopted and helped popularize the culture-civilization distinction. He adds, however, that "it is mostly Russian thinkers of the nineteenth century who elaborated upon it—such Slavophiles as Alexander Herzen and K. Leontiev who emphasised this distinction in an effort to define the true historical relationship between Russia and Europe."

8. See Riencourt (1958:269–91), where all these features are mentioned.

9. The emotional masses/Caesarism relationship recurs throughout the book, but see especially 148–49, 152–53.

10. In his *The Future in America* (1906:206–9), Wells had noted that "Caesarism and a splitting into contending Caesarisms" was unlikely in the United States. The growth of science, and the development of education more generally, meant that "the forces of intelligence," not "brute instinct, and individualistic disorder," were likely to prevail.

    Also, see Paul A. Carter (1989:214).

11. Abraham Lincoln's relationship to Caesarism would later be the subject of psychoanalytical interpretations by George B. Forgie (1979:55–87), and Dwight G. Anderson (1982:68–78). For critical comments on their arguments, see Richard O. Curry (1984).

12. See especially 253, 257, 259, 263–65 on Franklin Roosevelt as a Caesarian-like figure.

13. The best account of the controversy over "imperial Rome and progressive America", from which I have learned a great deal, is in Paul A. Carter (1989:207–30). I am leaning heavily on his discussion and references in this paragraph. For a critical estimate, see Bruce Collins (1990).

14. See Abbott (1923:146–47) on how the power of the Roman Senate and its "many safeguards against Caesarism" was finally "broken in the last century of the Republic when certain democratic magistrates made an appeal directly to the popular assembly. To this move on the part of the executive we have had an analogue on several occasions when the chief executive of the United States or of a state has made a popular appeal to the voters in his struggle with a legislative body." In a footnote to this discussion of "some political and social problems common to the Romans and to modern peoples," Abbott mentions "Governor Hughes of New York State and presidents Roosevelt and Wilson" as some of the American "executives who have appealed directly to the voters" (174).

15. On Perot as an "electronic Caesar" see Ronnie Dugger (1992); on Perot's "watery Caesarism," G.F. Will (1992); on his "corruption" of populism, Sean Wilentz (1993).

16. Riencourt's analogy had been anticipated by H.J. Haskell in his "The New Deal in Old Rome: How Government in the Ancient World Tried to Deal with Modern Problems" (1939). Haskell acknowledged the "profound differences between the Mediterranean world of Rome and the world today" but insisted that Roman government had "adopted a series of economic policies, some of them strikingly like those of the New Deal. They could not be identified by their modern names by pre-depression historians. But there they were—the Farm Debt Conciliation Committee, Resettlement Administration, Public Works Administration, Food Relief..." (Haskell 1939:5; also 237–41, an appendix devoted to the "Chronology of Roman New Deal Measures and Other Economic Experiments."

Historians of ancient Rome will tend to ridicule such parallels. Perhaps, however, we should look beyond their veracity to their significance in keeping ancient Rome alive in the minds of self-improving readers. This is what Riencourt also sought to do.

17. I have omitted the emphasis in the original.

18. Clinton Rossiter's *Constitutional Dictatorship* remains an exceptionally valuable contribution. Though Rossiter persuasively demonstrated the strength of American institutions to preserve liberty or regain it once immediate crises had passed (he would claim that in contrast with crisis-rule in Germany, Britain and France, "constitutional dictatorship" was in the American case "a figure of speech"), he remained concerned that the "independent president" could "present a serious potential danger to the American people" (1948:286–87). Part of that danger sprang from "the boundless grant of executive authority found in the Constitution;" but another part lay in the scope such authority afforded a determined and energetic president to impose his personal stamp on the nation in times of national emergency.

19. By Arthur Selwyn Miller: see, especially, his chapter on "Caesarism Triumphant" in Miller (1981:123–41).

20. On Mussolini and Caesarism, see Spengler's ambivalent assessment (1934:185–88). Also of interest are Emerton ([1925] 1964:57–63); Nomad ([1932] 1968:262–310); Seldes (1935); and the literature cited in Carter (1989:220–25). Fascist apologists were quick to seize opportunities for ingratiation. "He calls himself Benito Mussolini, but he could be seen instead as Alexander the Great and Caesar, Socrates and Plato, Virgil and Lucretius, Horace and Tacitus, Kant and Nietzsche, Marx and Sorel, Machiavelli and Napoleon" etc (O. Dinale, quoted in De Giorgi [1984:325–26, n. 12]). The 1937 bimillenary of the birth of Augustus was also actively orchestrated and appropriated by the Italian fascists: Galsterer (1990:3, n.5).

21. The quote comes from Ernst Nolte ([1963] 1969:522) in a section devoted to Hitler's "distant models." The response to Hitler from German and other critics who invoked the Caesar analogy was briefly discussed in my Introduction. See also Dahlke (1968:96–97), and Dickson (1994:127–31).

22. In his autobiography, published over three decades later, Mosley (1968:326–7) reaffirmed his view of the "merit of this speech."

23. The link between Caesarism and a "great personality" is also hinted at (210–11) where Gramsci writes of "charismatic 'men of destiny'," and the "charismatic leader," expressions that remind one of Max Weber. Though the uses of "Caesarism" by the Italian Marxist and the German liberal nationalist are very different in meaning, Gramsci does mention Weber in the "Notebooks" and cites the *locus classicus* of Weber's examination of Caesarism: "Parliament and Government in a Reconstructed Germany:" 19, 228 (both unnumbered footnotes). The tantalizing question is whether Gramsci's use of the term "charisma" might have been inspired by Weber (remembering that "charisma" is not a term that Weber uses in "Parliament and Government").

24. Gramsci also remarks (220) that "Caesarism is a polemical-ideological formula and not a canon of historical interpretation," 220, a comment difficult to square with the rest of Gramsci's very theoretical-historical account.

25. To be precise, Gramsci portrays the Caesarism of Caesar and Napoleon I as possessing "a quantitative/qualitative character," but it is the qualitative aspect that his discussion highlights.

26. "The Caesarism of Caesar and Napoleon I was, so to speak, of a quantitative/

qualitative character; in other words it represented the historical phase or passage in which the innovations were so numerous, and of such a nature, that they
represented a complete revolution" (222).

27. Gramsci also says that Caesarism may be "of an intermediate and episodic
character" (222).

28. Schwarz (1985); Hall and Schwarz (1985); Hall (1983b).

   Gramsci's theory of Caesarism was also extended, by James Overton, to
Newfoundland's experience of "Commission" government between 1934–1949,
the period in which the country was ruled by a "Commission appointed by and
responsible to the British Government in Westminster" (Overton 1990:85). However, the political causes of this "dictatorship"—as it was actually called at the
time—appear in Overton's account to lie less in an "equilibrium of forces," than
in a convergence of classes and groupings that had concluded that "responsible
government" was unworkable.

29. Schwarz uses the lower case.

30. And 53: "The character of the government from 1918 to 1922 was one of
unremitting reaction, in which there occurred a momentary fusion of the caesarist
elements which had marked political developments in the previous decade."

   That the Lloyd George coalitions were Caesarist is also accepted by Robin
Wilson (1985:164).

31. I have been unable to find a single British reference to Margaret Thatcher as a
Caesarist figure, though the derisory comment by Hugo Young about "the
Thatcher Imperium," (*The Guardian*, 26/7 January 1986) came fairly close.
Continental interpreters, however, were less reticent. Edgardo Bartoli, explaining the Westland scandal to an Italian audience, remarked that the incident
revealed "Mrs. Thatcher's Caesarism...in crisis," (*La Repubblica* 26/27 January
1986) meaning the prime minister's "decisionism," her predisposition to bypass
the legitimate rights of her cabinet members as a collegial body to make policy,
her bossy "presidential" style of leadership.

   The neo-Gramscian designation of the Thatcherite experiment was expressed
in the concept of "authoritarian populism," coined by Stuart Hall. The literature
on "authoritarian populism"—a notion quite close to many nineteenth-century
views of Caesarism—is abundant, but see especially S. Hall ([1979] 1983a: 19–
39); S. Hall (1982:1–19); and the debate between Hall and Bob Jessop et al. in
New Left Review (NLR) 147, (September-October, 1984:32–60), *NLR 151*, (May-
June, 1985:115–24), *NLR 153*, (September-October, 1985:87–101).

32. The founders of the SDP were four disillusioned members of the British Labour
Party: David Owen, Shirley Williams, William Rodgers and Roy Jenkins. For an
excellent short analysis, see Robert Behrens (1989).

33. Hall's article was entitled "The 'Little Caesars' of Social Democracy," and can
now be conveniently found in S. Hall and M. Jacques (eds.) (1983:309–21). It
was originally composed and published some six months before the formation
of the Liberal-SDP Alliance; hence Hall's remarks pertain exclusively to the
SDP. (The reprinted article in Hall and Jacques [1983], is a slightly amended
version of the *Marxism Today* piece. It mentions the Alliance on its first page
but this is an editorial updating only; the significance of the Alliance itself
remains untheorized in the amended version.)

34. Hall (1983b:311) = Gramsci (1971:210).

35. "Statements" is presumably a misprint.

36. There is also an equivocation in Hall's account about what these fundamental
forces are; sometimes they seem to refer to classes; at other times to parties;

sometimes to a class (the "working class and its allies") and a politico-ideological formation ("Thatcherism").

37. The quote comes from Eric Hobsbawm's analysis, "Labour's Lost Millions," in *Marxism Today*, (October 1983b:7–13, at 7)."Only 35% of skilled workers voted Labour: down by more than a quarter [from the general election of 1979]. Only 39% of trade unionists supported the party they had founded: a similar drop. Women had shown a slight swing to Labour in 1979, but in 1983 they abandoned the party at a greater rate than men. 41% of the young (first-time voters aged 18–22) had chosen Labour in 1979...But in 1983...(o)nly 17% of first-time voters chose Labour, 3% less than those who chose the Alliance, 11% less than the Tories—while almost half did not bother to vote at all. Of those who bothered to vote only 29% put their cross against Labour candidates," (I have omitted some emphases).

38. See Behrens (1989:92).

39. Hall proved to be more perceptive in his conjecture (1983:321) that the real significance of the SDP may lie in its moderating impact on the Labour Party and the neutralization of socialism that would follow. The new style Labour Party of the mid-to-late 1990s has adopted most of the SDP program of the early 1980s.

40. Karl A. Wittfogel's study of the same name was published three years after Gerth's and Mill's *Character and Social Structure*. For Wittfogel's view of Caesar, Diocletian, and Orientalism, see Wittfogel (1957:208–12).

41. The expression "Diocletian Empire" is itself very odd, suggesting as it does something quite different from the Roman Empire under Diocletian.

42. The essay was left unfinished by Neumann who died before he could complete it.

43. Neumann uses the lower case.

44. For a helpful discussion of the functions and powers of these respective magistracies, see H.F. Jolowicz ([1932] 1967:43–55).

45. This paragraph is based on Clinton Rossiter (1948:15–28).

46. I have dealt at greater length with modern notions of "dictatorship" in Baehr (1993).

47. Cf. Donald Dudley's *Roman Society* (1975:263–94), which refers to the period A.D. 193–337, as that of the "totalitarian state."

48. Neumann says on 248 that "under modern conditions, every dictatorship tends to be a totalitarian dictatorship."

49. The tendency to conflate Caesarism and totalitarian regimes, or at least not to clearly distinguish between them, is evident in Jeremiah Wolpert's (1965:690–95) "sociology of authority."

50. Neumann (1957:238).

51. Neumann (1957:236, 245).

52. Neumann (1957:244, 253).

53. Philip Thody is a literary critic by vocation, but his study of "French Caesarism" is not concerned, as one might have expected, with political rhetoric, but with the common crises and institutional patterns evinced by the four regimes he considers. It thus falls very much under the general rubric of political sociology.

54. Most French writers this century who have examined the rule of Napoleon I and Napoleon III, and of De Gaulle, have preferred the designation "Bonapartism" to "Caesarism." See, for instance, the influential work of René Rémond (1969).

55. The crux of Thody's argument is that France has been predisposed towards *coups d'état* because of a deficient political culture. From the French Revolution

to 1958, civilians proved themselves either incompetent or unwilling to take command of the state in a period of national emergency—be it domestic turmoil or foreign invasion. What distinguishes Caesarism from the junta tradition of South American states, Thody claims, is that Caesarism rules predominantly through civilians, and is in good part a result of the "invitation" to govern by civilian politicians under pressure.

France's militaristic syndrome, Thody believes, is probably now at an end, thanks to the resilient and flexible political structures enshrined in the constitution of the Fifth Republic.

56. Or in those influenced by his casuistry: see Guenther Roth's redescription of American city Caesarism as a kind of "neopatrimonialism" (Roth 1985:227) which is itself a redescription of Weber's concept of "plebiscitarianism." Rendering Caesarism as a form of "populist dictatorship" (Canovan 1981:137) retains the dangerous overtones of the original term and to that extent is preferable to the Weberian lexicon; however, as I shall show in the next section, it is doubtful whether Julius Caesar actually was a "populist" in the sense employed by modern political theorists.

57. The historical basis of many of Gramsci's own claims about ancient Rome is itself open to question. An example is his contention (Gramsci 1971:17) that "the change in the condition of the social position of the intellectuals in Rome between Republican and Imperial times (a change from an aristocratic-corporate to a democratic-bureaucratic régime) is due to Caesar, who granted citizenship to doctors and to masters of liberal arts so that they would be more willing to live in Rome and so that others should be persuaded to come there." This view of Caesar's significance contrasts, incidentally, with Gramsci's more debunking assessment of the Roman in the note on "Caesar and Caesarism" published in *Passato e presente* ([1951] 1966:189–90). Rebutting Emilio Bodrero's claims of Caesar's historical greatness, Gramsci argues that Caesar's Gallic conquest and other actions paved the way for Italy's disintegration. Quintin Hoare and Geoffrey Nowell Smith (1971:219, n. 9) are probably right to see in these remarks a critical reference to Mussolini's own illusions of grandeur.

58. The first date supposedly marks the overthrow of the Etruscan dynasty and the creation of the Republic; the second, the final act in the struggle of wealthy plebeians to break into the citadel of senatorial power: henceforth they and their erstwhile patrician enemies would rule the Republic together, and the elite of both orders would constitute the Roman "nobility," that is, "descendants of all those who at some time had held the highest public office, whether in the form of the dictatorship, the consulship, or the consular tribunate" (Gelzer [1912, 1915] 1969:52).

59. The latter date symbolises the importance that historians of antiquity attach to the tribunate of Tiberius Gracchus and the agrarian reform movement he inaugurated. More on him below.

60. Thirty-one was the year in which Octavian vanquished Antony's forces at the battle of Actium.

61. In this interpretation I follow Gelzer ([1921] 1968:6–26), and P.A. Brunt ([1971] 1978, chapter 1).

62. Gabba (1976a:5). Gabba claims that, before Marius's reforms, there were two major reductions in the census minimum, the first around 214–212, the second around 133–123 (5–7, 176 n.61). That interpretation is, however, contested by Brunt (1962:74, n. 55).

63. Gabba (1976a:11). The word "continuity" is misleading if one follows Brunt's

view (1962:80–1) that the average length of time a man would serve in the legions during the Late Republic would probably be about six to seven years. Both authors would nonetheless agree that, in contrast to the old militia system in which *assidui* were to be discharged after a year, terms of service were indeed protracted.

64. See Brunt (1978:8). *Urban* plebs formed only a fraction of the men serving in the legions. Freedmen, constituting the majority of plebs in Rome in the Late Republic, were ineligible for military service (though in an emergency they might be conscripted), and those free born urban citizens who were drafted into the army procured for themselves a reputation for being refractory and undisciplined.

65. See the appendix to P.A. Brunt and J.M. Moore's edition of *Res Gestae Divi Augusti* (1967:83–85) for the contrast between *imperium* and mere *potestas*.

66. On the political status of the Roman and Latin colonies, see H.H. Scullard ([1959] 1976:16–19).

67. A.H.M. Jones ([1965] 1974:117, 119). Converting *denarii* into modern currency is arithmetically hazardous but Brunt ([1971] 1978:14) says that in the second century, 400 *denarii* possibly represented the value of "a cottage, garden and some personal belongings."

68. I will not rehearse here the confrontation between *equites* and senators that had occasion to ignite from time to time in the Middle and Late Republic. It is dealt with in detail by Brunt in *Social Conflicts in the Roman Republic* (1978:69–73, 87–88, 95–96) and in Brunt ([1962] 1969:117–37). Suffice it to note that the conflict turned, first, on the monopolistic position of the Senate to grant state contracts to *equites*, and to insist that the original provisions of the agreement were fully observed (*equite* contractors would sometimes request that the agreement be revoked or amended if the execution of the contract were proving especially onerous); and second, on the struggle to control the law (particularly the extortion) courts. One might add that *equites* wished to be treated by senators with a dignity befitting their wealth. In virtually every other respect the orders' interests, including their economic interests, "were identical" (Brunt 1971:69): both groups desired a stable and hierarchical society, and both invested their excess wealth in land. They belonged to the same, economically dominant, landed, propertied class, and were often bound by ties of friendship, marriage and culture. Originally, *equites* ("knights") denoted those men who formed the army's citizen cavalry (Jolowicz 1967:77), but in the Late Republic the term referred simply to "all free-born citizens outside the Senate worth 400,000 HSS or more" (Brunt 1969:117. HSS = *sesterces*; 400,000 HSS = 100,000 *denarii*.)

Apart from the stratum within their order known as *publicani* (see below), *equites* were in principle eligible for senatorial office: Marius and Cicero hailed from *equite* families. Before Sulla's day, only few equites rose to the Senate, a body which up to that time was almost caste-like in its exclusivity; after Sulla's dictatorship in the eighties, increasing numbers of *equites* were recruited, though at first few managed to attain anything better than the lower magistracies. However, "from Caesar's time they swarmed into the *curia*" (Brunt 1969:120), occupying the highest positions and, from then on, increasingly displaced the hitherto supreme nobility.

69. The tax system was radically overhauled, and the power of the *publicani* dramatically curtailed, by Augustus. See Jones (1970:95, 118–19); also Brunt (1969:135) who shows that the process started under Caesar.

70. Popular theater and the circus became even more important once the Republic ended, for in a political system bereft of popular assemblies and elections, the theatre and games offered the crucial space in which popular demands, complaints and irreverences might be voiced. The subject is well examined by Alan Cameron. A comedy might witness actors deploying, and audience responding to, subversive *double entendres*, as in the case when a reference "to 'an old goat licking the does' was twisted into an allusion to Tiberius's supposed debaucheries on Capri." Another stratagem was the presentation of petitions "to the emperor at the circus and theatre—petitions to which we was morally obliged at least to reply." The institution of the petition was embedded in a complex structure of ritual and expectation and "it was a rash ruler who ignored or (worse) slighted such manifestations of public opinion." If petitions were refused, an explanation was expected: a "tablet from the emperor's own hand" was deemed the most courteous medium of communication, a herald one of the most perfunctory. From the stance of the emperor, too, the theatre and games had their own distinct advantages: they acted as foundries of legitimation and aggrandizement; they functioned as a conduit of information relaying the crowd's mood, and as a safety-valve of aggression; and they afforded the emperor with the golden opportunity to cultivate *civilitas*, that precious ability "to behave in a natural, unassuming way, as a citizen among his fellows. If an emperor could but master the popular touch, at the games he could be his own propaganda incarnate. The Roman people were in no doubt that monarchy was what they wanted, but they wanted a *Republican* monarch" (Cameron 1973:4–10).
      On plebeian "counter-theater" in England, see E.P. Thompson (1974:400–1), and on the symbolism of popular protest, Thompson (1978:158–61).
71. The following comments are restricted to the *clientela* system insofar as it affected individuals; however, the system could, and with the warlords often did, extend to communities, cities and regions both inside Italy and outside of it. On this see Ernst Badian (1958), especially his remarks on Pompey (252–84); also the review of Badian's book by Gabba (1976b).
72. Also p. 343 where Ste. Croix observes that there "were in fact many situations where a relationship which was in reality that of patron and client in some form would not be so called, for fear of giving offence;" thus "a real gentleman would expect to be called his patron's 'friend' (*amicus*), not his client…" The extent of the *clientela* is often obscured by these norms of politeness.
73. For example, "when they drove Cinna out of the city and set in train the series of events that led to Sulla's dictatorship, when they carried the Gabinian law by violence and thus gave Pompey his great command which proved fateful for the Republic, and when their continual turbulence in the fiftiess finally promoted the accord between Pompey and the optimates from which the civil war of 49 issued" (Brunt 1978:152–53).
74. Claude Nicolet ([1976] 1980:137–38) has observed the "remarkable fact that throughout the period [88–30] we find no instance of an insurrectional military movement instigated from below (whether by officers or private soldiers) with the object of setting up a 'military government.'" In other words, though armies intervened in Roman politics during periods of crisis, they did so not on their own account, but as the instruments of high ranking politician-generals like Marius, Sulla, Pompey, and Caesar.
75. L.R. Taylor (1949:12; also 20–21, 192–93, n. 52).
76. As Gelzer (1968:13) says, it is significant that the nomenclature of *optimates* and *populares* was "applied only to the politicians and never to their supporters,

whom each side called upon for help in the struggle for votes in the popular assembly."

77. I take the names directly from Ste. Croix (1981:353).

78. Ste. Croix (1981:352); cf. Ronald Syme's review of "M. Gelzer, Caesar der Politiker und Staatsmann," orig. 1944, reprinted in R. Syme (1979a:149–71, at 151–52).

79. *Pro Sestio* XLV.97–8 (= Cicero 1958:167–69).

80. *Pro Sestio* XLV.96 (= Cicero 1958:167).

81. *Pro Sestio* XLIX.105 (= Cicero 1958:179).

82. *Pro Sestio* XLVI.99 (= Cicero 1958:171).

83. *Pro Sestio* XLIX.105 (= Cicero 1958:179).

84. See Jones ([1970] 1977:3). On the political status of the "allies" (*socii*) see Jolowicz (1967:63–66).

85. Jolowicz (1967:27–55) for this interpretation, together with a useful dissection of senatorial powers.

86. Examples include the murder of Tiberius and Gaius Gracchus, and the crushing of the Catiline conspiracy.

87. On all this see Ste. Croix (1981:335–36).

88. Tribunes who acted as Caesar's agents included Rullus, Labienus, Vatinius, and, arguably most importantly, Curio and Antony. On Caesar's assiduous use of the tribunes as a vehicle for his own career see Gelzer (1968:42, 45, 69, 173, 176–79, 182, 189–90, 309–10).

89. On *libertas* see Syme ([1939] 1974:155), "a vague and negative notion—freedom from the rule of a tyrant or a faction." The word was widely and cynically used: "Nobody ever sought power for himself and the enslavement of others without invoking *libertas* and such fair names."

90. Margaret Canovan points out that these two themes by themselves are actually too nebulous to constitute any single species of populism. As she says, "'the people'…is one of the slipperiest concepts in the political vocabulary, capable of meaning many different things in different circumstances. It can refer (as it did in *narodnichestvo* or in Peasant Party rhetoric) to the peasants; to the 'producers' of U.S. Populist platforms; to Perón's *descamisados*; to the electorate…; to the nation; to everyone except one's political opponents; or quite frequently (and often deliberately) to no determinate group at all" (295). Antielitism is only "marginally more precise," though "the rhetoric of the underdog, the pathos of the 'little man,' his struggles, and his virtues" (295, 297) would seem to be a constant. However, what is actually necessary to constitute a populism is not the simple coalescence of these rather ambiguous motifs but they way they are specifically articulated and socially contextualized. Hence with regard to what Canovan calls "populist dictatorship" (137)—a rubric under which she chooses to place not only Perónism and the populism of Huey Long, but also "Caesarism" and "Bonapartism"—we see (a) a specific kind of leadership or regime which is at once autocratic, genuinely popular to subordinate groups (150) and vocal in its claim to embody popular sovereignty (its legitimising principle); (b) a related kind of mobilization from above, which is not tantamount to saying that the masses so mobilized are merely the passive and irrational instruments of the populist demagogue (142).

    The rhetoric of populism is also explored and emphasized, within a framework that owes much to Louis Althusser and Gramsci, by Ernesto Laclau (1977:143–98).

91. Also Gelzer (1969:54) who agrees on this date as a watershed. Yet see also

Gelzer p.20, and especially pp.32–33 where Caesar's *popularis* tendencies are implied to have been apparent as early as 68.

92. Simplicity in oratory as well as in the written word would, of course, only have magnified his effectiveness as a *popularis*. On his oratory and oratorical training, see Jane F. Gardner's Introduction to Caesar (1982:25).

93. The *Gallic War* (= *The Conquest of Gaul*), Caesar's other book of commentaries, was published in 51 but the rhetoric of the *popularis* is muted in its pages. This is what one would expect. In 51 Caesar had yet to experience his final rupture with the *optimate* dominated Senate; he was still pursuing constitutional means to achieve his objectives. Reconciliation was his desire, albeit on terms that would guarantee his dignity and personal security. An antagonistically phrased diatribe against the Senate would have wrecked this strategy. Even so, he cannot resist the occasional barbed comment, for example, the speech he puts in the mouth of Ariovistus (the chieftain of the Suebians) which implies senatorial treachery in Rome: see *Conquest of Gaul* I.44 = Caesar 1982:53.

94. One must not, however, exaggerate this quality. In the last years of his life Caesar evinced a damaging insensitivity on more than one occasion: e.g. his, greatly resented, dismissal of the tribunes Flavus and Marullus; his badly bungled personalized attack on the deceased Cato; his inability to quash rumours of his royal aspirations.

95. I follow Gelzer (1968:191, n.1).

96. *Civil War* I.9 (= Caesar 1967:40). He has previously remarked, "it pained me to see the privilege conferred on me by the Roman people being insultingly wrested from me by my enemies."

97. *Civil War* I.22 (= Caesar 1967:46–47).

98. *Civil War* I.22 (= Caesar 1967:47). Also Gelzer 1968:190: "Caesar's propaganda now tirelessly repeated that the state was being enslaved by a small group obstinate in its hatred towards him, while he himself stood for the free expression of their will by the Senate and the popular assembly. Thus he hoped to be able to discredit his opponents in the eyes of public opinion..."

99. *Civil War* I.7 (= Caesar 1967:39). Also I.85 (= 78) with the constant repetition of the word "me."

100. *Civil War* I.9 (= Caesar 1967:40).

101. *Civil War* III.91 (= Caesar 1967:152).

102. The order of priority is also evident in the *Civil War* I.7 (= Caesar 1967:39) when Caesar writes that "The men of the Thirteenth legion clamoured that they were ready to avenge the wrongs done to their general and to the tribunes."

103. For an attempt to apply the concept of "plebiscitary Caesarism" to Roman conditions, see Karl Loewenstein (1973:214–16). Plebiscitary Caesarism is itself a subtype of "monocracy" in Loewenstein's view, a kind of rule distinguished from monarchy by its nondynastic status, and from autocracy by its quasi-constitutionalism (223).

104. The Roman polity consisted of thirty-one rural and four urban tribes: Taylor (1949:50); yet see Brunt (1978:62).

105. I omit consideration of the *comitia curiata*, a fourth assembly, because by the Late Republic its political power had waned to virtual insignificance: Jolowicz (1967:16–18, 23).

106. For details of this body's five "classes" and the "centuries" into which the classes were subdivided, see Jolowicz (1967:18–19).

107. See Jolowicz (1967:18–19), and Taylor (1949:55–57) for details of the weighting system as it related to wealth. On the counting procedures of the assemblies,

see Jolowicz (16) and note also his remark: "We thus have the strange result that in the later republic there were three bodies all equally capable of passing binding statues, three sovereign legislatures, as we should call them, the *comitia centuriata* and *tributa*, consisting of the same people, though organised differently, and the *concilium plebis*, consisting almost entirely of the same people (for the patricians must by 287 have become a numerically insignificant minority), and meeting like the *comitia tributa* by tribes:" (22–23).

108. The precursor of the Roman *popularis* was the Greek "demagogue," another touchstone of Weber's ideal-type of charisma in general, and "plebiscitary democracy" in particular. The plausibility of conceptualising the Greek demagogues in this Weberian manner is effectively criticized on logical and historical grounds by Moses Finley (1985).

109. Writing of the benefits conferred on members of Caesar's Gallic army, Brunt (1978:142) remarks: "Booty had enriched them already, and they hoped to grow richer. They were not disappointed." As dictator, "Caesar roughly doubled the pay of all soldiers, bringing it up to 225 *denarii* a year. His veterans were to receive on discharge not only parcels of land but gratuities of 5,000 or 6,000 *denarii* at his triumph in 46, with proportionately more for officers. Their attachment to him outlasted his life; they were passionate for revenge on his assassins."

110. Most twentieth century historians of antiquity would agree with Syme (1974:52) that, insofar as private property was concerned, "Caesar was not a revolutionary."

111. However, Caesar's reduction of those entitled to receive gratis the corn dole from 320,000 to 150,000 does not seem to have adversely affected the Roman plebs. "Account must be taken of the fact that many needy persons left to settle overseas [in the colonization program] (about 80,000), while large numbers fell in the civil war" (Yavetz 1969:46).

112. This description is a montage drawn from Yavetz (1969:51–52, 98, 106, 137–39).

113. Details in Yavetz (1983:192–94, 199–200, 207). Yavetz notes (194) that "Even though the masses remained loyal to Caesar's memory, the anti-Caesarian tribunes were still popular after the Ides of March." For occasions when Caesar attracted the antagonism of the plebs, see also Gelzer (1968:79, 88, 149, 209–10, 319–20).

114. As they tended to remain to all the *populares*: see Ste. Croix (1981:353–54) for evidence of the erection of statues, the formation of cults, the establishment of shrines, etc. that followed the killings of popular champions. The intense and protracted devotion the plebs exhibited for their fallen leaders contradicts the common view of mass fickleness.

115. Suetonius I.87 (= 1980:45).

116. "Augustus" and *princeps civitatis* (which Octavian was also called) are words that do not lend themselves well to accurate translation, but see Nock (1934:483) who says that "between man and god it [Augustus] represents just such a compromise as does *princeps* between citizen and king." Also Brunt and Moore (eds.). (1967:77–78) on the "three nuances" of the name Augustus.

117. The ambivalence, and its consequences for propaganda during the Principate, is nicely brought out in Syme ([1950] 1979b:205–17): "The artifice of Augustus is patent. He exploited the divinity of the parent and paraded the titulature 'Divi filius.' For all else, Caesar the proconsul and Dictator was better forgotten" (214).

118. The centrality of military coercion in the case of Julius Caesar strongly contrasts with the position of those French leaders who are often referred to in social and political literature as "Caesarist". Eric Hobsbawm ([1967] 1977:180) has made the point that "Napoleon III was not even a soldier, and his rise to power owes little to the military; if they supported him in 1851 it was because he was *already* the effective government. The army which raised marshall Pétain to power was German and not French. As for General de Gaulle he freed himself of the military conspirators who brought him to power as soon as he could, and subordinated the army to civilian control in the usual way, and with little trouble. He called on it again in 1968, but evidently...without reviving its political ambitions." Also, see Thody, who largely concurs with Alfred Cobban's judgement that "of all the revolutions or *coups d'état* between 1815 and 1958 [in France], none was made and none was prevented by the army. The initiative had to come from civilians" (quoted in Thody [1989:165, n. 2]).

119. On Caesar's military prowess see Suetonius I.55 (= 1980:34–35); Plutarch (II 1992:209–10, 215); Yavetz (1983:161–65); Gelzer (1968: 198, 235–36, 243–44); Brunt (1978:142).

     Caesar's name continues to evoke the idea of great military leadership, as for instance in William Manchester's *American Caesar: Douglas MacArthur 1880–1964* (1979, esp. 8). However it is "praetorianism," much more than "Caesarism," that has appeared to exercise the interest of theorists of the military: see, for instance, D.C. Rapoport (1962:72–74); A. Perlmutter and V.P. Bennett (eds.) 1980: part II; S.E. Finer ([1962] 1976:187). Chapter 12 of Finer's study is particularly valuable in showing how modern military interventions, which he dates from the French Revolution, contrast with their antique, Renaissance, and seventeenth-century predecessors.

120. An important discussion is Syme (1979c:88–119, esp. 96–110); also Syme (1974:78–96). To the outrage of the oligarchy, Caesar also promoted centurions and freedmen to the Senate but, as Syme's prosopographical researches show, the number of men who came from those groups was tiny.

121. The extent and pace of Caesar's legislative program was extraordinary: between 49–44, thirty eight laws, decrees, and other measures are "associated with Caesar's name" (Yavetz 1983:57). It is little wonder that "there was not enough time to keep to the usual complicated procedure. In particular he often shortened the transactions of the Senate by merely informing the senior members of his plans and, if he called a meeting of the whole body, he simply announced his decisions to it and without any discussion these were then entered in the archives as senatorial decrees" (Gelzer 1968:290).

122. Gelzer (1968:320) says that "*Dictator perpetuus*, a new concept and one incompatible with the Republican constitution, in essentials amounted to the same as *rex* but avoided this hated word."

123. The quote is from Syme (1974:73). Also 76 on the foreign kings and monarchical aspirants who supported Caesar.

124. The limits of moral obligation, however, are also plain enough: Lily Ross Taylor (1949:175) points out that the sixty or so senators who conspired to kill Caesar consisted largely of men he had pardoned.

125. The statement is quoted by Gelzer (1968:269).

126. It is likely that one motive behind this dispersal policy was to prevent the veterans "when opportunity offered, from plotting revolts" (Yavetz 1983:142, and 141 on which I have been relying for this paragraph).

127. Yavetz (1983:15). The quotes from Cicero are taken, respectively, from p. 174

and 15. Though the term "syncretism" is clumsy, I have preferred it to Yavetz's use of *Gleichschaltung* ("synchronization"), a word with strong fascist overtones.

128. On the range of Augustus' powers, see Jones (1977:55, 60–61, 80–87, 92–93, 106–9); also Syme (1974:404–6, 475).

129. On the controversy over when this was granted see Brunt and Moore (eds.) (1967:10–11). (The authors settle on 23 B.C.)

130. The extent of this rupture remains a subject of great controversy among historians of the ancient world. Christian Meier, for instance, has argued that Rome of the Late Republic approximated "a crisis without an alternative" an expression which is not meant to deny the possibility of different courses of action in the Late Republic but rather their limited purchase in a situation of structural impasse. Reforms were possible, but "one thing could not be done: no new force could be created that was capable of placing the obsolete and largely ineffectual inherited [senatorial republican] order on a new footing." The alternative finally came after Caesar's murder, the civil war that followed, and the erosion to the point of destruction of republican institutions. Its form was the monarchy of the Augustan *Principate* (Meier [1982] 1995:491–96; Meier 1990:54–70).

131. See Jones (1977:10, 25, 31, 66, 82).

132. A point made by Ste. Croix (1981:354, 362, 371).

133. My comments ignore strict chronology which was as follows: Tiberius (A.D. 14–37), Gaius (Caligula) (37–41), Claudius (41–54) and Nero (54–68).

Bibliography

Dates in square brackets in the main text denote original year of publication.

Abbott, F.F. 1923. *Roman Politics*. Boston: Marshall Jones Company.

Adair, D. 1974a. "Fame and the founding fathers." In D. Adair, *Fame and the Founding Fathers*, pp.3–25. New York: W.W. Norton and Co, edited by T. Colbourn.

Adair, D. 1974b. "A note on certain of Hamilton's pseudonyms." In D. Adair, *Fame and the Founding Fathers*, edited by T. Colbourn, pp. 272–85. New York: W.W. Norton and Co.

Addison, J. 1928. *Cato. A Tragedy*. In J. Hampden, ed., *Eighteenth-Century Plays*, pp. 5–51. London: Dent and Sons.

Anderson, D.G. 1982. *Abraham Lincoln: The Quest for Immortality*. New York: Alfred A. Knopf.

Anderson P, 1974. *Passages from Antiquity to Feudalism*. London: New Left Books.

Antoni, C. 1962. *From History to Sociology: The Transition in German Historical Thinking*, translated by H.V. White. London: Merlin Books.

Appleby, J. 1986. "Republicanism in old and new contexts," *William and Mary Quarterly*, vol. XLIII, no.1:20–34.

Arendt, H. 1958. *The Human Condition*. Chicago: University of Chicago Press.

Arendt, H. 1979. *The Origins of Totalitarianism,* new edition with added prefaces. San Diego: Harcourt Brace.

Arendt, H. 1990. *On Revolution*. Harmondsworth: Penguin.

Arendt, H. 1993. "Tradition and the modern age." In H. Arendt, *Between Past and Future: Eight Exercises in Political Thought*, pp.17–40. Harmondsworth: Penguin.

Aristotle. 1962. *The Politics*, translated with an introduction by T.A. Sinclair. Harmondsworth: Penguin.

Bacon, F. 1860. "Of the Wisdom of the Ancients" In *The Works of Francis Bacon*, vol. XIII, pp. 83–172, collected and edited by J. Spedding, R.L. Ellis, and D. D. Heath. Boston: Brown and Taggard.

Bacon, F. 1909a. "Of honor and reputation." In F. Bacon, *Essays or Counsels Civil and Moral*, pp.129–30. New York: P.F. Collier and Sons.

Bacon, F. 1909b. "Of fame." In F. Bacon, *Essays or Counsels Civil and Moral*, pp.140–42. New York: P.F. Collier and Sons.

Bacon, F. 1974. "Of the proficiencies and advancement of learning, Divine and human." In A. Johnston, ed., *Francis Bacon: The Advancement of Learning and New Atlantis*, pp.3–212. Oxford: Clarendon Press.

Badian, E. 1958. *Foreign Clientelae (264–70 B.C.)*. Oxford: Clarendon Press.

Baehr, P. 1988. "Max Weber as a critic of Bismarck." *European Journal of Sociology*, vol. 29, no. 1:149–64.

Baehr, P. 1989. "Weber and Weimar: the 'Reich President' proposals." *Politics*, vol. 9, no. 1:20–25.

Baehr, P. 1993. "Dictatorship." In W. Outhwaite and T. Bottomore, eds., *The Blackwell Dictionary of Twentieth-Century Thought*, pp.158–61. Oxford: Basil Blackwell.

Baehr, P. and M. O'Brien. 1994. "Founders, classics and the concept of a canon." *Current Sociology*, vol. 42, no. 1:1–151.

Bailyn, B. 1992. *The Ideological Origins of the American Revolution*, enlarged edition. Cambridge, Mass.: Harvard University Press.

Bagehot, W. 1963. *The English Constitution*, with an introduction by R.H.S. Crossman. Glasgow: Fontana.Collins.

Bagehot, W. 1968a. "Caesareanism as it now exists." In *The Collected Works of Walter Bagehot*, vol. 4., ed. N. St. John-Stevas, pp.111–116. London: The Economist.

Bagehot, W. 1968b. "The collapse of Caesarism." In *The Collected Works of Walter Bagehot*, vol. 4., ed. N. St. John-Stevas, pp.155–159. London: The Economist.

Bagehot, W. 1968c. "The American Constitution at the present crisis." In *The Collected Works of Walter Bagehot*, vol. 4, ed. N. St. John-Stevas, pp. 283–313. London: The Economist.

Bagehot, W. 1968d. "Mr. Gladstone and the People." In *The Collected Works of Walter Bagehot*, vol. 3, ed. N. St. John-Stevas, pp. 461–464. London: The Economist.

Bagehot, W. 1978. "The Crédit Mobilier and banking companies in France." In *The Collected Works of Walter Bagehot*, vol. 10, ed. N. St. John-Stevas, pp. 341–371. London: The Economist.

Barnett, A. 1982. *Iron Britannia: Why Parliament Waged its Falklands War*. London: Allison and Busby.

Barnett, C. 1978. *Bonaparte*. London: Allen and Unwin.

Baron, H. 1966. *The Crisis of the Early Italian Renaissance: Civic Humanism and Republican Liberty in an Age of Classicism and Tyranny*. Princeton, New Jersey: Princeton University Press.

Bauer, B. 1877. *Christus und die Caesaren: Der Ursprung des Christenthums aus dem römischen Griechenthum*. Berlin: Eugen Grosser.

Bauer, B. 1880. *Das Urevangelium und die Gegner der Schrift: "Christus und die Caesaren."* Berlin: Eugen Grosser.

Baumgarten, E. 1964. *Max Weber: Werk und Person*. Tübingen: J.C.B. Mohr (Paul Siebeck).

Beetham, D. 1978. "From Socialism to Fascism: the relation between theory and practice in the work of Robert Michels," Parts I and II. *Political Studies*, 1:3–24; 2:161–81.

Beetham, D. 1985. *Max Weber and the Theory of Modern Politics*, second edition. Cambridge: Polity Press.

Beetham, D. 1989. "Max Weber and the liberal political tradition." *European Journal of Sociology*, vol. 30, no. 2:311–323.

Beetham, D. 1991. *The Legitimation of Power*. Atlantic City, NJ: Humanities Press International, Inc.

Behrens, R. 1989. "The Centre: Social Democracy and Liberalism." In L. Tivey and A. Wright , eds., *Party Ideology in Britain*, pp.74–101. London and New York: Routledge.

Bellamy, R. 1987. *Modern Italian Social Theory: Ideology and Politics from Pareto to the Present*. Cambridge: Polity Press.

Bellamy, R. 1992. *Liberalism and Modern Society: A Historical Argument*. Philadelphia: Pennsylvania State University Press.

Bendix, R. and Roth, G. 1971. eds. *Scholarship and Partisanship: Essays on Max Weber*. Berkeley: University of California Press.

Bergeron, L. 1981. *France Under Napoleon*, translated by R.R. Palmer. Princeton, NJ: Princeton University Press.

Berghahn, V.R. 1984. *Militarism: The History of an International Debate, 1861– 1979*. Cambridge: Cambridge University Press.

Bernstein, E. 1961. *Evolutionary Socialism: A Criticism and Affirmation*, introduction by S. Hook, translated by E.C. Harvey. New York: Schocken Books.

Berst, C.A. 1994. "Caesar and Cleopatra: an anatomy of greatness." In H. Bloom, ed., *Julius Caesar*, pp. 113–26. New York: Chelsea House Publishers.

Betts, R.F. 1971. "The allusion to Rome in British imperialist thought of the late nineteenth and early twentieth centuries." *Victorian Studies*, 15, 2:149–59.

Birch, A.H. 1964. *Representative and Responsible Government: An Essay on the British Constitution*. London: George Allen and Unwin.

Birch, A.H. 1971. *Representation*. London: Pall Mall Press.

Bismarck, O. von. 1898. *Bismarck, The Man and the Statesman: Being the Reflections and Reminiscences of Otto Prince von Bismarck*, vols. I and II, translated from the German under the supervision of A.J. Butler. London: Smith, Eldoer, and Co.

Blackbourn, D. and Eley, G. 1984. *The Peculiarities of German History*. Oxford: Oxford University Press.

Blake, W. 1958. *William Blake: A Selection of Poems and Letters*, ed., J. Bronowski. Harmondsworth: Penguin.

Blissett, W. 1956. "Lucan's Caesar and the Elizabethan Villain." *Studies in Philology*, 53:553–75.

Blissett, W. 1957. "Caesar and Satan." *Journal of the History of Ideas*, 18:221–32.

Blits, J.H. 1981. "Caesarism and the end of Republican Rome: *Julius Caesar*, Act I, scene i." *Journal of Politics*, vol. 43:40–55.

Bloom, H., ed. *Julius Caesar*. New York: Chelsea House Publishers.

Bock, G. Skinner, Q. and Viroli, M., eds. 1990. *Machiavelli and Republicanism*. Cambridge: Cambridge University Press.

Bocock, R. 1976. *Freud and Modern Society*. Sunbury-on-Thames: Nelson.

Bogdanor, V., ed. 1983. *Coalition Government in Western Europe*. London: Heinemann Educational Books.

Bonaparte, Louis. 1856a. "L'Idée Napoléonienne." In *Oeuvres de Napoléon III*, vol. 1:3–13. Paris: Henri Plon.

Bonaparte, Louis. 1856b. "Des Idées Napoléoniennes." In *Oeuvres de Napoléon III*, vol. 1:17–233. Paris: Henri Plon.

Bonaparte, Louis. 1856c. "Extinction du Paupérisme." In *Oeuvres de Napoléon III*, vol. 2. 109–151. Paris: Henri Plon.

Bonaparte, Louis. 1865. *Histoire de Jules César*, 2 vols. Paris: Henri Plon.

Bonaparte, Louis. 1972. *The Political and Historical Works of Louis Napoleon Bonaparte*, 2 vols. New York: Howard Fertig.

Bonaparte, N. 1954. *Napoleon's Letters*, edited and translated by J.M. Thompson. London: J. M. Dent and Sons.

Bonaparte, N. 1986. *Napoleon's Memoirs*, edited by. S. de Chair. London: The Soho Book Company.

Bramsted, E.K. and Melhuish, K.J., eds. and transl. 1978. *Western Liberalism: A History in Documents from Locke to Croce*. London and New York: Longman.

Braun, H.J. 1983. "Political Economy and Social Legislation in Germany, ca. 1870–1890." *History of European Ideas*, 4, 1:51–60.

Brecht, B. 1961. *Tales from the Calendar*, translated by Y. Kapp and M. Hamburger. London: Methuen and Co. Ltd.

Brecht, B. 1969. *Die Geschäfte des Herrn Julius Caesar. Romanfragment.* Frankfurt am Main: Suhrkamp Verlag.

Brecht, B. 1979. *The Threepenny Opera*, translated and edited by R. Mannheim and J. Willett. London: Eyre Methuen.

Brecht, B. 1980. *Mother Courage and Her Children*, edited by J. Willett and R. Mannheim, translated by J. Willett. London: Eyre Methuen.

Briggs, A. 1979. "The language of 'mass' and 'masses' in nineteenth-century England." In D.E. Martin and D. Rubinstein, eds., *Ideology and the Labour Movement: Essays Presented to John Saville*, pp.62–83. London: Croon Helm.

Brockhaus, F.A. 1883. *Brockhaus' Conversations Lexikon*, thirteenth edition. Leipzig: F.A. Brockhaus.

Brunt, P.A. 1962. "The Army and the Land in the Roman Revolution." *Journal of Roman Studies*, 52:69–86.

Brunt, P.A. 1969. "The Equites in the Late Republic." In R. Seager, ed., *The Crisis of the Roman Republic*, pp.117–37. Cambridge: W. Heffer and Sons.

Brunt, P.A. 1978. *Social Conflicts in the Roman Republic*. London: Chatto and Windus.

Brunt, P. and Moore, J.M., eds. 1967. *Res Gestae Divi Augusti: The Achievements of the Divine Augustus*, translated, with an introduction and commentary by the editors. Oxford: Oxford University Press.

Bryce, J. 1927. *The American Commonwealth*, vols. I and II. New York: Macmillan.

Burckhardt, J. 1929. *Die Zeit Constantins des Großen.* In Jacob Burckhardt Gesamtausgabe, vol. 2, edited by Felix Stähelin. Deutsche Verlagsanstalt: Berlin and Leipzig.

Burckhardt, J. 1949. *The Age of Constantine the Great*, translated by M. Hadas. London: Routledge and Kegan Paul.

Burckhardt, J. 1959. *Judgements on History and Historians*, translated by H. Zohn. London: George Allen and Unwin Ltd.

Burke, E. 1968. *Reflections on the Revolution in France*, edited by C.C. O'Brien. Harmondsworth: Penguin.

Burns, E.M. 1954. "The philosophy of history of the founding fathers." *The Historian*, vol. 16:142–68.

Byron, G.G. 1885. *Childe Harold's Pilgrimage*, edited by H.F. Tozer. Oxford: Clarendon Press.

Byron, G.G. ND (= No Date.) "The Deformed Transformed. A Drama." In *The Poetical Works of Lord Byron*, pp. 516–532. London: Frederick Warne and Co.

Caesar. 1967. *The Civil War*, translated with an introduction by J.F. Gardner. Harmondsworth: Penguin.

Caesar. 1982. *The Conquest of Gaul*, translated by S.A. Handford, revised with a new introduction by J. F. Gardner. Harmondsworth: Penguin.

Cameron, A. 1973. *Bread and Circuses: The Roman Emperor and his People.* London: King's College.

Camic, C. 1986. "The matter of habit." *American Journal of Sociology* 91 (5):1039–87.

Canovan, M. 1981. *Populism*. London: Junction Books.

Canovan, M. 1992. *Hannah Arendt: A Reinterpretation of Her Political Thought*. Cambridge: Cambridge University Press.

Carducci, G. 1939. "Il Cesarismo. [Leggendo la introduzione alla vita di Cesare scritta da Napoleone III.]" In G. Carducci, *Opere*, Edizione Nazionale, vol. III, pp. 24–25. Bologna: Nicola Zanichelli.

Carr, W. 1979. *A History of Germany, 1815–1945*, second edition. London: Edward Arnold.

Carter, P.A. 1989. *Revolt Against Destiny: An Intellectual History of the United States*. New York: Columbia University Press.

Cassius Dio. 1987. *The Roman History: The Reign of Augustus*, translated by I. Scott-Kilvert, with an introduction by J. Carter. Harmondsworth: Penguin.

Chateaubriand, F-R de. 1965. *The Memoirs of Chateaubriand*, selected, translated, and with an introduction by R. Baldick. Harmondsworth: Penguin.

Cicero. 1926. *Philippics*, translated by C.A. Ker. London: William Heinemann Ltd.

Cicero. 1928. *De Re Publica, De Legibus*, translated by C.W. Keyes. London: William Heinemann Ltd.

Cicero. 1945. *Tusculan Disputations*, translated by J.E. King. London: William Heinemann Ltd.

Cicero. 1958. *Pro Sestio and In Vatinium*, translated by R. Gardner. London: William Heinemann Ltd.

Cicero. 1971. *Selected Works*, translated with an introduction by M. Grant. Harmondsworth: Penguin.

Cicero. 1991. *On Duties*, edited and translated by M.T. Griffin and E.M. Atkins. Cambridge: Cambridge University Press.

Cobban, A. 1939. *Dictatorship: Its History and Theory*. London: Jonathan Cape.

Cobban, A. 1965. *A History of Modern France*, vol. 2: 1799–1871. Second Edition. Harmondsworth: Penguin.

Cole, A. and P. Campbell. 1989. *French Electoral Systems and Elections since 1789*. Aldershot: Gower.

Collins, B. 1990. "Come to bury Caesarism." *Times Higher Education Supplement* 27 July, p. 19.

Collins, R. 1986. *Weberian Sociological Theory*. Cambridge: Cambridge University Press.

Congrès de Jurisconsultes Catholiques. 1885. *Césarisme et Socialisme D'État*. Baratier et Dardelet: Grenoble.

Conrad, J. 1927. *Joseph Conrad: Life and Letters*, vol. I, edited by G. Jean-Aubry. London: William Heinemann, Ltd.

Conrad, J. 1963. *Nostromo: A Tale of the Seaboard*. Harmondsworth: Penguin.

Constant, B. 1988. "The Spirit of Conquest and Usurpation and their Relation to European Civilization." In B. Fontana, ed. and transl., *Constant: Political Writings*. Cambridge: Cambridge University Press.

Cooke, J.E. 1960. "Alexander Hamilton's authorship of the 'Caesar' letters." *William and Mary Quarterly*, vol. XVII, no. 1:78–85.

Cortés, J.D. 1879. *Essays on Catholicism, Liberalism, and Socialism: Considered in their Fundamental Principles*, translated by W. M'Donald. Dublin: M.H. Gill and Son.

Coulanges, F. de. 1916. *The Ancient City*, translated by W. Small. London: Simpkin, Marshall, Hamilton Kent and Co.

Craig, G.A. 1981. *Germany, 1866–1945*. Oxford: Oxford University Press.

Crankshaw, E. 1981. *Bismarck*. New York: Viking Press.

Crawford, M. 1978. *The Roman Republic*. Glasgow: Fontana.

Croce, B. 1934. *History of Europe in the Nineteenth Century*, translated by H. Furst. London: George Allen and Unwin Ltd.

Crossman, R.H.S. 1963. "Introduction" to W. Bagehot, *The English Constitution*, pp. 1–57. Glasgow: Fontana Collins.

Curry, R.O. 1984. "Conscious or unconscious Caesarism?: A critique of recent scholarly attempts to put Abraham Lincoln on the analyst's couch." *Journal of the Illinois State Historical Society*, vol. 77, no. 1:67–71.

Dahlke, H. 1968. *Cäsar bei Brecht. Eine vergleichende Betrachtung*. Berlin: Aufbau.

De Giorgi, F. 1984. "Scienze umane e concetto storico: il Cesarismo." *Nuova Rivista Storica*, vol. 68, nos. 3–4: 323–354.

Disraeli, B. 1833. *What is He?* A new edition, revised. London: James Ridgway and E. Lloyd.

Dickson, K.A. 1994. "Brecht on Julius Caesar." In H. Bloom , ed., *Julius Caesar*, pp. 127–38. New York: Chelsea House Publishers.

Dorpalen, A. 1964. *Hindenburg and the Weimar Republic*. Princeton, N.J.: Princeton University Press.

Dos Passos, J. 1960. *U.S.A. (The 42nd Parallel; Nineteen Nineteen; The Big Money)*, illustrated by R. Marsh. Boston: Houghton Mifflin.

Draper, H. 1977. *Karl Marx's Theory of Revolution*, vol. I: *State and Bureaucracy*. New York: Monthly Review Press.

Draper, T. "Presidential wars." *The New York Review of Books*, September 26, 1991, pp.64–74.

Dudley, D. 1975. *Roman Society*. Harmondsworth: Penguin.

Dugger, R. 1992. "Electronic Caesar?" *The Nation*, June 15:813–815.

Dülffer, J. 1976."Bonapartism, fascism and National Socialism." *Journal of Contemporary History*, 11:109–28.

Eley, G. 1976 "Defining social imperialism: use and abuse of an idea." *Social History*, 3,(October):265–90.

Eley, G. 1980. *Reshaping the German Right*. New Haven: Yale University Press.

Elias, N. 1978. *The History of Manners*, vol. I, *The Civilizing Process*, translated by E. Jephcott. Oxford: Basil Blackwell.

Elkins, S. and E. Mckitrick. 1961. "The founding fathers: young men of the revolution." *Political Science Quarterly*, vol. LXXVI, no. 2, pp.181–216.

Emerson, R.W. 1990. "Shakespeare; or, the poet." In *Ralph Waldo Emerson*, edited by Richard Poirier, pp.329–42. Oxford: Oxford University Press.

Emerton, E. 1964. *Humanism and Tyranny: Studies in the Italian Trecento*. Gloucester, Mass.: Peter Smith.

Engels, F. 1968a. "Preface to the Peasant War in Germany." In *Karl Marx Frederick Engels: Selected Works in One Volume*, pp. 235–41. London: Lawrence and Wishart Ltd.

Engels, F. 1968b. "The Origin of the family, Private Property and the State." In *Karl Marx Frederick Engels Selected Works in One Volume*, pp.449–583. London: Lawrence and Wishart Ltd.

Engels, F. 1978. "Two years of a revolution; 1848 and 1849." In Karl Marx and Frederick Engels, *Collected Works*, vol. 10:353–69. New York: International Publishers.

Engels, F. 1988. "The Housing Question." In Karl Marx and Frederick Engels, *Collected Works*, vol. 23:317–91. New York: International Publishers.

Eyck, E. 1968. *Bismarck and the German Empire*, third edition. London: Unwin University Books.

Ferrand, J. 1904. *Césarisme et Démocratie. L'Incompatibilité entre notre régime administratif et notre régime politique*. Paris: Plon-Nourrit.

Ferrero, G. 1909. *The Greatness and Decline of Rome*, vol. I: *The Empire Builders*, translated by A.E. Zimmern. New York: G.P. Putnam's Sons.

Ferrero, G. 1933. *The Life of Caesar*, translated by A.E. Zimmern. New York: G.P. Putnam's Sons.

Ferrero, G. 1972. *Militarism*, with a new introduction by S.E. Cooper. New York: Garland Publishing, Inc.

Finer, S.E. 1976. *The Man on Horseback: The Role of the Military in Politics*, second enlarged edition. Harmondsworth: Penguin.

Fink. Z.S. 1945. *The Classical Republicans: An Essay on the Recovery of a Pattern of Thought in Seventeenth-Century England*, second edition. Northwestern University Press.

Finley, M.I., ed. 1974. *Studies in Ancient Society*. London: Routledge and Kegan Paul.

Finley, M.I. 1977. "The Ancient City: From Fustel de Coulanges to Max Weber and Beyond." *Comparative Studies in Society and History*, XIX:305–27.

Finley, M.I. 1985. "Max Weber and the Greek City-State." In *Ancient History: Evidence and Models*, pp. 88–103. London: Chatto and Windus.

Fogt, H. 1977. *Max Weber-Wirkung und Bedeutung, 1890–1933* (Unpublished Master's thesis, Munich University).

Ford, F.L. 1970. *Europe, 1780–1830*. London: Longmans.

Ford, P.L. 1970. *Essays on the Constitution of the United States*. New York: Burt Franklin.

Forgie, G.B. 1979. *Patricide in the House Divided: A Psychological Interpretation of Lincoln and His Age*. New York: W.W. Norton and Co.

Fowler, W.W. 1904. *Julius Caesar and the Foundation of the Roman Imperial System*. London: G.P. Putnam's Sons.

Frankfurt Institute for Social Research. 1973. *Aspects of Sociology*, with a preface by M. Horkheimer and T.W. Adorno, translated by J. Viertel. London: Heinemann.

Froude, J.A. 1879. *Caesar: A Sketch*. New York and London: Harper and Brothers.

Gabba, E. 1976a. "The origins of the professional army at Rome: the 'proletarii' and Marius' reform." In E. Gabba, *Republican Rome, The Army and the Allies*, pp. 1–19, translated by P.J. Cuff. Oxford: Basil Blackwell.

Gabba, E. 1976b. "Review of E. Badian, 'Foreign Clientelae,' Oxford 1958." In E. Gabba, *Republican Rome, The Army and the Allies*, pp. 162–170, translated by P.J. Cuff. Oxford: Basil Blackwell.

Galsterer, H. 1990. "A man, a book, and a method: Sir Ronald Syme's *Roman Revolution* after fifty years." In K.A. Raaflaub and M. Toher , eds., *Between Republic and Empire: Interpretations of Augustus and his Principate*, pp.1–20. Berkeley: University of California Press.

Gay, P. *The Cultivation of Hatred. The Bourgeois Experience Victoria to Freud*, vol. 3. New York: W.W. Norton and Co.

Gelzer, M. 1968. *Caesar: Politician and Statesman*, translated by P. Needham. Oxford: Basil Blackwell.

Gelzer, M. 1969. *The Roman Nobility*, translated by R. Seager. Oxford: Basil Blackwell.

Gerth, H. and Mills, C. Wright. 1954. *Character and Social Structure: The Psychology of Social Institutions*. London:Routledge and Kegan Paul.

Gesche, H. 1976. *Caesar*. Darmstadt: Wissenschaftliche Buchgesellschaft.

Geyl. P. 1965. *Napoleon: For and Against*, translated by O. Renier. Harmondsworth: Penguin.

Gibbon, E. 1910. *The History of the Decline and Fall of the Roman Empire*, vol. I. London: Dent.

Giddens, A. 1972. *Politics and Sociology in the Thought of Max Weber*. London: Macmillan.

Giorgi, F. de. 1984. "Scienze umane e concetto storico: il Cesarismo." *Nuova Rivista Storica*, vol. 68, nos. 3–4:323–354.

Goethe, J.W. von. 1966. *Conversations and Encounters*, edited and translated by D. Luke and R. Pick. Chicago: H. Regnery Co.

Goethe, J.W. von. 1985. "Caesar". In Johann Wolfgang Goethe, *Sämtliche Werke*, bd. 4, *Dramen 1765–1775*, p. 123, edited by P. Huber and D. Borchmeyer. Frankfurt am Main: Deutscher Klassiker Verlag.

Goethe, J.W. von. 1988. *Roman Elegies and The Diary*, bilingual edition, verse translation by D. Luke, introduction by H.R. Vaget. London: Libris.

Goldman, E. 1969. "Minorities versus Majorities." In *Anarchism and Other Essays*, pp. 69–78, with a new introduction by R. Drinnon. New York: Dover Publications. Inc.

Goldman, H.S. 1993. "Weber's ascetic practices of the self." In H. Lehmann and G. Roth, eds., *Weber's Protestant Ethic: Origins, Evidence, Contexts*, pp.161–177. Cambridge: Cambridge University Press.

Goldstein, R.J. 1983. *Political Repression in 19th Century Europe*. London: Croom Helm.

Gollwitzer, H. 1952. "Der Cäsarismus Napoleons III. im Widerhall der öffentlichen Meinung Deutschlands." *Historische Zeitschrift*, 173:23–75.

Gollwitzer, H. 1987. "The Caesarism of Napoleon III as seen by public opinion in Germany." *Economy and Society*, vol. 16, no. 3:357–404, translated by Gordon C. Wells (translation of Gollwitzer 1952).

Govan, T.P. 1975. "Alexander Hamilton and Julius Caesar: a note on the use of historical evidence." *William and Mary Quarterly*, vol. XXXII, no. 3:475–80.

Gramsci, A. 1966. *Passato e presente*, edited by F. Platone. Turin: Giulio Einaudi.

Gramsci, A. 1971. *Selections from the Prison Notebooks of Antonio Gramsci*, edited and translated by Q. Hoare and G.N. Smith. London: Lawrence and Wishart.

Groh, D. 1972. "Cäsarismus, Napoleonismus, Bonapartismus, Führer, Chef, Imperialismus." In O. Brunner, W. Conze, and R. Koselleck, eds., *Geschichtliche Grundbegriffe. Historisches Lexikon zur politisch-sozialen Sprache in Deutschland*, vol. 1, pp.726–71. Stuttgart: Ernst Klett.

Grumach, E. 1949. *Goethe und die Antike. Eine Sammlung*, 2 vols. Berlin: Walter de Gruyter and Co.

Guarnieri, C. 1983. "Cesarismo." In N. Bobbio, N. Matteucci, and Gianfranco Pasquino, eds., *Dizionario di politica*, 2nd ed., pp. 155–57. Turin: UTET.

Guicciardini, Francesco. 1965. *Selected Writings*, edited and introduced by Cecil Grayson, translated by Margaret Grayson. London: Oxford University Press.

Guizot, F. 1887. *History of Civilization*, vol. II. London, translated by W. Hazlitt. New York: D. Appleton and Co.

Gummere, R.M. 1962. "The classical ancestry of the United States Constitution." *American Quarterly*, vol. 14, pp.3–18.

Gundelfinger (= Gundolf), F. 1904. *Caesar in der deutschen Literatur*. Berlin: Mayer and Müller.

Gundolf, F. 1928. *The Mantle of Caesar*, translated by J.W. Hartmann. New York: The Vanguard Press.

Gundolf, F. 1968. *Caesar im neunzehnten Jahrhundert*. In F. Gundolf, Caesar, pp. 278–360. Düsseldorf and Munich: Helmut Küpper.

Gunn, J.A.W. 1983. *Beyond Liberty and Property: The Process of Self-Recognition in Eighteenth-Century Political Thought*. Kingston and Montreal:McGill-Queen's University Press.

Hadley, H.S. 1923. *Rome and the World Today*, second and revised edition. New York: G.P. Putnam's Sons.

Hailsham, Q. 1976. *Elective Dictatorship*. London:British Broadcasting Corporation.

Hall, S. 1982. "The Battle for Socialist Ideas in the 1980s." *Socialist Register 1982*. eds. M. Eve and D. Musson, pp.1–19. London: Merlin Press.

Hall, S. 1983a. "The Great Moving Right Show." In S. Hall and M. Jacques, eds., *The Politics of Thatcherism*, pp.19–39. London: Lawrence and Wishart.

Hall, S. 1983b. "The 'Little Caesars' of Social Democracy." In S. Hall and M. Jacques, eds., *The Politics of Thatcherism*, pp.309–21. London: Lawrence and Wishart.

Hall, S. 1985. "Authoritarian Populism: A Reply to Jessop et al." *New Left Review*, 151 (May-June):115–24.

Hall, S. and Jacques, M. 1983. *The Politics of Thatcherism*. London: Lawrence and Wishart.

Hall, S. and Schwarz, B. 1985. "State and Society, 1880–1930." In M. Langan and B. Schwarz, eds., *Crises in the British State 1880–1930*, pp.7–32. London: Hutchinson.

Hammer, K. and Hartmann, P.C. eds. 1977. *Der Bonapartismus. Historisches Phänomen und politischer Mythos*. Munich: Artemis Verlag.

Hammond, N.G.L. and Scullard, H.H., eds. 1970. *The Oxford Classical Dictionary*, second edition. Oxford: Oxford University Press.

Harrington, J. 1992. "The Commonwealth of Oceana." In *The Commonwealth of Oceana and A System of Politics*, pp.1–266, edited and translated by J.G.A. Pocock. Cambridge: Cambridge University Press.

Haskell, H.J. 1939. *The New Deal in Old Rome: How Government in the Ancient World Tried to Deal with Modern Problems*. New York: Alfred A. Knopf.

Hegel, G.W.F. 1956. *The Philosophy of History*, preface by C. Hegel, translated by J. Sibree with a new introduction by C.J. Friedrich. New York: Dover Publications.

Held, D. 1987. *Models of Democracy*. Cambridge: Polity Press.

Hennis, W. 1983. "Max Weber's 'Central Question.'" *Economy and Society*, 12, 2:135–80, translated by K. Tribe.

Hennis, W. 1988. *Max Weber: Essays in Reconstruction*, translated by K. Tribe. London: Allen and Unwin.

Herold, J.C. 1955. *The Mind of Napoleon: A Selection from his Written and Spoken Words*, edited and translated by J.C. Herold. New York: Columbia University Press.

Hintze, O. 1975. *The Historical Essays of Otto Hintze*, edited with an introduction by F. Gilbert, translators various. New York: Oxford University Press.

Hobsbawm, E.J. 1977. "Civilians versus military in twentieth-century politics." In E.J. Hobsbawm, *Revolutionaries: Contemporary Essays*, pp. 77–191. London: Quartet Books.

Hobsbawm, E.J. 1983a. "Mass-Producing Traditions: Europe, 1870–1914." In E. Hobsbawm and T. Ranger, eds., *The Invention of Tradition*, pp.263–307. Cambridge: Cambridge University Press.

Hobsbawm, E.J. 1983b. "Labor's Lost Millions." *Marxism Today*, (October):7–13.

Hobson, J.A. 1909. *The Crisis of Liberalism: New Issues of Democracy*. London: P.S. King and Son.

Hochhuth, R. 1987. *Täter und Denker. Profile und Probleme von Cäsar bis Jünger*. Stuttgart: Deutsche Verlags-Anstalt.

Hofmann, H. 1977. "Das Problem der cäsaristischen Legitimität im Bismarckreich."

In K. Hammer and P.C. Hartmann,. eds., *Der Bonapartismus. Historisches Phänomen und politischer Mythos*, pp. 77–101. Munich: Artemis Verlag.

Hughes, H. Stuart. 1962. *Oswald Spengler: A Critical Estimate*, revised edition. New York: Charles Scribner's Sons.

Hugo, Victor. n.d. "Napoléon le Petit." In *Oeuvres Complètes de Victor Hugo, Histoire*, vol. 1. Paris: Hetzel and Quantin.

Hume, D. 1953. *David Hume's Political Essays*, edited by C. W. Hendel. New York: Bobbs-Merrill.

Hunt, G and Scott, J.B., eds. 1970. *The Debates in the Federal Convention of 1787 Which Framed the Constitution of the United States of America*. Westport, Conn.: Greenwood Press.

Janssen, J., ed. 1868. *J.F. Böhmer, Leben, Briefe und kleinere Schriften*, vol. 1. Freiburg: Herder.

Jessop, B., Bonnett, K., Bromley, S., Ling, T. 1984. "Authoritarian Populism, Two Nations, and Thatcherism." *New Left Review*, 147 (September-October):32–60.

Jessop, B. 1985. "Thatcherism and the Politics of Hegemony: a Reply to Stuart Hall." *New Left Review,* 153:87–101.

Jolowicz, H.F. 1967. *Historical Introduction to the Study of Roman Law*. Cambridge: Cambridge University Press.

Jones, A.H.M. 1977. *Augustus*. London: Chatto and Windus.

Jones, A.H.M. 1974. "Ancient empires and the economy: Rome." In A.H.M. Jones, *The Roman Economy: Studies in Ancient Economic and Administrative History*, edited by P.A. Brunt, pp.114–39. Oxford: Basil Blackwell.

Käsler, D. *Max Weber: An Introduction to His Life and Work*, translated by P. Hurd. Cambridge: Polity Press.

Kitchen, M. 1976. *The Silent Dictatorship: The Politics of the German High Command under Hindenburg and Ludendorff, 1916–1918*. London: Croom Helm.

Knight, W.F. Jackson. 1958. "Introduction," Virgil, *The Aeneid*, pp. 11–24. Harmondsworth: Penguin.

Knox, B. ed. 1993a. *The Norton Book of Classical Literature*. New York: W.W. Norton and Co.

Knox, B. 1993b. *The Oldest Dead White European Males*. New York: W.W. Norton and Co.

Koch, H.W. 1984. *A Constitutional History of Germany in the Nineteenth and Twentieth Centuries*. London: Longman.

Koebner, R. and Schmidt, H.D. 1964. *Imperialism: The Story and Significance of a Political Word, 1840–1960*. Cambridge: Cambridge University Press.

Kramnick, I. 1987. "Editor's Introduction." In J. Madison, A. Hamilton and J. Jay. 1987. *The Federalist Papers*, pp. 11–82. Harmondsworth: Penguin.

Kramnick, I. 1988. "The 'Great National Discussion': The Discourse of Politics in 1787." *William and Mary Quarterly* vol. XLV, no. 1:3–32.

Kristeller, P.O. 1961. *Renaissance Thought: The Classic, Scholastic and Humanistic Strains*. New York: Harper.

Laclau, E. 1977. "Towards a theory of populism." In E. Laclau, *Politics and Ideology in Marxist Theory*, pp.143–98. London: New Left Books.

Ladendorf, O. 1906. *Historisches Schlagwörterbuch*, with an introduction by H.- G. Schumann. Berlin: Walter de Gruyter and Co.

Larousse, P. 1867. *Grand dictionnaire universal du XIXe siècle*, vol. 3. Paris: Pierre Larousse.

Larousse, 1971. *Grand Larousse de la langue française*, vol. I. Paris: Librairie Larousse.

Lasch, C. 1991. *The True and Only Heaven: Progress and Its Critics*. New York: W.W. Norton and Co.

Lazzaro, G. 1862. *Il Cesarismo e l'Italia*. Naples: Stabilimento Tipografico dei Classici Italiani.

Le Bon, G. 1960. *The Crowd*, with a new introduction by R.K. Merton. New York: Viking Press.

Lehmann, H. and Roth, G. 1993. *Weber's Protestant Ethic: Origins, Evidence, Contexts*. Cambridge: Cambridge University Press.

Lepenies, W. 1988. *Between Literature and Science: The Rise of Sociology*, translated by R.J. Hollingdale. Cambridge: Cambridge University Press.

Lenihan, J.H. 1992. "English classics for Cold War America." *Journal of Popular Film and Television*, 20, 3:42–51.

Lenin, V.I. 1964. *Collected Works*, vol. 25. Moscow: Progress Publishers.

Le Normand, M.A. 1895. *The Historical and Secret Memoirs of the Empress Josephine*, vol. I. London: H.S. Nichols.

Litto, F.M. 1966. "Addison's *Cato* in the Colonies." *William and Mary Quarterly*, vol. XXIII, no. 3:431–449.

Littré, E. 1873. *Dictionnaire de la langue française*, vol. I. Paris: Littré.

Livy. 1965. *The War with Hannibal* (= Books XXI-XXX of the *History of Rome*), translated by A. de Sélincourt, edited with an introduction by Betty Radice. Harmondsworth: Penguin.

Livy. 1971. *The Early History of Rome* (= Books I-V of the *History of Rome*), translated by A. de Sélincourt, with an introduction by R.M. Ogilvie. Harmondsworth: Penguin.

Livy. 1982. *Rome and Italy* (= Books VI-X of the *History of Rome*), translated and annotated by B. Radice, with an introduction by R.M. Ogilvie. Harmondsworth: Penguin.

Loewenstein, K. 1973. *The Governance of Rome*. The Hague: Martinus Nijhoff.

Locke, J. 1967. *Two Treatises of Government*. 2nd edition, edited by P. Laslett. Cambridge: Cambridge University Press.

Loftis, J.C. 1963. *The Politics of Drama in Augustan England*. Oxford: Clarendon Press.

Low, S. 1904. *The Governance of England*. London: T. Fisher Unwin.

Lowi, T.J. 1985. "Presidential Power: Restoring the Balance." *Political Science Quarterly*, 100, 2:185–213.

Lucan. 1956. *Pharsalia*, translated by R. Graves. Harmondsworth: Penguin.

Luttwak, E. 1994. "Programmed to fail." *London Review of Books*, 22 December, pp. 10–11.

Lutz, D.S. 1984. "The relative influence of European writers on late eighteenth-century American political thought." *American Political Science Review*, vol. 78, pp. 189–97.

Macaulay, T.B. 1913. *Historical Essays Contributed to the Edinburgh Review*. London: Oxford University Press.

Machiavelli, N. 1965. *The Art of War*, a revised edition of the E. Farneworth translation, with an introduction by N. Wood. New York: Bobbs-Merrill.

Machiavelli, N. 1970. *The Discourses*, edited with an introduction by B. Crick, translated by L. J. Walker, S.J., with revisions by B. Richardson. Harmondsworth: Penguin.

Machiavelli, N. 1972. *The Prince*. In J. Plamenatz, ed., *Machiavelli: The Prince, Selections from the Discourses and Other Writings*, translated by A. Gilbert, pp. 57–135. London: Fontana Collins.

MacIntyre, A.C. 1995. *After Virtue: A Study in Moral Theory*. London: Gerald Duckworth and Company Ltd.

McCarthy, G.E. 1990. *Marx and the Ancients: Classical Ethics, Social Justice, and*

Nineteenth-Century Political Economy. Savage, Md.: Rowman and Littlefield Publishers, Inc.

McCarthy, G.E., ed. 1992. *Marx and Aristotle: Nineteenth Century German Social Theory and Classical Antiquity.* Savage, Md.: Rowman and Littlefield Publishers, Inc.

McClelland, J.S. 1989. *The Crowd and the Mob: From Plato to Canetti.* London: Unwin Hyman.

McCullough, C. 1991. *The First Man in Rome.* New York: Avon Books.

McCullough, C. 1992. *The Grass Crown.* New York: Avon Books.

McCullough, C. 1994. *Fortune's Favorites.* New York: Avon Books.

McKenzie, J.L. 1965. *Dictionary of the Bible.* London: Collier Macmillan.

McLachlan, J. 1976. "Classical names, American identities." In J.W. Eadie, ed., *Classical Traditions in Early America*, pp.81–97. Ann Arbor: University of Michigan Press.

McManners, J. 1966. *Lectures on European History, 1789–1914.* Oxford: Blackwell.

Madison, J, A. Hamilton and J. Jay. 1987. *The Federalist Papers*, edited with an introduction by I. Kramnick. Harmondsworth: Penguin.

Maistre, J. de. 1974. *Considerations on France*, translated by R.A. Lebrun. Montreal and London: McGill-Queen's University Press.

Maistre, J. de. 1993. *St Petersburg Dialogues: Or Conversations on the Temporal Government of Providence*, translated and edited by R.A. Lebrun. Montreal and Kingston: McGill-Queen's University Press.

Magraw, R. 1983. *France 1814–1915: The Bourgeois Century.* Oxford: Fontana.

Manchester, W. 1979. *American Caesar: Douglas MacArthur, 1880–1964.* London: Hutchinson and Co.

Mandel, E. 1962. *Marxist Economic Theory*, translated by B. Pearce. London: Merlin Press.

Mangoni, L. 1979. "Per una definizione del fascismo: i concetti di bonapartismo e cesarismo." *Italia Contemporanea*, 31, 135:17–52.

Mann, M. 1986. *The Sources of Social Power*, vol. I: *A History of Power from the Beginning to A.D. 1760.* Cambridge: Cambridge University Press.

Markham, F. 1963. *Napoleon.* New York: New American Library.

Marx, K. 1968a. "Vorwort [zur zweiten Ausgabe (1869) 'Der achtzehnte Brumaire des Louis Bonaparte'." In *K. Marx-F. Engels Werke*, vol. 16:358–60. Berlin: Dietz Verlag.

Marx, K. 1968b. "Der Bürgerkrieg in Frankreich." In *K. Marx-F. Engels Werke*, vol. 17:319–65. Berlin: Dietz Verlag.

Marx, K. 1969. "Der achtzehnte Brumaire des Louis Bonaparte." In *K. Marx-F. Engels Werke*, vol. 8:115–207. Berlin: Dietz Verlag.

Marx, K. 1973a. "The Class Struggles in France:1848–1850." In *Surveys from Exile*, pp.35–142, translated by P. Jackson, edited and introduced by D. Fernbach. Harmondsworth: Penguin.

Marx, K. 1973b. "The Eighteenth Brumaire of Louis Bonaparte. In *Surveys from Exile*, pp.143–249, translated by B. Fowkes, edited and introduced by D. Fernbach. Harmondsworth: Penguin.

Marx, K. 1974. "The Civil War in France." In *The First International and After*, pp.187–268, edited and introduced by D. Fernbach. Harmondsworth: Penguin.

Marx, K. 1976. *Capital*, vol. I, translated by B. Fowkes. Harmondsworth: Penguin.

Marx, K. 1978. "The constitution of the French Republic adopted November 4, 1848." In Karl Marx and Frederick Engels, *Collected Works*, vol. 10:567–80. New York: International Publishers.

Marx, K. 1980a. "The France of Bonaparte the Little." In Karl Marx and Frederick Engels, *Collected Works*, vol. 14: 615–20. New York: International Publishers.

Marx, K. 1980b. "Peace or war." In Karl Marx and Frederick Engels, *Collected Works*, vol. 16:256–57. New York: International Publishers.

Marx, K. 1981. *Capital*, vol. III, translated by D. Fernbach. Harmondsworth: Penguin.

Marx, K. 1984. "France's financial situation." In Karl Marx and Frederick Engels, *Collected Works*, vol. 19:82–85, translated by H. Mins. New York: International Publishers.

Marx, K. 1986a. "The French Crédit Mobilier I." In Karl Marx and Frederick Engels, *Collected Works*, vol. 15, pp.8–13. New York: International Publishers.

Marx, K. 1986b. "The French Crédit Mobilier II." In Karl Marx and Frederick Engels, *Collected Works*, vol. 15, pp.14–18. New York: International Publishers.

Marx, K. 1986c. "The attempt upon the life of Bonaparte." In Karl Marx and Frederick Engels, *Collected Works*, vol. 15, pp. 453–58. New York: International Publishers.

Marx, K. 1986d. "The rule of the Pretorians." In Karl Marx and Frederick Engels, *Collected Works*, vol. 15, pp. 464–67. New York: International Publishers.

Marx, K. 1986e. "Pelissier's mission to England." In Karl Marx and Frederick Engels, *Collected Works*, vol. 15, pp.482–84. New York: International Publishers.

Marx, K. 1986f. "Political parties in England. Situation in Europe." In Karl Marx and Frederick Engels, *Collected Works*, vol. 15, pp. 566–69. New York: International Publishers.

Marx, K. and Engels, F. 1968. *Selected Works in One Volume*, translators various. London: Lawrence and Wishart.

Marx, K. and Engels, F. 1973. "Manifesto of the Communist Party," translated by S. Moore. In *The Revolutions of 1848*, edited and introduced by D. Fernbach. Harmondsworth: Penguin.

Marx, K and Engels, F. 1975. *Marx-Engels Selected Correspondence*, third edition, translated by I. Lasker. Moscow: Progress Publishers.

Marx, K and Engels, F. 1978. "Address of the Central Authority to the League." In Karl Marx and Frederick Engels, *Collected Works*, vol. 10:371–77. New York: International Publishers.

Mayer, J.P. 1956. *Max Weber and German Politics*. London: Faber and Faber Ltd.

Mazzini, G. 1908a. "Byron and Goethe." In *Life and Writings of Joseph Mazzini*, six vols., vol. 6 *Critical and Literary*: 61–94. London: Smith, Elder, and Co.

Mazzini, G. 1908b. "Thoughts upon democracy in Europe." In *Life and Writings of Joseph Mazzini*, six vols., vol. 6 *Critical and Literary*:98–214. London: Smith, Elder, and Co.

Mazzini, G. 1939. "Il Cesarismo." In G. Mazzini, *Opere*, vol. II, pp.791–807, edited by L. Salvatorelli. Milan: Rizzoli.

Medvedev, R. 1981. "The dictatorship of the proletariat." In *Leninism and Western Socialism*, pp. 29–93, translated by A.D.P.Briggs. London: Verso.

Meier, C. 1990. "C. Caesar Divi filius and the formation of the alternative in Rome." In K.A. Raaflaub and M. Toher , eds., *Between Republic and Empire: Interpretations of Augustus and His Principate*, pp.54–70. Berkeley: University of California Press.

Meier, C. 1995. *Caesar*, translated from the German by D. McLintock. New York: Basic Books.

Meyer, E. 1978. *Caesars Monarchie und das Principat des Pompejus*. Darmstadt: Wissenschaftliche Buchgesellschaft.

Meyer, W. 1975. *Demokratie und Cäsarismus. Konservatives Denken in der Schweiz zur Zeit Napoleons III*. Bern and Frankfurt a.M.: Herbert and Peter Lang.

Meyers Enzyklopädisches Lexikon. 1972, vol. 5. With special contributions by W. Bauer, R. Kaiser and K. Rahner. Mannheim: Lexikonverlag.

Michels, R. 1915. *Political Parties*, translated by E. and C. Paul. New York: Dover.

Mill, J.S. 1971. "On Liberty." In *Essential Works of John Stuart Mill*, edited by M. Lerner, pp. 255–360. New York: Bantam Books, Inc.

Miller, A.S. 1981. *Democratic Dictatorship: The Emergent Constitution of Control*. Westport, Conn.: Greenwood Press.

Milton, J. 1991. "A Defence of the People of England." In M. Dzelzainis, ed. *John Milton: Political Writings*, pp.51–254, translated by C. Gruzelier.

Mitchell, A. 1977. "Bonapartism as a Model for Bismarckian Politics." *Journal of Modern History*, 49, 2:181–99.

Milano, P., ed. 1977. *The Portable Dante*. New York: Viking Penguin.

Mitzman, A. 1970. *The Iron Cage: An Historical Interpretation of Max Weber*. New York: Alfred Knopf.

Momigliano, A. 1956. "Per un riesame della storia dell'idea di Cesarismo." In *Radio Italiana*, edited by Cesare Nel Bimillenario Della Morte. Turin: Edizioni Radio Italiana.

Momigliano, A. 1962. "J. Burckhardt e la parola 'Cesarismo.'" *Rivista Storica Italiana*, LXXIV. pp.369–71.

Momigliano, A. 1977. "The instruments of decline." *Times Literary Supplement*, (April 8) pp.435–36.

Mommsen, T. 1911. *The History of Rome*, vol. 4, translated by W.P. Dickson. London:J.M. Dent and Sons.

Mommsen, T. 1952. "'Last Wishes.' A codicil to the will of Theodor Mommsen." *Past and Present* (February 1) pp.71.

Mommsen, W.J. 1963. "Zum Begriff der 'plebiszitären Führerdemokratie' bei Max Weber." *Kölner Zeitschrift für Soziologie und Sozialpsychologie*, 15:295–322.

Mommsen, W.J. 1974. *The Age of Bureaucracy: Perspectives on the Political Sociology of Max Weber*. Oxford: Basil Blackwell.

Mommsen, W.J. 1981. "Max Weber and Roberto Michels: An asymmetrical partnership." *European Journal of Sociology*, XXII, pp.100–16.

Mommsen, W.J. 1984. *Max Weber and German Politics, 1890–1920*, translated by M.S. Steinberg. Chicago: University of Chicago Press.

Montesquieu. 1965. *Considerations on the Causes of the Greatness of the Romans and their Decline*, translated, with an introduction and notes, by D. Lowenthal. New York: Free Press.

Montesquieu. 1967. *Considérations sur les causes de la Grandeur des Romains et de leur décadence*. Paris: Éditions Garnier Frères, edited, with an introduction and notes, by G. Truc.

Montesquieu. 1989. *The Spirit of the Laws*, edited and translated by A. Cohler, B. Miller, and H. Stone. Cambridge: Cambridge University Press.

Mosley, O. 1968. *My Life*. London: Thomas Nelson and Sons.

Mosse, G.L. 1971. "Caesarism, Circuses and Monuments." *Journal of Contemporary History*, 6,2:167–82.

Mount, F. 1992. *The British Constitution Now*. London: William Heinemann.

Mouzelis, N.P. 1986. *Politics in the Semi-Periphery: Early Parliamentarism and Late Industrialisation in the Balkans and Latin America*. London: Macmillan.

Mullett, C.F. 1939–40. "Classical influences on the American Revolution." *Classical Journal*, vol. 35, no. 1:92–104.

Myers, A.R. 1975. *Parliaments and Estates in Europe to 1789*. London: Thames and Hudson.

Namier, L. 1958. "The first mountebank dictator." In L. Namier, *Vanished Suprema-*

cies: Essays on European History 1812–1918, pp. 54–64. London. Hamish Hamilton.

Naumann, F. 1964. *Werke*, vol. 5. Cologne: Westdeutscher Verlag.

Neumann, A. 1934. *Der neve Cäsar*. Amsterdam: Verlag Allert De Lange.

Neumann, F. [1942] [1944] 1983. *Behemoth: The Structure and Practice of National Socialism, 1933–1944*. New York: Octagon Books.

Neumann, F. 1964. "Notes on the theory of dictatorship." In F. Neumann, ed. H. Marcuse, *The Democratic and the Authoritarian State: Essays in Political and Legal Theory*. pp. 233–56. Glencoe, Illinois: Free Press.

Nicolet, C. 1980. *The World of the Citizen in Republican Rome*, translated by P.S. Falla. Berkeley and Los Angeles: University of California Press.

Nietzsche, F. 1956. *The Birth of Tragedy and the Genealogy of Morals*, translated by F. Golffing. New York: Anchor Books.

Nietzsche, F. 1966. "Zur Genealogie der Moral." In F. Nietzsche, *Werke in Drei Bänden*, vol. 2:763–900. Munich: Carl Hanser.

Nietzsche, F. 1968. *Twilight of the Idols and The Anti-Christ*, translated by R.J. Hollingdale. Harmondsworth: Penguin.

Nietzsche, F. 1973. *Beyond Good and Evil*, translated by R.J. Hollingdale. Harmondsworth: Penguin.

Nietzsche, F. 1982. *Daybreak: Thoughts on the Prejudices of Morality*, translated by R.J. Hollingdale with an introduction by Michael Tannera. Cambridge: Cambridge University Press.

Nock, A.D. 1934. "Religious developments from the close of the Republic to the reign of Nero." In S.A. Cook, F.E. Adcock, and M.P. Charlesworth, eds., *Cambridge Ancient History*, vol. X. *The Augustan Empire, 44 B.C.-A.D. 70*, pp.465–511. Cambridge: Cambridge University Press.

Nolte, E. 1969. *Three Faces of Fascism: Action Française, Italian Fascism, National Socialism*, translated by L. Vennewitz. New York: New American Library.

Nomad, M. 1968. *Rebels and Renegades*. New York: Books for Libraries Press Inc.

O'Brien, C.C. 1994. *On the Eve of the Millenium*. Concord, Ontario: House of Anansi Press, Ltd.

Ortega y Gasset, J. 1957. *The Revolt of the Masses*. New York: W.W. Norton and Co.

Ostrogorski, M. 1970. *Democracy and the Organization of Political Parties*, vols. I and II, translated by F. Clarke. New York: Haskell House Publishers.

Overton, J. 1990. "Economic crisis and the end of democracy: politics in Newfoundland during the Great Depression." *Labour/Le Travail*, 26:85–124.

Ovid. 1955. *The Metamorphoses of Ovid*, translated with an introduction by M.M. Innes. Harmondsworth: Penguin.

Owen, D. 1984. *A Future That Will Work*. Harmondsworth: Penguin.

Owens, M.T. 1984. "A further note on certain of Hamilton's pseudonyms: the 'love of fame' and the use of Plutarch." *Journal of the Early Republic*, 4,3:275–86.

Oxford English Dictionary. 1971. *The Compact Edition of the Oxford English Dictionary* (complete text). Oxford: Oxford University Press.

Palgrave, R.H. Inglis, ed. 1908. *Dictionary of Political Economy*, vol. III, second edition. London: Macmillan.

Parker, H.T. 1965. *The Cult of Antiquity and the French Revolutionaries*. New York: Octagon Books, Inc.

Parkin, F. 1982. *Max Weber*. Chichester: Ellis Horwood.

Parsons, T. 1949. *The Structure of Social Action*. New York: Free Press.

Perez-Diaz, V.M. 1978. *State, Bureaucracy and Civil Society: A Critical Discussion of the Political Theory of Karl Marx*. London: Macmillan.

Perlmutter, A. and Bennett, V.P., eds. 1980. *The Political Influence of the Military.* New Haven: Yale University Press.

Peterson, M.D. 1975. *The Portable Thomas Jefferson.* New York: Viking Penguin.

Pierard, R.V. 1982. "Culture versus Civilization: A Christian critique of Oswald Spengler's Cultural Pessimism." *Fides et Historia,* vol. 14, no. 2: 37–49.

Plato. 1955. *The Republic,* translated with an introduction by H.D.P. Lee. Harmondsworth: Penguin.

Plutarch. 1992. *Plutarch's Lives,* vols. I and II, the Dryden translation edited and revised by Arthur Hugh Clough. New York: Modern Library.

Polan, A.J. 1984. *Lenin and the End of Politics.* London: Methuen and Co. Ltd.

Polybius. 1979. *The Rise of the Roman Empire,* translated by I. Scott-Kilvert, selected with an introduction by F.W. Walbank. Harmondsworth: Penguin.

Pocock, J.G.A. 1975. *The Machiavellian Moment: Florentine Political Thought and the Atlantic Republican Tradition.* Princeton, N.J.: Princeton University Press.

Pocock, J.G.A. 1976. "Comment." In J.W. Eadie, ed., *Classical Traditions in Early America,* pp.255–261. Ann Arbor: University of Michigan Press.

Pocock, J.G.A. 1977. "Historical Introduction." In *The Political Works of James Harrington,* edited with an introduction by J.G.A. Pocock, pp.1–152. Cambridge: Cambridge University Press.

Poulantzas, N. 1973. *Political Power and Social Classes,* translated by T. O'Hagan with the assistance of D. McLellan, A. de Casparis, and B. Grogan. London: New Left Books.

Poulantzas, N. 1974. *Fascism and Dictatorship,* translated by J. White. London: New Left Books.

Poulantzas, N. 1976. *The Crisis of the Dictatorships,* translated by D. Fernbach. London: New Left Books.

Price, R. 1973. "The senses of *Virtù* in Machiavelli." *European Studies Review,* 3, 4:315–45.

Proudhon, P.J. 1883. *Césarisme et Christianisme. De l'an 45 avant J.-C. a l'an 476 après,* 2 vols., with a preface by J.A. Langlois. Paris: Marpon and Flammarion.

Proudhon, P.J. 1969. *Selected Writings of Pierre-Joseph Proudhon,* edited with an introduction by S. Edwards, translated by E. Fraser. London: Macmillan and Co.

Quincey, T. De. 1877. The Works of *Thomas De Quincey,* vol. VI. New York: Hurd and Houghton.

Raab, F. 1964. *The English Face of Machiavelli: a Changing Interpretation 1500–1700.* London: Routledge and Kegan Paul.

Rahe, P.A. 1992. *Republics Ancient and Modern: Classical Republicanism and the American Revolution.* Chapel Hill and London: University of North Carolina Press.

Rapoport, D.C. "A Comparative Theory of Military and Political Types." In S.P. Huntington, ed., *Changing Patterns of Military Politics,* pp.71–101. New York: Free Press.

Reinhold, M. 1975. *The Classick Pages: Classical Reading of Eighteenth-Century Americans.* University Park: Pennsylvania State University Press.

Rémond, R. 1969. *La droite en France.* Paris: Aubier-Montaigne.

Richter, M. 1981. "Modernity and its Distinctive Threats to Liberty: Montesquieu and Tocqueville on New Forms of Illegitimate Domination." In M. Hereth, and J. Höffken, eds., *Alexis de Tocqueville—Zur Politik in der Demokratie,* pp. 61–80. Baden-Baden: Nomos Verlagsgesellschaft.

Richter, M. 1982. "Toward a Concept of Political Illegitimacy: Bonapartist Dictatorship and Democratic Legitimacy." *Political Theory,* 10, 2:185–214.

Richter, M. 1988. "Tocqueville, Napoleon, and Bonapartism." In A.S. Eisenstadt, ed.,

Reconsidering Tocqueville's Democracy in America, pp.110–145. New Brunswick and London: Rutgers University Press.

Riencourt, A. de. 1958. *The Coming Caesars*. London: Jonathan Cape.

Riesebrodt, M. 1981. "Bibliographie zur Max Weber Gesamtausgabe." *Prospekt der Max Weber Gesamtausgabe*. Tübingen: J.C.B. Mohr (Paul Siebeck).

Robert, P. 1966. *Dictionnaire alphabétique et analogique de la langue française*. Paris: Le Robert.

Robbins, C.A. 1959. *The Eighteenth-century Commonwealthman: Studies in the Transmission, Development and Circumstances of English Liberal Thought from the Restoration of Charles II until the War with the Thirteen Colonies*. Cambridge, Mass.: Harvard University Press.

Robbins, C.A., ed. 1969. *Two English Republican Tracts*. Cambridge: Cambridge University Press.

Röhl, J.C.G. 1967. *Germany without Bismarck: The Crisis of Government in the Second Reich, 1890–1900*. London: B.T. Batsford Ltd.

Romieu, M.A. 1850. *L'ère des Césars*, second edition. Paris: Ledoyen.

Romieu, M.A. 1851. *Le spectre rouge de 1852*. Paris: Ledoyen.

Roscher, W. 1892. *Politik Geschichtliche Naturlehre der Monarchie, Aristokratie und Demokratie*. Stuttgart: J.C. Cotta.

Rossiter, C. 1948. *Constitutional Dictatorship*. Princeton: Princeton University Press.

Rostovtzeff, M. 1975. *Rome*. Oxford: Oxford University Press.

Roth, G. 1977. Review of M. Weber, *The Agrarian Sociology of Ancient Civilizations*, *American Journal of Sociology*, 83,3:766–69.

Roth, G. 1985. "Marx and Weber on the United States—Today." In R.J. Antonio and R.M. Glassman, eds., *A Weber-Marx Dialogue*, pp.215–33. Kansas: University Press of Kansas.

Roth, G. 1993. "Weber the would-be Englishman: Anglophilia and family history." In H. Lehmann and G. Roth., *Weber's Protestant Ethic: Origins, Evidence, Contexts*, pp.83–121. Cambridge: Cambridge University Press.

Rousseau, J.J. 1993a. *The Social Contract*. In G.D.H. Cole, ed., *The Social Contract and Discourses*, pp.181–309, translated and Introduced by G.D.H. Cole, revised and augmented by J.H. Brumfitt and J.C. Hall, updated by P.D. Jimack. London: J.M. Dent.

Rousseau, J.J. 1993b. *Political Economy*. In G.D.H. Cole, ed., *The Social Contract and Discourses*, pp.128–168. London: J.M. Dent.

Rubel, M. 1960. *Karl Marx devant le bonapartisme*. Paris: Mouton.

Runciman, W.G. 1983. "Capitalism without classes: the case of classical Rome." *British Journal of Sociology*, 34, 2:157–77.

Rush, B. 1947. "Observations on the government of Pennsylvania." In D.D. Runes, ed., *The Selected Writings of Benjamin Rush*, pp.54–84. New York: Philosophical Library.

Rush, B. 1951. *Letters of Benjamin Rush*, vol. I: 1761–1792, edited by L.H. Butterfield. Princeton, N.J.: Princeton University Press.

Rüstow, F.W. 1879. *Der Cäsarismus. Sein Wesen und sein Schaffen*. Zurich: Cäsar Schmidt.

Ste. Croix, G.E.M. de. 1981. *The Class Struggle in the Ancient Greek World from the Archaic Age to the Arab Conquests*. London: Gerald Duckworth and Company Ltd.

Sallust. 1963. *The Jugurthine War; The Conspiracy of Catiline*, translated with an introduction by S.A. Handford. Harmondsworth: Penguin.

Salutati, C. 1925. "De Tyranno." In E. Emerton, *Humanism and Tyranny: Studies in the Italian Trecento*, pp.70–116, translated by E. Emerton. Gloucester, Mass.: Peter Smith.

Sandel, M.J. 1996. "America's search for a new public philosophy." *The Atlantic Monthly*, March 1996:57–74.

Scaff, L.A. 1980–81. "Max Weber and Robert Michels." *American Journal of Sociology*, 86,6:190–215.

Scaff. L.A. 1982. "On Richter 'Toward a concept of political illegitimacy.'" *Political Theory*, 11, 1:133–5.

Scaff, L.A. 1984. "Weber before Weberian Sociology." *British Journal of Sociology*, 35,2:190–215.

Scaff, L.A. 1989. *Fleeing the Iron Cage: Culture, Politics and Modernity in the Thought of Max Weber*. Berkeley: University of California Press.

Schäffle, A. 1896. *Bau und Leben des sozialen Körpers*, vols. I and II, second edition. Tübingen:Lauppschen Buchhandlung.

Schapiro, L. 1972. *Totalitarianism*. London: Macmillan.

Schlesinger, A.M. 1973. *The Imperial Presidency*. Boston: Houghton Mifflin.

Schluchter, W. "Value-neutrality and the ethic of responsibility." In. G. Roth and W. Schluchter, eds., *Max Weber's Vision of History*, pp.65–116, translated by G. Roth. Berkeley: University of California Press.

Schmitt, C. 1976. *The Concept of the Political*, translation, introduction, and notes by G. Schwab. New Brunswick, N.J.: Rutgers University Press.

Schmitt, C. 1978. *Die Diktatur. Von den Anfängen des modernen Souveränitätsgedankens bis zum proletarischen Klassenkampf*. Berlin: Duncker and Humblot.

Schmitt, C. 1985. *Political Theology: Four Chapters on the Concept of Sovereignty*, translated and introduced by G. Schwab. Cambridge, Mass.: MIT Press.

Schulz, G. 1963. *Zwischen Demokratie und Diktatur. Verfassungspolitik und Reichsreform in der Weimar Republik*, vol. I. Berlin: De Gruyter.

Schuster, R., ed. 1978. *Deutsche Verfassungen*, ninth edition. Munich: Goldmann.

Schwarz, B. 1985. "Conservatism and 'caesarism,' 1903–22." In M. Langan and B. Schwarz, eds., pp. 33–62. *Crises in the British State 1880–1930*. London: Hutchinson.

Scullard, H.H. 1976. *From the Gracchi to Nero: A History of Rome from 133 B.C. to A.D. 68*, fourth edition. London: Methuen and Co. Ltd.

Seldes, G. 1935. *Sawdust Caesar: The Untold History of Mussolini and Fascism*. New York and London: Harper and Brothers Publishers.

Senior, N.W. 1871. *Journals kept in France and Italy from 1848–1852*, 2 vols., second edition, edited by M.C.M. Simpson. London: Henry S. King and Co.

Shaw, G.B. 1963. *Caesar and Cleopatra: A History in Four Acts*. In Bernard Shaw, *Complete Plays with Prefaces*, vol. III, pp.357–481. New York: Dodd, Mead and Company.

Sheehan, J.J. 1968. "Political Leadership in the German Reichstag, 1871–1918." *American Historical Review*, 74:511–28.

Shklar, J.N. 1990." Montesquieu and the new republicanism." In G. Bock, Q. Skinner, and M. Viroli , eds., *Machiavelli and Republicanism*, pp. 265–279. Cambridge: Cambridge University Press.

Singer, P. 1981. *The Expanding Circle*. Oxford: Oxford University Press.

Skinner, Q. 1969. "Meaning and understanding in the history of ideas." *History and Theory*, 8:5–53.

Skinner, Q. 1978. *The Foundations of Modern Political Thought*, vol. I: *The Renaissance*. Cambridge: Cambridge University Press.

Skinner, Q. 1981. *Machiavelli*. Oxford: Oxford University Press.

Skinner, Q. 1986. "The paradoxes of political liberty." In *The Tanner Lectures on Human Values*, VII, pp.227–50. Salt Lake City: University of Utah Press.

Skinner, Q. 1990. "Machiavelli's *Discorsi* and the pre-humanist origins of republican ideas." In G. Bock, Q. Skinner, and M. Viroli , eds., *Machiavelli and Republicanism*, pp. 121–141. Cambridge: Cambridge University Press.

Soboul, A. 1977. *A Short History of the French Revolution 1789–1799*, translated by G. Symcox. Berkeley: University of California Press.

Sorel, Georges. 1950. *Reflections on Violence*, translated by T.E. Hulme and J. Roth, with an introduction by E.A. Shils. New York: Collier Books.

Spencer, M.E. 1979. "Marx on the State: The Events in France between 1848–1850." *Theory and Society*, 7:167–98.

Spengler, O. 1926–28. *The Decline of the West*, vols. I and II, translated by C.F. Atkinson. London: George Allen and Unwin Ltd.

Spengler, O. 1934. *The Hour of Decision*, translated by C.F. Atkinson. New York: Alfred A. Knopf.

Spengler, O. 1967. "Pessimism?" In *Oswald Spengler: Selected Essays*, introduced and translated by D.O. White, pp. 133–54. Chicago: Henry Regnery Company.

Staël, Madame de. 1964. *Madame de Staël on Politics, Literature and National Character*, translated, edited, and with an introduction by M. Berger. London: Sidgwick and Jackson.

Stendhal. 1971. *La Chartreuse de Parme*. Paris: Bordas.

Stendhal. 1956. *A Life of Napoleon*, translated by R. Gant. London: The Rodale Press.

Stern, J.P. 1975. *Hitler: The Führer and the People*. Glasgow: Fontana Collins.

Storing, H.J. 1981. *The Complete Anti-Federalist*, vols. I-VII, edited, with commentary and notes, by H.J. Storing, with the assistance of M. Dry. Chicago: University of Chicago Press.

Stourzh, G. 1970. *Alexander Hamilton and the Idea of Republican Government*. Stanford, Cal.: Stanford University Press.

Strauss, L. 1963. *On Tyranny*, revised and enlarged edition. Glencoe, Ill.: Free Press.

Struve, W. 1973. *Elites Against Democracy: Leadership Ideals in Bourgeois Political Thought in Germany 1890–1933*. Princeton, N.J.: Princeton University Press.

Stürmer, M. *Regierung und Reichstag im Bismarckstaat 1871–1880. Cäsarismus oder Parlamentarismus*. Düsseldorf: Droste Verlag.

Stürmer, M. 1977a. "Caesar's Laurel Crown—the case for a Comparative Concept." *Journal of Modern History*, 49, 2:203–7.

Stürmer, M. 1977b. "Krise, Konflikt, Entscheidung. Die Suche nach dem neuen Cäsar als europäisches Verfassungsproblem." In K. Hammer and P.C. Hartmann,. eds., *Der Bonapartismus. Historisches Phänomen und politischer Mythos*, pp. 102–18. Munich: Artemis Verlag.

Suetonius. 1980. *The Twelve Caesars* (illustrated edition), translated by R. Graves, revised with an introduction by M. Grant, captions, essays, and picture research by S. Maccormack. Harmondsworth:Penguin.

Syme, R. 1964. *Sallust*. Berkeley: University of California Press.

Syme, R. 1974. *The Roman Revolution*. Oxford: Oxford University Press.

Syme, R. 1979a. "M. Gelzer, Caesar der Politiker und Staatsmann". In R. Syme, *Roman Papers*, vol. I, pp.149–71, edited by E. Badian. Oxford: Clarendon Press.

Syme, R. 1979b. "A Roman post-mortem. An inquest on the fall of the Roman Republic." In R. Syme, *Roman Papers*, vol. 1, pp.205–17, edited by E. Badian. Oxford: Clarendon Press.

Syme, R. 1979c. "Caesar, the senate, and Italy." In R. Syme, *Roman Papers*, vol. 1, pp. 88–119, edited by E. Badian. Oxford: Clarendon Press.

Tacitus. 1948. *The Agricola and the Germania*, translated with an introduction by H. Mattingly. Harmondsworth: Penguin.

Tacitus. 1964. *The Histories*, translated by K. Wellesley. Harmondsworth: Penguin.

Tacitus. 1977. *The Annals of Imperial Rome*, translated by M. Grant. Harmondsworth: Penguin.

Tanner, T. 1993. "Shakespeare: The Greek and Roman Plays". In William Shakespeare, *Tragedies*, vol. 2, pp.xi-cxi. London: David Campbell Publishers Ltd.

Taylor. A.J.P. 1945. *The Course of German History: A Survey of the Development of Germany since 1815*. London: Hamish Hamilton.

Taylor, A.J.P. 1967. "Metternich." In *Europe: Grandeur and Decline*, pp.22–26, Harmondsworth: Penguin.

Taylor, L.R. 1949. *Party Politics in the Age of Caesar*. Berkeley, Los Angeles: University of California Press.

Tenbruck, F.H. 1987. "Max Weber and Eduard Meyer." In W.J. Mommsen and J. Osterhammel , eds., *Max Weber and His Contemporaries*, pp.234–267, translated by S. Whimster. London: Unwin Hyman.

Thody, P. 1989. *French Caesarism from Napoleon I to Charles de Gaulle*. London: Macmillan.

Thompson, E.P. 1974. "Patrician society, plebeian culture." *Journal of Social History* 7:382–405.

Thompson, E.P. 1978. "Eighteenth-century English society: class struggle without class?" *Social History*, 3, 2:133–65.

Thompson, J.M. 1954. *Napoleon's Letters*, selected, translated and edited by J.M. Thompson. London: Dent.

Thompson, J.M. 1955. *Louis Napoleon and the Second Empire*. New York: Farrar, Straus, and Cudahy.

Thornton, A.P. 1985. *The Imperial Idea and Its Enemies: A Study in British Power*. Second Edition. London: Macmillan.

Thucydides. 1972. *History of the Peloponnesian War*, translated by Rex Warner with an introduction and notes by M.I. Finley. Harmondsworth: Penguin.

Tocqueville, A. de. 1969. *Democracy in America*, edited by J.P. Mayer and translated by G. Lawrence. New York: Harper and Row.

Tocqueville, A. de. 1970. *Recollections*, edited by J.P. Mayer and A.P. Kerr, introduction by J.P. Mayer, translated by G. Lawrence. New York: Doubleday and Co.

Tocqueville, A. de. 1985. *Alexis de Tocqueville: Selected Letters on Politics and Society,* edited by R. Boesche, translated by J. Toupin and R. Boesche. Berkeley: University of California Press.

Tönnies, F. 1917. *Der englische Staat und der deutsche Staat*. Berlin: Karl Curtius.

Tozer, H.F. 1885. "Introduction" to Byron, *Childe Harold*. Oxford: Clarendon Press.

Treitschke, H. von. 1916. *Politics*, 2 vols., translated by B. Dugdale and T. de Bille, with an introduction by A.J. Balfour. New York: Macmillan.

Tribe, K. 1989. "Introduction." to K. Tribe, ed., *Reading Weber*, pp.1–14. London: Routledge.

Trotsky, L. 1972. *The Revolution Betrayed*, fifth edition, translated by M. Eastman. New York: Pathfinder Press.

Trotsky, L. 1975. *The Struggle Against Fascism in Germany*, translators various. Harmondsworth: Penguin.

Trotsky, L. 1977. *History of the Russian Revolution*, translated by M. Eastman. London: Pluto Press.

Turner, F.M. 1986. "British politics and the demise of the Roman Republic: 1700–1939," *The Historical Journal*, vol. 29, no. 3:577–599.

Villedieu, E. 1880. *Le Césarisme Jacobin. Les droits de l'Église et le droit national.* Paris: Jules Gervais.

Virgil. 1958. *The Aeneid*, translated with an introduction by W.F. Jackson Knight. Harmondsworth: Penguin.

Viroli, M. 1990. "Machiavelli and the republican idea of politics." In G. Bock, Q. Skinner and M. Viroli , eds., *Machiavelli and Republicanism*, pp. 143–71. Cambridge: Cambridge University Press.

Voegelin, E. 1949. "On Tyranny." *The Review of Politics*, vol. 11:241–244.

Voltaire, 1964. *La mort de César*, edited by A-M. Rousseau. Paris: Societé D'Édition D'Enseignement Supérieur.

Voltaire, 1994. *Political Writings*, edited and translated by D. Williams. Cambridge: Cambridge University Press.

Ward, A. 1964. "The Tory view of Roman history." In C. Camden, ed., *Studies in English Literature 1500–1900*, vol. IV, pp.413–56. New York: Rice University Press.

Warner, R. 1958. *The Young Caesar*. Boston: Little, Brown and Co.

Warner, R. 1960. *Imperial Caesar*. Boston: Little, Brown and Co.

Weber, Marianne. 1988. *Max Weber: A Biography*, translated by H. Zohn. New Brunswick: Transaction Books.

Weber, Max. 1897. "Agrarverhältnisse im Altertum." in J.Conrad et al., eds., *Handwörterbuch der Staatswissenschaften*, second supplementary volume. Jena. pp.1–18.

Weber, Max. 1920. *Gesammelte Aufsätze zur Religionssoziologie*, vol. I. Tübingen: J.C.B. Mohr (Paul Siebeck).

Weber, Max. 1924a. *Gesammelte Aufsätze zur Soziologie und Sozialpolitik*, edited by Marianne Weber. Tübingen: J.C.B. Mohr (Paul Siebeck).

Weber, Max. 1924b. *Gesammelte Aufsätze zur Sozial- und Wirtschaftsgeschichte.* Tubingen, edited by Marianne Weber. Tübingen: J.C.B. Mohr (Paul Siebeck).

Weber, Max. 1930. *The Protestant Ethic and the Spirit of Capitalism*, translated by T. Parsons. London: George Allen and Unwin.

Weber, Max. 1936. *Jugendbriefe*, edited with an introduction by Marianne Weber. Tübingen: J.C.B. Mohr (Paul Siebeck).

Weber, Max. 1949. "'Objectivity' in social science and social policy." In M. Weber, *The Methodology of the Social Sciences*, edited and translated by E.A. Shils and H.A. Finch, with a foreword by E.A. Shils, pp.49–112. New York: Free Press.

Weber, Max. 1951a. *The Religion of China*, translated and edited by H.H. Gerth, with an introduction by C.K. Yang. New York: Free Press.

Weber, Max. 1951b. *Gesammelte Aufsätze zur Wissenschaftslehre*, second edition, edited by J. Winckelmann. Tübingen: J.C.B. Mohr (Paul Siebeck).

Weber, Max. 1958. *Gesammelte Politische Schriften*, second edition, edited by J. Winckelmann. With a Preface by Th. Heuss. Tübingen: J.C.B. Mohr (Paul Siebeck).

Weber, Max. 1964. *Wirtschaft und Gesellschaft. Grundriss der verstehenden Soziologie*, vols. I and II (paperback edition, based on the 1956 fourth edition), edited by J. Winckelmann. Cologne and Berlin: Kiepenheuer and Witsch.

Weber, Max. 1970a. "Politics as a Vocation". In *From Max Weber*, edited and translated by H.H. Gerth and C. Wright Mills, pp.77–128. London: Routledge and Kegan Paul.

Weber, Max. 1970b. "Science as a Vocation". In *From Max Weber*, edited and translated by H.H. Gerth and C. Wright Mills, pp.129–56.

Weber, Max. 1970c. "The Social Psychology of the World Religions." In *From Max Weber*, edited and translated by H.H. Gerth and C. Wright Mills, pp.267–301.

Weber, Max. 1970d. "National Character and the Junkers." In *From Max Weber*, edited and translated by H.H. Gerth and C. Wright Mills, pp. 386–95.

Weber, Max. 1970e. "Capitalism and Rural Society in Germany." In *From Max Weber*, edited and translated by H.H. Gerth and C. Wright Mills, pp. 363–85.

Weber, Max. 1971. "Stellungnahme zur Flottenumfrage der Allgemeinen Zeitung." In M. Weber, *Gesammelte Politische Schriften*, third edition, edited by J. Winckelmann, with a preface by Th. Heuss. Tübingen: J.C.B. Mohr (Paul Siebeck).

Weber, Max. 1972. "Socialism." In *Max Weber: The Interpretation of Social Reality*, edited by J.E.T. Eldridge, translated by D. Hÿtch, pp. 191–219. London: Thomas Nelson and Sons.

Weber, Max. 1975. *Roscher and Knies: The Logical Problems of Historical Economics*, translated by G. Oakes. New York: Free Press.

Weber, Max. 1976. *The Agrarian Sociology of Ancient Civilizations*, translated by R.I. Frank. London: Verso.

Weber, Max. 1978a. *Parliament and Government in a Reconstructed Germany*, translated by G. Roth. In Max Weber 1978b, pp. 1381–1469.

Weber, Max. 1978b. *Economy and Society*, vols. I and II, edited by G. Roth and C. Wittich, translators various. Berkeley: University of California Press.

Weber, Max. 1980. "The national state and economic policy." *Economy and Society*, 9,4:428–49, translated by B. Fowkes.

Weber, Max. 1981. "Some Categories of Interpretative Sociology." *Sociological Quarterly*, 22:151–80, translated by E. Graber.

Weber, Max. 1986. "The Reich President." *Social Research*, 53,1:128–32, translated by G.C. Wells.

Weber, Max. 1988. "Deutschland unter den europäischen Weltmächten." In Max Weber, *Zur Politik im Weltkrieg. Schriften und Reden 1914–1918. Studienausgabe der Max Weber-Gesamtausgabe*, vol. I.15, edited by W.J. Mommsen in collaboration with Gangolf Hübinger, pp.61–78. Tübingen: J.C.B. Mohr (Paul Siebeck).

Weber, Max. 1995a. "Bourgeois democracy in Russia." In M. Weber, *The Russian Revolutions*, translated and edited by G.C. Wells and P. Baehr, pp.41–147. Cambridge: Polity Press.

Weber, Max. 1995b. "Russia's transition to pseudo-constitutionalism." In M. Weber, *The Russian Revolutions*, translated and edited by G.C. Wells and P. Baehr, pp. 148–240. Cambridge: Polity Press.

Wehler, H.U. 1970. "Bismarck's Imperialism 1862–1890." *Past and Present*, 48:119–55, translated by N. Porter, J. Sheehan, and T.W. Mason.

Weil, S. 1963. *Gravity and Grace*. London: Routledge.

Wells, H.G. 1906. *The Future in America*. New York and London: Harper and Brothers Publishers.

Wells, H.G. 1961. *Outline of History: Being a Plain History of Life and Mankind*, vols. 1 and 2, revised and brought up to date by R. Postgate. New York: Garden City Books.

Wilder, T. 1948. *The Ides of March*. New York: Harper.

Wilentz, S. 1993. "Pox Populi." *The New Republic*, August 9, pp. 29–35.

Williams, R. [1958] 1963. *Culture and Society, 1780–1950*. Harmondsworth: Penguin.

Williams, R. 1976. *Keywords: A Vocabulary of Culture and Society*. Glasgow: Fontana.

Will, G. 1992. "The Veep and the Blatherskite." *Newsweek*, June 29, p. 72.

Wills, G. 1984. *Cincinnatus: George Washington and the Enlightenment*. New York: Doubleday and Company, Inc.

Wilson, R. "Imperialism in Crisis; the 'Irish Dimension'." In M. Langan and B.

Schwarz, eds., *Crises in the British State, 1880–1930*, pp.151–78. London: Hutchinson.

Wippermann, W. 1983. *Die Bonapartismustheorie von Marx und Engels*. Stuttgart: Klett-Cotta.

Wittfogel, K.A. 1957. *Oriental Despotism: A Comparative Study of Total Power*. New Haven, CT: Yale University Press.

Wolin, S. 1981. "Max Weber: Legitimation, Method and the Politics of Theory." *Political Theory*, 9,3:401–24.

Wolpert, J.F. 1965. "Toward a sociology of authority." In A.W. Gouldner, ed., *Studies in Leadership: Leadership and Democratic Action*, pp.679–701. New York: Russell and Russell, Inc.

Wood, G. 1972. *The Creation of the American Republic, 1776–1787*. New York: W.W. Norton and Co.

Woodcock, G. 1987. *Pierre-Joseph Proudhon: A Biography*. Montreal: Black Rose Books.

Wootton, D. 1986. *Divine Right and Democracy: An Anthology of Political Writings in Stuart England*. Harmondsworth: Penguin.

Worden, B. 1982. "Classical republicanism and the Puritan revolution." In H. Lloyd-Jones, V. Pearl and B. Worden, eds., *History and Imagination: Essays in Honor of H.R. Trevor-Roper*, pp. 182–200. New York: Holmes and Meier Publishers.

Worden, B. 1990. "Milton's republicanism and the tyranny of heaven." In G. Bock, Q. Skinner and M. Viroli , eds., *Machiavelli and Republicanism,* pp. 225–45. Cambridge: Cambridge University Press.

Worden, B. 1991. "English republicanism." In *The Cambridge History of Political Thought 1450–1700*, pp. 443–475, edited by J.H. Burns, with the assistance of Mark Goldie. Cambridge: Cambridge University Press.

Yavetz, Z. 1969. *Plebs and Princeps*. Oxford: Clarendon Press.

Yavetz, Z. 1983. *Julius Caesar and his Public Image*. London: Thames and Hudson.

Zeldin, T. 1958. *The Political System of Napoleon III*. London: Macmillan.

Zeldin, T. 1979. *France 1848–1945: Politics and Anger*. Oxford: Oxford University Press.

Index